CALIFORNIA
REAL ESTATE PRACTICE

Kathryn Haupt
Megan Dorsey

ROCKWELL PUBLISHING COMPANY

TABLE OF CONTENTS

CHAPTER

1

REAL ESTATE AGENCY RELATIONSHIPS

AGENCY AND AGENCY LAW

- Agency relationships
- Agent's duties to the principal
- Agent's duties to third parties
- Other legal effects of agency

HOW AN AGENCY IS CREATED AND TERMINATED

AGENCY DISCLOSURES

- Historical background
- Disclosure requirements
- Acting in accordance with the disclosures
- Licensee acting as a principal

TYPES OF REAL ESTATE AGENCY RELATIONSHIPS

- Seller agency
- Buyer agency
- Dual agency
- Finder or middleman

INTRODUCTION

You have just closed a sale. The seller was thrilled with the sales price; the buyers are happy to be moving into their dream house. Your broker is beaming with approval. Her office will now reach this month's sales goal, thanks to your sale. And you can't wait to take your commission check to the bank.

But wait! Now the buyer is talking to her attorney about breach of agency duties and threatening to cancel the contract because of undisclosed material facts. The Department of Real Estate has notified you that it has received a complaint against you: the seller is claiming that you failed to disclose your agency status. Plus, the seller is refusing to pay the commission. Your broker is worried about a lawsuit, and she thinks that it's all your fault. What a disaster!

What went wrong? In this hypothetical situation, as sometimes in real life, there was confusion about agency relationships and what they meant for the real estate licensee. In today's increasingly complicated legal environment, it is crucial to understand the practical aspects of agency relationships. In this chapter, we will discuss real estate agency law, the ways in which agency relationships can be established, agency disclosure requirements, and the different types of agency relationships.

AGENCY AND AGENCY LAW

Agency law is the body of statutes and court decisions that govern agency relationships in a wide variety of contexts. For example, agency law applies to the relationship between lawyer and client, or between trustee and beneficiary. It is also the legal basis for a real estate agent's relationship with his or her clients.

AGENCY RELATIONSHIPS

An **agent** is a person who has been authorized by a **principal** to represent the principal in dealings with **third parties**. A real estate agent's principal may be a real estate seller, buyer, landlord, or tenant. A real estate agent's principal may also be called his or her **client**. When a real estate agent negotiates with buyers or tenants on a client's behalf, those third parties are sometimes called **customers**.

EXAMPLE: Sullivan asks Broker Harris to find a buyer for her house. Harris shows Sullivan's house to Brown, who makes an offer to purchase the house. Sullivan is Harris's client, or principal; Harris is Sullivan's agent; and Brown is the customer or third party.

The term "real estate agent" is commonly used to refer to either a licensed real estate broker or a licensed real estate salesperson. Technically, however, only a broker can be the agent of a member of the public (a seller, buyer, landlord, or tenant). When a real estate salesperson works with a seller (for example), the salesperson does so as an agent of her broker, not as the agent of the seller. The broker is legally responsible for the actions of the salesperson. So even though the salesperson as well as the broker may be referred to as the seller's agent, strictly speaking only the broker is the seller's agent in the eyes of the law. Although this technical distinction doesn't necessarily make much difference in the day-to-day work of a salesperson, it should be kept in mind.

In many residential sales transactions, one real estate licensee acts as the **seller's agent** and another licensee acts as the **buyer's agent**. A licensee may also act as a **dual agent**, representing both the seller and the buyer in the same transaction. And in some cases a licensee may prefer not to act as the agent of either party, choosing instead to act merely as a middleman or **finder**. We'll discuss each of these roles in more detail later in this chapter.

Why does it matter which party in a transaction a real estate licensee is representing? Because an agency relationship has a number of very important legal implications. For a third party, dealing with the agent can be the legal equivalent of dealing with the principal. For instance, if an agent is authorized to do so, she can enter into a contract that will be legally binding on the principal. And if the agent makes a mistake or commits fraud, the principal could be held liable to a third party who was injured by the agent's action. Perhaps most importantly, an agent owes special legal duties to her principal that she does not owe to third parties. We'll cover each of these issues in more detail. Let's start with the agent's legal duties.

AGENT'S DUTIES TO THE PRINCIPAL

The duties that agents owe to their principals are called fiduciary duties. A **fiduciary** is a person who occupies a position of special trust in relation to another person. An agent owes the principal these five basic fiduciary duties:

- utmost care,
- obedience and good faith,
- accounting,
- loyalty, and
- disclosure of material facts.

A real estate agent owes his client(s) these duties regardless of whether he is representing the seller, the buyer, or both parties. Fiduciary duties are owed from the time the agency relationship begins until the transaction closes or the agency terminates for some other reason.

UTMOST CARE. An agent owes her principal the duty of utmost care in carrying out the agency. A real estate agent is required to act with the level of care and skill generally expected of a competent real estate agent. If her performance fails to meet that standard, she may be found liable for any harm to the principal that results from her negligence.

OBEDIENCE AND GOOD FAITH. An agent must obey the principal's instructions and carry them out in good faith, with honesty and integrity. The agent's actions must conform to the purpose and intent of the instructions. If a real estate agent fails to obey the client's instructions, the agent (or the agent's broker) may be held liable for any loss to the client that results.

ACCOUNTING. Agents must be able to account to their clients for all funds (or other valuables) entrusted to their care. These are referred to as **trust funds**. California's Real Estate Law requires brokers to report to their clients on the status of all trust funds on a regular basis. They must also avoid mixing, or **commingling**, trust funds with their own funds.

LOYALTY. The duty of loyalty means that agents must put the interests of their clients above their own interests and above the interests of any other party. An agent must not make any **secret profits** from the agency. For example, it is a breach of agency duty for a broker to list a property for less than it is worth, secretly buy it from the principal through an intermediary, and then sell it for a profit.

One of the most important aspects of the duty of loyalty is the requirement of **confidentiality**. An agent may not disclose any confidential information about the principal, even after the agency relationship terminates. Information is generally considered confidential if it was:

1. given to the agent by the principal in confidence, and/or
2. acquired by the agent during the course of or on account of the fiduciary relationship.

Confidential information cannot be disclosed to other parties or otherwise used in a manner that is detrimental to the principal.

EXAMPLE: A buyer privately tells her agent that she is independently wealthy and can easily afford the listing price, but would like to offer $5,000 less than the listing price as an opening offer. The buyer's agent must keep this information confidential, since it was told to the agent in confidence, and revealing the information to the seller would not be in the buyer's best interest.

Of course, information is not confidential if it is already available to the general public. Also, information is not confidential if the principal is required by law to disclose it. For example, as we'll discuss later in this chapter and in Chapter 2, the seller in a real estate transaction is required to make a number of disclosures to the buyer. One kind of information that must be disclosed is the presence of latent defects in the property. A **latent defect** is a problem that would not be discovered by ordinary inspection.

Information about latent defects must never be concealed on the grounds that the information is confidential. Because the principal would be legally obligated to disclose a latent defect to buyers, by definition it is not confidential information.

EXAMPLE: A seller tells Parker, his agent, that the roof of his house leaks during heavy rain, and asks her not to mention this information to prospective buyers. Although this was told to Parker in confidence, she is legally obligated to disclose it to buyers.

Confidential information about a principal must not be disclosed even after the transaction has ended. This is particularly important if a person who once was an agent's principal is now represented by another agent.

EXAMPLE: Agent Vance helped Torino purchase an expensive house. While Vance was representing him, Torino told Vance a considerable amount of confidential information about his extensive financial holdings.

Over a year later, Vance is representing Cortez in the sale of an investment property. Torino, who is now represented by another agent, is interested in buying Cortez's property. Vance knows that Torino is extremely wealthy and can easily afford to pay the property's full listing price. But because this knowledge is based on confidential information he learned while he was acting as Torino's agent, Vance cannot disclose this to his current client, Cortez. This is true even though Vance's agency relationship with Torino ended a long time ago.

DISCLOSURE OF MATERIAL FACTS. While an agent must not disclose the principal's confidential information to third parties, the agent is required to disclose all material facts that she is aware of to the principal. For a real estate agent, a **material fact** is any information that affects the value or desirability of the property, or that could affect the principal's decision as to whether or not to enter into a transaction. Material facts that must be disclosed to the principal include:

- all offers to purchase the property,
- the true value of the property, and
- any relationship between the agent and another party.

A seller's agent must present all offers to the principal in a timely manner. It's the seller, not the agent, who decides whether an offer is acceptable. The duty to present all offers continues even after the property is subject to an existing contract.

EXAMPLE: Seller Sanders has just accepted an offer from Buyer Barton. Garcia, the listing agent, receives another written offer for the same property from Buyer Bell. Garcia has a duty to present Bell's offer to Sanders, even though Sanders has already accepted Barton's offer.

A seller's agent must also inform his principal of the property's true value. Since sellers usually rely on their agent's advice in setting a listing price, an agent could arrange to collect a secret profit by telling the seller that the property is worth less than it actually is. This would be a breach of the agent's fiduciary duties.

Any **conflicts of interest** must also be disclosed to the principal. For instance, the seller's agent must inform the seller if there is any relationship between the agent and a prospective buyer. And this disclosure must be made before the principal decides whether to accept the buyer's offer. If the buyer is a friend, relative, or business associate of the agent, or a company in which the agent has an interest, there may be a conflict of interest. The principal has the right to have this information when making his decision.

An agent isn't merely expected to disclose material facts to the principal, but also to discuss the ramifications of the information, to help the principal make sound decisions. However, a real estate agent's advice should not exceed the agent's expertise. For example, a real estate agent must never offer legal advice; when appropriate, she should recommend that the principal consult with a real estate attorney.

AGENT'S DUTIES TO THIRD PARTIES

Even though an agent owes her principal the duties of loyalty and obedience, she may not lie to or mislead other parties in order to achieve a better result for her principal. In fact, the agent owes certain legal duties to other parties. These include the duty of reasonable care and skill and the duty of good faith and fair dealing.

REASONABLE CARE AND SKILL. An agent owes the duty of utmost care to his principal, but he also owes the duty of reasonable care and skill to third parties. Again, the standard that a real estate agent will be measured against is the degree of care and skill that would be expected of a reasonably competent real estate agent. If an agent harms a third party because of carelessness or incompetence, he may held liable to the third party for the harm caused by his negligence.

GOOD FAITH AND FAIR DEALING. The duty of good faith and fair dealing requires a real estate agent to be honest with third parties she deals with on behalf of the principal. Making inaccurate statements or misrepresentations to customers would be a breach of this duty. Even an unintentional misrepresentation may constitute fraud. The party to whom the misrepresentation was made would have the right to rescind the transaction and/or sue for damages.

Not only the real estate agent but also the principal has a duty of good faith and fair dealing. If a seller or a buyer makes misrepresentations to the other party, the other party can rescind the transaction and/or sue for damages.

Disclosure of material facts. It's the duty of good faith and fair dealing that requires seller's agents and sellers to disclose material facts to prospective buyers. They must disclose any information that materially affects the value, desirability, or intended use of the property, unless the information should already be apparent to buyers. Of course, this includes latent defects: problems with the property that wouldn't be obvious to a buyer during a casual inspection. The seller and the seller's agent cannot conceal latent defects; they must disclose them even if the buyer doesn't specifically ask about them.

In most residential transactions, the seller is required to give the buyer a transfer disclosure statement. This requirement applies to all sales of one- to four-unit residential properties, except for new homes in subdivisions being sold for the first time, or properties sold through court order such as probate or foreclosure. We will discuss the transfer disclosure statement in more detail in Chapter 2.

Note that you can usually be held liable for failure to disclose a material fact only if it is a fact that you are aware of, and only if the fact is not readily apparent or ascertainable by the other party. Also, you aren't required to explain the ramifications of a material fact to a third party; you're only required to disclose the fact itself.

If it's unclear whether or not an observed condition is a latent defect, it is always best to err on the side of disclosure. Even small problems should be disclosed, because they might indicate a much bigger problem when considered together.

Example: The seller's agent notices that the house is built on a hillside that consists mostly of fill dirt, which can be unstable. There is netting further down the hill that was probably used to shore up slumping soil. Also, the surface of the garage floor is somewhat uneven.

The agent should consider these facts to be latent defects and disclose them. Although they do not conclusively show that the property is at risk for landslides, taken together they are red flags that suggest a possible geologic hazard.

FIG. 1.1   REAL ESTATE LICENSEE'S AGENCY DUTIES

FIDUCIARY DUTIES OWED ONLY TO THE PRINCIPAL
- UTMOST CARE
- OBEDIENCE AND GOOD FAITH
- ACCOUNTING
- LOYALTY AND CONFIDENTIALITY
- DISCLOSURE OF MATERIAL FACTS

DUTIES OWED TO THIRD PARTIES
- REASONABLE CARE AND SKILL
- GOOD FAITH AND FAIR DEALING
- VISUAL PROPERTY INSPECTION AND DISCLOSURE OF LATENT DEFECTS AND OTHER MATERIAL FACTS

The disclosure of latent defects cannot be waived by the buyer or the buyer's agent. Even if there is an "as is" clause in the deposit receipt, the seller and the seller's agent must still reveal all known latent defects.

INVESTIGATION OR INSPECTION. An agent generally isn't required to search for and discover material facts that she doesn't already know. For instance, an agent does not need to investigate a party's financial position, or to verify statements that come from a reliable source, such as a title insurance company.

One important exception is that California law requires real estate agents to perform a reasonably competent and diligent visual inspection of the property being sold, if it is a residential property with one to four units. Any latent defects or other material facts discovered during the inspection must be reported to a prospective buyer.

WHAT NEED NOT BE DISCLOSED. Certain types of information can stigmatize a property, even though they have no actual effect on the property's condition or title. California law specifically provides that a seller or a seller's agent does not have to disclose to prospective buyers that the property was occupied by someone who had AIDS or was HIV-positive. If a buyer asks whether anyone with AIDS lives or lived in the seller's house, you should explain that answering that question could violate fair housing laws. The same response is appropriate for questions about race, creed, or color (see Chapter 3).

State law also provides that it is not necessary to disclose to buyers that someone died on the property more than three years ago, no matter what the cause of death was. However, if there has been a death on the property within the last three years, and the death could affect the desirability of the property, you should disclose it. In addition, if the buyer asks you about the subject directly, you must answer truthfully.

> **EXAMPLE:** Agent Kipling is showing Buyer Green a house. Green has three children and wants a safe family home to live in. Kipling knows that the property he's showing Green was the site of a brutal homicide-suicide ten years ago. This information does not have to be disclosed to Green, because the deaths occurred more than three years ago.
>
> Note, however, that if Green asks Kipling whether any crimes have occurred on the property, Kipling will have to answer honestly.

OTHER LEGAL EFFECTS OF AGENCY RELATIONSHIPS

An agency relationship has other significant legal implications beyond the issue of agency duties. As we mentioned earlier, for a third party, dealing with an agent can be the legal equivalent of dealing with the principal. When an agent who is authorized to do so signs a document or makes a promise, it's as if the principal signed or promised. The principal is bound by the agent's actions if they are within the actual or apparent scope of the agency. Third parties are expected to inquire into the actual scope of the agent's authority, however. If they fail to do so, the principal will usually not be liable for actions that exceeded the agent's authority.

In addition, communication to an agent is the legal equivalent of communication to the principal. If a third party gives the agent information about a certain problem or requirement, the principal is deemed to have been informed of it—even if the agent never actually passed the information on to the principal. This is called the **imputed knowledge** rule; the agent's knowledge is imputed to the principal.

Furthermore, under certain circumstances, if an agent does something wrong, the principal may be held liable to third parties for harm resulting from the agent's actions. This is called **vicarious liability**. Vicarious liability may apply whether or not the principal approved or knew of the agent's acts, either before or after the fact.

EXAMPLE: Broker Burroughs is representing Sawyer in the sale of her property. While inspecting the property, Burroughs notices indications of previous flooding. Sawyer doesn't know about the flooding, and Burroughs doesn't tell either Sawyer or prospective buyers about the problem.

Hassan purchases Sawyer's property, and soon afterward it floods again. Hassan must pay a repair bill of $5,000. Hassan can sue both Burroughs and Sawyer. Sawyer may be held vicariously liable for her agent's failure to disclose a material fact to the buyer.

If the third party prevails in a lawsuit based on vicarious liability, the agent and principal will usually be jointly liable for the full amount of the damages. In other words, either of them can be required to pay the full amount if the other does not pay his or her share. This is called **joint and several liability**. However, if the principal did nothing wrong, the principal may turn around and sue the agent for the amount the principal had to pay to the injured party.

EXAMPLE: Continuing with the previous example, the court awards Hassan $5,000 in damages. To prevent a judgment lien from attaching to the property she currently owns, Sawyer (the seller) pays the full $5,000 to Hassan. But since Sawyer actually did nothing wrong herself and wasn't aware that Burroughs was withholding information, she may now sue Burroughs (her agent) for the $5,000 that she had to pay to Hassan.

It isn't always easy to collect a judgment from the defendant in a lawsuit, and these liability rules address that problem. In a situation like the one in the example, the problem of collecting money from the broker has effectively been transferred from the buyer (the third party) to the seller—the agent's principal. This creates an incentive for someone who hires an agent to pay attention to how the agency is being carried out, instead of purposefully remaining ignorant of the agent's misconduct.

Note that when it's a real estate salesperson rather than a broker whose action harms a third party, both the salesperson's broker and the client (the seller or buyer) could be held liable. The broker would be vicariously liable as the salesperson's principal, and the client would be vicariously liable as the broker's principal.

To summarize, you can see how important it is to know which party you are representing in a real estate transaction. The existence of an agency relationship has an effect on all of the following concerns:

- the extent of the duties you owe to a particular party in the transaction;
- whether your actions will be binding on a party;
- whether information communicated to you is deemed to have been communicated to a party; and
- whether, under some circumstances, a party may be held liable for your actions.

HOW AN AGENCY IS CREATED AND TERMINATED

Since agency duties arise when an agency relationship begins and last until it ends, you need to know how agency relationships are created and terminated.

CREATING AN AGENCY

The key requirement for the creation of an agency relationship is very simple: the consent of both parties. There are three different ways to establish an agency:

1. **express agreement** (the principal appoints someone to act as an agent, and the agent accepts the appointment);
2. **ratification** (the principal gives approval after the fact to acts performed by a person who was without authority to act for the principal); or
3. **estoppel** (when it would be unfair to a third party to deny an agent's authority because the principal allowed the third party to believe there was an agency relationship).

The vast majority of real estate agency relationships are created by express agreement, either with a listing agreement, a buyer representation agreement (discussed later in this chapter), or a property management agreement (see Chapter 11). A power of attorney is another way of creating an agency by express agreement; real estate agents do not ordinarily have power of attorney for their clients, however.

A real estate agency relationship may also be created inadvertently. This can happen if the seller's agent acts as if she's representing the buyer, leading the buyer to believe that the agent represents him instead of the seller. This is known as an **agency by implication**, because the agent's actions imply that she's the buyer's agent. To avoid unfairness to the buyer, the agent cannot deny the existence of this agency relationship. But since the agent is already representing the seller, this creates an **inadvertent dual agency**.

> **EXAMPLE:** Salesperson Phillips has been working with the Glenn family for a few weeks, showing them a number of houses that they might want to buy and providing them with a lot of information and advice. Phillips doesn't have a signed buyer representation agreement with the Glenns, and in fact he is acting as the sellers' agent in connection with all of these properties. But he doesn't explain that to the Glenns, and they develop the impression that Phillips is acting as their agent.
>
> Under these circumstances, a court could hold that Phillips has become the Glenns' agent by implication. As a result, since Phillips was already acting as the sellers' agent, he has created an inadvertent dual agency.
>
> When the Glenns find a house that they really like, they tell Phillips that they're willing to pay the full listing price but would like to begin by offering $15,000 less. This puts Phillips in a very awkward position. He would be breaching his fiduciary duties to the sellers if he didn't tell them what the Glenns said about the price. However, the Glenns disclosed that information to him because they believed he was their agent and would keep it confidential. So if Phillips does repeat the Glenns' remarks to the sellers, he would be breaching his fiduciary duties to the Glenns.

Inadvertent dual agency was once a common problem. But as we'll discuss shortly, agency disclosure laws have done much to prevent it.

TERMINATING AN AGENCY

An agency relationship may be terminated either by the actions of the parties or through the operation of law. Once an agency has been terminated, the agent is no longer authorized to represent the principal.

TERMINATION BY THE PARTIES. Since agency requires the consent of both the principal and the agent, they can end the agency relationship at any time. This may occur by mutual agreement, revocation, or renunciation.

MUTUAL AGREEMENT. In some cases, the principal and the agent simply agree to end the agency. If the agency was originally established with a written document, it's advisable to formally terminate it in writing, too.

REVOCATION. A principal may revoke an agent's authority at any time. Under some circumstances, however, the revocation may be a breach of contract. In that case, the principal may be liable to the agent for damages resulting from the breach of contract.

> **EXAMPLE:** Davidson decides she distrusts and dislikes the broker she listed her house with, but their exclusive listing won't expire for another two months. Even though Davidson could terminate the listing unilaterally, revoking the broker's authority to represent her, it would be much better if she could get the broker to agree to the termination instead. A unilateral revocation would be a breach of the listing agreement, and the broker could sue Davidson for his commission.

RENUNCIATION. An agent also has the right to terminate the agency relationship unilaterally, without the principal's consent. This is called renouncing the agency. Like revocation, renunciation may be a breach of contract, and the agent could end up owing the principal damages for the breach. But damages are usually not an issue when a real estate broker renounces an agency.

TERMINATION BY OPERATION OF LAW. An agency relationship can terminate by operation of law, without any action on the part of the principal or agent. This can happen as a result of the expiration of the agency, fulfillment of purpose, death or incapacity, or the extinction of the subject matter.

EXPIRATION. If an agency agreement has a termination date, the agent's authority to represent the principal terminates automatically when the expiration date arrives. If there is no termination date, the agency will be deemed to expire within a reasonable time. How long a period is considered reasonable will depend on the circumstances and may be decided by a court.

Note that an agency agreement without a termination date can usually be ended by either party without liability for damages; unilateral termination does not represent a breach of the agreement. In some situations, the other party could ask for reimbursement of expenses incurred in the course of the agency.

FULFILLMENT OF PURPOSE. An agency relationship terminates automatically (before its expiration date) when its purpose has been fulfilled. A listing agreement, for example, is fulfilled when the sale of the listed property closes. The real estate agent's services are no longer needed.

DEATH OR INCAPACITY. An agency also terminates before it expires if either the principal or the agent dies or becomes legally incapacitated (mentally incompetent). As a general rule, the agent's authority to act on behalf of the principal ends at the moment that the principal dies or is declared incompetent by a court, even if the agent is not informed of the event until later on.

EXTINCTION OF SUBJECT MATTER. If the subject matter of an agency is destroyed or otherwise ceases to exist, the agency terminates. For example, the subject matter of a property management agreement is the principal's property. If the principal sells the property, the agent's authority terminates.

FIG. 1.2 CREATION AND TERMINATION OF AGENCY

AGENCY RELATIONSHIPS CAN BE CREATED BY:
- EXPRESS AGREEMENT
- RATIFICATION
- ESTOPPEL
- IMPLICATION (MAY LEAD TO INADVERTENT DUAL AGENCY)

AGENCY RELATIONSHIPS CAN BE TERMINATED BY:
- MUTUAL AGREEMENT
- REVOCATION BY THE PRINCIPAL
- RENUNCIATION BY THE AGENT
- EXPIRATION OF THE AGENCY TERM
- FULFILLMENT OF PURPOSE
- DEATH OR INCAPACITY OF THE PRINCIPAL OR THE AGENT
- EXTINCTION OF THE SUBJECT MATTER

Agency Disclosure

We began this chapter with an example of what can happen to a real estate agent when there is confusion concerning the agency relationships in a transaction: loss of the commission, a lawsuit (perhaps even more than one), and disciplinary action. The best way to prevent confusion is with proper agency disclosure. Agency disclosure should make it clear to all parties who is representing whom, and it is required by state law.

Historical Background

At one time, most listing agreement forms published by multiple listing services had a provision called the "unilateral offer of subagency." Under this provision not only the listing broker, but all of the agents involved in a sale, represented the seller. Agents from the MLS who showed the seller's property to prospective buyers, including the selling agent (the one who ultimately found the buyer for the property), were considered agents of the listing broker and subagents of the seller. A **subagent** is the agent of an agent. If an agent is authorized to appoint subagents, then the principal may be bound by and liable for the actions of a subagent.

Even though in most transactions all of the agents were representing the seller, many buyers believed that the agent who was showing them homes was their agent, not the seller's. This was understandable, since the agent was often working so closely with the buyers. As we explained earlier, this situation could give rise to an inadvertent dual agency and cause some serious problems. The buyers might disclose confidential information to the agent showing them a home, and the agent—as a subagent of the seller—was duty bound to pass the information on to the seller. This came as an unpleasant surprise to the buyers.

As it became more widely understood that buyers weren't being represented by the selling agent, more and more buyers wanted to have agents of their own. Multiple listing services changed the language in their listing agreements to make it easier for MLS members to establish buyer agency relationships. In most listing agreements, the unilateral offer of subagency was replaced with a "cooperation and compensation" clause. Under this clause, other members of an MLS who attempted to

FIG. 1.3 AGENCY DISCLOSURE FORM

CALIFORNIA ASSOCIATION OF REALTORS®

DISCLOSURE REGARDING
REAL ESTATE AGENCY RELATIONSHIPS
(As required by the Civil Code)
(C.A.R. Form AD, Revised 10/01)

When you enter into a discussion with a real estate agent regarding a real estate transaction, you should from the outset understand what type of agency relationship or representation you wish to have with the agent in the transaction.

SELLER'S AGENT

A Seller's agent under a listing agreement with the Seller acts as the agent for the Seller only. A Seller's agent or a subagent of that agent has the following affirmative obligations:
To the Seller:
A Fiduciary duty of utmost care, integrity, honesty, and loyalty in dealings with the Seller.
To the Buyer and the Seller:
(a) Diligent exercise of reasonable skill and care in performance of the agent's duties.
(b) A duty of honest and fair dealing and good faith.
(c) A duty to disclose all facts known to the agent materially affecting the value or desirability of the property that are not known to, or within the diligent attention and observation of, the parties.

An agent is not obligated to reveal to either party any confidential information obtained from the other party that does not involve the affirmative duties set forth above.

BUYER'S AGENT

A selling agent can, with a Buyer's consent, agree to act as agent for the Buyer only. In these situations, the agent is not the Seller's agent, even if by agreement the agent may receive compensation for services rendered, either in full or in part from the Seller. An agent acting only for a Buyer has the following affirmative obligations:
To the Buyer:
A fiduciary duty of utmost care, integrity, honesty, and loyalty in dealings with the Buyer.
To the Buyer and the Seller:
(a) Diligent exercise of reasonable skill and care in performance of the agent's duties.
(b) A duty of honest and fair dealing and good faith.
(c) A duty to disclose all facts known to the agent materially affecting the value or desirability of the property that are not known to, or within the diligent attention and observation of, the parties.

An agent is not obligated to reveal to either party any confidential information obtained from the other party that does not involve the affirmative duties set forth above.

AGENT REPRESENTING BOTH SELLER AND BUYER

A real estate agent, either acting directly or through one or more associate licensees, can legally be the agent of both the Seller and the Buyer in a transaction, but only with the knowledge and consent of both the Seller and the Buyer.

In a dual agency situation, the agent has the following affirmative obligations to both the Seller and the Buyer:
(a) A fiduciary duty of utmost care, integrity, honesty and loyalty in the dealings with either the Seller or the Buyer.
(b) Other duties to the Seller and the Buyer as stated above in their respective sections.

In representing both Seller and Buyer, the agent may not, without the express permission of the respective party, disclose to the other party that the Seller will accept a price less than the listing price or that the Buyer will pay a price greater than the price offered.

The above duties of the agent in a real estate transaction do not relieve a Seller or Buyer from the responsibility to protect his or her own interests. You should carefully read all agreements to assure that they adequately express your understanding of the transaction. A real estate agent is a person qualified to advise about real estate. If legal or tax advice is desired, consult a competent professional.

Throughout your real property transaction you may receive more than one disclosure form, depending upon the number of agents assisting in the transaction. The law requires each agent with whom you have more than a casual relationship to present you with this disclosure form. You should read its contents each time it is presented to you, considering the relationship between you and the real estate agent in your specific transaction.

This disclosure form includes the provisions of Sections 2079.13 to 2079.24, inclusive, of the Civil Code set forth on the reverse hereof. Read it carefully.

I/WE ACKNOWLEDGE RECEIPT OF A COPY OF THIS DISCLOSURE AND CHAPTER 2 OF TITLE 9 OF PART 4 OF DIVISION 3 OF THE CIVIL CODE.

BUYER/SELLER _____ Date _____ Time _____ AM/PM

BUYER/SELLER _____ Date _____ Time _____ AM/PM

AGENT _____ By _____ Date _____
         (Please Print)   (Associate-Licensee or Broker Signature)

THIS FORM SHALL BE PROVIDED AND ACKNOWLEDGED AS FOLLOWS (Civil Code § 2079.14):
•When the listing brokerage company also represents the Buyer, the Listing Agent shall give one AD form to the Seller and one to the Buyer.
•When Buyer and Seller are represented by different brokerage companies, then the Listing Agent shall give one AD form to the Seller and the Buyer's Agent shall give one AD form to the Buyer and one AD form to the Seller.

SEE REVERSE SIDE FOR FURTHER INFORMATION

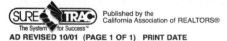 **SURE TRAC** The System for Success™

Published by the
California Association of REALTORS®

AD REVISED 10/01 (PAGE 1 OF 1) PRINT DATE

Reviewed by _____ Date _____

EQUAL HOUSING OPPORTUNITY

DISCLOSURE REGARDING REAL ESTATE AGENCY RELATIONSHIPS (AD PAGE 1 OF 1)

Reprinted with permission, California Association of Realtors®. No endorsement implied.

CHAPTER 2 OF TITLE 9 OF PART 4 OF DIVISION 3 OF THE CIVIL CODE

2079.13 As used in Sections 2079.14 to 2079.24, inclusive, the following terms have the following meanings:
(a) "Agent" means a person acting under provisions of title 9 (commencing with Section 2295) in a real property transaction, and includes a person who is licensed as a real estate broker under Chapter 3 (commencing with Section 10130) of Part 1 of Division 4 of the Business and Professions Code, and under whose license a listing is executed or an offer to purchase is obtained. **(b)** "Associate licensee" means a person who is licensed as a real broker or salesperson under Chapter 3 (commencing with Section 10130) of Part 1 of Division 4 of the Business and Professions Code and who is either licensed under a broker or has entered into a written contract with a broker to act as the broker's agent in connection with acts requiring a real estate license and to function under the broker's supervision in the capacity of an associate licensee. The agent in the real property transaction bears responsibility for his or her associate licensees who perform as agents of the agent. When an associate licensee owes a duty to any principal, or to any buyer or seller who is not a principal, in a real property transaction, that duty is equivalent to the duty owed to that party by the broker for whom the associate licensee functions. **(c)** "Buyer" means a transferee in a real property transaction, and includes a person who executes an offer to purchase real property from a seller through an agent, or who seeks the services of an agent in more than a casual, transitory, or preliminary manner, with the object of entering into a real property transaction. "Buyer" includes vendee or lessee. **(d)** "Dual agent" means an agent acting, either directly or through an associate licensee, as agent for both the seller and the buyer in a real property transaction. **(e)** "Listing agreement" means a contract between an owner of real property and an agent, by which the agent has been authorized to sell the real property or to find or obtain a buyer. **(f)** "Listing agent" means a person who has obtained a listing of real property to act as an agent for compensation. **(g)** "Listing price" is the amount expressed in dollars specified in the listing for which the seller is willing to sell the real property through the listing agent. **(h)** "Offering price" is the amount expressed in dollars specified in an offer to purchase for which the buyer is willing to buy the real property. **(i)** "Offer to purchase" means a written contract executed by a buyer acting through a selling agent which becomes the contract for the sale of the real property upon acceptance by the seller. **(j)** "Real property" means any estate specified by subdivision (1) or (2) of Section 761 in property which constitutes or is improved with one to four dwelling units, any leasehold in this type of property exceeding one year's duration, and mobilehomes, when offered for sale or sold through an agent pursuant to the authority contained in Section 10131.6 of the Business and Professions Code. **(k)** "Real property transaction" means a transaction for the sale of real property in which an agent is employed by one or more of the principals to act in that transaction, and includes a listing or an offer to purchase. **(l)** "Sell," "sale," or "sold" refers to a transaction for the transfer of real property from the seller to the buyer, and includes exchanges of real property between the seller and buyer, transactions for the creation of a real property sales contract within the meaning of Section 2985, and transactions for the creation of a leasehold exceeding one year's duration. **(m)** "Seller" means the transferor in a real property transaction, and includes an owner who lists real property with an agent, whether or not a transfer results, or who receives an offer to purchase real property of which he or she is the owner from an agent on behalf of another. "Seller" includes both a vendor and a lessor. **(n)** "Selling agent" means a listing agent who acts alone, or an agent who acts in cooperation with a listing agent, and who sells or finds and obtains a buyer for the real property, or an agent who locates property for a buyer or who finds a buyer for a property for which no listing exists and presents an offer to purchase to the seller. **(o)** "Subagent" means a person to whom an agent delegates agency powers as provided in Article 5 (commencing with Section 2349) of Chapter 1 of Title 9. However, "subagent" does not include an associate licensee who is acting under the supervision of an agent in a real property transaction.

2079.14 Listing agents and selling agents shall provide the seller and buyer in a real property transaction with a copy of the disclosure form specified in Section 2079.16, and, except as provided in subdivision (c), shall obtain a signed acknowledgement of receipt from that seller or buyer, except as provided in this section or Section 2079.15, as follows: **(a)** The listing agent, if any, shall provide the disclosure form to the seller prior to entering into the listing agreement. **(b)** The selling agent shall provide the disclosure form to the seller as soon as practicable prior to presenting the seller with an offer to purchase, unless the selling agent previously provided the seller with a copy of the disclosure form pursuant to subdivision (a). **(c)** Where the selling agent does not deal on a face-to-face basis with the seller, the disclosure form prepared by the selling agent may be furnished to the seller (and acknowledgement of receipt obtained for the selling agent from the seller) by the listing agent, or the selling agent may deliver the disclosure form by certified mail addressed to the seller at his or her last known address, in which case no signed acknowledgement of receipt is required. **(d)** The selling agent shall provide the disclosure form to the buyer as soon as practicable prior to execution of the buyer's offer to purchase, except that if the offer to purchase is not prepared by the selling agent, the selling agent shall present the disclosure form to the buyer not later than the next business day after the selling agent receives the offer to purchase from the buyer.

2079.15 In any circumstance in which the seller or buyer refuses to sign an acknowledgement of receipt pursuant to Section 2079.14, the agent, or an associate licensee acting for an agent, shall set forth, sign, and date a written declaration of the facts of the refusal.

2079.17 (a) As soon as practicable, the selling agent shall disclose to the buyer and seller whether the selling agent is acting in the real property transaction exclusively as the buyer's agent, exclusively as the seller's agent, or as a dual agent representing both the buyer and the seller. This relationship shall be confirmed in the contract to purchase and sell real property or in a separate writing executed or acknowledged by the seller, the buyer, and the selling agent prior to or coincident with execution of that contract by the buyer and the seller, respectively. **(b)** As soon as practicable, the listing agent shall disclose to the seller whether the listing agent is acting in the real property transaction exclusively as the seller's agent, or as a dual agent representing both the buyer and seller. This relationship shall be confirmed in the contract to purchase and sell real property or in a separate writing executed or acknowledged by the seller and the listing agent prior to or coincident with the execution of that contract by the seller.
(c) The confirmation required by subdivisions (a) and (b) shall be in the following form.

_____ is the agent of (check one): ☐ the seller exclusively; or ☐ both the buyer and seller.
(Name of Listing Agent)

_____ is the agent of (check one): ☐ the buyer exclusively; or ☐ the seller exclusively; or
(Name of Selling Agent if not the same as the Listing Agent)   ☐ both the buyer and seller.

(d) The disclosures and confirmation required by this section shall be in addition to the disclosure required by Section 2079.14.

2079.18 No selling agent in a real property transaction may act as an agent for the buyer only, when the selling agent is also acting as the listing agent in the transaction.

2079.19 The payment of compensation or the obligation to pay compensation to an agent by the seller or buyer is not necessarily determinative of a particular agency relationship between an agent and the seller or buyer. A listing agent and a selling agent may agree to share any compensation or commission paid, or any right to any compensation or commission for which an obligation arises as the result of a real estate transaction, and the terms of any such agreement shall not necessarily be determinative of a particular relationship.

2079.20 Nothing in this article prevents an agent from selecting, as a condition of the agent's employment, a specific form of agency relationship not specifically prohibited by this article if the requirements of Section 2079.14 and Section 2079.17 are complied with.

2079.21 A dual agent shall not disclose to the buyer that the seller is willing to sell the property at a price less than the listing price, without the express written consent of the seller. A dual agent shall not disclose to the seller that the buyer is willing to pay a price greater than the offering price, without the express written consent of the buyer. This section does not alter in any way the duty or responsibility of a dual agent to any principal with respect to confidential information other than price.

2079.22 Nothing in this article precludes a listing agent from also being a selling agent, and the combination of these functions in one agent does not, of itself, make that agent a dual agent.

2079.23 A contract between the principal and agent may be modified or altered to change the agency relationship at any time before the performance of the act which is the object of the agency with the written consent of the parties to the agency relationship.

2079.24 Nothing in this article shall be construed to either diminish the duty of disclosure owed buyers and sellers by agents and their associate licensees, subagents, and employees or to relieve agents and their associate licensees, subagents, and employees from liability for their conduct in connection with acts governed by this article or for any breach of a fiduciary duty or a duty of disclosure.

(AD BACKER)

find a buyer for a property were authorized to act as cooperating agents and share in the listing broker's compensation. This did not necessarily create an agency relationship between the seller and the cooperating agents; instead, a cooperating agent could choose whether he or she would represent the buyer or the seller in a particular transaction.

In spite of this change in listing agreements, most cooperating agents still acted as the seller's agent, and many buyers were still confused. To address this problem directly, a number of state legislatures, including California's, passed agency disclosure laws. These laws require real estate agents to disclose which party they are representing in a transaction. The agency disclosure laws have done much to reduce buyers' confusion over who (if anyone) is representing them. As a result, inadvertent dual agency is now a much less common problem.

AGENCY DISCLOSURE REQUIREMENTS

California's agency disclosure law, adopted in 1988, applies to transactions involving residential property with one to four dwelling units. It requires the real estate agents to disclose their agency status to the parties and give them two different written disclosures: an agency disclosure form and an agency confirmation statement.

AGENCY DISCLOSURE FORM. The agency disclosure form is essentially a consumer information form for real estate sellers and buyers. It explains the legal duties of a seller's agent, a buyer's agent, and a dual agent. The back of the form sets forth the provisions of the agency disclosure law. An example of this form is shown in Figure 1.3.

A listing agent is required to provide a copy of this general disclosure form to a seller before the seller signs a listing agreement. A selling agent must give the form to a buyer as soon as practical, and before the buyer signs an offer to purchase. The selling agent must also give the form to the seller as soon as practical before presenting the buyer's offer to the seller. (If the selling agent isn't dealing directly with the seller, the selling agent can deliver the form to the seller through the listing agent or by certified mail.) Each disclosure form must be signed by the party who receives it, to acknowledge receipt. The agent who furnished the form must also sign it and keep a copy for her transaction records.

FIG. 1.4   AGENCY CONFIRMATION STATEMENT

CALIFORNIA ASSOCIATION OF REALTORS®

CONFIRMATION REAL ESTATE AGENCY RELATIONSHIPS

(As required by the Civil Code)

Subject Property Address

The following agency relationship(s) is/are hereby confirmed for this transaction:

LISTING AGENT: _____

is the agent of (check one):
- ❑ the Seller exclusively; or
- ❑ both the Buyer and Seller

SELLING AGENT: _____

(if not the same as Listing Agent)

is the agent of (check one):
- ❑ the Buyer exclusively; or
- ❑ the Seller exclusively; or
- ❑ both the Buyer and Seller

I/WE ACKNOWLEDGE RECEIPT OF A COPY OF THIS CONFIRMATION.

Seller _____ Date _____   Buyer _____ Date _____

Seller _____ Date _____   Buyer _____ Date _____

Listing Agent _____ By _____ Date _____
       (Please Print)   (Associate Licensee or Broker-Signature)

Selling Agent _____ By _____ Date _____
       (Please Print)   (Associate Licensee or Broker-Signature)

A REAL ESTATE BROKER IS QUALIFIED TO ADVISE ON REAL ESTATE. IF YOU DESIRE LEGAL ADVICE, CONSULT YOUR ATTORNEY.

This form is available for use by the entire real estate industry. It is not intended to identify the user as a REALTOR®. REALTOR® is a registered collective membership mark which may be used only by members of the NATIONAL ASSOCIATION OF REALTORS® who subscribe to its Code of Ethics.

The copyright laws of the United States (17 U.S. Code) forbid the unauthorized reproduction of this form by any means, including facsimile or computerized formats.
Copyright © 1987-1997, CALIFORNIA ASSOCIATION OF REALTORS®

Published and Distributed by:
REAL ESTATE BUSINESS SERVICES, INC.
a subsidiary of the CALIFORNIA ASSOCIATION OF REALTORS®
525 South Virgil Avenue, Los Angeles, California 90020

Page _____ of _____ Pages.

OFFICE USE ONLY
Reviewed by Broker
or Designee _____
Date _____

EQUAL HOUSING OPPORTUNITY

CONFIRMATION REAL ESTATE AGENCY RELATIONSHIPS (AC-6 PAGE 1 OF 1) REVISED 1987

Reprinted with permission, California Association of Realtors®. No endorsement implied.

Notice that the agency disclosure form does not indicate which party the agent who provides it is representing in this particular transaction. That specific disclosure is made in the agency confirmation statement.

AGENCY CONFIRMATION STATEMENT. As soon as it's practical to do so, a real estate agent is required to disclose to each party in a particular transaction which party or parties he is representing in the transaction. The initial disclosure may be spoken rather than written, but each party must sign a written agency confirmation statement before signing a deposit receipt form (a purchase agreement).

This confirmation statement may be included in the deposit receipt form, as long as it's clearly presented in a separate agency disclosure paragraph. Alternatively, the confirmation statement may be a separate document. The parties' signatures on the deposit receipt or the separate agency confirmation document indicate that they understand and accept the stated agency relationships.

Figure 1.4 shows an example of an agency confirmation form. This would be used if the deposit receipt form didn't have an agency confirmation provision. Each agent checks off which party he or she represents and signs the document. Both the seller and the buyer also sign it to acknowledge receipt of a copy.

ACTING IN ACCORDANCE WITH THE DISCLOSURES

The disclosures mandated by state law are fairly straightforward. However, once the disclosures have been made, a real estate agent also must act in accordance with them. This can be more difficult than it sounds.

EXAMPLE: Carville is the listing agent for Sharp's house; he represents only the seller. Carville discloses this fact, in writing, to Blaine, a potential buyer.

But Carville and Blaine get along well, and over the course of a few days he acts more and more like Blaine's agent. He gives Blaine a lot of advice about making an offer and negotiating the best terms. Blaine begins to rely on Carville's advice, and by the time Blaine is ready to make an offer on Sharp's house, he feels confident that Carville is working in his (Blaine's) best interests.

In this case, even though Carville properly disclosed his status as the seller's agent, his actions may have implied an agency relationship with Blaine and created an inadvertent dual agency. If Blaine or Sharp later became dissatisfied with the transaction, either of them could accuse Carville of breaching his agency duties.

As this example shows, the agency disclosure law has not completely eliminated the problem of inadvertent dual agency.

If a real estate agent's conduct is not consistent with her agency disclosure, she may be subject to disciplinary action by the Department of Real Estate, and the following sanctions may be imposed:

- suspension or revocation of her real estate license; and/or
- a fine of up to $10,000.

LICENSEE ACTING AS A PRINCIPAL

As a real estate agent, when you're selling or buying property for yourself, you should make some special disclosures to the other party. You should disclose that you are a licensed real estate agent and that you are selling or buying the property for your own benefit. If you're buying property in order to fix it up and resell it, inform the seller that you plan to make a profit off it. If you're selling property that you have a direct or indirect ownership interest in, you must disclose the extent of your interest to the buyer. Make all of these disclosures in writing. It's also a good idea to recommend that the other party seek independent legal advice and an independent appraisal.

Don't try to act as the other party's agent. Disclose your licensed status, but avoid using your business cards, brokerage stationery, or other items that may create the impression that you're acting in your capacity as a real estate licensee.

In certain situations, you might change your role from agent to principal. For example, this would happen if you decided to buy one of your own listings. Then it would be especially important to explain your conflict of interest to the seller and strongly advise her to consult a lawyer about the transaction. If you are planning to resell the property at a profit, disclose the amount of profit you expect to make and obtain the seller's consent. Again, do all of this in writing.

Your broker may have specific office policies about buying or selling your own property. If so, you should become familiar with them and follow them. Ask your broker to review any contracts involved before you make or accept an offer.

TYPES OF AGENCY RELATIONSHIPS

Now let's examine more closely the three basic types of real estate agency relationships: seller agency, buyer agency, and dual agency. We'll also discuss how a real estate licensee can act as a finder instead of as an agent.

SELLER AGENCY

Seller agency, which is ordinarily established with a listing agreement, is the traditional type of real estate agency. As we explained earlier, at one time all of the agents involved in a typical residential transaction—the listing agent, the selling agent, and any other cooperating agents—were representing the seller. It was relatively uncommon for residential buyers to be represented by an agent.

Now the "cooperation and compensation" clause is a standard provision in listing agreements, and many licensees choose to represent buyers. However, a property's listing agent still always represents the property's seller. And unless a licensee specifically enters into an agency agreement with a buyer, he still may be presumed to be acting as the seller's agent.

SELLER'S AGENT'S DUTIES TO SELLER. A licensee acting as a seller's agent owes fiduciary duties to the seller. During the agency, she must use her best efforts to promote the seller's interests. While marketing the property, she must use utmost care and obey the seller's instructions. She must not disclose any confidential information obtained from the seller to third parties.

SERVICES TO BUYERS. A seller's agent must always treat a prospective buyer fairly and in good faith. But the agent must not act as if she is representing the buyer. While the seller's agent must fully disclose all material facts and answer the buyer's questions honestly, the agent should not give the buyer advice. For example, it would obviously be inappropriate for the seller's agent to suggest to the buyer how much to offer for the listed property.

Even so, there are many services that a seller's agent can provide to a buyer without violating his fiduciary duties to the seller. In fact, these services actually promote the interests of the seller, because they increase the chances of a sale and then enable the sales transaction to close smoothly. The services a seller's agent can offer a buyer include:

- discussing the buyer's housing needs;
- showing the property to the buyer;
- answering questions about the property and the neighborhood;
- discussing financing alternatives;
- furnishing copies of documents that affect the property (such as CC&Rs and easements);
- explaining the process of presenting the offer, negotiation, and closing the transaction; and
- referring the buyer to other professionals, if necessary.

PRE-EXISTING RELATIONSHIPS. A seller's agent can provide all of these services without creating an agency relationship with the buyer. However, sometimes the seller's agent has had a previous relationship with the buyer. In this situation it may be difficult for the agent to represent the seller's interests without feeling some loyalty to the buyer as well.

> **EXAMPLE:** Agent Jensen helped Sterling sell her home. Sterling was so pleased with Jensen's work, she wants him to help her find her next home. Jensen selects a suitable property that he has listed and shows it to Sterling.
>
> Under the circumstances, it would be easy for Sterling to assume that Jensen is acting as her agent. But unless otherwise agreed, Jensen is only the seller's agent, and he should emphasize this fact to Sterling. Jensen should disclose his agency relationship with the seller to Sterling, remind Sterling that he is obligated to tell the seller any material information Sterling reveals to him, and emphasize to Sterling that he will be representing the seller in all negotiations.

Remember, however, that if an agent learns confidential information from the principal during the agency relationship, he cannot disclose that information to others even after the termination of the agency relationship. So Jensen cannot tell his current client, the seller, things that he knows about Sterling because he used to be her agent.

BUYER AGENCY

Buyer agency became increasingly popular over the last decade, as buyers grew familiar with the advantages of agency representation. Some buyers want more than the services a seller's agent can provide to a customer. They want advice on how much to offer for a particular home and someone to help them negotiate the terms of the sale. When represented by their own agents, buyers can relax and divulge key information about their housing needs and financial condition, knowing the agent must keep these matters confidential.

BENEFITS OF BUYER AGENCY. The benefits of a buyer agency relationship can be broken down into four categories:

- agency duties,
- objective advice,
- help with negotiations, and
- access to more properties.

AGENCY DUTIES. A buyer's agent owes fiduciary duties to the buyer rather than to the seller. For many buyers, the loyalty their agent owes them is the most important benefit of a buyer agency relationship. A buyer's agent must put the buyer's interests ahead of anyone else's, and any private information the buyer discloses to the agent must be kept confidential.

EXAMPLE: Ashworth is a first-time home buyer. Broker Donnelly is helping him find a home. Donnelly shows him a home he's very interested in. Its listing price is $359,000 and Ashworth could easily afford a home that costs $30,000 more. Donnelly must put Ashworth's interests before her own, so she encourages him to make an offer on the home, even though she would receive a larger commission if he purchased a more expensive property.

Ashworth is eager to buy the home and suggests making a full price offer. Donnelly is pretty sure Ashworth can get the property for less than the listing price, so she advises him to start by offering $354,000. Even though Donnelly knows Ashworth is willing to pay the full listing price, she is obligated to keep that information confidential. If she had been the seller's agent, she would have been required to disclose this information to the seller.

OBJECTIVE ADVICE. Seller's agents develop expert sales techniques that are designed to convince the buyer to sign on the dotted line. Buyer's agents, on the other hand, are free to advise the buyer on the pros and cons of purchasing any given home.

EXAMPLE: The Whittiers looked very seriously at two homes before they purchased a third one. Their agent, Smith, gave them invaluable advice throughout the house-hunting process.

The Whittiers responded emotionally to the beautiful landscaping and lovely interior of the first home, and they were immediately ready to make a full price offer. Then Smith helped them look into the property taxes, heating costs, and upkeep, and the Whittiers realized that the house would cost too much to maintain.

The second home they were interested in was much more affordable, but Smith made sure they got all the pertinent information about the structural condition of the house. Once they realized how much it would cost to replace the roof and what three previous termite infestations meant, they quickly decided against the purchase.

The third home seemed ideal, even after Smith helped them evaluate all the information about it. Because Smith was familiar with the housing market, he advised the Whittiers to offer $8,000 less than the listing price. Their offer was accepted and the transaction closed without a hitch. If it weren't for Smith's objective advice, they might have ended up with a property that wasn't right for them.

HELP WITH NEGOTIATIONS. While some buyers are happiest when they're dickering over a sales price, many buyers are decidedly uncomfortable negotiating for a home they want. They are afraid to offer full price, because they don't want to pay too much for the home. On the other hand, they are afraid to make an offer that's too low, for fear of offending the seller and ruining any chance of reaching an agreement. A buyer's agent is extremely useful during the negotiation phase. The agent can use her knowledge of the real estate market to help the buyer get the property on the best possible terms.

EXAMPLE: The Browns are first-time buyers. They have decided to make an offer on a starter home, but they are unsure about how much to offer. Their agent, Cohen, knows the going price for similar homes and suggests an amount for a strategic opening offer. She also discusses other important terms of the offer, such as the amount of the good faith deposit, the closing date, and how the parties will divide the closing costs. With her help, the Browns are able to purchase the home on very favorable terms.

ACCESS TO MORE PROPERTIES. A buyer's agent who enters into a written representation agreement with the buyer (see below) will usually be compensated if the buyer purchases any home, even one that isn't listed with a broker. So a buyer's agent may pursue less traditional means of searching for properties, considering properties that are for sale by owner, properties with open listings, and properties in foreclosure or probate proceedings.

EXAMPLE: McHugh has very specific housing requirements. Among other things, he wants lake frontage, a boat ramp, an outbuilding to use as a shop, and fruit trees. A property with these features in McHugh's price range simply can't be found through the multiple listing service.

McHugh enters into a buyer representation agreement with Morris and agrees to pay a commission if Morris finds him a property that is not listed with the MLS. Morris scours legal notices for foreclosure, bankruptcy, and estate sales. He also carefully reviews "for sale by owner" (FSBO) ads in the local and regional papers. Finally, after driving through several lakeshore neighborhoods, he spots a FSBO that meets most of McHugh's requirements.

McHugh makes an offer on the house and the seller accepts it. McHugh is overjoyed to have found the home he wants, and he's glad to pay Morris's commission.

BUYER REPRESENTATION AGREEMENTS. If a buyer and a broker choose to create a buyer agency relationship, they should enter into a written **representation agreement** that sets forth the rights and duties of both parties. Naturally, these include the agent's duty to use his professional expertise to locate a property for the buyer and negotiate the terms of the sale, and also the circumstances in which the buyer will be required to compensate the agent. Most buyer representation agreements contain other important provisions as well. These may include:

- the term of the agreement;
- the general characteristics of the property the buyer wants;
- a price range for the property;
- any warranties or representations made by the agent; and
- how the buyer agency relationship will affect the agent's relationship with other property buyers and sellers.

An example of a buyer representation agreement is shown in Figure 1.5. This form authorizes the broker to locate properties and show them to the buyer, present offers on the buyer's behalf, assist in the negotiation process, and assist the buyer in obtaining financing, inspections, and escrow services.

The agreement shown in Figure 1.5 also provides that the agent may show the buyer properties listed with the agent's own firm. In that case, the salesperson's broker will become a dual agent and is required to immediately disclose the dual agency to the buyer. (See the section on in-house transactions in the discussion of dual agency later in this chapter.) The buyer also acknowledges that other salespersons affiliated with the broker may represent different buyers in competing transactions involving the same property, but that the broker will not reveal either party's negotiating position to the other party.

Another provision often found in buyer representation agreements is one regarding warranties and representations. Generally, the buyer agrees to be responsible for investigating and inspecting the property. The buyer's agent refuses to make any warranties or representations regarding the value of any property or its suitability for the buyer's purposes.

BUYER'S AGENT'S COMPENSATION. Naturally, real estate agents are concerned about how they will be compensated for their time and effort. The way a seller's agent is compensated is well established: the seller agrees to pay the listing broker a percentage of the sales price when the prop-

FIG. 1.5   BUYER REPRESENTATION AGREEMENT

CALIFORNIA ASSOCIATION OF REALTORS®

BUYER BROKER REPRESENTATION AGREEMENT
(C.A.R. Form BR, Revised 4/02)

1.   **RIGHT TO REPRESENT:** _____ ("Buyer")
     grants _____ ("Broker")
     beginning on (date) _____ and ending **(i)** upon written notice by either party, **(ii)** upon completion of a resulting transaction, or **(iii)** one year (or ☐ _____) from the beginning date, whichever occurs first ("Representation Period"), the non-exclusive and revocable right, on the terms specified in this Agreement, to represent Buyer in acquiring real property or a manufactured home. Broker agrees to exercise due diligence and reasonable efforts to fulfill the following authorizations and obligations. Broker will perform its obligations under this Agreement through the individual signing for Broker below, who is either Broker individually or an associate-licensee (an individual licensed as a real estate salesperson or broker who works under Broker's real estate license). Buyer agrees that Broker's duties are limited by the terms of this Agreement, including those limitations set forth in paragraphs 3 and 4.

2.   **AGENCY RELATIONSHIPS:**
     A.   DISCLOSURE: If the property being sought includes residential property with one-to-four dwelling units, Buyer acknowledges receipt of the "Disclosure Regarding Real Estate Agency Relationships" form prior to entering into this Agreement.
     B.   BUYER REPRESENTATION: Broker will represent, as described in this Agreement, Buyer in any resulting transaction.
     C.   (1) POSSIBLE DUAL AGENCY WITH SELLER: (C(1) APPLIES UNLESS C(2)(i) or (ii) is checked below.)
     Depending on the circumstances, it may be necessary or appropriate for Broker to act as an agent for both Buyer and a seller, exchange party, or one or more additional parties ("Seller"). Broker shall, as soon as practicable, disclose to Buyer any election to act as a dual agent representing both Buyer and Seller. If Buyer is shown property listed with Broker, Buyer consents to Broker becoming a dual agent representing both Buyer and Seller with respect to those properties. In event of dual agency, Buyer agrees that: **(a)** Broker, without the prior written consent of Buyer, will not disclose to Seller that Buyer is willing to pay a price greater than the price offered; **(b)** Broker, without the prior written consent of Seller, will not disclose to Buyer that Seller is willing to sell property at a price less than the listing price; and **(c)** other than as set forth in (a) and (b) above, a dual agent is obligated to disclose known facts materially affecting the value or desirability of the Property to both parties.
     OR (2) SINGLE AGENCY ONLY: (APPLIES ONLY IF (i) or (ii) is checked below.)
     ☐ **(i) Broker's firm lists properties for sale:** Buyer understands that this election will prevent Broker from showing Buyer those properties that are listed with Broker's firm or from representing Buyer in connection with those properties. In any resulting transaction in which Seller's property is not listed with Broker's firm, Broker will be the exclusive agent of Buyer and not a dual agent also representing Seller.
     OR ☐ **(ii) Broker's firm DOES NOT list property:** Entire brokerage firm only represents buyers and does not list property. In any resulting transaction, Broker will be the exclusive agent of Buyer and not a dual agent also representing Seller.
     D.   OTHER POTENTIAL BUYERS: Buyer understands that other potential buyers may, through Broker, consider, make offers on or acquire the same or similar properties as those Buyer is seeking to acquire. Buyer consents to Broker's representation of such other potential buyers before, during and after the term of this Agreement, or any extension thereof.
     E.   CONFIRMATION: If the Property includes residential property with one-to-four dwelling units, Broker shall confirm the agency relationship described above, or as modified, in writing, prior to or coincident with Buyer's execution of a Property Contract.

3.   **BROKER AUTHORIZATIONS AND OBLIGATIONS:**
     A.   Buyer authorizes Broker to: (i) locate and present selected properties to Buyer, present offers authorized by Buyer, and assist Buyer in negotiating for acceptance of such offers, **(ii)** assist Buyer with the financing process, including obtaining loan pre-qualification; **(iii)** upon request, provide Buyer with a list of professionals or vendors who perform the services described in the attached Buyer's Inspection Advisory; **(iv)** order reports, and schedule and attend meetings and appointments with professionals chosen by Buyer; **(v)** provide guidance to help Buyer with the acquisition of property; and **(vi)** obtain a credit report on Buyer.
     B.   For property transactions of which Broker is aware and not precluded from participating in by Buyer, Broker shall provide and review forms to create a property contract ("Property Contract") for the acquisition of a specific property ("Property"). With respect to such Property, Broker shall: (i) if the Property contains residential property with one-to-four dwelling units, conduct a reasonably competent and diligent on-site visual inspection of the accessible areas of the Property (excluding any common areas), and disclose to Buyer all facts materially affecting the value or desirability of such Property that are revealed by this inspection; **(ii)** deliver or communicate to Buyer any disclosures, materials or information received by, in the personal possession of or personally known to the individual signing for Broker below during the Representation Period; and **(iii)** facilitate the escrow process, including assisting Buyer in negotiating with Seller. Unless otherwise specified in writing, any information provided through Broker in the course of representing Buyer has not been and will not be verified by Broker. Broker's services are performed in compliance with federal, state and local anti-discrimination laws.

4.   **SCOPE OF BROKER DUTY:**
     A.   While Broker will perform the duties described in paragraph 3B, Broker recommends that Buyer select other professionals, as described in the attached Buyer's Inspection Advisory, to investigate the Property through inspections, investigations, tests, surveys, reports, studies and other available information ("Inspections") during the transaction. Buyer agrees that these Inspections, to the extent they exceed the obligations described in paragraph 3B, are not within the scope of Broker's agency duties. Broker informs Buyer that it is in Buyer's best interest to obtain such Inspections.

Buyer's Initials (_____)(_____)
Broker's Initials (_____)(_____)

Reviewed by _____ Date _____

EQUAL HOUSING OPPORTUNITY

BUYER BROKER REPRESENTATION AGREEMENT (BR PAGE 1 OF 2)

Buyer: _____   Date: _____

B. Buyer acknowledges and agrees that Broker: **(i)** does not decide what price Buyer should pay or Seller should accept; **(ii)** does not guarantee the condition of the Property; **(iii)** does not guarantee the performance, adequacy or completeness of Inspections, services, products or repairs provided or made by Seller or others to Buyer or Seller; **(iv)** shall not be responsible for identifying defects that are not known to Broker and either **(a)** are not visually observable in reasonably accessible areas of the Property or **(b)** are in common areas; **(v)** shall not be responsible for identifying the location of boundary lines or other items affecting title; **(vi)** shall not be responsible for verifying square footage, representations of others or information contained in Inspection reports; **(vii)** shall not be responsible for providing legal or tax advice regarding any aspect of a transaction entered into by Buyer in the course of this representation; and **(viii)** shall not be responsible for providing other advice or information that exceeds the knowledge, education and experience required to perform real estate licensed activities. Buyer agrees to seek legal, tax, insurance, title and other desired assistance from appropriate professionals.

C. Broker owes no duty to inspect for common environmental hazards, earthquake weaknesses, or geologic and seismic hazards. If Buyer receives the booklets titled "Environmental Hazards: A Guide for Homeowners, Buyers,Landlords and Tenants," "The Homeowner's Guide to Earthquake Safety," or "The Commercial Property Owner's Guide to Earthquake Safety," the booklets are deemed adequate to inform Buyer regarding the information contained in the booklets and, other than as specified in 3B above, Broker is not required to provide Buyer with additional information about the matters described in the booklets.

5. BUYER OBLIGATIONS:

A. Buyer agrees to timely view and consider properties selected by Broker and to negotiate in good faith to acquire a property. Buyer further agrees to act in good faith toward the completion of any Property Contract entered into in furtherance of this Agreement. Within **5 (or** ☐ _____**) calendar days** from the execution of this Agreement, Buyer shall provide relevant personal and financial information to Broker to assure Buyer's ability to acquire Property. If Buyer fails to provide such information, or if Buyer does not qualify financially to acquire Property, then Broker may cancel this Agreement in writing. Buyer has an affirmative duty to take steps to protect him/herself, including discovery of the legal, practical and technical implications of discovered or disclosed facts, and investigation of information and facts which are known to Buyer or are within the diligent attention and observation of Buyer. Buyer is obligated to and agrees to read all documents provided to Buyer. Buyer agrees to seek desired assistance from appropriate professionals, selected by Buyer, such as those referenced in the attached Buyer's Inspection Advisory.

B. Buyer shall notify Broker in writing of any material issue to Buyer, such as, but not limited to, Buyer requests for information on, or concerns regarding, any particular area of interest or importance to Buyer ("Material Consideration").

C. **Buyer agrees to (i) indemnify, defend and hold Broker harmless from all claims, disputes, litigation, judgments, costs and attorney fees arising from any incorrect information supplied by Buyer, or from any Material Consideration that Buyer fails to disclose in writing to Broker and (ii) pay for reports, Inspections and meetings arranged by Broker on Buyer's behalf.**

D. Buyer is advised to read the attached Buyer's Inspection Advisory for a list of items and other concerns that typically warrant Inspections or investigation by Buyer or other professionals.

E. Other Brokers: Buyer represents that Buyer has not entered into an exclusive representation agreement with another brokerage to represent Buyer in acquiring real property or manufactured house except _____ .

6. TIME TO BRING LEGAL ACTION: Legal action for breach of this Agreement, or any obligation arising therefrom, shall be brought no more than two years from the expiration of the Representation Period or the date such cause of action arises, whichever occurs first.

7. OTHER TERMS AND CONDITIONS, including ATTACHED SUPPLEMENTS: ☐ Buyer's Inspection Advisory (C.A.R. Form BIA)
_____
_____

8. ENTIRE CONTRACT: All understandings between the parties are incorporated in this Agreement. Its terms are intended by the parties as a final, complete and exclusive expression of their agreement with respect to its subject matter, and may not be contradicted by evidence of any prior agreement or contemporaneous oral agreement. This Agreement may not be extended, amended, modified, altered or changed, except in writing signed by Buyer and Broker. In the event that any provision of this Agreement is held to be ineffective or invalid, the remaining provisions will nevertheless be given full force and effect. This Agreement and any supplement, addendum or modification, including any copy, whether by copier, facsimile, NCR or electronic, may be signed in two or more counterparts, all of which shall constitute one and the same writing.

Buyer acknowledges that Buyer has read, understands, accepts and has received a copy of this Agreement.

Buyer _____   Date _____
Address _____ City _____ State _____ Zip _____
Telephone _____ Fax _____ E-mail _____

Buyer _____   Date _____
Address _____ City _____ State _____ Zip _____
Telephone _____ Fax _____ E-mail _____

Real Estate Broker (Firm) _____
By (Agent) _____   Date _____
Address _____ City _____ State _____ Zip _____
Telephone _____ Fax _____ E-mail _____

THIS FORM HAS BEEN APPROVED BY THE CALIFORNIA ASSOCIATION OF REALTORS® (C.A.R.). NO REPRESENTATION IS MADE AS TO THE LEGAL VALIDITY OR ADEQUACY OF ANY PROVISION IN ANY SPECIFIC TRANSACTION. A REAL ESTATE BROKER IS THE PERSON QUALIFIED TO ADVISE ON REAL ESTATE TRANSACTIONS. IF YOU DESIRE LEGAL OR TAX ADVICE, CONSULT AN APPROPRIATE PROFESSIONAL.

This form is available for use by the entire real estate industry. It is not intended to identify the user as a REALTOR®. REALTOR® is a registered collective membership mark which may be used only by members of the NATIONAL ASSOCIATION OF REALTORS® who subscribe to its Code of Ethics.

SURE TRAC
The System for Success™

Published by the
California Association of REALTORS®

BR REVISED 4/02 (PAGE 2 OF 2)

Reviewed by _____ Date _____

EQUAL HOUSING OPPORTUNITY

BUYER BROKER REPRESENTATION AGREEMENT   (BR PAGE 2 OF 2)

erty is sold. If another brokerage is involved in bringing the sale about, the listing broker and the selling broker will split the commission.

The arrangements for paying a buyer's agent's fee are not so clear-cut. There are three common methods of compensating a buyer's agent:

- a seller-paid fee,
- a buyer-paid fee, and
- a retainer.

The buyer and the buyer's agent may agree to one of these methods, or a combination of two or more methods.

SELLER-PAID FEE. Under the terms of most listing agreements, the buyer's agent will be paid by the seller, as a result of a commission split. The seller pays the commission to the listing agent, and the listing agent then splits the commission with the buyer's agent. This arrangement is based on a provision found in most listing agreements that entitles any cooperating agent who procures a buyer to receive the selling broker's portion of the commission, regardless of which party that cooperating agent represents. (The source of the commission does not determine the identity of the agent's principal.)

> **EXAMPLE:** Seller Forbes lists his property with Broker Winston. He agrees to pay Winston a commission of 7% of the sales price. The listing agreement includes a clause that entitles any cooperating broker who procures a buyer to be paid the selling broker's portion of the commission.
>
> Broker Lopez is representing Buyer Brown. Brown offers $200,000 for Forbes's house and Forbes accepts the offer. When the transaction closes, the $14,000 commission paid by Forbes is split between Winston and Lopez. Accepting a share of the commission paid by the seller does not affect Lopez's agency relationship with the buyer.

Since the commission split arrangement does not change the amount of the commission the seller is obligated to pay, sellers rarely object to paying the buyer's agent's fee in this way. Most buyer representation agreements provide that the buyer's agent will be paid by a commission split if the buyer purchases a home that is listed through a multiple listing service.

BUYER-PAID FEE. Buyer representation agreements may also provide for a buyer-paid fee. The fee may be based on an hourly rate, an arrangement that turns the agent into a consultant. Alternatively, a buyer's agent may charge a percentage fee, requiring the buyer to pay the agent a percentage of the purchase price of the property as a commission. A third possibility is a flat fee—a specified sum that is payable if the buyer purchases a property found by the broker.

Many buyer representation agreements provide that the buyer's agent will accept a commission split if one is available, but that the buyer will pay the fee if the purchased property was unlisted (for example, if the property was for sale by owner). In some situations, a buyer promises to pay a flat fee to a broker but then purchases a property that is subject to a commission split. If the commission split only covers a part of that fee, the buyer will need to pay the broker the difference.

RETAINER. Some agents insist on a retainer—a fee paid up front—before agreeing to a buyer agency relationship. The retainer is usually nonrefundable, but will be credited against any fee or commission that the buyer's agent becomes entitled to.

DUAL AGENCY

As you know, a dual agency relationship exists when an agent represents both the seller and the buyer in the same transaction. A dual agent owes fiduciary duties to both principals. However, because the interests of the buyer and the seller nearly always conflict, it is difficult to represent them both without being disloyal to one or the other.

> **EXAMPLE:** Woodman represents both the buyer and the seller in a real estate transaction. The seller informs Woodman that she is in a big hurry to sell and will accept any reasonable offer. The buyer tells Woodman that he is very interested in the house and is willing to pay the full listing price. Should Woodman tell the buyer about the seller's eagerness to sell? Should Woodman tell the seller about the buyer's willingness to pay full price?

In fact, it is really impossible for a dual agent to fully represent both parties. Thus, a dual agent should explain to both of her principals that neither of them will receive full representation. Certain facts must necessarily be withheld from each party; the dual agent cannot divulge confidential information about one party to the other. California law specifically provides that a dual agent cannot tell the buyer that the seller is willing to sell for less than the listing price unless the seller consents to the disclosure in writing. Nor can the dual agent tell the seller that the buyer is willing to pay less than the offered price without the buyer's written consent.

IN-HOUSE TRANSACTIONS. Sometimes a dual agency arises in connection with an in-house transaction. An in-house transaction exists when the listing agent and the selling agent both work for the same broker. The listing agent, of course, represents the seller, and if the selling agent is representing the buyer, then their broker becomes a dual agent.

> **EXAMPLE:** Salesperson Werner, who works for Broker Black, is acting as Buyer Miller's agent. They've looked at many houses. Finally, Werner shows Miller a house listed by Salesperson Nagano, who also works for Broker Black. Miller decides to make an offer on the house. Salesperson Werner will continue to represent Buyer Miller; Salesperson Nagano will continue to represent the seller; and Broker Black will be considered a dual agent.

FIG. 1.6   TYPES OF REAL ESTATE AGENCY

SELLER'S AGENT
- OWES FIDUCIARY DUTIES ONLY TO THE SELLER

BUYER'S AGENT
- OWES FIDUCIARY DUTIES ONLY TO THE BUYER

DUAL AGENT
- OWES FIDUCIARY DUTIES TO BOTH SELLER AND BUYER
- MUST NOT DISCLOSE CONFIDENTIAL INFORMATION TO EITHER PARTY

FINDER OR MIDDLEMAN
- INTRODUCES BUYER TO SELLER
- OWES FIDUCIARY DUTIES TO NEITHER PARTY

DUAL AGENCY DISCLOSURE. Before acting as a dual agent, a broker must have the informed written consent of both parties to the transaction. Acting as a dual agent without full disclosure and written consent is a violation of California's Real Estate Law, and may lead to disciplinary action.

Real estate licensees should be especially careful about their agency disclosures in this context. Buyers and sellers, eager to get on with the business of buying and selling a home, may agree to a dual agency without really understanding what it means. They may accept the agent's explanation at face value and sign an agency confirmation statement without question. Later, one party may feel that his or her interests were neglected and that agency duties were breached. This kind of disappointment often leads to legal action.

FINDER OR MIDDLEMAN

It's possible for a real estate licensee to be involved in a transaction without forming an agency relationship with either party. This happens when a licensee acts as a **finder** or **middleman**. In order to be considered a finder rather than an agent, the licensee can have no involvement in the transaction beyond arranging an introduction between the seller and a prospective buyer.

A licensee acting as a finder does not owe fiduciary duties to either party. Any activity aside from a mere introduction, such as participating in the negotiations, will create an agency relationship. Forming an agency relationship without the proper disclosure can lead to disciplinary action and the loss of the finder's fee.

Note that it is not necessary to be a real estate licensee to act as a finder and collect a finder's fee. Again, however, the finder must do nothing more than introduce the parties. If an unlicensed person did anything beyond that, she would be acting as a real estate licensee without a license and could face penalties from the Real Estate Commissioner.

CHAPTER SUMMARY

1. When a real estate licensee enters into an agency relationship, he owes fiduciary duties to his principal. These include the duty of utmost care, obedience and good faith, accounting, loyalty and confidentiality, and disclosure of material facts.

2. A real estate licensee owes third parties the duties of reasonable care and skill and good faith and fair dealing. Both a seller's agent and the seller must disclose latent defects and other material facts to prospective buyers.

3. California law requires real estate agents to perform a reasonably competent and diligent visual inspection of the property and disclose any problems they discover to the buyer.

4. In California, real estate agents must disclose to the parties in a transaction which party they are representing. The parties must be given an agency disclosure form, and they must also sign an agency confirmation form or provision in the deposit receipt.

5. A seller agency relationship is ordinarily created with a listing agreement. A buyer agency relationship should also be created by written agreement. A licensee may act as a dual agent with the written consent of both parties, but must be careful not to create a dual agency inadvertently.

6. A real estate licensee (or an unlicensed person) may collect a finder's fee for introducing a seller and a buyer. A finder is not considered to be an agent and does not owe fiduciary duties to either party.

CHAPTER QUIZ

1. The listing agent knows that a suicide took place in the house four years ago. A buyer specifically asks the agent if he knows about any deaths that have occurred on the property. The agent says he's not aware of any. What duty has the agent breached?

    a. The duty to disclose material facts

    b. The duty of reasonable care and skill

    c. The duty of good faith and fair dealing

    d. None; the agent acted properly

2. Under California law, which of the following would not have to be disclosed as a latent defect?

    a. The agent found indications of flooding in the basement during a visual inspection

    b. A person diagnosed with AIDS lived on the property until last year

    c. The property was the site of an illegal drug lab, and chemical residues may linger

    d. The roof of the house leaks during heavy rains

3. The duty of accounting does not include which of the following responsibilities?

    a. To disclose the terms of the listing salesperson's share of the commission

    b. To be able to account for all funds or valuables entrusted to the broker

    c. To avoid commingling trust funds with the broker's own funds

    d. To report to clients on the status of all trust funds regularly

4. A buyer's agent is most commonly compensated with:

    a. an hourly rate

    b. a seller-paid commission split

    c. a retainer

    d. a flat fee

5. Which of the following situations clearly does not involve dual agency?

   a. A listing agent gives advice to prospective buyers about how much to offer for the property

   b. A licensee introduces a seller to a prospective buyer without providing further representation

   c. A buyer and a seller consent in writing to be represented by the same broker

   d. A broker employs both the selling agent, who is representing the buyer in this transaction, and the listing agent, who represents the seller

6. The seller's agent does not have to:

   a. present an offer that is below the listing price

   b. present an offer if the seller already has a higher offer for the same property

   c. seek additional offers when the property is subject to an existing sales contract

   d. disclose material facts she learns after the sales contract has been signed

7. Whether or not you have an agency relationship with a particular party in a transaction does not affect:

   a. whether that party may be held liable for your actions

   b. the extent of the duties you owe to that party

   c. whether your actions will be binding on that party

   d. whether you are required to answer that party's questions in good faith

8. Proper agency confirmation may be made:

   a. anywhere in the deposit receipt

   b. in a separate document

   c. in a separate paragraph in the deposit receipt

   d. Both b and c

9. Which of the following is not one of the basic types of real estate agency relationships in California?

    a. Net agency

    b. Seller agency

    c. Dual agency

    d. Buyer agency

10. Which of the following situations involves a change from one type of agency relationship to another?

    a. A finder explains to the seller and the buyer that she is acting only as a facilitator in the transaction

    b. The buyer's agent receives the selling broker's share of the commission, even though the commission was paid by the seller

    c. A real estate agent representing a buyer shows the buyer one of her own listings

    d. A buyer representation agreement provides that the buyer's agent will accept a commission split if available, but otherwise the buyer will pay the agent's fee

ANSWER KEY

1. c. The agent was not required to disclose the suicide as a material fact, because it took place more than three years ago. But by responding untruthfully to a specific question, the agent breached the duty of good faith and fair dealing that he owes to potential buyers.

2. b. An agent may not disclose that a property was occupied by a person who had AIDS or was HIV-positive. Other problems that may affect the value or desirability of the property are material facts and must be disclosed as latent defects.

3. a. The duty of accounting requires a broker to account for all trust funds she holds. The broker must keep the client updated as to the status of the funds. She must also avoid commingling them with her personal or general business funds. (The listing salesperson's share of the brokerage commission does not have to be disclosed to the client.)

4. b. Unless the property was unlisted, a buyer's agent is ordinarily compensated with a portion of the commission paid by the seller to the listing agent.

5. b. A finder can avoid creating an agency relationship with either party by providing no services beyond introducing them to one another. A dual agency can be created through express agreement or inadvertently. In an in-house transaction, the broker becomes a dual agent (but the listing agent continues to represent only the seller and the selling agent continues to represent only the buyer).

6. c. The seller's agent is not required to seek additional offers once the seller has entered into a purchase agreement.

7. d. An agency relationship with one of the parties in a transaction does not allow you to give false or misleading information to third parties, even on your principal's orders.

8. d. The agency confirmation statement may be included in the deposit receipt or provided in a separate document. If it is incorporated into the deposit receipt, it must be in a separate paragraph.

9. a. The basic types of real estate agency relationships in California are seller agency, buyer agency, and dual agency.

10. c. A listing agent always represents the seller. So when a buyer's agent shows the buyer one of her own listings, a dual agency is created. The agent must disclose this to both parties and obtain their written consent.

LISTING AGREEMENTS AND PROPERTY DISCLOSURES

TYPES OF LISTING AGREEMENTS

- Open listings
- Exclusive agency listings
- Exclusive right to sell listings

ELEMENTS OF A LISTING AGREEMENT

- Basic legal requirements
- Provisions of a typical listing agreement form
- Modifying a listing agreement

MANDATORY DISCLOSURES CONCERNING THE PROPERTY

- Transfer disclosure statement
- Environmental hazards booklet
- Natural hazard disclosure statement
- Residential earthquake hazards report
- Lead-based paint disclosure
- Smoke detector and water heater disclosures
- Supplemental statutory disclosure form
- Mello-Roos lien disclosure

INTRODUCTION

Real estate agents love to get new listings. Each listing can generate a lot of business activity:

- When you submit a listing agreement to the multiple listing service, all of the agents who belong to the MLS can start looking for a buyer.
- When a new "For Sale" sign shows up in a neighborhood, "drive-by" buyers will call your office for more information.
- When you hold an open house for the listed property, you attract potential buyers and sellers that you may be able to do business with in the future.
- And when the listed property sells, you get a portion of the commission, no matter who finds the buyer.

Obtaining a listing is a positive and financially rewarding experience. There are a variety of techniques you can learn to help you get listings; these methods are thoroughly explained in courses and books on sales techniques. However, using a listing agreement properly and fulfilling the legal obligations it imposes are just as important as finding an interested seller to list with you. If you aren't thoroughly familiar with the terms of your listing agreement form and able to use it correctly, your career may get off to a very rocky start.

This chapter describes the different types of listing agreements, the elements of a valid listing agreement, and the standard provisions that are found in most listing agreement forms. It also discusses the transfer disclosure statement form that you will give to sellers to fill out when they list their property with you. The chapter also covers a variety of other disclosures that California law requires sellers to make to prospective buyers.

TYPES OF LISTING AGREEMENTS

A **listing agreement** is a written employment contract between a property owner and a real estate broker. The owner hires the broker to find a buyer (or a tenant) who is **ready, willing, and able** to buy (or lease) the property on the owner's terms.

There are three different types of listing agreements:

- the open listing,
- the exclusive agency listing, and
- the exclusive right to sell listing.

OPEN LISTING AGREEMENTS

Open listings are rarely used in residential transactions these days, but you still need to understand how they work. Under an open listing, the seller is obligated to pay your broker a commission only if you are the **procuring cause** of the sale. The procuring cause is the person who is primarily responsible for bringing about the agreement between the seller and a ready, willing, and able buyer. To be the procuring cause, you usually must have personally negotiated the offer that the seller accepts, or an offer that meets the seller's stated terms.

An open listing is rarely in the best interests of either the real estate agent or the seller. Here are some of the disadvantages of open listings:

- A seller may enter into open listings with as many brokers as he wants. Only the broker whose salesperson makes the sale is entitled to a commission; the other brokers and their sales agents are not compensated for their time and effort. And if the seller himself makes the sale, he does not have to pay any of the brokers.
- Since a listing agent has little assurance of earning a commission from an open listing, she might not put as much effort into marketing the property.
- If agents working for two competing brokers negotiate with the person who ends up buying the property, there may be a dispute over which agent was the procuring cause.

Because of these problems, open listings are generally used only when a seller is unwilling to execute an exclusive agency or exclusive right to sell listing.

EXCLUSIVE AGENCY LISTING AGREEMENTS

In an exclusive agency listing, the seller agrees to list with only one broker, but retains the right to sell the property herself without being

---

FIG. 2.1   TYPES OF LISTING AGREEMENTS

OPEN LISTING
- SELLER MAY GIVE OPEN LISTINGS TO SEVERAL BROKERS
- ONLY THE BROKER WHOSE AGENT WAS THE PROCURING CAUSE IS COMPENSATED

EXCLUSIVE AGENCY LISTING
- SELLER GIVES LISTING TO ONLY ONE BROKER
- NO COMPENSATION IF SELLER FINDS A BUYER WITHOUT HELP
- LISTING BROKER COMPENSATED IF ANYONE OTHER THAN SELLER FINDS A BUYER

EXCLUSIVE RIGHT TO SELL LISTING
- SELLER GIVES LISTING TO ONLY ONE BROKER
- LISTING BROKER COMPENSATED IF ANYONE FINDS A BUYER

---

obligated to pay the broker a commission. The broker is entitled to a commission if anyone other than the seller finds a buyer for the property, but not if the seller finds the buyer without the help of an agent.

Exclusive agency listings are uncommon in residential transactions because they present the chance of a commission dispute between the seller and the broker as to who was the procuring cause of the sale.

EXCLUSIVE RIGHT TO SELL LISTING AGREEMENTS

In an exclusive right to sell listing, the seller agrees to list with only one broker, and that broker is entitled to a commission if the property sells during the listing term, regardless of who finds the buyer. Even if the seller makes the sale directly, without the help of an agent, the broker is still entitled to the commission.

Not surprisingly, the exclusive right to sell listing is the type preferred by most brokers. It provides the most protection for the listing broker, and the potential for conflict with the seller over who was the procuring cause is limited. The brokers involved in the transaction might disagree about who's entitled to the selling broker's share of the commission, but the seller will have to pay the listing broker in any event.

Because of these advantages, the great majority of residential listing agreements are exclusive right to sell listings.

ELEMENTS OF A LISTING AGREEMENT

When you go to a listing appointment, you take along the listing agreement form used by your office. It is probably a form provided by your local multiple listing service or Association of Realtors®. Brokers rarely use their own individual listing forms, and you certainly aren't expected to come up with one yourself. (If you did, you would be guilty of the unauthorized practice of law.) Even so, you should understand the basic legal requirements for a valid listing agreement. Later in the chapter we will look at the standard provisions found in a typical listing agreement form.

BASIC LEGAL REQUIREMENTS

Of course, a listing agreement must have all of the elements that are required for any valid contract: competent parties, offer and acceptance, consideration, and a legal purpose. In addition, a listing agreement should:

- identify the property to be sold,
- include terms of sale,
- establish the broker's authority,
- establish the broker's compensation,
- specify the listing's termination date, and
- be in writing and signed by the seller.

IDENTIFY THE PROPERTY. The property must be clearly identified in the agreement. Of course, it's best to use a legal description. A street address is useful, but not adequate by itself. After you fill in the property's street address, you should fill in or attach the property's legal description as well. You can get the property's legal description from a title insurance company or from the seller's deed.

TERMS OF SALE. A listing agreement should indicate what kind of offer the seller wants from prospective buyers. Most importantly, the agreement should state the listing price—that is, the cash price that the seller would like for the property. It should also state any other terms of sale the seller requires (for example, a closing date after January 1) or is willing to provide (for example, secondary financing, or assumption of an existing loan).

The seller ought to specify any terms that would affect whether or not he'd be willing to accept an offer. Otherwise, he could become liable for the brokerage commission if he refuses an offer that meets all the stated terms of sale but is nonetheless undesirable.

The listing agreement should also state what property will and will not be included in the sale. This applies especially to any items of personal property that the seller intends to leave behind for the buyer, and to any fixtures that the seller intends to remove.

BROKER'S AUTHORITY. Since the listing agreement is an employment contract, it should specify the listing agent's duties and the scope of her authority. Typically, a broker is given the authority to list the property with a multiple listing service, advertise the property, cooperate with buyers' agents, and receive offers and good faith deposits on the seller's behalf.

PROMISE OF COMPENSATION. Of course, the seller's promise to compensate the broker is a key provision in a listing agreement. The conditions of payment should be clearly stated. For example, the seller could promise to pay the broker when the broker has found a ready, willing, and able buyer, or not until a contract is signed, or not unless a sale actually closes. A **ready, willing, and able buyer** is one who:

1. makes an offer to purchase that meets the seller's terms, and
2. is financially able to complete the transaction.

In addition to the conditions of payment, the listing agreement should state the amount or rate of the listing broker's compensation. The compensation—the brokerage commission—is usually stated as a specified percentage of the sales price, but it may be a specified dollar amount instead.

In listing agreements for one- to four-unit residential properties, state law requires a provision in boldface type stating that the amount or rate of the commission is not fixed by law, and is negotiable between the seller and broker.

In a **net listing**, the seller stipulates a certain net amount that she wants from the sale of the property. If the sales price exceeds that net figure, the listing agent is entitled to keep the excess as his compensation. In California, net listings are allowed only if the listing agent discloses the amount of his commission to the seller before the seller becomes committed to the transaction.

> **EXAMPLE:** Warshaw wants you to sell her home. She wants to get $235,000 from the sale, and she says you can have anything over that. In other words, if you can sell the property for $245,000, you get a $10,000 commission. If you sell the property for $250,000, you get a $15,000 commission.
>
> It is legal to take Warshaw's listing on this basis only if you inform her how much your commission will amount to before she accepts an offer to purchase.

Net listings are generally disfavored because they give unscrupulous brokers an opportunity to take advantage of clients who don't know the true value of their property.

TERMINATION DATE. California law requires an exclusive agency or exclusive right to sell listing agreement to have a definite termination date. There is no minimum or maximum listing period; the parties may agree to whatever listing period suits their needs. But the listing period's termination date must be included in the listing agreement.

IN WRITING. California's statute of frauds requires all listing agreements to be in writing and signed by the seller. Without a written, signed listing agreement, the broker can't sue for the commission. Note, however, that the writing requirement doesn't mean that you must have a formal listing agreement. Some notes jotted on a piece of paper could be sufficient.

> **EXAMPLE:** George runs into his old friend Brad. Brad wants to put his house up for sale, and he's delighted to discover that George is now a real estate broker. He wants to list his property with George right away.
>
> George doesn't have a listing agreement form with him, so he jots down the following on a piece of paper: "I will pay George Hanson 6% of the selling price when he finds a ready, willing, and able buyer for the only piece of property I own—Hillshire Orchards—in Fresno County." Brad signs the paper. This would probably be enforceable in California, as long as Brad is legally competent and the description is sufficient to identify the property.

PROVISIONS OF A TYPICAL LISTING AGREEMENT FORM

Of course, printed listing agreement forms contain much more information than the handwritten note in the example above. Let's take a look at the many provisions found in a typical listing form.

In California (as in most states), there is no single standard listing agreement form. Various forms are available from multiple listing services, brokers' associations, and general publishers of legal forms. Although these forms have many elements in common, there may also be significant differences between them. You must be sure to learn the provisions of the specific form used by your broker.

The following is a general discussion of provisions likely to be encountered in a typical form, but any given form might omit some of these provisions and include others not discussed here. As an example, an exclusive right to sell listing form published by the California Association of Realtors® is shown in Figure 2.2.

BROKER'S AUTHORITY AND LISTING PERIOD. The first section in a listing agreement form usually identifies the parties, establishes the broker's agency authority, and specifies the date on which the listing period will expire.

BROKER'S NAME. Although a listing agreement form is frequently filled out and signed by a salesperson, the listing agreement is actually a contract between the seller and the broker. Remember, only a broker may directly contract with members of the public for brokerage services (see Chapter 1).

AGENCY AUTHORITY. Even though the most commonly used type of listing agreement is called an "exclusive right to sell" listing, it does not literally give the broker authority to sell the property. It is up to the seller to accept an offer and transfer the property to the buyer.

> **EXAMPLE:** You take a listing on Sorenson's house. Wilson is very interested in purchasing the house, and he makes an offer that meets all of Sorenson's terms. You do not have the authority to accept this offer; you only have the authority to present the offer to Sorenson. Sorenson will choose whether or not to accept the offer.

Typically, the listing agreement also gives the broker authority to accept good faith deposits from prospective buyers on behalf of the seller.

FIG. 2.2 EXCLUSIVE RIGHT TO SELL LISTING AGREEMENT FORM

CALIFORNIA ASSOCIATION OF REALTORS®

RESIDENTIAL LISTING AGREEMENT
(Exclusive Authorization and Right to Sell)
(C.A.R. Form LA, Revised 10/02)

1. **EXCLUSIVE RIGHT TO SELL:** _____ ("Seller")
   hereby employs and grants _____ ("Broker")
   beginning (date) _____ and ending at 11:59 P.M. on (date) _____ ("Listing Period")
   the exclusive and irrevocable right to sell or exchange the real property in the City of _____,
   County of _____, California, described as: _____
   _____ ("Property").

2. **ITEMS EXCLUDED AND INCLUDED:** Unless otherwise specified in a real estate purchase agreement, all fixtures and fittings that are attached to the Property are included, and personal property items are excluded, from the purchase price.
   ADDITIONAL ITEMS EXCLUDED: _____
   ADDITIONAL ITEMS INCLUDED: _____
   Seller intends that the above items be excluded or included in offering the Property for sale, but understands that: **(i)** the purchase agreement supersedes any intention expressed above and will ultimately determine which items are excluded and included in the sale; and **(ii)** Broker is not responsible for and does not guarantee that the above exclusions and/or inclusions will be in the purchase agreement.

3. **LISTING PRICE AND TERMS:**
   A. The listing price shall be: _____
   _____ Dollars ($ _____).
   B. Additional Terms: _____
   _____

4. **COMPENSATION TO BROKER:**
   Notice: The amount or rate of real estate commissions is not fixed by law. They are set by each Broker individually and may be negotiable between Seller and Broker (real estate commissions include all compensation and fees to Broker).
   A. Seller agrees to pay to Broker as compensation for services irrespective of agency relationship(s), either ☐ _____ percent of the listing price (or if a purchase agreement is entered into, of the purchase price), or ☐ $ _____,
   AND _____, as follows:
   (1) If Broker, Seller, cooperating broker, or any other person procures a buyer(s) who offers to purchase the Property on the above price and terms, or on any price and terms acceptable to Seller during the Listing Period, or any extension.
   (2) If Seller, within _____ calendar days **(a)** after the end of the Listing Period or any extension, or **(b)** after any cancellation of this Agreement, unless otherwise agreed, enters into a contract to sell, convey, lease or otherwise transfer the Property to anyone ("Prospective Buyer") or that person's related entity: **(i)** who physically entered and was shown the Property during the Listing Period or any extension by Broker or a cooperating broker; or **(ii)** for whom Broker or any cooperating broker submitted to Seller a signed, written offer to acquire, lease, exchange or obtain an option on the Property. Seller, however, shall have no obligation to Broker under paragraph 4A(2) unless, not later than **3 calendar days** after the end of the Listing Period or any extension or cancellation, Broker has given Seller a written notice of the names of such Prospective Buyers.
   (3) If, without Broker's prior written consent, the Property is withdrawn from sale, conveyed, leased, rented, otherwise transferred, or made unmarketable by a voluntary act of Seller during the Listing Period, or any extension.
   B. If completion of the sale is prevented by a party to the transaction other than Seller, then compensation due under paragraph 4A shall be payable only if and when Seller collects damages by suit, arbitration, settlement or otherwise, and then in an amount equal to the lesser of one-half of the damages recovered or the above compensation, after first deducting title and escrow expenses and the expenses of collection, if any.
   C. In addition, Seller agrees to pay Broker: _____
   D. **(1)** Broker is authorized to cooperate with and compensate brokers participating through the multiple listing service(s) ("MLS"): **(i)** in any manner; **OR (ii)** (if checked) by offering MLS brokers: either ☐ _____ percent of the purchase price, or ☐ $ _____.
   (2) Broker is authorized to cooperate with and compensate brokers operating outside the MLS in any manner.
   E. Seller hereby irrevocably assigns to Broker the above compensation from Seller's funds and proceeds in escrow. Broker may submit this agreement, as instructions to compensate Broker pursuant to paragraph 4A, to any escrow regarding the Property involving Seller and a buyer, Prospective Buyer or other transferee.
   F. **(1)** Seller represents that Seller has not previously entered into a listing agreement with another broker regarding the Property, unless specified as follows: _____
   (2) Seller warrants that Seller has no obligation to pay compensation to any other broker regarding the Property unless the Property is transferred to any of the following individuals or entities: _____
   _____
   (3) If the Property is sold to anyone listed above during the time Seller is obligated to compensate another broker: **(i)** Broker is not entitled to compensation under this agreement; and **(ii)** Broker is not obligated to represent Seller in such transaction.

Seller acknowledges receipt of a copy of this page.
Seller's Initials (_____)(_____)

Reviewed by _____ Date _____

LA REVISED 10/02 (PAGE 1 OF 3) Print Date

RESIDENTIAL LISTING AGREEMENT-EXCLUSIVE (LA PAGE 1 OF 3)

Property Address: _____ Date: _____

5. **OWNERSHIP, TITLE AND AUTHORITY:** Seller warrants that: **(i)** Seller is the owner of the Property; **(ii)** no other persons or entities have title to the Property; and **(iii)** Seller has the authority to both execute this agreement and sell the Property. Exceptions to ownership, title and authority are as follows: _____ .

6. **MULTIPLE LISTING SERVICE:** Information about this listing will (or ☐ will not) be provided to the MLS of Broker's selection. All terms of the transaction, including financing, if applicable, will be provided to the selected MLS for publication, dissemination and use by persons and entities on terms approved by the MLS. Seller authorizes Broker to comply with all applicable MLS rules. MLS rules allow MLS data to be made available by the MLS to additional Internet sites unless Broker gives the MLS instructions to the contrary.

7. **SELLER REPRESENTATIONS:** Seller represents that, unless otherwise specified in writing, Seller is unaware of: **(i)** any Notice of Default recorded against the Property; **(ii)** any delinquent amounts due under any loan secured by, or other obligation affecting, the Property; **(iii)** any bankruptcy, insolvency or similar proceeding affecting the Property; **(iv)** any litigation, arbitration, administrative action, government investigation or other pending or threatened action that affects or may affect the Property or Seller's ability to transfer it; and **(v)** any current, pending or proposed special assessments affecting the Property. Seller shall promptly notify Broker in writing if Seller becomes aware of any of these items during the Listing Period or any extension thereof.

8. **BROKER'S AND SELLER'S DUTIES:** Broker agrees to exercise reasonable effort and due diligence to achieve the purposes of this agreement. Unless Seller gives Broker written instructions to the contrary, Broker is authorized to order reports and disclosures as appropriate or necessary and advertise and market the Property by any method and in any medium selected by Broker, including MLS and the Internet, and, to the extent permitted by these media, control the dissemination of the information submitted to any medium. Seller agrees to consider offers presented by Broker, and to act in good faith to accomplish the sale of the Property by, among other things, making the Property available for showing at reasonable times and referring to Broker all inquiries of any party interested in the Property. Seller is responsible for determining at what price to list and sell the Property. **Seller further agrees to indemnify, defend and hold Broker harmless from all claims, disputes, litigation, judgments and attorney fees arising from any incorrect information supplied by Seller, or from any material facts that Seller knows but fails to disclose.**

9. **DEPOSIT:** Broker is authorized to accept and hold on Seller's behalf any deposits to be applied toward the purchase price.

10. **AGENCY RELATIONSHIPS:**
    A. Disclosure: If the Property includes residential property with one-to-four dwelling units, Seller shall receive a "Disclosure Regarding Agency Relationships" form prior to entering into this agreement.
    B. Seller Representation: Broker shall represent Seller in any resulting transaction, except as specified in paragraph 4F.
    C. Possible Dual Agency With Buyer: Depending upon the circumstances, it may be necessary or appropriate for Broker to act as an agent for both Seller and buyer, exchange party, or one or more additional parties ("Buyer"). Broker shall, as soon as practicable, disclose to Seller any election to act as a dual agent representing both Seller and Buyer. If a Buyer is procured directly by Broker or an associate licensee in Broker's firm, Seller hereby consents to Broker acting as a dual agent for Seller and such Buyer. In the event of an exchange, Seller hereby consents to Broker collecting compensation from additional parties for services rendered, provided there is disclosure to all parties of such agency and compensation. Seller understands and agrees that: **(i)** Broker, without the prior written consent of Seller, will not disclose to Buyer that Seller is willing to sell the Property at a price less than the listing price; **(ii)** Broker, without the prior written consent of Buyer, will not disclose to Seller that Buyer is willing to pay a price greater than the offered price; and **(iii)** except for (i) and (ii) above, a dual agent is obligated to disclose known facts materially affecting the value or desirability of the Property to both parties.
    D. Other Sellers: Seller understands that Broker may have or obtain listings on other properties, and that potential buyers may consider, make offers on, or purchase through Broker, property the same as or similar to Seller's Property. Seller consents to Broker's representation of sellers and buyers of other properties before, during and after the end of this agreement.
    E. Confirmation: If the Property includes residential property with one-to-four dwelling units, Broker shall confirm the agency relationship described above, or as modified, in writing, prior to or concurrent with Seller's execution of a purchase agreement.

11. **SECURITY AND INSURANCE:** Broker is not responsible for loss of or damage to personal or real property, or person, whether attributable to use of a keysafe/lockbox, a showing of the Property, or otherwise. Third parties, including, but not limited to, appraisers, inspectors, brokers and prospective buyers, may have access to, and take videos and photographs of, the interior of the Property. Seller agrees: **(i)** to take reasonable precautions to safeguard and protect valuables that might be made accessible during showings of the Property; and **(ii)** to obtain insurance to protect against these risks. Broker does not maintain insurance to protect Seller.

12. **KEYSAFE/LOCKBOX:** A keysafe/lockbox is designed to hold a key to the Property to permit access to the Property by Broker, cooperating brokers, MLS participants, their authorized licensees and representatives, authorized inspectors, and accompanied prospective buyers. Broker, cooperating brokers, MLS and Associations/Boards of REALTORS® are **not** insurers against injury, theft, loss, vandalism or damage attributed to the use of a keysafe/lockbox. Seller does (or if checked ☐ does not) authorize Broker to install a keysafe/lockbox. If Seller does not occupy the Property, Seller shall be responsible for obtaining occupant(s)' written permission for use of a keysafe/lockbox.

13. **SIGN:** Seller does (or if checked ☐ does not) authorize Broker to install a FOR SALE/SOLD sign on the Property.

14. **EQUAL HOUSING OPPORTUNITY:** The Property is offered in compliance with federal, state and local anti-discrimination laws.

15. **ATTORNEY FEES:** In any action, proceeding or arbitration between Seller and Broker regarding the obligation to pay compensation under this agreement, the prevailing Seller or Broker shall be entitled to reasonable attorney fees and costs from the non-prevailing Seller or Broker, except as provided in paragraph 19A.

16. **ADDITIONAL TERMS:** _____
_____
_____

17. **MANAGEMENT APPROVAL:** If an associate licensee in Broker's office (salesperson or broker-associate) enters into this agreement on Broker's behalf, and Broker or Manager does not approve of its terms, Broker or Manager has the right to cancel this agreement, in writing, within 5 days after its execution.

18. **SUCCESSORS AND ASSIGNS:** This agreement shall be binding upon Seller and Seller's successors and assigns.

Seller acknowledges receipt of a copy of this page.
Seller's Initials (_____)(_____)

LA REVISED 10/02 (PAGE 2 OF 3)

Reviewed by _____ Date _____

RESIDENTIAL LISTING AGREEMENT-EXCLUSIVE (LA PAGE 2 OF 3)

Property Address: _____   Date: _____

19. DISPUTE RESOLUTION:

A.   MEDIATION: Seller and Broker agree to mediate any dispute or claim arising between them out of this agreement, or any resulting transaction, before resorting to arbitration or court action, subject to paragraph 19B(2) below. Paragraph 19B(2) below applies whether or not the arbitration provision is initialed. Mediation fees, if any, shall be divided equally among the parties involved. If, for any dispute or claim to which this paragraph applies, any party commences an action without first attempting to resolve the matter through mediation, or refuses to mediate after a request has been made, then that party shall not be entitled to recover attorney fees, even if they would otherwise be available to that party in any such action. THIS MEDIATION PROVISION APPLIES WHETHER OR NOT THE ARBITRATION PROVISION IS INITIALED.

B.   ARBITRATION OF DISPUTES: (1) Seller and Broker agree that any dispute or claim in Law or equity arising between them regarding the obligation to pay compensation under this agreement, which is not settled through mediation, shall be decided by neutral, binding arbitration, including and subject to paragraph 19B(2) below. The arbitrator shall be a retired judge or justice, or an attorney with at least 5 years of residential real estate law experience, unless the parties mutually agree to a different arbitrator, who shall render an award in accordance with substantive California Law. The parties shall have the right to discovery in accordance with Code of Civil Procedure §1283.05. In all other respects, the arbitration shall be conducted in accordance with Title 9 of Part III of the California Code of Civil Procedure. Judgment upon the award of the arbitrator(s) may be entered in any court having jurisdiction. Interpretation of this agreement to arbitrate shall be governed by the Federal Arbitration Act.

(2) EXCLUSIONS FROM MEDIATION AND ARBITRATION: The following matters are excluded from mediation and arbitration hereunder: **(i)** a judicial or non-judicial foreclosure or other action or proceeding to enforce a deed of trust, mortgage, or installment land sale contract as defined in Civil Code §2985; **(ii)** an unlawful detainer action; **(iii)** the filing or enforcement of a mechanic's lien; and **(iv)** any matter that is within the jurisdiction of a probate, small claims, or bankruptcy court. The filing of a court action to enable the recording of a notice of pending action, for order of attachment, receivership, injunction, or other provisional remedies, shall not constitute a waiver of the mediation and arbitration provisions.

"NOTICE: BY INITIALING IN THE SPACE BELOW YOU ARE AGREEING TO HAVE ANY DISPUTE ARISING OUT OF THE MATTERS INCLUDED IN THE 'ARBITRATION OF DISPUTES' PROVISION DECIDED BY NEUTRAL ARBITRATION AS PROVIDED BY CALIFORNIA LAW AND YOU ARE GIVING UP ANY RIGHTS YOU MIGHT POSSESS TO HAVE THE DISPUTE LITIGATED IN A COURT OR JURY TRIAL. BY INITIALING IN THE SPACE BELOW YOU ARE GIVING UP YOUR JUDICIAL RIGHTS TO DISCOVERY AND APPEAL, UNLESS THOSE RIGHTS ARE SPECIFICALLY INCLUDED IN THE 'ARBITRATION OF DISPUTES' PROVISION. IF YOU REFUSE TO SUBMIT TO ARBITRATION AFTER AGREEING TO THIS PROVISION, YOU MAY BE COMPELLED TO ARBITRATE UNDER THE AUTHORITY OF THE CALIFORNIA CODE OF CIVIL PROCEDURE. YOUR AGREEMENT TO THIS ARBITRATION PROVISION IS VOLUNTARY."

"WE HAVE READ AND UNDERSTAND THE FOREGOING AND AGREE TO SUBMIT DISPUTES ARISING OUT OF THE MATTERS INCLUDED IN THE 'ARBITRATION OF DISPUTES' PROVISION TO NEUTRAL ARBITRATION."

| Seller's Initials ____ / ____ | Broker's Initials ____ / ____ |

20. ENTIRE CONTRACT: All prior discussions, negotiations and agreements between the parties concerning the subject matter of this agreement are superseded by this agreement, which constitutes the entire contract and a complete and exclusive expression of their agreement, and may not be contradicted by evidence of any prior agreement or contemporaneous oral agreement. If any provision of this agreement is held to be ineffective or invalid, the remaining provisions will nevertheless be given full force and effect. This agreement and any supplement, addendum or modification, including any photocopy or facsimile, may be executed in counterparts.

By signing below, Seller acknowledges that Seller has read, understands, accepts and has received a copy of this agreement.

Seller _____   Date _____
Address _____ City _____ State _____ Zip _____
Telephone _____ Fax _____ E-mail _____

Seller _____   Date _____
Address _____ City _____ State _____ Zip _____
Telephone _____ Fax _____ E-mail _____

Real Estate Broker (Firm) _____
By (Agent) _____   Date _____
Address _____ City _____ State _____ Zip _____
Telephone _____ Fax _____ E-mail _____

SURE TRAC
The System for Success™

Published by the
California Association of REALTORS®

EQUAL HOUSING OPPORTUNITY

LA REVISED 10/02 (PAGE 3 OF 3)

| Reviewed by _____ Date _____ |

RESIDENTIAL LISTING AGREEMENT-EXCLUSIVE (LA PAGE 3 OF 3)

LISTING PERIOD. A listing agreement ordinarily includes a termination date. This is especially important for exclusive listing agreements, because an exclusive listing effectively prevents the seller from hiring a different agent until it expires. (If the seller hired another agent, she might end up owing a commission to both the first agent and the new one.) As we said earlier, a termination date is required by law in an exclusive listing agreement in California, although the listing period can be whatever the seller and the listing agent agree to.

Of course, a listing agreement may terminate before its termination date even without a sale of the property. This can happen in a number of different ways, generally corresponding to the ways in which any agency relationship can terminate (see Chapter 1):

- termination by mutual agreement of the seller and the broker;
- revocation by the seller;
- renunciation by the broker;
- death, mental incompetence, or bankruptcy of the seller or broker; or
- the loss of the broker's license.

The seller and the listing broker may terminate the listing by mutual agreement at any time. Alternatively, the seller may revoke the listing agreement by firing the broker whenever he wishes. As we discussed in Chapter 1, revocation of an agency agreement may be a breach of contract. In the case of a listing agreement, this could mean that the seller will be required to pay the broker's commission.

On the other hand, the listing broker can renounce the listing agreement. Like revocation, renunciation would constitute a breach of contract, in which case the broker could be liable for the seller's resulting damages (if any).

PROPERTY DESCRIPTION. As we discussed earlier, a listing agreement should include the property's correct legal description. If the legal description is lengthy, you should photocopy the description on a separate piece of paper or an addendum form and attach it to the listing agreement, writing "See attached" or "See addendum" in the space provided for a description on the form. Remember that any attachments or addenda to a contract must be signed or initialed by the seller.

COMMISSION. A listing agreement form usually includes a blank in which to fill in the percentage or amount of the broker's commission. It also explains how and when the broker earns the commission. An exclusive right to sell listing might provide that the broker will earn a commission if any of these events occur:

1. during the listing period, the broker (or another agent in the MLS) secures a buyer who is willing to buy on the exact terms specified by the seller in the listing agreement or on other terms acceptable to the seller (in other words, a ready, willing, and able buyer);
2. the seller sells, exchanges, or enters into a contract to sell or exchange the property during the term of the listing agreement; or
3. the seller sells the property within a certain period (for example, six months) after the expiration date of the listing agreement to anyone who first became aware of the property through any advertising or other marketing activities of the broker (or other agents in the MLS).

The agreement is also likely to provide that MLS members are considered "cooperating brokers" and may act as the agent of the buyer, as the agent of the seller, or in some other capacity as agreed to by the parties. No matter which party the selling agent represents, he or she will be entitled to the selling office's share of the commission. On the form shown in Figure 2.2, the seller has the option of specifying how cooperating brokers will be compensated.

Most deposit receipts provide that if the buyer breaches the contract, the seller will be entitled to keep the good faith deposit as liquidated damages (see Chapter 5). Listing agreements commonly provide that under those circumstances the deposit will first be applied to cover any costs incurred (title and escrow expenses, for example); then the seller and the broker will split the remainder of the deposit, with half going to the broker as compensation for the broker's services.

Under the terms of many listing agreement forms, the seller agrees not to interfere with the broker's right to market the property. For example, if the seller leases the property, grants an option on the property, or enters into any other agreement that might interfere with selling the property, she will be liable for the full commission.

SAFETY CLAUSE. Number three on the list shown above is an example of a safety clause (sometimes called a "protection period clause," "protection clause," or "extender clause"). Occasionally, behind the listing agent's back, a buyer and a seller agree to postpone entering into a contract until after the listing expires, to save the cost of the broker's commission. A safety clause prevents this strategy from working (unless the buyer and seller are willing to wait a long time).

Safety clauses differ from one listing agreement form to another. Sometimes the obligation to pay a commission after the listing has expired is triggered only when the property is sold to a buyer that the agent actually negotiated with during the listing period.

> **EXAMPLE:** You have listed Baker's property. The safety clause in your listing agreement applies only to buyers you've negotiated with.
>
> One buyer, Abrams, is very interested in Baker's property. You present her offer to Baker and spend a few days trying to negotiate the terms of the sale. Finally, Abrams decides that she isn't willing to raise her final offer by the extra $1,000 that Baker wants, and she walks away from the property. Another buyer, Thornwood, sees your "For Sale" sign posted on the property and calls you on the phone to ask some questions about the property. You have no further contact with Thornwood, who doesn't seem very interested in the property after all.
>
> Suppose Abrams buys the property after your listing agreement with Baker expires. Since you actually negotiated with Abrams, your safety clause applies and Baker owes you a commission. On the other hand, if Thornwood were to purchase the property, Baker would not owe you a commission. Under the terms of the listing agreement, since you never actually negotiated with Thornwood, the safety clause does not apply.

Some safety clauses are broader and require the seller to pay a commission if the property is sold within a specified period of time to anyone who learned about it in any way that can be traced to the listing broker or an MLS agent.

> **EXAMPLE:** Returning to the previous example, now suppose that the safety clause in the listing requires the seller to pay the commission if the property is sold to anyone who learned of it from you or another MLS agent. With this type of safety clause, if Thornwood were to buy Baker's property during the period of time covered by the safety clause, Baker would still owe you a commission. Even though you never actually negotiated with Thornwood, he learned the property was

for sale because of your "For Sale" sign and then contacted you to find out more about the property.

Some safety clauses provide safeguards for the seller. For example, you may be required to give the seller a list of all the potential buyers you had contact with during the listing period. Or the safety clause might state that a commission will not be due if the property is listed with another real estate broker during the extension period. This protects the seller from becoming liable for two commissions.

EXAMPLE: Your listing agreement with Baker expires and Baker immediately lists the property with a new agent. Shortly afterwards, Abrams (a buyer you negotiated with before your listing expired) purchases the property. Under some safety clauses, Baker could be held liable for two commissions—one to you (because of your safety clause) and one to the new agent (under the terms of the new agent's listing agreement). But your safety clause excluded this kind of situation, so Baker only owes a commission to the new listing agent.

SELLER'S WARRANTIES. Most listing agreement forms have some warranties or representations by the seller. These may include:

- a warranty stating that the seller has the right to sell the property on the terms stated in the listing agreement;
- a warranty stating that the information about the property included in the listing is accurate; and
- a representation stating that there are no undisclosed encumbrances against the property, such as loan delinquencies, special assessments, or pending legal actions.

There is usually also a "hold harmless" clause to protect the broker. This clause states that the seller takes responsibility for the information given and will indemnify the broker against any losses caused by errors or omissions.

EXAMPLE: You have listed Carr's property. You are unaware of the fact that the roof leaks, and the seller doesn't include this information in the listing agreement. The Bolts purchase the property, and when they discover the leaky roof, they sue both Carr and you. Since you relied on the information in the listing agreement and had no reason to doubt it, Carr will be obligated to reimburse you for any damages you are required to pay the buyers because of his omission.

MULTIPLE LISTING PROVISION. Most listing agreements include a provision alerting the seller to the fact that you will be submitting the listing to your local multiple listing service. It reminds the seller that the information in the listing is not confidential; it will be circulated among the members of the MLS and will be publicly available on the Internet.

The multiple listing service is not a party to the listing agreement. Its only function is to provide information about the property to other MLS members. The MLS will not be responsible for verifying any information provided by the seller or the listing agent.

AGENCY RELATIONSHIPS. The "Agency Relationships" paragraph in the listing agreement form in Figure 2.2 states that the broker will represent the seller. The form then goes on to describe when a dual agency situation may arise: when the property is sold to a buyer represented by the same broker and/or by the same listing agent. The seller gives her consent to this dual agency situation. The seller also acknowledges that a dual agent is not permitted to disclose either party's negotiating position to the other party without written consent. (Dual agency is discussed in Chapter 1.)

ACCESS AND KEYBOXES. A listing agreement form typically gives you the right to enter the property at reasonable times so you can show it to prospective buyers. And since other MLS members will be acting as cooperating agents—helping to find a buyer—they need a way to gain access to the property as well. Keyboxes are the standard method of facilitating access to listed properties when the owners aren't home. Thus, MLS listing forms usually include a provision authorizing the installation of a keybox on the property and permitting MLS agents to enter and show the home. It's common to include a disclaimer of liability for any loss of or damage to the seller's property that may occur because of misuse of a keybox.

In many listing agreement forms, the seller agrees to take precautions to secure valuables within the house during showings, and to obtain insurance needed to protect the contents of the house. Most sellers already have homeowner's insurance, but they should notify the insurer that the property is for sale and that open houses will be held during the selling process.

ATTORNEYS' FEES. Many listing agreement forms provide that if either the broker or the seller has to resort to a lawsuit to enforce the contract, the attorneys' fees of the party who wins the lawsuit must be paid by the other party.

DISPUTE RESOLUTION. Some listing forms include a provision that, if initialed, requires the parties to attempt to settle any dispute using alternative methods such as mediation or arbitration rather than a lawsuit. Either party may refuse to initial such a clause, though, and retain the right to pursue legal action in a court of law instead.

Mediation and arbitration are frequently confused. In mediation, a neutral party helps the parties find a mutually satisfactory solution; the mediator does not impose a solution on the parties. By contrast, arbitration is overseen by a third party (usually a retired judge) who hears evidence and then issues a decision that is binding on both parties. The advantage that arbitration has over a lawsuit is that it can resolve a case much more quickly than the court system generally can.

LISTING INFORMATION. Most listing agreement forms used by multiple listing services are accompanied by a **listing input sheet**. The purpose of a listing input sheet is to generate detailed information about the property and the listing that will be distributed in the MLS publications. Much of the information is coded to make computer input easier.

All of the following basic information is typically required on a listing input sheet for residential property:

- the property address,
- the location on a coded map,
- the architectural style of the home,
- the listing price,
- identification of the listing agent,
- the expiration date of the listing,
- the age of the home,
- the number of bedrooms,
- the number of bathrooms,
- the county tax identification number,
- the commission split,
- the name of the present occupant, and
- the name, address, and phone number of the owner.

The rest of the input sheet usually has spaces to fill in or boxes to check off to describe a wide variety of property features and amenities. There is also a place for information about any existing encumbrances and the annual property taxes.

SIGNATURES. A listing agreement should be signed by both parties, the listing broker and the seller. When you prepare a listing agreement form, you will sign on behalf of your broker. Write your broker's name (as licensed) on the line labeled "Agent" and sign your own name on the "By" line underneath.

If more than one person owns the property, make sure that all of them sign the form.

> **EXAMPLE:** You are preparing a listing agreement for property owned by the Mastersons, a married couple. Unless both the husband and the wife sign the listing agreement form, the contract might turn out to be unenforceable.

In some cases, the sellers are unsure of the names of all the owners. For example, this might happen if the property was inherited by several people, or if it is owned by a partnership. If the sellers seem at all uncertain, or if you simply want to double-check the ownership, you have three options:

1. get a copy of the deed or other title instrument from the seller;
2. check with a title company; or
3. check the county's tax records.

RECEIPT OF COPY. You are required by law to give a copy of any document you prepare to the parties at the time of signature. So a listing agreement form often includes the seller's acknowledgment of receipt of a copy of the agreement.

MODIFYING A LISTING AGREEMENT

Once a listing agreement (or any contract) has been signed, it can be modified only with the written consent of all of the parties.

> **EXAMPLE:** You and the Mastersons signed a listing agreement. Two days later, all of you decide to change the listing's expiration date. You've agreed that a 90-day listing would be more appropriate than a 60-day

listing. So you cross out the old expiration date on the form and write in a new expiration date. To make this change legally effective, you must write your initials and the date beside the change, and both of the Mastersons must do the same.

In some cases it is acceptable to modify simple terms in a listing agreement by crossing out what was filled in and replacing it with new information (as long as all parties initial and date the change, as in the example above). However, if your multiple listing service makes available an amendment form specifically designed for changing the terms of a listing agreement, it's a better practice to use that. Of course, the amendment form must also be signed and dated by all parties to the original agreement.

MANDATORY DISCLOSURES CONCERNING THE PROPERTY

When real property is sold, California law requires certain information about the property to be disclosed to potential buyers. The disclosures necessary for a particular transaction may include:

- a transfer disclosure statement,
- an environmental hazards booklet,
- a natural hazard disclosure statement,
- a residential earthquake hazards report,
- a lead-based paint disclosure,
- special disclosures regarding smoke detectors and water heaters,
- a supplemental statutory disclosure form, and
- disclosure of Mello-Roos liens.

TRANSFER DISCLOSURE STATEMENT

California requires sellers of residential property to give their buyers a comprehensive disclosure form called a **real estate transfer disclosure statement**. For the purposes of this disclosure law, a residential transaction is a sale, exchange, or option to purchase that involves a dwelling with up to four units. The law applies to single-family homes, multifamily properties with up to four units, homes for sale by owner, mobile homes, and condominiums and cooperatives. A transfer disclosure statement isn't required for the sale of new construction in a subdivision where a public report has been delivered, or for a sale pursuant to court order, such as a probate sale or a foreclosure. Also exempt from this requirement are transfers between spouses or co-owners, transfers to lineal descendants, and sales to or from a government entity.

In the transfer disclosure statement, the seller is required to share her knowledge about the condition of the buildings and utilities, the existence of easements or other encumbrances, and a wide variety of other issues concerning the property's physical condition and title. Buyers should understand that the statement is merely a disclosure of information; it does not serve as a warranty by the seller or the seller's agents.

An example of a transfer disclosure statement form is shown in Figure 2.3. The content of the form is prescribed by statute, so neither a seller nor an agent should ever change the form's wording. Some cities and counties require additional disclosures; in that case, the standard local disclosure form should be used in addition to the state form.

FILLING OUT THE FORM. The "Seller's Information" section takes up the majority of the transfer disclosure statement form. You should explain the purpose of the disclosure statement to the sellers you represent, but you shouldn't fill out any part of the Seller's Information section for them. If you did, you could be held liable for any inaccuracies.

The first part of the Seller's Information section is a checklist of features that are present on the property. The next part asks if the seller knows of any problems with the basic structural or functional components of the property, such as the frame, the foundation, and the plumbing and electrical systems.

Next, the seller must check "Yes" or "No" to answer sixteen questions concerning other potential problems, such as environmental concerns, drainage problems, zoning issues, private restrictions, and lawsuits that may affect the property. If the seller answers "Yes" to any of these questions, she is required to provide more information (attaching additional sheets of paper if necessary).

The last page of the transfer disclosure statement has sections to be completed by the listing agent and the selling agent (the agent who obtained the offer), if there are agents involved in the transaction. Each agent must perform a visual inspection of the property and list any problems he or she observes that require disclosure (see Chapter 1).

FIG. 2.3 TRANSFER DISCLOSURE STATEMENT

CALIFORNIA ASSOCIATION OF REALTORS®

REAL ESTATE TRANSFER DISCLOSURE STATEMENT
(CALIFORNIA CIVIL CODE §1102, ET SEQ.)
(C.A.R. Form TDS, Revised 10/03)

THIS DISCLOSURE STATEMENT CONCERNS THE REAL PROPERTY SITUATED IN THE CITY OF _____
_____, COUNTY OF _____, STATE OF CALIFORNIA,
DESCRIBED AS _____.
THIS STATEMENT IS A DISCLOSURE OF THE CONDITION OF THE ABOVE DESCRIBED PROPERTY IN COMPLIANCE
WITH SECTION 1102 OF THE CIVIL CODE AS OF (date) _____. IT IS NOT A WARRANTY OF ANY
KIND BY THE SELLER(S) OR ANY AGENT(S) REPRESENTING ANY PRINCIPAL(S) IN THIS TRANSACTION, AND IS
NOT A SUBSTITUTE FOR ANY INSPECTIONS OR WARRANTIES THE PRINCIPAL(S) MAY WISH TO OBTAIN.

I. COORDINATION WITH OTHER DISCLOSURE FORMS

This Real Estate Transfer Disclosure Statement is made pursuant to Section 1102 of the Civil Code. Other statutes require disclosures, depending upon the details of the particular real estate transaction (for example: special study zone and purchase-money liens on residential property).

Substituted Disclosures: The following disclosures and other disclosures required by law, including the Natural Hazard Disclosure Report/Statement that may include airport annoyances, earthquake, fire, flood, or special assessment information, have or will be made in connection with this real estate transfer, and are intended to satisfy the disclosure obligations on this form, where the subject matter is the same:

☐ Inspection reports completed pursuant to the contract of sale or receipt for deposit.
☐ Additional inspection reports or disclosures: _____

II. SELLER'S INFORMATION

The Seller discloses the following information with the knowledge that even though this is not a warranty, prospective Buyers may rely on this information in deciding whether and on what terms to purchase the subject property. Seller hereby authorizes any agent(s) representing any principal(s) in this transaction to provide a copy of this statement to any person or entity in connection with any actual or anticipated sale of the property.

THE FOLLOWING ARE REPRESENTATIONS MADE BY THE SELLER(S) AND ARE NOT THE REPRESENTATIONS OF THE AGENT(S), IF ANY. THIS INFORMATION IS A DISCLOSURE AND IS NOT INTENDED TO BE PART OF ANY CONTRACT BETWEEN THE BUYER AND SELLER.

Seller ☐ is ☐ is not occupying the property.

A. The subject property has the items checked below (read across):

☐ Range	☐ Oven	☐ Microwave
☐ Dishwasher	☐ Trash Compactor	☐ Garbage Disposal
☐ Washer/Dryer Hookups		☐ Rain Gutters
☐ Burglar Alarms	☐ Smoke Detector(s)	☐ Fire Alarm
☐ TV Antenna	☐ Satellite Dish	☐ Intercom
☐ Central Heating	☐ Central Air Conditioning	☐ Evaporator Cooler(s)
☐ Wall/Window Air Conditioning	☐ Sprinklers	☐ Public Sewer System
☐ Septic Tank	☐ Sump Pump	☐ Water Softener
☐ Patio/Decking	☐ Built-in Barbecue	☐ Gazebo
☐ Sauna		
☐ Hot Tub	☐ Pool	☐ Spa
☐ Locking Safety Cover*	☐ Child Resistant Barrier*	☐ Locking Safety Cover*
☐ Security Gate(s)	☐ Automatic Garage Door Opener(s)*	☐ Number Remote Controls _____
Garage: ☐ Attached	☐ Not Attached	☐ Carport
Pool/Spa Heater: ☐ Gas	☐ Solar	☐ Electric
Water Heater: ☐ Gas	☐ Water Heater Anchored, Braced, or Strapped*	
Water Supply: ☐ City	☐ Well	☐ Private Utility or
Gas Supply: ☐ Utility	☐ Bottled	Other _____
☐ Window Screens	☐ Window Security Bars ☐ Quick Release Mechanism on Bedroom Windows*	

Exhaust Fan(s) in _____ 220 Volt Wiring in _____ Fireplace(s) in _____
☐ Gas Starter _____ ☐ Roof(s): Type: _____ Age: _____ (approx.)
☐ Other: _____
Are there, to the best of your (Seller's) knowledge, any of the above that are not in operating condition? ☐ Yes ☐ No. If yes, then describe. (Attach additional sheets if necessary): _____

(*see footnote on page 2)

TDS REVISED 10/03 (PAGE 1 OF 3) Print Date

Buyer's Initials (_____)(_____)
Seller's Initials (_____)(_____)

Reviewed by _____ Date _____

EQUAL HOUSING OPPORTUNITY

REAL ESTATE TRANSFER DISCLOSURE STATEMENT (TDS PAGE 1 OF 3)

Reprinted with permission, California Association of Realtors®. No endorsement implied.

Property Address: _____ Date: _____

B. Are you (Seller) aware of any significant defects/malfunctions in any of the following? ☐ Yes ☐ No. If yes, check appropriate space(s) below.

☐ Interior Walls ☐ Ceilings ☐ Floors ☐ Exterior Walls ☐ Insulation ☐ Roof(s) ☐ Windows ☐ Doors ☐ Foundation ☐ Slab(s)
☐ Driveways ☐ Sidewalks ☐ Walls/Fences ☐ Electrical Systems ☐ Plumbing/Sewers/Septics ☐ Other Structural Components
(Describe: _____

_____

_____)

If any of the above is checked, explain. (Attach additional sheets if necessary.): _____

_____

_____

_____

*This garage door opener or child resistant pool barrier may not be in compliance with the safety standards relating to automatic reversing devices as set forth in Chapter 12.5 (commencing with Section 19890) of Part 3 of Division 13 of, or with the pool safety standards of Article 2.5 (commencing with Section 115920) of Chapter 5 of Part 10 of Division 104 of, the Health and Safety Code. The water heater may not be anchored, braced, or strapped in accordance with Section 19211 of the Health and Safety Code. Window security bars may not have quick release mechanisms in compliance with the 1995 edition of the California Building Standards Code.

C. Are you (Seller) aware of any of the following:

1. Substances, materials, or products which may be an environmental hazard such as, but not limited to, asbestos, formaldehyde, radon gas, lead-based paint, mold, fuel or chemical storage tanks, and contaminated soil or water on the subject property . . . . ☐ Yes ☐ No
2. Features of the property shared in common with adjoining landowners, such as walls, fences, and driveways, whose use or responsibility for maintenance may have an effect on the subject property . . . . ☐ Yes ☐ No
3. Any encroachments, easements or similar matters that may affect your interest in the subject property . . . . ☐ Yes ☐ No
4. Room additions, structural modifications, or other alterations or repairs made without necessary permits . . . . ☐ Yes ☐ No
5. Room additions, structural modifications, or other alterations or repairs not in compliance with building codes . . . ☐ Yes ☐ No
6. Fill (compacted or otherwise) on the property or any portion thereof . . . . ☐ Yes ☐ No
7. Any settling from any cause, or slippage, sliding, or other soil problems . . . . ☐ Yes ☐ No
8. Flooding, drainage or grading problems . . . . ☐ Yes ☐ No
9. Major damage to the property or any of the structures from fire, earthquake, floods, or landslides . . . . ☐ Yes ☐ No
10. Any zoning violations, nonconforming uses, violations of "setback" requirements . . . . ☐ Yes ☐ No
11. Neighborhood noise problems or other nuisances . . . . ☐ Yes ☐ No
12. CC&R's or other deed restrictions or obligations . . . . ☐ Yes ☐ No
13. Homeowners' Association which has any authority over the subject property . . . . ☐ Yes ☐ No
14. Any "common area" (facilities such as pools, tennis courts, walkways, or other areas co-owned in undivided interest with others) . . . . ☐ Yes ☐ No
15. Any notices of abatement or citations against the property . . . . ☐ Yes ☐ No
16. Any lawsuits by or against the Seller threatening to or affecting this real property, including any lawsuits alleging a defect or deficiency in this real property or "common areas" (facilities such as pools, tennis courts, walkways, or other areas co-owned in undivided interest with others) . . . . ☐ Yes ☐ No

If the answer to any of these is yes, explain. (Attach additional sheets if necessary.): _____

_____

_____

_____

Seller certifies that the information herein is true and correct to the best of the Seller's knowledge as of the date signed by the Seller.

Seller_____ Date _____

Seller_____ Date _____

Copyright © 1991-2003, CALIFORNIA ASSOCIATION OF REALTORS®, INC.
TDS REVISED 10/03 (PAGE 2 OF 3)

Buyer's Initials (_____)(_____)
Reviewed by _____ Date _____

REAL ESTATE TRANSFER DISCLOSURE STATEMENT (TDS PAGE 2 OF 3)

Property Address: _____ Date: _____

III. AGENT'S INSPECTION DISCLOSURE
(To be completed only if the Seller is represented by an agent in this transaction.)

THE UNDERSIGNED, BASED ON THE ABOVE INQUIRY OF THE SELLER(S) AS TO THE CONDITION OF THE PROPERTY AND BASED ON A REASONABLY COMPETENT AND DILIGENT VISUAL INSPECTION OF THE ACCESSIBLE AREAS OF THE PROPERTY IN CONJUNCTION WITH THAT INQUIRY, STATES THE FOLLOWING:

☐ Agent notes no items for disclosure.

☐ Agent notes the following items: _____
_____
_____
_____
_____

Agent (Broker Representing Seller) _____ By _____ Date _____
    (Please Print)   (Associate Licensee or Broker Signature)

IV. AGENT'S INSPECTION DISCLOSURE
(To be completed only if the agent who has obtained the offer is other than the agent above.)

THE UNDERSIGNED, BASED ON A REASONABLY COMPETENT AND DILIGENT VISUAL INSPECTION OF THE ACCESSIBLE AREAS OF THE PROPERTY, STATES THE FOLLOWING:

☐ Agent notes no items for disclosure.

☐ Agent notes the following items: _____
_____
_____
_____

Agent (Broker Obtaining the Offer) _____ By _____ Date _____
    (Please Print)   (Associate Licensee or Broker Signature)

V. BUYER(S) AND SELLER(S) MAY WISH TO OBTAIN PROFESSIONAL ADVICE AND/OR INSPECTIONS OF THE PROPERTY AND TO PROVIDE FOR APPROPRIATE PROVISIONS IN A CONTRACT BETWEEN BUYER AND SELLER(S) WITH RESPECT TO ANY ADVICE/INSPECTIONS/DEFECTS.

I/WE ACKNOWLEDGE RECEIPT OF A COPY OF THIS STATEMENT.

Seller _____ Date _____ Buyer _____ Date _____
Seller _____ Date _____ Buyer _____ Date _____
Agent (Broker Representing Seller) _____ By _____ Date _____
    (Please Print)   (Associate Licensee or Broker Signature)
Agent (Broker Obtaining the Offer) _____ By _____ Date _____
    (Please Print)   (Associate Licensee or Broker Signature)

SECTION 1102.3 OF THE CIVIL CODE PROVIDES A BUYER WITH THE RIGHT TO RESCIND A PURCHASE CONTRACT FOR AT LEAST THREE DAYS AFTER THE DELIVERY OF THIS DISCLOSURE IF DELIVERY OCCURS AFTER THE SIGNING OF AN OFFER TO PURCHASE. IF YOU WISH TO RESCIND THE CONTRACT, YOU MUST ACT WITHIN THE PRESCRIBED PERIOD.

A REAL ESTATE BROKER IS QUALIFIED TO ADVISE ON REAL ESTATE. IF YOU DESIRE LEGAL ADVICE, CONSULT YOUR ATTORNEY.

SURE TRAC
The System for Success™

Published by the
California Association of REALTORS®

Reviewed by _____ Date _____

EQUAL HOUSING
OPPORTUNITY

TDS REVISED 10/03 (PAGE 3 OF 3)

REAL ESTATE TRANSFER DISCLOSURE STATEMENT (TDS PAGE 3 OF 3)

The final part of the form encourages the buyer and seller to have professional inspections of the property performed, and to include appropriate provisions regarding the inspections (such as a contingency clause) in the purchase contract.

Timing and Effect of Disclosure. The buyer must ordinarily be given the disclosure statement as soon as practicable after the deposit receipt is signed and before transfer of title. (Note that the disclosure statement does not become part of the purchase contract between the parties.) The buyer may not waive the right to receive a completed statement, even if the property is being sold subject to an "as is" clause. If there's more than one agent involved in the transaction, it's the selling agent's responsibility to deliver the statement to the buyer, unless the seller instructs otherwise.

Within three business days after personal delivery of a completed disclosure statement, or five days after the completed statement is deposited in the mail, the buyer can either accept the disclosure or rescind the deposit receipt. The choice between acceptance and rescission is completely up to the buyer. If he does not like the information in the disclosure for any reason, however trivial, he can rescind the agreement.

If the buyer decides to rescind the agreement, he must notify the seller or the seller's real estate agent in writing. The buyer will then be entitled to a full refund of the good faith deposit.

If the buyer is not given a disclosure statement, the transaction is still valid, but the person who failed to comply with the disclosure law (either the seller or one of the agents) will be liable for any damages the buyer suffers as a result.

When Circumstances Change. After the buyer accepts the transfer disclosure statement, information may come to light that makes the statement inaccurate.

Example: Stein and O'Neil signed a deposit receipt. Stein filled out the transfer disclosure statement and gave it to O'Neil. O'Neil examined the statement, was satisfied with it, and decided to go ahead with the purchase. Two weeks later, Stein discovers that the roof has started leaking. Since this wasn't disclosed in the transfer disclosure statement she gave O'Neil, the disclosure statement is no longer accurate.

When this happens, the seller may either give the buyer an amended disclosure statement, or else fix the problem so that the disclosure statement is made accurate once again. If the seller amends the disclosure statement, the buyer again has three or five days (depending on the delivery method) to either accept the amended disclosure statement or rescind the deposit receipt.

> **EXAMPLE:** Stein gives O'Neil an amended disclosure statement, this time listing the true condition of the roof. O'Neil, who has had second thoughts about buying the property anyway, decides to rescind the deposit receipt.

Once the sale has closed, the buyer can no longer rescind, even if new information is discovered.

DISCLOSURE OF LATENT DEFECTS. The transfer disclosure statement does not limit the responsibility of the seller and the real estate agent to disclose latent defects and other material facts to the buyer. Even if there's no question on the disclosure statement form about a particular problem, the seller and the agent must disclose it if they are aware of it.

ENVIRONMENTAL HAZARDS BOOKLET

As we've discussed, the disclosures that must be made in the transfer disclosure statement include any specific environmental problems on the property that the seller or the agents are aware of. In addition, the seller or the seller's agent should also make sure the buyer receives a copy of a pamphlet prepared by the Department of Real Estate entitled "Environmental Hazards: A Guide for Homeowners, Buyers, Landlords, and Tenants." If the buyer is given this general information pamphlet, the seller and the seller's agent do not need to provide further information regarding environmental hazards, beyond the disclosure of known problems on the property.

NATURAL HAZARD DISCLOSURE STATEMENT

Additional disclosures are required for properties that are at higher risk for natural disasters, such as earthquakes or landslides. These hazards should be disclosed separately on the natural hazards disclosure statement, rather than on the transfer disclosure statement.

FIG. 2.4 NATURAL HAZARD DISCLOSURE STATEMENT

CALIFORNIA ASSOCIATION OF REALTORS®

NATURAL HAZARD DISCLOSURE STATEMENT
(C.A.R. Form NHD, Revised 10/99)

This statement applies to the following property: _____

The transferor and his or her agent(s) disclose the following information with the knowledge that even though this is not a warranty, prospective transferees may rely on this information in deciding whether and on what terms to purchase the subject property. Transferor hereby authorizes any agent(s) representing any principal(s) in this action to provide a copy of this statement to any person or entity in connection with any actual or anticipated sale of the property.

The following are representations made by the transferor and his or her agent(s) based on their knowledge and maps drawn by the state and federal governments. This information is a disclosure and is not intended to be part of any contract between the transferee and transferor.

THIS REAL PROPERTY LIES WITHIN THE FOLLOWING HAZARDOUS AREA(S): (Check the answer which applies.)

A SPECIAL FLOOD HAZARD AREA (Any type Zone "A" or "V") designated by the Federal Emergency Management Agency.

Yes _____   No _____   Do not know and information not available from local jurisdiction _____

AN AREA OF POTENTIAL FLOODING shown on a dam failure inundation map pursuant to Section 8589.5 of the Government Code.

Yes _____   No _____   Do not know and information not available from local jurisdiction _____

A VERY HIGH FIRE HAZARD SEVERITY ZONE pursuant to Section 51178 or 51179 of the Government Code. The owner of this property is subject to the maintenance requirements of Section 51182 of the Government Code.

Yes _____   No _____

A WILDLAND AREA THAT MAY CONTAIN SUBSTANTIAL FOREST FIRE RISKS AND HAZARDS pursuant to Section 4125 of the Public Resources Code. The owner of this property is subject to the maintenance requirements of Section 4291 of the Public Resources Code. Additionally, it is not the state's responsibility to provide fire protection services to any building or structure located within the wildlands unless the Department of Forestry and Fire Protection has entered into a cooperative agreement with a local agency for those purposes pursuant to Section 4142 of the Public Resources Code.

Yes _____   No _____

AN EARTHQUAKE FAULT ZONE pursuant to Section 2622 of the Public Resources Code.

Yes _____   No _____

A SEISMIC HAZARD ZONE pursuant to Section 2696 of the Public Resources Code.

Yes (Landslide Zone) _____

   No _____   Map not yet released by state _____

Yes (Liquefaction Zone) _____

THESE HAZARDS MAY LIMIT YOUR ABILITY TO DEVELOP THE REAL PROPERTY, TO OBTAIN INSURANCE, OR TO RECEIVE ASSISTANCE AFTER A DISASTER.

THE MAPS ON WHICH THESE DISCLOSURES ARE BASED ESTIMATE WHERE NATURAL HAZARDS EXIST. THEY ARE NOT DEFINITIVE INDICATORS OF WHETHER OR NOT A PROPERTY WILL BE AFFECTED BY A NATURAL DISASTER. TRANSFEREE(S) AND TRANSFEROR(S) MAY WISH TO OBTAIN PROFESSIONAL ADVICE REGARDING THOSE HAZARDS AND OTHER HAZARDS THAT MAY AFFECT THE PROPERTY.

The information in this box is not part of the statutory form.
☐ (if checked) The representations made in this form are based upon information provided by an independent third-party report provided as a substituted disclosure pursuant to California Civil Code §1103.4. Neither the seller nor the seller's agent (1) has independently verified the information contained in this form and the report or (2) is personally aware of any errors or inaccuracies in the information contained on this form.

Transferor represents that the information herein is true and correct to the best of the transferor's knowledge as of the date signed by the transferor.

Signature of Transferor _____   Date _____

Agent represents that the information herein is true and correct to the best of the agent's knowledge as of the date signed by the agent.

Signature of Agent _____   Date _____

Signature of Agent _____   Date _____

Transferee represents that he or she has read and understands this document.

Signature of Transferee _____   Date _____

SURE TRAC The System for Success™

Published by the
California Association of REALTORS®

NHD REVISED 10/99 (PAGE 1 OF 1) Print Date

Reviewed by _____ Date _____

EQUAL HOUSING OPPORTUNITY

NATURAL HAZARD DISCLOSURE STATEMENT (NHD PAGE 1 OF 1)

Reprinted with permission, California Association of Realtors®. No endorsement implied.

An example of a natural hazards disclosure statement form is shown in Figure 2.4. If a property is in an earthquake fault zone, a seismic hazard zone (an area subject to landslides or liquefaction), an area designated a flood hazard area or subject to potential flooding in the event of a dam failure, or an area with high forest fire risks, the seller should check "Yes" for that particular hazard.

Whereas the seller and agents can rely on their own knowledge when they fill out the transfer disclosure statement, they can't do that for the natural hazard disclosure statement. They must consult the appropriate maps, issued by the state or federal government, to determine whether or not the property is located in a hazard area.

Buyers have the same rescission rights in connection with the natural hazard disclosure statement that they have in connection with the transfer disclosure statement. In other words, they can rescind the deposit receipt within three days after receiving the natural hazard disclosure statement in person, or within five days after the statement is mailed to them.

RESIDENTIAL EARTHQUAKE HAZARDS REPORT

For one- to four-unit residences built prior to January 1, 1960, the listing agent must give the buyer a copy of a pamphlet published by the California Seismic Safety Commission entitled "The Homeowner's Guide to Earthquake Safety." The guide contains a disclosure form called the Residential Earthquake Hazards Report, which the seller should complete and give to the buyer. The disclosure form asks the seller whether seismic retrofitting has been performed on the house, and also whether the property is in an earthquake fault zone or seismic hazard zone.

LEAD-BASED PAINT DISCLOSURE

In sale or lease transactions that involve housing built before 1978, federal law requires the seller or landlord to disclose information about lead-based paint on the property to potential buyers or tenants. About three-quarters of the homes built before 1978 contain some lead-based paint. The paint is usually not dangerous if properly maintained, but if it deteriorates and is ingested, it may cause brain damage and organ damage in young children.

The federal law requires the seller of a dwelling built before 1978 to do all of the following:

- disclose the location of any lead-based paint in the home that he is aware of;
- provide a copy of any report concerning lead-based paint in the home, if the home has been inspected;
- give buyers a copy of a pamphlet on lead-based paint prepared by the U.S. Environmental Protection Agency; and
- allow buyers at least a ten-day period in which to have the home tested for lead-based paint.

A disclosure form such as the one shown in Figure 2.5 can be used to comply with this law. It must be signed by the parties and the agents, and it becomes part of the deposit receipt.

AGENT'S RESPONSIBILITIES. A real estate agent is required to ensure that the seller knows her obligations under the lead-based paint disclosure law and fulfills those obligations. It is also the agent's responsibility to make sure that the deposit receipt contains the required warnings, disclosures, and signatures.

PENALTIES. Sellers and real estate agents who fail to fulfill their obligations under the lead-based paint disclosure law may be ordered to pay the buyer treble damages (three times the amount of any actual damages suffered by the buyer). Civil and criminal penalties may also be imposed. Although a real estate agent may be held liable for a seller's failure to comply with the law, the agent isn't responsible for information withheld by the seller.

SMOKE DETECTOR AND WATER HEATER DISCLOSURES

California law requires single-family homes to have an operable smoke detector. In addition, water heaters are required to be braced, anchored, or strapped to prevent damage in an earthquake. The seller must complete disclosure forms that verify that the house being sold complies with each of these state laws, or with local ordinances if they are stricter than the state laws.

FIG. 2.5 LEAD-BASED PAINT DISCLOSURE

CALIFORNIA ASSOCIATION OF REALTORS®

LEAD-BASED PAINT AND LEAD-BASED PAINT HAZARDS DISCLOSURE, ACKNOWLEDGMENT AND ADDENDUM
For Pre-1978 Housing Sales, Leases, or Rentals
(C.A.R. Form FLD, Revised 1/03)

The following terms and conditions are hereby incorporated in and made a part of the: ☐ California Residential Purchase Agreement, ☐ Residential Lease or Month-to-Month Rental Agreement, or ☐ other: _____ _____,dated _____, on property known as: _____ ("Property") in which _____ is referred to as Buyer or Tenant and _____ is referred to as Seller or Landlord.

LEAD WARNING STATEMENT (SALE OR PURCHASE) Every purchaser of any interest in residential real property on which a residential dwelling was built prior to 1978 is notified that such property may present exposure to lead from lead-based paint that may place young children at risk of developing lead poisoning. Lead poisoning in young children may produce permanent neurological damage, including learning disabilities, reduced intelligent quotient, behavioral problems and impaired memory. Lead poisoning also poses a particular risk to pregnant women. The seller of any interest in residential real property is required to provide the buyer with any information on lead-based paint hazards from risk assessments or inspections in the seller's possession and notify the buyer of any known lead-based paint hazards. A risk assessment or inspection for possible lead-based paint hazards is recommended prior to purchase.

LEAD WARNING STATEMENT (LEASE OR RENTAL) Housing built before 1978 may contain lead-based paint. Lead from paint, paint chips and dust can pose health hazards if not managed properly. Lead exposure is especially harmful to young children and pregnant women. Before renting pre-1978 housing, lessors must disclose the presence of lead-based paint and/or lead-based paint hazards in the dwelling. Lessees must also receive federally approved pamphlet on lead poisoning prevention.

1. SELLER'S OR LANDLORD'S DISCLOSURE

I (we) have no knowledge of lead-based paint and/or lead-based paint hazards in the housing other than the following:
_____
_____
_____
_____

I (we) have no reports or records pertaining to lead-based paint and/or lead-based paint hazards in the housing other than the following, which, previously or as an attachment to this addendum have been provided to Buyer or Tenant: _____
_____
_____

I (we), previously or as an attachment to this addendum, have provided Buyer or Tenant with the pamphlet "Protect Your Family From Lead In Your Home" or an equivalent pamphlet approved for use in the State such as "The Homeowner's Guide to Environmental Hazards and Earthquake Safety."

For Sales Transactions Only: Buyer has 10 days, unless otherwise agreed in the real estate purchase contract, to conduct a risk assessment or inspection for the presence of lead-based paint and/or lead-based paint hazards.

I (we) have reviewed the information above and certify, to the best of my (our) knowledge, that the information provided is true and correct.

_____   Date _____
Seller or Landlord

_____   Date _____
Seller or Landlord

FLD REVISED 1/03 (PAGE 1 OF 2) Print Date

Buyer's Initials (_____)(_____)
Seller's Initials (_____)(_____)

EQUAL HOUSING OPPORTUNITY

| Reviewed by _____ Date _____ |

LEAD-BASED PAINT AND LEAD-BASED PAINT HAZARDS DISCLOSURE (FLD-11 PAGE 1 OF 2)

Property Address: _____ Date _____

2. LISTING AGENT'S ACKNOWLEDGMENT

Agent has informed Seller or Landlord of Seller's or Landlord's obligations under §42 U.S.C. 4852d and is aware of Agent's responsibility to ensure compliance.

I have reviewed the information above and certify, to the best of my knowledge, that the information provided is true and correct.

_____   By _____
Agent (Broker representing Seller)Please Print   Associate-Licensee or Broker Signature   Date

3. BUYER'S OR TENANT'S ACKNOWLEDGMENT

I (we) have received copies of all information listed, if any, in 1 above and the pamphlet "Protect Your Family From Lead In Your Home" or an equivalent pamphlet approved for use in the State such as "The Homeowner's Guide to Environmental Hazards and Earthquake Safety." **If delivery of any of the disclosures or pamphlet referenced in paragraph 1 above occurs after Acceptance of an offer to purchase, Buyer has a right to cancel pursuant to the purchase contract. If you wish to cancel, you must act within the prescribed period.**

For Sales Transactions Only: Buyer acknowledges the right for 10 days, unless otherwise agreed in the real estate purchase contract, to conduct a risk assessment or inspection for the presence of lead-based paint and/or lead-based paint hazards; OR, (if checked) ☐ Buyer waives the right to conduct a risk assessment or inspection for the presence of lead-based paint and/or lead-based paint hazards.

I (we) have reviewed the information above and certify, to the best of my (our) knowledge, that the information provided is true and correct.

_____   _____   _____   _____
Buyer or Tenant   Date   Buyer or Tenant   Date

4. COOPERATING AGENT'S ACKNOWLEDGMENT

Agent has informed Seller or Landlord, through the Listing Agent if the property is listed, of Seller's or Landlord's obligations under §42 USC 4852d and is aware of Agent's responsibility to ensure compliance.

I have reviewed the information above and certify, to the best of my knowledge, that the information provided is true and correct.

_____   By _____
Agent (Broker obtaining the Offer)   Associate-Licensee or Broker Signature   Date

SURE TRAC
The System for Success™

Published by the
California Association of REALTORS®

FLD REVISED 1/03 (PAGE 2 OF 2)

Reviewed by _____ Date _____

LEAD-BASED PAINT AND LEAD-BASED PAINT HAZARDS DISCLOSURE (FLD-11 PAGE 2 OF 2)

SUPPLEMENTAL STATUTORY DISCLOSURE FORM

California state law requires a number of other disclosures that don't have their own disclosure forms. It may be necessary to disclose that:

- the property is located in a commercial or industrial zone,
- the property is affected by a nearby airport,
- the property is near a former military site that may have live munitions on it,
- illegal controlled substances were released on the property, or
- a death occurred on the property within the last three years.

Many organizations publish a supplemental disclosure form that can be used to make any of these disclosures.

MELLO-ROOS LIEN DISCLOSURE

The Mello-Roos Community Facilities Act is a state law that allows communities to form special taxing districts and make special assessments to provide public services and facilities such as police protection and parks. When property that is subject to a Mello-Roos assessment lien is sold, the lien must be disclosed to the buyer.

Ordinarily, the seller complies with this requirement by obtaining a copy of the tax notice from the local agency that levied the special assessment. If the seller or listing agent delivers a copy of this notice to the buyer, no further disclosure is required. Even so, it's generally a good idea to disclose the lien on the transfer disclosure statement as well.

CHAPTER SUMMARY

1. The listing agreement is an employment contract between the seller and the real estate broker. The seller agrees to pay the broker a stated commission if a ready, willing, and able buyer is found during the listing period.

2. The three basic types of listing agreements are the open listing, the exclusive agency listing, and the exclusive right to sell listing. The type of listing determines the circumstances under which the broker is entitled to be paid a commission.

3. A listing agreement must be in writing. It should identify the property to be sold, specify the listing price and other terms of sale, state the broker's authority, include a promise to compensate the broker, set a termination date, and be signed by the seller.

4. The listing agreement should also state the items included and excluded, the conditions under which the commission will be paid, and the seller's warranties and representations regarding the accuracy of the information provided about the property.

5. A safety clause provides that the seller will be liable for the broker's commission if the property is sold during a certain period after the listing expires to a buyer the broker dealt with during the listing period.

6. When residential property is sold, the seller is required to give the buyer a transfer disclosure statement, disclosing any problems concerning the title or condition of the property. On the basis of the information in the disclosure statement, the buyer may choose to rescind the deposit receipt.

7. Other disclosures concerning the property that may be required in a transaction include a natural hazard disclosure statement, a residential earthquake hazards report, a lead-based paint disclosure, smoke detector and water heater disclosures, and a Mello-Roos lien disclosure. A supplemental form may be used for disclosures that do not call for their own separate form.

CHAPTER QUIZ

1. One disadvantage of an open listing agreement is that it:

    a. does not state the broker's compensation as a fixed amount

    b. requires the agent to put more effort into marketing the property

    c. may lead to a dispute over which agent was the procuring cause, if the seller gives the listing to more than one broker

    d. prevents sellers from listing their property with as many brokers as they want

2. Which of the following types of listings offers the listing agent the greatest protection?

    a. Open listing

    b. Exclusive agency listing

    c. Exclusive right to sell listing

    d. Non-exclusive listing

3. A typical listing agreement form does not authorize the broker to:

    a. act as the agent of the seller

    b. accept good faith deposits from prospective buyers on behalf of the seller

    c. accept an offer to purchase the property

    d. submit offers to purchase to the seller

4. A hold harmless clause:

    a. protects the broker in that the seller takes responsibility for information given in the listing

    b. relieves the agent from liability for any theft or damage during an open house

    c. states that the seller will pay the agent's attorney fees if the seller loses a legal dispute with the agent regarding payment of a commission

    d. contains a warranty that there are no undisclosed encumbrances against the property

5. A transfer disclosure statement:

   a. is considered part of the listing agreement

   b. is considered part of the purchase contract between the seller and the buyer

   c. provides warranty protection to a buyer who acts in reliance on the statement

   d. reflects the seller's knowledge of the condition of the property and the title

6. A safety clause (protection clause or extender clause) might provide that:

   a. the seller must pay a commission if the property is sold within the extension period to a buyer you negotiated with during the listing period

   b. the seller will not owe you a commission if the property is listed with another broker during the extension period

   c. the provision will not be enforceable unless you give the seller a list of all potential buyers you negotiated with during the listing period

   d. All of the above

7. Which of the following disclosures does not require a separate disclosure form?

   a. Disclosure that the property is in a flood hazard zone

   b. Disclosure of a Mello-Roos lien

   c. Disclosure of presence of lead-based paint

   d. Disclosure that the house has not been seismically retrofitted

8. The purpose of a listing input sheet is to:

   a. explain the agency relationships of MLS members to the seller

   b. allow the MLS to verify the accuracy of information about the listing

   c. gather information about the property for distribution in MLS publications

   d. disclose information the seller is required to give to the buyer

9. With respect to the transfer disclosure statement, all of the following statements concerning the buyer's rights are true, except:

   a. If the buyer rescinds the deposit receipt based on the disclosure statement, she gives up her good faith deposit

   b. The buyer can rescind the deposit receipt if she does not like something in the disclosure statement, no matter how trivial

   c. The buyer has three days after personal delivery of the disclosure statement to accept it or rescind the deposit receipt

   d. If the seller fails to provide a disclosure statement, the transaction is still valid but the seller may be liable for any damages suffered by the buyer as a result

10. If new information comes to light that makes the transfer disclosure statement inaccurate:

    a. the seller is required to take action to fix the problem so that the disclosure statement is accurate again

    b. the seller does not have to give the buyer an amended disclosure statement if he can correct the problem so that the original statement is accurate again

    c. the buyer must accept the amended disclosure statement if she accepted the original disclosure statement

    d. the buyer has the right to rescind the deposit receipt after the sale closes

Answer Key

1. c. Because a seller can give open listings to more than one broker, they can lead to disputes over which agent was the procuring cause of a sale.

2. c. An exclusive right to sell listing pays a commission to the listing broker regardless of whether the property is sold by one of his own agents, an agent working for another broker, or the seller herself. This provides the most protection to the listing agent.

3. c. Under the terms of nearly any listing agreement, the broker may submit offers to the seller, but only the seller can accept an offer. A broker cannot ordinarily accept an offer and create a contract that will be binding on the seller.

4. a. In a hold harmless clause, the seller takes responsibility for the information given to the listing agent in the listing agreement.

5. d. In filling out a transfer disclosure statement, a seller relies on her own knowledge of the property's condition and title. The disclosure statement is not part of the listing agreement or the deposit receipt, and it does not establish any warranties.

6. d. In addition to protecting the broker's commission for a specified period after the listing expires, a safety clause may also contain protections for the seller, such as the ones described in options b and c.

7. b. Disclosure of a Mello-Roos lien can be made simply by providing the buyer with a copy of the tax notice from the taxing authority that levied the assessment. Special forms should be used for each of the other disclosures.

8. c. The listing input sheet is filled in with information for the MLS to distribute to its members and use in listing the property. The MLS does not verify the information or take legal responsibility for it.

9. a. Within three days after receiving the transfer disclosure statement or five days after the statement is deposited in the mail, the buyer may rescind the deposit receipt for any reason without penalty. If a disclosure statement is not provided, the buyer can rescind the agreement at any time until closing, but not after closing.

10. b. The seller has two choices. He can either give the buyer an amended disclosure statement, or else he can correct the problem to make the original disclosure statement accurate again.

3

LISTING REGULATIONS

INTRODUCTION

The previous chapter covered two of the main legal issues you face when you take a listing: the validity of the listing agreement, and the disclosures concerning the property that the seller is required to make to buyers. But those are by no means the only legal issues you may confront as a listing agent. What would happen if the seller refused to pay your commission? Could you sue her? What should you do if the seller indicates that she doesn't want you to show the property to non-white buyers? What if you suspect there's an environmental problem with the property?

A wide variety of laws affect real estate listing and marketing practices, and you'll need to be familiar with them if you're going to avoid some of the pitfalls of selling real estate. They include the Real Estate Law, antidiscrimination laws, antitrust laws, and environmental laws. In this chapter, we'll discuss the provisions of these laws that pertain to listing and marketing properties and to brokerage commissions.

THE REAL ESTATE LAW

California's Real Estate Law includes rules concerning payment of brokers' commissions and control of listings.

COMMISSIONS

As you know, a seller ordinarily pays the brokerage commission to the listing broker. In most cases, the listing broker then pays a share of the commission to his own agent (the listing agent) and another share to the selling broker. The selling broker, in turn, pays a share of what she received to her own agent (the selling agent).

These steps are necessary because the Real Estate Law allows a broker to share a commission only with another licensed broker or with one of his own affiliated sales agents. A broker may not pay any compensation directly to a sales agent who is affiliated with another broker. Payment must be made to that agent's broker, who then pays the agent.

EXAMPLE: You work for Broker Winston. You found a buyer for a property that was listed by an agent working for Broker Andreas. When the sale closes, the seller pays Andreas a $10,000 commission.

Of that $10,000, Andreas gets to keep $2,500 for herself. She will pay her own agent (the one who listed the property) another $2,500. She pays the other $5,000 to your broker, Winston, because Winston is the selling broker. Winston pays you $2,500, because you found the buyer. It would be unlawful for Andreas to pay your $2,500 directly to you. Your compensation must come from your own broker.

Note that a real estate salesperson is not allowed to share her compensation with another salesperson, whether they work for different brokers or the same broker. If two sales agents are going to split a commission, the split must be handled by their broker or brokers.

A valid written agency agreement (either a listing agreement or a buyer representation agreement) is required before a broker can sue for a commission. Only the broker can sue the seller (or buyer, if appropriate) for the commission. A salesperson can't sue a principal for a commission. However, if the broker fails to pay the salesperson's share of the commission, the salesperson can sue the broker for it.

Ownership of a Listing

Under the Real Estate Law, only a broker can directly represent a member of the public (see Chapter 1). As a result, even though a listing agreement is usually prepared and signed by a salesperson, the listing is in the name of the broker and belongs to the broker.

EXAMPLE: You work for Broker Yamaguchi. You are making a listing presentation to Piper. He decides to list his property with you, and you and he both sign the listing agreement form. However, the listing agreement is actually a contract between Yamaguchi and Piper. When you sign the form, you are signing it as an agent of Yamaguchi.

Because the listing agreement is between the broker and the seller, if the salesperson who took the listing goes to work for another broker, the listing stays with the original broker.

EXAMPLE: You don't want to work for Yamaguchi anymore, so you start working for Broker Wilder instead. Piper's listing agreement was with Yamaguchi, not with you, so Yamaguchi keeps the listing.

ANTIDISCRIMINATION LAWS

Fair housing laws and other antidiscrimination laws affect both how you obtain listings and how you market properties once they are listed. Before we discuss the impact of these laws on listing and marketing practices, we'll review the basic provisions of the main federal and state antidiscrimination laws that apply in real estate transactions.

FEDERAL FAIR HOUSING ACT

The Federal Fair Housing Act, part of the Civil Rights Act of 1968, makes it illegal to discriminate on the basis of **race, color, religion, sex, national origin, handicap**, or **familial status** in the sale or lease of residential property, or in the sale or lease of vacant land for the construction of residential buildings. The law also prohibits discrimination in advertising, lending, real estate brokerage, and other services in connection with residential real estate transactions.

PROHIBITED ACTS. The Fair Housing Act prohibits any of the following actions if they are done on the basis of race, color, religion, sex, national origin, handicap, or familial status:

- refusing to rent or sell residential property after receiving a bona fide offer;
- refusing to negotiate for the sale or rental of residential property, or otherwise making it unavailable;
- changing the terms of sale or lease for different potential buyers or tenants;
- using advertising that indicates a preference or intent to discriminate;
- representing that property is not available for inspection, sale, or rent when it is in fact available;
- discrimination by an institutional lender in making a housing loan;
- limiting participation in a multiple listing service or similar service;
- coercing, intimidating, threatening, or interfering with anyone on account of his or her enjoyment, attempt to enjoy, or encouragement or assistance to others in enjoying the rights granted by the Fair Housing Act.

The discriminatory practices known as blockbusting, steering, and redlining are also prohibited.

1. **BLOCKBUSTING:** This occurs when someone tries to induce home-owners to list or sell their properties by predicting that people of another race (or disabled people, people of a particular ethnic background, etc.) will be moving into the neighborhood, and that this will have undesirable consequences, such as a higher crime rate or lower property values. The blockbuster then profits by purchasing the homes at reduced prices, or (in the case of a real estate agent) by collecting commissions on the induced sales. Blockbusting is also known as **panic selling**.

2. **STEERING:** This refers to channeling prospective buyers or tenants toward or away from specific neighborhoods based on their race (or religion, national origin, etc.) in order to maintain or change the character of those neighborhoods.

3. **REDLINING:** This is a refusal to make a loan because of the racial or ethnic composition of the neighborhood in which the proposed security property is located. Rejection of a loan application must be based on objective financial considerations concerning the buyer or the property.

EXEMPTIONS. There are some exemptions from the Fair Housing Act. However, these exemptions are very limited and apply only rarely. The most important thing to remember about the exemptions is that they *never* apply when a real estate agent is involved in a transaction.

ENFORCEMENT. The Fair Housing Act is enforced by the Department of Housing and Urban Development (HUD), through its Office of Fair Housing and Equal Opportunity. In California, HUD may also refer complaints to the California Department of Fair Employment and Housing.

When someone is held to have violated the Fair Housing Act, a court may issue an injunction ordering the violator to stop the discriminatory conduct. The violator may also be ordered to pay compensatory damages and attorneys' fees to the injured party. In addition, the violator may be required to pay punitive damages to the injured party, or a civil penalty to the government. The civil penalty can range from a maximum of $10,000 for a first offense to $50,000 for the third offense within seven years.

CALIFORNIA STATE ANTIDISCRIMINATION LAWS

Real estate agents must also comply with the state laws that prohibit discrimination. These include the Unruh Civil Rights Act, the Fair Employment and Housing Act, and the Housing Financial Discrimination Act. In addition, California's Real Estate Law and the Commissioner's regulations prohibit discrimination by real estate licensees.

UNRUH CIVIL RIGHTS ACT. One major state antidiscrimination law affecting real estate agents in California is the Unruh Civil Rights Act, which applies to business establishments. A brokerage is a business establishment, so the professional activities of real estate agents are subject to this law.

The Unruh Civil Rights Act prohibits any discrimination based on **race, color, religion, ancestry, national origin, sex, disability, medical condition,** or **age**. In transactions related to housing, business establishments are also not allowed to discriminate based on **sexual orientation, marital status, familial status**, or **source of income**.

Apartment and condominium complexes are also considered business establishments, so they must comply with the law. There is an exemption, however, for developments that qualify as housing for senior citizens. Developments that meet the requirements of the senior housing exemption may discriminate on the basis of age and familial status to exclude families with children (but they cannot discriminate against other protected groups).

PENALTIES. If someone is found to have violated the Unruh Act, they will be liable for the injured party's actual damages and attorney's fees. If the discrimination is still ongoing, the guilty party may be ordered to cease and desist from discriminatory actions. The violator may also have to pay up to three times the amount of actual damages or $4,000, whichever is less.

FAIR EMPLOYMENT AND HOUSING ACT. The Fair Employment and Housing Act, also known as the **Rumford Act**, makes it unlawful to discriminate in the selling or leasing of housing. It applies not only to real estate agents and housing developments, but also to individual property owners.

The Fair Employment and Housing Act specifically prohibits a seller or landlord from asking about the **race, color, religion, sex, sexual orientation, marital status, national origin, ancestry, familial status,** or **disability** of any prospective buyer or tenant. You should refuse to answer such a question from a seller or landlord.

The law also specifically prohibits anyone from advertising housing for sale or rent in discriminatory terms. This includes advertising that suggests a preference for a particular group.

EXAMPLE: A landlord places an advertisement listing an apartment for rent. The ad states: "Married couples only, please." The landlord has violated the Fair Employment and Housing Act.

EXEMPTIONS. There are a few exemptions from the Fair Employment and Housing Act. It doesn't apply to accommodations operated by non-profit religious, fraternal, or charitable organizations. It also doesn't apply when part of a single-family, owner-occupied home is rented to a single boarder.

EXAMPLE: Judy is a 75-year-old widow who owns a house and lives alone. She has extra space and needs some additional income, so she decides to rent out a room in her house. Judy believes she will only feel comfortable with another single, older woman as a tenant. She places an advertisement specifically looking for such a tenant. This is permissible under the Fair Employment and Housing Act.

PENALTIES. Housing discrimination complaints are investigated by the Department of Fair Employment and Housing. If necessary, the Department will issue an accusation and a hearing will be held. A violator who is found guilty may be ordered to sell or lease the property or a similar property to the injured party. Additionally, the violator may be required to pay the injured party actual damages plus a civil penalty of $10,000 to $50,000.

HOUSING FINANCIAL DISCRIMINATION ACT. Another state law you should be aware of is the Housing Financial Discrimination Act, also known as the **Holden Act**. Under this law, a lender must make a lending decision based on the merits of the borrower and the security property, rather than on the property's neighborhood or location.

The Holden Act prohibits lenders from considering the racial, ethnic, religious, or national origin composition of the neighborhood. Like the Federal Fair Housing Act, this makes the practice of redlining illegal. The Holden Act also bars lenders from discriminating based on race, color, sex, marital status, national origin, or ancestry.

CALIFORNIA REAL ESTATE LAW. In addition to the federal and state laws already discussed, real estate licensees must comply with the antidiscrimination provisions of the Real Estate Law and the Commissioner's regulations. Both the statute and the regulations prohibit discrimination by real estate agents.

Under the Real Estate Law, a licensee who engages in discriminatory activity is subject to disciplinary action by the Department of Real Estate. If a broker or salesperson violates the fair housing or civil rights laws, his or her license could be suspended or revoked. Furthermore, the licensee could face a fine of up to $10,000.

COMMISSIONER'S REGULATIONS. The Real Estate Commissioner's regulations contain a list of prohibited discriminatory conduct. If the conduct is based on discrimination against a protected group, it is against the law for a real estate licensee to:

- refuse to negotiate for the sale, rental, or financing of the purchase of real estate, or otherwise make it unavailable;
- refuse or fail to show, rent, sell, or finance the purchase of real estate;
- refuse or fail to provide information to any person about a property;
- discriminate in the sale, purchase, or negotiation of real estate;
- discriminate in the terms and conditions of a real estate transaction;
- discriminate in providing services or facilities in connection with a real estate transaction;
- represent that property is not available for inspection, sale, or rental when it is in fact available;

- act to delay, hinder, or avoid a real estate transaction;
- make any effort to encourage discrimination in a real estate transaction;
- refuse or fail to cooperate with another real estate licensee in a transaction;
- ask any question or make any statement that expresses or implies an intent to discriminate;
- make any effort to interfere with any person in the exercise of their rights;
- solicit sales, rentals, or listings in a discriminatory manner;
- discriminate in informing persons of waiting lists or other procedures with respect to the future availability of real estate;
- make any effort to discourage or prevent a real estate transaction;
- provide information or advice concerning real estate in a discriminatory manner;
- refuse to accept a listing or application for financing;
- enter into an agreement or carry out instructions with the understanding that a person may be discriminated against;
- advertise property in a way that indicates a discriminatory preference or limitation;
- selectively advertise property in a manner that causes discrimination;
- quote or charge a different price, rental, or deposit amount;
- discriminate in making any determination of financial ability or in processing a loan application;
- advise a person of the value of a property based on neighborhood characteristics related to a protected class;
- discriminate against owners or tenants in providing property management services;
- make any effort to instruct or encourage other licensees to engage in discriminatory acts; or
- assist any person in a real estate transaction where there are reasonable grounds to believe that the person intends to discriminate.

The Commissioner's regulations cover just about every activity a real estate agent might engage in. Note that the discriminatory conduct in this list normally violates other antidiscrimination laws as well.

FIG. 3.1   COMPARISON OF ANTIDISCRIMINATION LAWS

FEDERAL FAIR HOUSING ACT

- APPLIES TO RESIDENTIAL REAL ESTATE TRANSACTIONS

- PROTECTED CLASSES: RACE, COLOR, RELIGION, SEX, NATIONAL ORIGIN, HANDICAP, OR FAMILIAL STATUS

- NO EXEMPTIONS FOR TRANSACTIONS INVOLVING REAL ESTATE AGENTS

UNRUH CIVIL RIGHTS ACT

- APPLIES TO BUSINESS ESTABLISHMENTS, INCLUDING REAL ESTATE BROKERAGES

- PROTECTED CLASSES: RACE, COLOR, RELIGION, ANCESTRY, NATIONAL ORIGIN, SEX, DISABILITY, MEDICAL CONDITION, AGE, SEXUAL ORIENTATION, MARITAL STATUS, FAMILIAL STATUS, OR SOURCE OF INCOME

- EXEMPTION FOR HOUSING FOR SENIOR CITIZENS

FAIR EMPLOYMENT AND HOUSING ACT (RUMFORD ACT)

- APPLIES TO THE SALE OR LEASE OF HOUSING

- PROTECTED CLASSES: RACE, COLOR, RELIGION, SEX, SEXUAL ORIENTATION, MARITAL STATUS, NATIONAL ORIGIN, ANCESTRY, FAMILIAL STATUS, OR DISABILITY

COMPLYING WITH FAIR HOUSING LAWS

As you can see, these antidiscrimination laws cover a lot of territory. You must become familiar with their provisions and know what activities are prohibited. And you must remember that violating an antidiscrimination law does not require intent; if you do something that is considered discriminatory, you may be found guilty of violating the law even if you had good intentions.

EXAMPLE: You're giving a listing presentation at the seller's home. The sellers are from Central America and speak only limited English. You do not speak Spanish. During the listing presentation, you feel increasingly uncomfortable because of the communication barrier. When you finish your presentation, the sellers tell you they want to list their property with you right away. Somewhat awkwardly, you suggest that they may want to list their property with an agent who speaks Spanish. You explain tactfully that you have a very difficult time understanding them and believe that they would be happier with a Spanish-speaking agent. They insist that they want to list with you. You tell them, in all honesty, that you think another agent would be able to give them better service. Your well-intentioned refusal to list their property could be regarded as discrimination on the basis of national origin, and you could be found guilty of violating federal or state antidiscrimination laws.

To help you avoid unintentional discrimination, we'll discuss some basic guidelines to follow when you list property and when you advertise the properties you list.

COMPLIANCE WHEN LISTING PROPERTY. When you're taking a listing, you should remember the following general rules.

Never say or imply that the presence of persons of a particular protected class (race, national origin, etc.) in a neighborhood could or will result in:

- lower property values;
- a change in the composition of the neighborhood;
- a more dangerous neighborhood; or
- a decline in the quality of the schools in the neighborhood.

EXAMPLE: Chadwick is making a listing presentation to Thompson, a homeowner who is considering selling her property but isn't sure this is the right time. During the presentation, Chadwick says to Thompson, "I hear your neighbor, Bowen, has an offer on his house from a minority couple. You know, it might be a good idea to get your house listed and an offer nailed down before any minority families move into the neighborhood. That way, you can get the best price for your house. If you wait until Bowen's house is sold—well, you just might not get as much for your house." This is an example of blockbusting. Chadwick has violated the antidiscrimination laws.

Remember that you can't refuse to list property in a market area served by your office because of the presence or absence of particular protected groups. Nor can you state or imply that a home will be more difficult (or easier) to sell based on the presence or absence of a particular group of people.

EXAMPLE: Norquist is discussing the listing price with the sellers. She tells them with enthusiasm, "Your house is in a great neighborhood! There aren't very many safe, white, middle-class neighborhoods left these days. Your home's really going to sell fast!" Norquist has just violated antidiscrimination laws.

Most agents would not act in an overtly discriminatory way; for example, they wouldn't turn away a prospective buyer because of the buyer's race. Yet some of those same agents might tell racial or ethnic jokes or make derogatory remarks about a particular group of people. Although these jokes or remarks don't necessarily indicate a willingness to actually discriminate in a transaction, a listener might assume that they do. And if an agent listens and says nothing while a seller, a buyer, or another agent makes discriminatory remarks or jokes, it can give the impression that the agent agrees with these discriminatory attitudes. Avoid participating in or going along with racial or ethnic slurs, no matter what the source.

Before taking a listing, be sure to discuss the fair housing laws with the seller, and tell the seller that you will strictly abide by them. Ask the seller to make a firm commitment to comply with the fair housing laws. If the seller refuses to do so, you should refuse to take the listing. The same holds true if the seller makes remarks that suggest that he might act in a discriminatory manner.

EXAMPLE: You're making a listing presentation to the Boyds, a white couple who live in a predominantly white neighborhood. While you are discussing the listing terms, Mr. Boyd says, "You know, we certainly want the best price for our house. But we want you to be pretty careful who you show it to. We spent a lot of time fixing up this house, and we raised our kids here. We don't really want to change the neighborhood. Our neighbors are good, traditional, hard-working folks. We don't want a buyer who would lower everybody else's property values. You know what we mean."

Even though the Boyds don't come out and say so, they could easily be implying that they would not accept an offer from a buyer with a different racial or ethnic background. Mr. Boyd's comments are red flags. You should discuss fair housing principles with the couple, emphasizing that equal opportunity is the law. If the Boyds seem uncomfortable with what you are saying, you should refuse to take the listing.

If you refuse a listing because you think the sellers would discriminate against potential buyers, you should immediately report that to your managing broker.

In your relationships with potential sellers, be sure to provide equal service without regard to the seller's race, creed, color, religion, national origin, ancestry, sex, marital status, familial status, age, or disability. You should always follow the same listing procedures no matter who your client is.

COMPLIANCE WHEN ADVERTISING PROPERTY. After you list a property, your next step is usually to advertise it. Keep in mind that you need to avoid discrimination in the way you market the property.

Sometimes apparently innocent statements or actions may be interpreted as discriminatory. Suppose that you're preparing and mailing out a flyer about your listing. You could be accused of discrimination if:

- you send flyers only to neighborhoods where the residents are all predominantly of the same race or ethnic background as the seller;
- you send them to all the neighboring properties except those owned by people of a particular race or ethnic background; or
- the wording of the flyer suggests that the recipient can control the type of person who will buy the property.

EXAMPLE: Your flyer says that a neighbor can, by referring potential buyers, "uphold the standards of the community." But you fail to specify what community standards you're referring to. Unless you clearly describe these standards in nondiscriminatory language, a reader might infer that he can control the race or ethnic background of the buyer. A court could rule that your flyer violates antidiscrimination laws.

As a real estate agent, you're likely to place many newspaper ads. Here are some things to watch out for when you're deciding on a newspaper advertising strategy after you take a listing.

- Your choice of newspapers could be seen as a form of racial steering.

  EXAMPLE: You've listed a home in a predominantly minority neighborhood. Your sellers are members of the minority group. You decide to advertise the property in the neighborhood weekly newspaper rather than the city newspaper or any other neighborhood weeklies. You feel this is the best choice, because you think other minority residents from the same neighborhood would be more interested in the home than residents of other neighborhoods. This is discriminatory.

- The choice of models you use in display advertising could also lead to charges of discrimination.

  EXAMPLE: A broker is the listing agent for a large, exclusive housing development. She advertises the homes in the development by putting display ads in the local paper. In every ad she places, the buyers and sellers are depicted only by white models, even though 38% of the city's population is non-white. The use of only white models could be grounds for a discrimination suit.

  When pictures of people are used in display advertising, you should take all reasonable steps to make sure that the pictures give the impression that the housing is open to everyone.

- All your residential advertising should contain the Equal Housing Opportunity logo or slogan. Your brochures, circulars, business cards, direct mail advertising, and all other forms of advertising should also include the Equal Housing Opportunity logo or slogan.

ACTIONS THAT DO NOT VIOLATE FAIR HOUSING LAWS. Certain actions may initially appear to violate antidiscrimination laws, but in fact are not considered to be violations. Here are some examples.

- You may provide information required by a federal, state, or local agency for data collection or civil rights enforcement purposes.

FIG. 3.2   FAIR HOUSING LOGO

EQUAL HOUSING OPPORTUNITY

- You may ask questions and provide information on forms in regard to marital status, in an effort to comply with the state's community property laws concerning the purchase, sale, or financing of real estate.

- You may ask questions or make statements as necessary to best serve the needs of a disabled person. This may include calling the attention of disabled clients or customers to particular buildings built or modified to meet their needs.

- You may use an affirmative marketing plan that tries to attract members of a particular group to an area or property that they might not otherwise be aware of. A brokerage or real estate board may also take affirmative steps to recruit minority employees or members.

EXAMPLE: The developer of a large, moderately priced subdivision located on the fringes of the metropolitan area contacts you to assist in the sale of properties in the subdivision. The developer encourages you to target your marketing efforts toward recent immigrants who might be looking for affordable entry-level housing. In your area, most of the recent immigrants are non-white and live in a few older urban neighborhoods. You could devote extra effort to advertising in immigrant community newspapers or leafletting these neighborhoods, as long as you also advertise in other neighborhoods or in newspapers of wider circulation.

• You may truthfully answer questions about the racial composition of neighborhoods, even if this results in unintentional racial steering. If a buyer expresses a desire not to be shown homes in a particular neighborhood, even if the buyer makes that decision because of the race or other characteristics of the residents, you are not obligated to show them homes in that neighborhood.

EXAMPLE: You are representing the Duvalls, who have only a limited amount of money to spend on their first home. You suggest a variety of neighborhoods where there are listings that fit their price range and other preferences, including the Greengate neighborhood. When Mr. Duvall asks about the people who live in Greengate, you truthfully respond that most of the residents belong to a particular immigrant group. Mr. Duvall says, "I'm not sure we'd feel comfortable there; we'd rather look in other areas." So long as you do not discourage the Duvalls from looking at properties in this neighborhood, you aren't required to show them houses in this area against their wishes.

AMERICANS WITH DISABILITIES ACT

To avoid discrimination and promote equal treatment, real estate licensees need to be familiar not only with the fair housing laws but also with the Americans with Disabilities Act. This federal law, which took effect in 1992, is intended to guarantee people with disabilities equal access to employment, goods, and services.

As we discussed, housing discrimination on the basis of handicap is prohibited under the Federal Fair Housing Act. The ADA has a broader application. Under this law, no one may be discriminated against on the basis of disability in any place of public accommodation.

Most significantly, this means places of public accommodation must be accessible to the disabled. Physical barriers to access must be removed, wheelchair ramps must be added, and restrooms and other facilities must be modified.

PLACES OF PUBLIC ACCOMMODATION. A wide variety of facilities open to the public, both publicly and privately owned, fall within the ADA's definition of public accommodation. Hotels, restaurants, retail stores, schools, theaters, and professional offices are all covered. For instance, the office of a real estate brokerage is open to the public and therefore must be accessible to people with disabilities.

ADA REQUIREMENTS. If you frequently deal with commercial or retail properties, it's particularly important to be familiar with the ADA's requirements. The person who owns, leases, or operates a place of public accommodation is legally responsible for the removal of barriers to accessibility, so you may have to advise clients about modifications that may be necessary on properties that they're considering purchasing or leasing.

Changes that the owner or tenant of a commercial property might need to make so that the building complies with the ADA include:

- creating an accessible entrance by installing ramps, adding parking spaces, or widening doorways;
- providing access to goods and services within a building by installing elevators, widening aisles, or adding Braille or raised-lettering signage;
- improving restrooms by adding larger stalls, grab bars, or more easily operated faucets and door handles; or
- relocating other features such as drinking fountains or pay phones so they are more easily reached.

Note that barrier removal is required only in public areas, and is not required where it is not "readily achievable." For example, the owner of a small, independently owned two-story retail business would not necessarily be required to install an elevator to the second story. However, the business would be required to make other accommodations to serve a disabled customer, such as having a salesperson bring items down to the customer on the first floor.

NEW CONSTRUCTION. If you are representing someone who plans to build a new building, you should be aware that all new construction of places of public accommodation must comply with ADA requirements.

Model homes are not ordinarily required to meet ADA requirements. However, if a model home is also serving as a sales office for a subdivision or complex, then the area used as a sales office would be considered a place of public accommodation.

ANTITRUST LAWS AND LISTING PRACTICES

As you go about the business of obtaining listings and negotiating listing terms, you need to be aware of the restrictions imposed by federal antitrust laws. The purpose of antitrust laws is to foster fair business practices among competitors. These laws are based on the belief that free enterprise and healthy competition are good both for individual consumers and for the economy as a whole.

The most important federal antitrust law is the **Sherman Antitrust Act**, which was passed in 1890. The Sherman Act prohibits any agreement that has the effect of restraining trade. This includes a **conspiracy**, which is defined in the law as two or more business entities participating in a common scheme, the effect of which is the restraint of trade.

The Sherman Act doesn't apply only to monolithic computer companies and oil companies. Since 1950, antitrust laws have also applied to the real estate industry. In a landmark case, the United States Supreme Court held that mandatory fee schedules established and enforced by a real estate board violated the Sherman Act (*United States v. National Association of Real Estate Boards*).

The penalties for violating antitrust laws are severe:

- If an individual is found guilty of violating the Sherman Act, he or she can be fined up to $350,000 and/or sentenced to three years' imprisonment.
- If a corporation is found guilty of violating the Sherman Act, it can be fined up to ten million dollars.

To avoid violations, you need to be aware of three types of prohibited activities. These are:

- price fixing,
- group boycotts, and
- tie-in arrangements.

PRICE FIXING

Price fixing is defined as the cooperative setting of prices or price ranges by competing firms. Real estate brokers can run afoul of the law against price fixing by setting, or appearing to set, uniform commission rates.

> **EXAMPLE:** Members of a local organization of real estate brokers decide that they should all insist on 7% commissions. They arrange for 7% to be pre-printed in all their listing forms, and when potential sellers question the commission rate, the real estate agents say, "It's the same rate everybody charges." This would be considered a blatant case of illegal price fixing.

One of the best ways to avoid the appearance of price fixing is to scrupulously avoid discussing commission rates with competing agents. (Note that it's a discussion between *competing* agents that is dangerous—it's all right for a broker to discuss commission rates with her own sales agents.) The only exception to this general rule is that two competing brokers may discuss a commission split in a cooperative sale. In other words, a listing broker and a selling broker may discuss what percentage of the sales commission each of them will receive.

Even casually mentioning that you're changing your commission rate could lead to antitrust problems.

> **EXAMPLE:** A prominent broker attends a meeting of the local real estate brokers' organization. He's asked to give a brief speech about his firm's sales goals. In the middle of his comments, he mentions that he's going to raise his firm's commission rate, even if nobody else raises theirs. The profitability of his firm depends on it.
>
> The broker's statements could be interpreted as an invitation to conspire to fix prices. If any other members of the brokers' organization follow his lead and raise their rates, they might be accused of accepting his invitation to fix prices.

As this example illustrates, a broker doesn't have to actually consult with other brokers to be accused of conspiring to fix commission rates. Merely mentioning, among competing brokers, an intent to increase rates could be enough to lead to an antitrust lawsuit.

When you're taking a listing, it's important to emphasize to the seller that the commission rate is freely negotiable. You should never imply that commission rates are set by law or by your local MLS or Board of Realtors®. Don't mention the rates of competing agents, either.

EXAMPLE: Harris is making a listing presentation to Bell. When Bell asks Harris about the commission, Harris casually says, "Oh, the commission rate is 7%." When Bell asks if she has to pay a 7% commission, Harris replies, "All the agents around here charge a 7% commission. In fact, if you and I agreed to a lower commission rate, I'm not even sure that the MLS would accept the listing." Harris has violated the antitrust laws.

Remember that in California, a listing agreement for a residential property with up to four units must have a provision in boldface type stating that the amount or rate of the commission is negotiable between the seller and broker, not fixed by law. (See Chapter 2.)

GROUP BOYCOTTS

Antitrust laws also prohibit group boycotts. A **group boycott** is an agreement between business competitors to exclude another competitor from fair participation in business activities. For example, an agreement between two or more real estate brokers to exclude another broker from fair participation in real estate activities would be a group boycott. The purpose of a group boycott is to hurt or destroy a competitor, and this is automatically unlawful under the antitrust laws.

A group boycott doesn't have to be based on a formal arrangement or carried out by a large group of people.

EXAMPLE: Barker and Jaffrey, two real estate brokers, meet to discuss an offer on a house. After discussing the offer, they begin talking about the business practices of a third broker, Hutton. Barker, angry with Hutton because of a past business transaction, claims that Hutton is dishonest. Barker says, "That sleazy jerk! I'll never do business with him again!" Jaffrey laughs. Barker then says, "You know, I've stopped returning Hutton's calls when he's asking about my listings. You should do the same thing. With any luck, the guy will be out of business in a few months." Jaffrey, who also disapproves of Hutton, agrees to go along with what Barker has suggested. Barker and Jaffrey could be found guilty of a conspiracy to boycott Hutton.

It's one thing to think another broker is dishonest or unethical and to choose to avoid her. It's another matter entirely to encourage other brokers to do the same. You should never tell clients or other agents not to work with a competing agent because (for example) you have doubts about that agent's competence or integrity.

It would also be considered a group boycott if a multiple listing service refused to allow a broker to become a member because he had a different kind of fee schedule. For example, an MLS can't refuse membership to a brokerage firm just because it charges a small flat fee for a listing, rather than a percentage of the sales price.

TIE-IN ARRANGEMENTS

Another type of business practice that antitrust laws prohibit is a tie-in arrangement. A **tie-in arrangement** is defined as an agreement to sell one product only on the condition that the buyer also purchases a different (or "tied") product.

> **EXAMPLE:** Fisher is a subdivision developer. Tyler, a builder, wants to buy a lot. Fisher tells Tyler that he will sell him a lot only if Tyler agrees that after Tyler builds a house on the lot, he will list the improved property with Fisher.

The type of agreement described in this example is called a **list-back agreement**. List-back agreements are not unlawful in themselves. But requiring a lot buyer to enter into a list-back agreement as a condition of the sale is a tie-in arrangement and violates the antitrust laws.

Another danger area for real estate agents is agreeing to manage property only if the owner agrees to list that property with you.

> **EXAMPLE:** Dahl, a broker, is negotiating a property management agreement with Heinz, a property owner. Dahl wants to include a clause in the agreement that provides that if Heinz ever decides to sell the managed property, he will list the property with Dahl. If Dahl tells Heinz that she'll enter into a management agreement only if it includes this listing clause, Dahl is violating the antitrust laws.

ENVIRONMENTAL ISSUES

As you saw in Chapter 2, the transfer disclosure statement calls for the disclosure of environmental hazards. Because of the growing concern about environmental hazards related to real estate—even residential real estate—it's important to discuss some of those hazards and the laws related to them. While you aren't expected to be an environmental expert, you should have a basic understanding of the environmental problems facing property owners and buyers today.

ENVIRONMENTAL LAWS

A number of federal and state environmental laws affect real estate agents and property sellers and buyers. We will just highlight some of the most important laws.

NATIONAL ENVIRONMENTAL POLICY ACT. The National Environmental Policy Act (NEPA) requires federal agencies to provide an **environmental impact statement** (EIS) for any action that may have a significant effect on the environment. NEPA applies to all types of federal development, such as construction projects, the building of highways, and waste control. NEPA also applies to private uses or developments that require the approval of a federal agency in the form of a license, a permit, or even a federal loan. In these cases, federal agencies may require submission of an EIS before approving the use or development.

An EIS should disclose the impact of the development on energy consumption, sewage systems, school population, drainage, water facilities, and other environmental, economic, and social factors.

CALIFORNIA ENVIRONMENTAL QUALITY ACT. California has its own version of NEPA, the California Environmental Quality Act (CEQA). This law applies to public or private projects that may have a significant effect on the environment.

To meet CEQA requirements, the public agency overseeing the project must prepare an environmental impact report (EIR), which is similar to the EIS required under NEPA. An EIR is not required only if the public agency overseeing the project rules that it will not have significant adverse effects.

CALIFORNIA COASTAL ACT. The California Coastal Act regulates development along the state's coastline. This law established the California Coastal Commission, which researches ways to protect the California coastline and controls development along the coast.

The Coastal Commission has several regional divisions that oversee coastal programs at the local level. No development is allowed in the coastal zone without a coastal development permit from the appropriate agency.

CERCLA. One of the most important environmental laws is the federal Comprehensive Environmental Response, Compensation and Liability Act (CERCLA). CERCLA concerns liability for environmental cleanup costs and has dramatically changed the way property buyers view potential environmental liability.

CERCLA is best known for its creation of a multibillion-dollar fund called **Superfund**. The purpose of Superfund is to clean up hazardous waste dumps and respond to spills of hazardous materials. CERCLA also created a process for identifying the parties who are responsible for cleanup costs. Cleanup costs may include both the cost of cleaning up a particular property and the cost of cleaning up any neighboring property that may have been contaminated by the hazardous substances.

The parties responsible for the cleanup may include both present and previous landowners. In some cases, the current owners of contaminated property may be required to pay for the cleanup even if they did not cause the contamination. A buyer who is considering purchasing property that may have been contaminated should consult an environmental engineer and/or an attorney specializing in environmental law.

CLEAN WATER ACT. Of particular concern to land developers is the federal law protecting **wetlands**—swamps, marshes, ponds, and similar areas where the soil is saturated for part of the year. Section 404 of the Clean Water Act makes it illegal for a private landowner to fill or drain wetlands on his property without obtaining a permit from the U.S. Army Corps of Engineers. Violations may be punished with an order to restore the wetlands, civil penalties, and even criminal sanctions.

The presence of a wetland is not necessarily a complete barrier to the development of a property, though. A landowner may fill a wetland for development if she creates or restores new wetlands elsewhere, so that there is no net loss of wetland area. Alternatively, the landowner may purchase the right to develop in wetland areas by paying into a government fund that is used to develop new wetlands elsewhere.

ENDANGERED SPECIES ACT. Both the federal government and the state of California have passed an Endangered Species Act. The purpose of these laws is to conserve habitats that shelter endangered or threatened species.

The federal and state governments each maintain their own lists of endangered species. A species may be included in either the federal list or the state list, or both. In California, there are dozens of listed species, many of which make their habitat primarily on private lands.

As with wetlands, however, the presence of an endangered species on a property does not completely bar development; private landowners may develop land supporting listed species if they agree to a Habitat Conservation Plan and undertake conservation measures. Landowners who agree to a plan and carry it out won't be required to take additional steps later on, even if the environmental circumstances change.

As a real estate agent, you should be familiar with the basic requirements of all of these environmental laws. And you shouldn't hesitate to refer prospective buyers of developable land to the U.S. Environmental Protection Agency, the U.S. Fish and Wildlife Service, or the California Department of Fish and Game if they have any questions as to whether these laws may limit how they can use the land.

ENVIRONMENTAL HAZARDS

Now let's take a look at some of the more common environmental hazards that real estate agents need to know about.

ASBESTOS. Asbestos was used for many years in insulation on plumbing pipes and heat ducts, and as general insulation material. It can also be found in floor tile and roofing material. In its original condition, asbestos is considered relatively harmless; but when asbestos dust filters into the air, it can cause lung cancer. Asbestos becomes a hazard in two ways: when it gets old and starts to disintegrate into a fine dust, and when it is damaged or removed during remodeling projects.

There are three methods of dealing with the presence of asbestos:

1. enclosure (this involves placing an airtight barrier between the asbestos and the rest of the space);
2. encapsulation (this involves covering the asbestos with an adhesive that will permanently seal in the asbestos fibers); or
3. removal.

Each of these three methods should only be undertaken by an experienced professional.

UREA FORMALDEHYDE. Until 1982, urea formaldehyde was used in foam insulation. It was banned because of the risk of illness caused by the formaldehyde gas released from the insulation. Urea formaldehyde foam insulation (UFFI) is not found in most American homes. If a home does contain UFFI, the health department can test the amount of formaldehyde gas being released from the insulation. UFFI can be removed, but new insulation and wall siding will have to be installed.

Urea formaldehyde may also be found in the adhesives used in pressed wood building materials, which are widely used in furniture, kitchen cabinets, and some types of paneling.

Urea formaldehyde may cause cancer, skin rashes, and breathing problems. However, it emits significant amounts of dangerous gas only in the first few years. Older urea formaldehyde materials are not considered dangerous.

RADON. Radon, a colorless, odorless gas, is actually present almost everywhere. It is found wherever uranium is deposited in the earth's crust. As uranium decomposes, radon gas is formed and seeps from the earth, usually into the atmosphere. However, radon sometimes collects in buildings. For example, radon may enter a house through cracks in the foundation or through floor drains. Exposure to dangerous levels of radon gas may cause lung cancer.

There are three ways to lower radon levels in a home:

1. sealing the holes and cracks that allow the gas to enter the home;
2. increasing ventilation to dilute the gas, especially in the areas where radon enters, such as the basement or crawl spaces; and
3. pressurizing the home to keep the gas out.

LEAD-BASED PAINT. Lead, though useful for many things, is extremely toxic to human beings. Children are especially susceptible to lead poisoning because they absorb it more quickly and have a more adverse reaction to its toxicity. Lead damages the brain, the kidneys, and the central nervous system.

The most common source of lead in the home is lead-based paint. Lead is now banned in consumer paint, but lead-based paint is still found in many homes built before 1978. As lead-based paint deteriorates, or if it is sanded or scraped, it forms a lead dust that accumulates inside and outside the home. This dust can be breathed in or ingested, increasing the risk of toxic lead exposure.

If there is lead-based paint in a home, it can be either eliminated or covered with non-lead-based paint. This requires special equipment and training; homeowners shouldn't try to handle the problem on their own.

In some cases, a seller or landlord is required by law to make disclosures concerning lead-based paint to prospective buyers or tenants. This disclosure law is discussed in Chapter 2.

UNDERGROUND STORAGE TANKS. Underground storage tanks are found not only on commercial and industrial properties, but also on residential properties. A storage tank is considered underground if 10% of its volume (including piping) is below the earth's surface. Probably the most common commercial use of underground storage tanks is for gas stations. Chemical plants, paint manufacturers, and other industries use underground storage tanks to store toxic liquids. In the residential setting, older homes used underground storage tanks to store fuel oil.

The principal danger from underground storage tanks is that when they grow old they begin to rust, leaking toxic products into the soil or, even more dangerously, into the groundwater.

Removing underground storage tanks and cleaning up the contaminated soil can be time-consuming and expensive. Both federal and state laws regulate the removal of storage tanks and the necessary cleanup.

WATER CONTAMINATION. Water can be contaminated by a variety of agents, including bacteria, viruses, nitrates, metals such as lead or mercury, fertilizers and pesticides, and radon. These contaminants may come from underground storage tanks, industrial discharge, urban area runoff, malfunctioning septic systems, and runoff from agricultural areas. Drinking contaminated water can cause physical symptoms that range from mild stomach aches to kidney and liver damage, cancer, and death.

If a homeowner uses a well as a water source, it should be tested by health authorities or private laboratories at least once a year. If well water becomes contaminated, a new well may have to be dug.

ILLEGAL DRUG MANUFACTURING. If property has been the site of illegal drug manufacturing, there may be substantial health risks for the occupants. The chemicals used to manufacture certain illegal drugs are highly toxic, and the effects of the contamination can linger for a long time.

If property is currently being used to manufacture illegal drugs, it can be seized by the government. This can occur even if the owner has no knowledge of the illegal drug activity.

> **EXAMPLE:** Meyers owns a single-family home that has been used as a rental property for several years. Unknown to Meyers, the current tenants are manufacturing illegal drugs in the basement of the home. The property could be seized by the government, even though Meyers knows nothing about the drug activity.

Of course, a property should not be listed or sold until any conditions that could subject the property to seizure have been eliminated.

MOLD. Mold is a commonplace problem, especially in damp parts of houses such as basements and bathrooms. For most people, the presence of mold does not cause any adverse effects. However, for people who are allergic to mold or who have respiratory problems, the presence of mold may render a house unlivable. You may hear references to "toxic mold," which is something of a misnomer; certain varieties of black mold can be particularly problematic for those who are sensitive to mold, but generally do not pose any more of a health hazard for most people than other types of mold.

Mold can never be completely eliminated, but it can be controlled by cutting off sources of moisture. Mold that is already growing can be removed by scrubbing with a water and bleach solution. Carpet or tile that is affected by mold may need to be removed and thrown out.

FIG. 3.3   ENVIRONMENTAL HAZARDS

ENVIRONMENTAL HAZARDS THAT MAY AFFECT HOMES
- ASBESTOS
- UREA FORMALDEHYDE
- RADON GAS
- LEAD-BASED PAINT
- UNDERGROUND STORAGE TANKS
- WATER CONTAMINATION
- ILLEGAL DRUG MANUFACTURING
- MOLD
- GEOLOGIC HAZARDS: LANDSLIDES, FLOODING, SUBSIDENCE, AND EARTHQUAKES

Awareness of mold has increased greatly in recent years, as a result of some high-profile lawsuits against builders or insurance companies, as well as news reports about contamination of public buildings such as schools and government offices. "Mold contingencies," where sale of a property is contingent upon not finding mold during the inspection process, are sometimes written into purchase agreements.

Mold problems that you're aware of should be treated as a latent defect and disclosed to prospective buyers. You should also disclose any knowledge of previous incidents of flooding or water damage, since that can start the growth of mold. Bear in mind that mold may grow out of sight, inside walls or heating ducts, and will not necessarily be discovered in an inspection, so your disclosure is particularly important.

GEOLOGIC HAZARDS. Geologic hazards are a significant concern for many property owners in California. Major potential geologic problems include landslides, flooding, subsidence, and earthquakes.

As with other environmental hazards, you should disclose any geologic hazards affecting a property as latent defects. In addition, information about designated hazard areas for flooding and earthquakes must be included in the natural hazards disclosure statement, which is discussed in Chapter 2.

LANDSLIDES. Probably the most costly geologic problem affecting homeowners is landslides. It's quite common for a house to be built close to the top of a cliff overlooking a body of water, in order to take advantage of the view. However, the weight of the house on unstable soil, particularly after heavy rainfall, can cause ground movement downhill, damaging the foundation or even tearing the house apart.

When you're dealing with a property located on or near a steep slope, you should always look for signs of ground movement. Tilting trees, active soil erosion, and cracking, dipping, or slumping ground are all indicators of slide activity. A property owner may take corrective steps, such as building retaining walls or rockeries, but they are expensive and unlikely to completely solve the problem.

If you see any evidence of landslide activity, it may be wise to consult with a geologist, in order to assess the magnitude of the problem. In addition, if you have listed a property where there is any evidence of ground movement, that should be considered a latent defect and disclosed to potential buyers.

FLOODING. Flooding can also be a serious problem for property owners. Whenever property is located in a flood plain—in the low-lying, flat areas immediately adjacent to a river—there is cause for concern. A prudent agent will check for signs of previous flood damage to structures, particularly in basements and foundations, and may want to check historical records to see how often flooding has been a problem.

SUBSIDENCE. Another potential geologic problem is subsidence, the collapse of ground into underground cavities. This can occur naturally, but only in areas of particularly porous bedrock. In most cases, subsidence is caused by man-made cavities. It may happen when forgotten underground storage tanks collapse, or when underground tanks have been removed but the soil has not been properly replaced. It is most common where mining has occurred. Over 50,000 abandoned mines exist throughout California, so before engaging in new construction in areas where mining once occurred, it may be advisable to obtain maps from government agencies that depict old mines.

EARTHQUAKES. Earthquakes are the least predictable and least controllable of geologic problems. They are also potentially the most destructive.

However, steps can be taken to protect buildings against earthquakes. In fact, seismic retrofitting can make a property more desirable and increase its value. The most important step in this process involves bolting elements of a home's wood frame to the underlying foundation. Many contractors are able to perform this type of work, and information about seismic retrofitting is widely available from state and local government agencies.

REAL ESTATE AGENT'S RESPONSIBILITIES

As you make your listing presentation and later prepare offers to purchase, you have two major responsibilities in regard to environmental issues:

1. to recognize potential environmental hazards, and
2. to recommend that the seller obtain the advice of an environmental attorney or other environmental expert.

If you are representing a seller whose property has environmental problems, it is better to have an attorney draft the appropriate disclosures instead of doing it yourself—if only to lessen your own liability. And if you represent buyers who are interested in purchasing a property with environmental problems, you need to make sure that they understand the potential risks of such a purchase. These risks should be explained to them by their attorney.

Naturally, contaminated property should only change hands after the cleanup has been completed. But even then, under federal environmental laws, the buyers may be assuming more potential liability than they are aware of. As the new owners of the property, the buyers may be held responsible for any additional cleanup costs, even though they had nothing to do with the contamination.

CHAPTER SUMMARY

1. California's Real Estate Law imposes certain restrictions on your listing activities. As a salesperson, you can be paid your commission only by your own broker. You can't be paid by other brokers or sales agents, or by the principal. And you may not sue the principal for a commission; only the broker may sue the principal.

2. A listing agreement belongs to the listing broker. It is a contract between the property seller and the broker; you sign the listing agreement only as an agent of your broker. Should you stop working for the listing broker, the listing remains with the broker. You can't take it with you to your new broker.

3. The Federal Fair Housing Act prohibits discrimination based on race, color, religion, sex, national origin, handicap, or familial status. In transactions related to housing, California antidiscrimination laws prohibit discrimination based on race, color, religion, ancestry, national origin, sex, disability, medical condition, age, sexual orientation, marital status, familial status, or source of income. Any discriminatory conduct by a real estate licensee is unlawful.

4. While dealing with potential clients and taking listings, you need to scrupulously follow all fair housing laws. Never imply that the presence of a particular group of residents will change property values or other characteristics of a neighborhood. Never refuse to list a property because of the seller's race, national origin, or another protected characteristic. Avoid any kind of discriminatory slur, including telling racial or ethnic jokes or passively listening to them. You should also discuss fair housing laws with the seller before taking a listing. If you think the seller may discriminate against potential purchasers, refuse to take the listing.

5. When you advertise listed properties, make sure that all your advertising complies with fair housing laws. Never send flyers or choose advertising media based on discriminatory ideas, and make sure any models included in ads do not have discriminatory implications. Remember to include the fair housing logo or slogan in your ads.

6. Antitrust laws prohibit price fixing, group boycotts, and tie-in arrangements. To avoid charges of price fixing, you should never discuss your commission rates with competing agents, and you must be sure to explain to sellers that the commission rate is fully negotiable. Never use a listing agreement form that has a commission amount or rate already set.

7. You should be familiar with the basic provisions of several environmental laws, including the National Environmental Policy Act (NEPA), the California Environmental Quality Act (CEQA), the California Coastal Act, and the Comprehensive Environmental Response, Compensation and Liability Act (CERCLA). CERCLA is particularly important, because it may impose liability on present owners for the cost of cleaning up hazardous substances, regardless of fault.

8. Environmental hazards you need to be aware of include asbestos, urea formaldehyde, radon, lead-based paint, underground storage tanks, water contamination, the effects of illegal drug manufacturing, and geologic problems. You must be able to recognize potential environmental hazards in a listed property, and advise the seller to consult an environmental professional when it is appropriate to do so.

CHAPTER QUIZ

1. Salesperson Jackson and Salesperson Robinson work for the same broker, Stellar Properties. They've both worked closely with a particular buyer. When that buyer finally purchases a house, Stellar Properties receives the selling broker's share of the commission and pays Jackson half of it. Jackson then gives half of her share of the commission to Robinson. This is:

   a. legal, because once a commission share has been paid to a salesperson, she is entitled to do whatever she wants with it

   b. legal, because agents are allowed to share compensation if they work for the same broker

   c. illegal, because a broker can share a commission only with another licensed broker

   d. illegal, because a commission split must be handled by the broker or brokers involved

2. Violations of the Rumford Act are investigated by the:

   a. Department of Real Estate

   b. Department of Fair Employment and Housing

   c. Department of Housing and Urban Development

   d. California Coastal Commission

3. Which of the following is not an example of illegal steering?

   a. An agent working with a buyer who has a disability calls his attention to a property with modifications that meet his needs

   b. An agent avoids showing an unmarried buyer houses in neighborhoods where most residents are married couples with children

   c. An agent working with a white couple doesn't tell them about homes in predominantly minority neighborhoods

   d. An agent working with a minority couple doesn't tell them about homes in predominantly white neighborhoods

4. Your advertising for residential properties should always include:

a. models from the same ethnic group as the residents of the neighborhood you are advertising in

b. models of a different ethnic background from the residents of the neighborhood you are advertising in

c. the Equal Housing Opportunity logo or slogan

d. a specific explanation of the standards of the community

5. Which of the following actions is most likely to be considered discriminatory?

a. When a white buyer asks about the racial composition of a neighborhood, an agent truthfully answers that it is predominantly minority

b. The listing agent for a home in a predominantly minority neighborhood decides to advertise only in the neighborhood newspaper because he thinks other minorities are most likely to be interested in the home

c. A brokerage uses a marketing plan to let minority buyers know about properties in predominantly white neighborhoods that they might not otherwise be aware of

d. A white couple expresses a desire not to be shown homes in a minority neighborhood, and their agent complies with their request

6. Which of the following is an example of price fixing?

a. A listing broker and a selling broker discuss a commission split in a cooperative sale

b. An agent making a listing presentation tells the seller that she is asking for a 7% commission, but emphasizes that the commission is negotiable

c. A broker holds a staff meeting with her sales agents to discuss commission rates for the office

d. A broker is having lunch with two other brokers and mentions that he is raising his commission rate, but there is no further discussion of the matter

7. Which law requires an environmental impact report (EIR) for projects that may have a significant effect on the environment?

   a. California Environmental Quality Act

   b. California Coastal Act

   c. Clean Water Act

   d. CERCLA

a

8. Which environmental law requires developers to obtain a permit from the U.S. Army Corps of Engineers?

   a. Clean Water Act

   b. Endangered Species Act

   c. National Environmental Policy Act

   d. California Coastal Act

a

9. Urea formaldehyde is found:

   a. in some floor tiles and roofing material

   b. wherever uranium is deposited in the earth's crust

   c. in the adhesives used in some pressed wood building materials

   d. in underground storage tanks

c

10. As a real estate agent, what is your responsibility with respect to environmental issues?

   a. Recognizing potential hazards and recommending that your clients obtain expert advice

   b. Making sure that an environmental impact statement is provided to the buyer

   c. Deciding what corrective action needs to be taken to solve the problem

   d. All of the above

a

ANSWER KEY

1. d. Two salespersons working for the same broker may split a commission, but the commission split must be handled by their broker. A salesperson can only receive a commission through his or her broker.

2. b. Under the Rumford Act, also known as the Fair Employment and Housing Act, housing discrimination complaints are investigated by the Department of Fair Employment and Housing.

3. a. An agent can legitimately bring properties that are specially suited to the needs of a disabled buyer to the buyer's attention.

4. c. Regardless of what type of advertising you use to market a home, it should always include the Equal Housing Opportunity logo or slogan.

5. b. Advertising can be considered discriminatory if it appears only in a publication directed toward the minority neighborhood where the property is located. The advertising should also appear where it will be seen by a broader spectrum of the population.

6. d. Any communication between competing brokers about prices could be considered an invitation to engage in price fixing, even if the brokers don't explicitly decide to cooperate in fixing prices.

7. a. The California Environmental Quality Act (CEQA) requires an EIR for projects that may have a significant effect on the environment.

8. a. The Clean Water Act makes it illegal for a private landowner to fill or drain wetlands without a permit from the U.S. Army Corps of Engineers.

9. c. Urea formaldehyde is found in the adhesives used in some pressed wood building materials, and also in some types of foam insulation.

10. a. If there are environmental issues concerning a property, you should always recommend that your clients seek expert advice from an environmental engineer or attorney.

CHAPTER 4

EVALUATING AND PRICING PROPERTY

THE AGENT'S ROLE IN PRICING PROPERTY

VALUE
- Types of value
- Value vs. price or cost

COMPETITIVE MARKET ANALYSIS
- Analyzing the seller's property
  - Neighborhood analysis
  - Site analysis
  - Building analysis
- Choosing comparable properties
- Making adjustments to the comparables
- Estimating market value
- Completing a CMA
- CMA form

THE PROBLEM OF A LOW APPRAISAL
- Request for reconsideration of value

INTRODUCTION

How quickly your listing sells, or whether it sells at all, depends largely on the listing price. How is a competitive listing price determined? If your seller insists on listing her home at a ridiculously inflated price, should you simply take the listing and hope for the best?

In this chapter, we will discuss the listing agent's role in evaluating and pricing a seller's home, the concept of value, and how to complete a competitive market analysis.

THE AGENT'S ROLE IN PRICING PROPERTY

It is your seller's responsibility—not yours—to decide on a listing price for his home. But the average seller does not have the knowledge or expertise to arrive at a realistic price. Your seller will depend on you for information and advice about this important decision. Without your expertise, the seller could easily underprice or overprice his property. Either of these mistakes could have serious consequences for you and for the seller.

> **EXAMPLE:** Jeffries is listing his home with you. He asks you for advice on setting a listing price, but you tell him that the price is up to him.
>
> Jeffries knows about a few houses in his neighborhood that have been for sale for many months. He believes the houses haven't sold because they are overpriced. He thinks his house is comparable to these other houses, but he wants a quick sale. So Jeffries sets his listing price by deducting $10,000 from the listing price of the other houses. He ends up listing his house for $320,000.
>
> Jeffries's house is actually very appealing and sells quickly at that price. When his house is appraised, he discovers to his dismay that it was actually worth about $350,000. He's very angry—he just lost $30,000, and he considers it entirely your fault. If he decided to sue your broker, the broker could lose the commission and might even have to pay additional damages as well.
>
> On the other hand, suppose that when Jeffries sets his listing price, he thinks his house is worth much more than it really is. With a listing price of $370,000, his house languishes on the market for several months. Finally, your listing agreement expires and Jeffries decides to list the property with another firm. Because of an inflated listing price, Jeffries waited in vain for a sale, you wasted a good deal of effort

trying to sell an overpriced house, and your reputation in the neighborhood suffered as your "For Sale" sign faded and was then removed without a "SOLD!" banner.

Your ability to suggest a competitive listing price is one of the most important services you can provide a seller. Your advice on a listing price will generally take the form of a **competitive market analysis** (CMA). A CMA compares your seller's house to other similar houses that are on the market or have recently sold. The listing or sales prices of those other houses help the seller set a realistic listing price for her own house.

A CMA is similar to an appraisal, *but it is not an appraisal.* As the listing agent, your role is very different from that of an appraiser. Your job is to provide the seller with information about the sales prices of similar homes. This is the information that is contained in your CMA. The seller uses this information to decide how much to ask for her property.

An appraiser, on the other hand, uses his professional experience to estimate the property's market value as of a specific date. The appraiser usually does this for a lender, to help the lender set a maximum loan amount for the loan applicant who wants to buy the property. The appraiser bases this estimate on a wide variety of data, including general social and economic data. An appraisal is much more complex than a competitive market analysis and is based on more information.

VALUE

The value of a home has many consequences for the owner. The value largely determines not only how much it costs to purchase the home, but also the financing, the property tax assessment, the insurance coverage, the potential rental rate, the eventual selling price, and the income tax consequences of its sale.

To estimate the value of a home, you need a general understanding of the concept of value. First of all, keep in mind that value is created by people. It is not so much the intrinsic qualities of an item that make it valuable, but rather our attitudes toward it. For example, if it were to begin raining gold instead of water, gold would become a nuisance and its value would disappear. Yet its intrinsic qualities would be the same whether it was a rare and precious metal or a too-common nuisance.

TYPES OF VALUE

Appraisers distinguish between several different types of value. A property's value can vary depending on which type of value is in question in a given situation. For example, **value in use** is the subjective value placed on a property by someone who owns or uses it. By contrast, **value in exchange** (commonly referred to as **market value**) is the objective value of a property in the eyes of the average person. The difference between these two types of value is one reason the seller needs your help in setting a listing price.

> **EXAMPLE:** Darnell owns a large old house that has been in her family for generations. Because of the history of the house, it is very valuable to Darnell. In other words, its value in use is very high. Yet if an objective third party were considering buying the house, he or she would not be willing to pay very much for it. The plumbing is poor and the design is very outdated. The property's value in exchange is not nearly as high as its value in use.

Real estate agents are concerned with value in exchange, or market value. Here is the most widely accepted definition of market value, taken from the Uniform Standards of Professional Appraisal Practice:

The most probable price which a property should bring in a competitive and open market under all conditions requisite to a fair sale, the buyer and seller each acting prudently and knowledgeably, and assuming the price is not affected by undue stimulus.

VALUE VS. PRICE OR COST

When you're estimating the value of property, always remember that there's an important distinction between market value and market price. **Market price** is the price actually paid for a property, regardless of whether the parties to the transaction were informed and acting free of unusual pressure. Market value, as you've seen, is what should be paid if a property is purchased and sold under all the conditions requisite to a fair sale.

Another related concept is that of cost. **Cost** is the amount of money that was paid to acquire the property and build the structures on it. A property's cost, value, and price may all be different.

EXAMPLE: A developer paid $75,000 for a parcel of vacant land and then spent $240,000 to build a house on the land. After the house was completed, the property was worth $350,000. But the developer needed some fast cash, so he sold the property at the "fire sale" price of $330,000. The cost of the house was $315,000, the value of the house was $350,000, and the price of the house was $330,000.

The basis for a good listing price for a home is its market value, not its original cost or purchase price. And the real estate agent's best tool for estimating market value is competitive market analysis.

COMPETITIVE MARKET ANALYSIS

Although competitive market analysis is not the only way to arrive at a listing price, there's a lot to recommend it. It has two key advantages over the "eyeball" approach to setting a listing price: it's reliable, and it's easy to explain.

With the eyeball approach, the real estate agent simply walks through the seller's house, observes its features, and then mentally compares them to features he's observed in other houses. The agent then decides on what he feels is a competitive price. A price reached in this way can be far from the true market value. Not only that, the agent does not have any data to support his conclusion if the seller questions him about it.

An estimate of value based on your gut feelings is especially problematic when the seller is expecting to get more for her property than it's worth. Unless you can back up your "low" estimate with facts and figures that are easy to understand, you will lose credibility as well as the seller's good will. So it's important to have a simple method of valuing property that is easy to apply and to explain.

In a formal appraisal, the appraiser may estimate the property's value by applying these three methods:

1. Cost approach to value: Estimating how much it would cost to build a similar structure, and then subtracting the depreciation that has accrued.
2. Income approach to value: Estimating value based on the income the property could potentially generate.
3. Sales comparison approach to value: Estimating value by comparing the property to similar properties that have recently sold.

The first two methods can be complicated, time-consuming, and difficult for a seller to understand. The third method, the sales comparison approach, is much simpler to use and easier for the seller to understand. In addition, the sales comparison approach is considered the most reliable method for appraising residential property. As a result, real estate agents have borrowed the sales comparison method of appraisal and modified it for their own use. This modified sales comparison method is called competitive market analysis, or CMA.

With a CMA, you estimate the value of your seller's property by comparing it to similar nearby properties that have sold recently or are for sale. CMAs are effective because an informed buyer acting free of pressure will not pay more for a particular property than she would have to pay for an equally desirable substitute property. Thus, if the seller is objective, he will base the listing price on the prices recently paid for similar properties in the same area.

The steps involved in completing a CMA include:

1. collecting and analyzing information about the seller's property;
2. choosing the comparable properties;
3. comparing the seller's property to the comparables and adjusting the value of the comparables accordingly; and
4. estimating a realistic listing price for the seller's property.

ANALYZING THE SELLER'S PROPERTY

The first step is to gather and study information about the seller's property. Naturally, you should pay the most attention to the elements that have the greatest impact on value. These elements fall into three categories:

1. the property's neighborhood,
2. the property (or site) itself, and
3. the improvements on the property.

As you collect information about the seller's property (sometimes called the **subject property**), keep in mind that you will need to gather the same information about the properties you choose as comparables.

NEIGHBORHOOD ANALYSIS. Few factors have as much impact on a property's value as its location, or neighborhood. A neighborhood is an area that contains similar types of properties; it may be residential, commercial, industrial, or agricultural. Its boundaries may be determined by physical obstacles (such as highways and bodies of water), land use patterns, the age and value of homes or other buildings, and/or the economic status of the residents.

Neighborhood characteristics set the upper and lower limits of a property's value. A high-quality property cannot overcome the adverse influence of a poor neighborhood. And the value of a relatively weak property is enhanced by a desirable neighborhood.

Here are some specific factors to look at when gathering data about a residential neighborhood:

1. **PERCENTAGE OF HOMEOWNERSHIP.** Is there a high degree of owner-occupancy, or do rental properties predominate? Owner-occupied homes are generally better maintained and less susceptible to deterioration.

2. **VACANT HOMES AND LOTS.** An unusual number of vacant homes or lots suggests a low level of interest in the area, which has a negative effect on property values. On the other hand, significant construction activity indicates strong interest in the area.

3. **CONFORMITY.** The homes in a neighborhood should be reasonably similar in style, age, size, and quality. Strictly enforced zoning and private restrictions promote conformity and protect property values.

4. **CHANGING LAND USE.** Is the neighborhood in the middle of a transition from residential use to some other type of use? If so, the properties may be losing their value.

5. **CONTOUR OF THE LAND.** Mildly rolling topography is preferable to terrain that is either monotonously flat or excessively hilly.

6. **STREETS.** Wide, gently curving streets are more appealing than narrow or straight streets. Streets should be hard-surfaced and well maintained.

7. **UTILITIES.** Does the neighborhood have electricity, gas, water, sewers, and telephones? What about cable television and high-speed Internet access?

8. **NUISANCES.** Not surprisingly, nuisances (odors, eyesores, industrial noises or pollutants, or exposure to unusual winds, smog, or fog) in or near a neighborhood hurt property values.

9. **Reputation.** Is the neighborhood considered prestigious, in comparison to others in the community? If so, that will increase property values.

10. **Proximity.** How far is it to traffic arterials and to important points such as downtown, employment centers, and shopping centers?

11. **Schools.** What schools serve the neighborhood? Are they highly regarded? Are they within walking distance? The quality of a school or school district can make a major difference in property values in a residential neighborhood.

12. **Public services.** How well is the neighborhood served by public transportation, police, and fire units?

13. **Governmental influences.** Does zoning in and around the neighborhood promote residential use and insulate the property owner from nuisances? How do the property tax rates compare with those of other neighborhoods nearby?

You can use a worksheet such as the one shown in Figure 4.1 to record your neighborhood information. Of course, as you gain more experience, you will become familiar with all of the neighborhoods in your area and their distinguishing characteristics. Before long, you will be able to gauge the effect of the neighborhood on a property's value as soon as you hear where the property is located.

Site Analysis. Studying the site of the subject property means collecting information about the following factors:

1. **Width.** This refers to the lot's measurements from one side boundary to the other. Width can vary from front to back, as in the case of a pie-shaped lot on a cul-de-sac.

2. **Frontage.** Frontage is the length of the front boundary of the lot, the boundary that abuts a street or a body of water. The amount of frontage can be an important consideration if it measures the property's access or exposure to something desirable.

3. **Depth.** Depth is the distance between the site's front boundary and its rear boundary. Greater depth (more than the norm) can mean greater value, but it doesn't always. For example, suppose

FIG. 4.1   NEIGHBORHOOD DATA FORM

NEIGHBORHOOD DATA

Property adjacent to:

NORTH___Plum Boulevard, garden apartments___

SOUTH___Cherry Street, single-family homes___

EAST___14th Avenue, single-family homes___

WEST___12th Avenue, single-family homes___

Population: __ increasing   __ decreasing   _x_ stable

Life cycle stage: __ integration _x_ equilibrium __ disintegration __ rebirth

Tax rate: __ higher   __ lower _x_ same as competing areas

Services: _x_ police   _x_ fire _x_ garbage __ other:_____

Average family size: _3.5_____

Occupational status: _White collar; skilled trades_____

Distance from:

Commercial areas _3 miles_____

Elementary school _6 blocks_____

Secondary school _1 mile_____

Recreational areas _2 miles_____

Cultural centers _3 miles_____

Places of worship _Methodist, Catholic, Baptist_____

Transportation _Bus stop 1 block; frequent service to downtown_

Freeway/highway _10 blocks_____

Typical Properties	Age	Price Range	Owner-occupancy
Vacant lots: 0%			
Single-family homes: 80%	20 yrs	$275,000-$340,000	93%
Apartments, 2- to 4-unit: 15%	10 yrs		
Apartments, over 4 units: 5%	5 yrs		
Non-residential: 0%			

Nuisances (odors, noise, etc.) _None_____

Environmental hazards (chemical storage, etc.) _None_____

Lot 1 and Lot 2 are the same, except that Lot 2 is deeper; Lot 2 is not necessarily more valuable than Lot 1. Each situation must be analyzed individually to determine whether more depth translates into greater value.

4. **AREA.** Area is the total size of the site, usually measured in square feet or acres. Comparisons between lots often focus on the features of frontage and area.

   Commercial land is usually valued in terms of frontage; that is, it is worth a certain number of dollars per front foot. Industrial land, on the other hand, tends to be valued in terms of square feet or acreage. Residential lots are measured both ways: by square feet or by acreage in most instances, but by front foot when the property abuts a lake or river, or some other desirable feature.

   Under certain circumstances, combining two or more adjoining lots to achieve greater width, depth, or area will make the larger parcel more valuable than the sum of the values of its component parcels. The increment of value that results when two or more lots are combined to produce greater value is called **plottage**. The process of assembling lots to increase their value is most frequently part of industrial or commercial land development.

5. **SHAPE.** Lots with uniform width and depth (such as rectangular lots) are almost always more useful than irregularly shaped lots; a standard shape is more versatile for building purposes. This is true for any kind of lot—residential, commercial, or industrial.

6. **TOPOGRAPHY.** A site is generally more valuable if it is aesthetically appealing. Rolling terrain is preferable to flat, monotonous land. On the other hand, if the site would be costly to develop because it sits well above or below the street or is excessively hilly, that lessens its value.

7. **POSITION AND ORIENTATION.** How a lot is situated relative to the surrounding area influences its value. Consider whether the site has a view, and how much sunshine it gets during the day. And is it sheltered, or exposed to the elements and/or to traffic noise?

FIG. 4.2   SITE DATA FORM

SITE DATA

Address ___10157 - 13th Avenue___

Legal description ___Lot 6, Block 4, Caldwell's Addition, vol. 72, pg. 25___

Dimensions ___50' x 200'___   Shape ___Rectangular___

Square feet ___10,000___   Street paving ___Asphalt___

Landscaping ___Adequate___   Topsoil ___Good___

Drainage ___Good___   Frontage ___(Street)___

Easements ___Utility S 15'___   Corner lot __ Inside lot _x_ View __

Encroachments ___Fence on west property line?___

Improvements: _x_ Driveway   _x_ Sidewalks   _x_ Curbs   __ Alley

Utilities: _x_ Electricity   __ Gas   _x_ Water   _x_ Sewers   _x_ Storm drains
              _x_ Telephone   _x_ Cable TV   _x_ High-speed Internet

---

8. **TITLE.** Of course, any title problems will have an adverse effect on the value of the property. When you examine the site, look for signs of easements or encroachments. If a utility company has an easement across the rear portion of the property, for example, this would reduce the value of the property in comparison to a similar property with no easement.

You may want to use a worksheet such as the one shown in Figure 4.2 to record the information you gather about the site.

BUILDING ANALYSIS. After examining the neighborhood and the site of the seller's property, the next step is to examine the improvements built on the property. For the typical residential property, this means a house and garage, and perhaps a garden shed or workshop. Here are some of the primary factors to analyze.

1. **CONSTRUCTION QUALITY.** Is the quality of the materials and workmanship good, average, or poor?

2. **AGE/CONDITION.** How old is the home? Is its overall condition good, average, or poor? Depending on the condition, the effective age of the home may be more or less than its actual age.

3. **SIZE OF HOUSE (SQUARE FOOTAGE).** This includes the improved living area, excluding the garage, basement, and porches.

4. **BASEMENT.** A functional basement, especially a finished basement, contributes to value. However, the amount a finished basement contributes to value is often not enough to recover the cost of the finish work.

5. **NUMBER OF ROOMS.** Add up the total number of rooms in the house, excluding bathrooms and basement rooms.

6. **NUMBER OF BEDROOMS.** The number of bedrooms has a major impact on value. For instance, if all else is equal, a two-bedroom home is worth considerably less than a three-bedroom home.

7. **NUMBER OF BATHROOMS.** A full bath is a wash basin, toilet, and bathtub, with or without a shower; a three-quarter bath is a wash basin, toilet, and shower (no tub); a half bath is a wash basin and toilet only. The number of bathrooms can have a noticeable effect on value.

8. **AIR CONDITIONING.** The presence of an air conditioning system and the system's condition are important in most areas of California.

9. **ENERGY EFFICIENCY.** With spiraling energy costs, an energy-efficient home is more valuable than a comparable one that is not. Energy-efficient features, such as double-paned windows, good insulation, and weather stripping, increase value.

10. **GARAGE OR CARPORT.** An enclosed garage is generally better than a carport. How many cars can it accommodate? Is there work or storage space in addition to space for parking? Is it possible to enter the home directly from the garage or carport, protected from the weather?

11. **DESIGN AND LAYOUT.** Is the floor plan functional and convenient? Are the design and layout attractive and efficient, or are there obvious design deficiencies that will decrease the value of the home? (We'll discuss design and layout in more detail in the next section of the chapter.)

You might want to use a form such as the one shown in Figure 4.3 to record the information you gather about the quality and condition of the improvements.

FIG. 4.3   BUILDING DATA FORM

BUILDING DATA

Address ____10157 - 13th Avenue_____

Age __7 years_____   Square feet __1,350_____

Number of rooms __6_____   Construction quality __very good___

Style ___ranch_____   General condition ___very good____

Feature	Good	Fair	Bad
Exterior: brick, frame, veneer, stucco, alum	x		
Foundation: slab, bsmt., crawl sp.	x		
Garage: attached, 1-car, 2-car, 3-car	x		
Patio, deck, porch, shed, other		x	
Interior (general condition)	x		
Walls: drywall, wood, plaster	x		
Ceilings	x		
Floors: wood, tile, lino, concrete, carpet		x	
Electrical wiring	x		
Heating: electric, gas, oil, other	x		
Air conditioning		x	
Fireplace(s) None			
Kitchen	x		
Bathroom(s) 2 full	x		
Bedroom(s) 1 large, 2 medium	x		

Additional amenities __Large windows in living areas_____

Design advantages___Convenient, sunny kitchen_____

Design flaws__Inadequate closets in the two smaller bedrooms___

Energy efficiency __Insulation, weather-stripping_____

Location	Living Rm	Dining Rm	Kitchen	Bedrms	Baths	Family Rm
Basement						
First floor	x	x	x	3	2	None
Second floor						
Attic						

Depreciation:

   Deferred maintenance ____Normal wear, except for deck railings___

   Functional obsolescence __No family room_____

   External obsolescence ___None_____

DESIGN AND LAYOUT. A well-designed house is one that is the right size, shape, and design to produce the maximum value. Here are some questions to ask yourself as you examine the design of a house.

GENERAL DESIGN. The number of bedrooms in a house usually determines which buyers will consider purchasing it. Keep in mind the family size of those potential buyers as you evaluate the house.

In relation to the number of bedrooms, is the house large enough overall? Are there enough bathrooms, and an adequate number of closets? Is there a separate family room, children's playroom, or other recreational space? Is there sufficient work space in the kitchen and laundry room, and is there storage space for cleaning and gardening tools? Are there enough windows and natural light, especially in the kitchen and other work or recreational spaces?

LIVING ROOM AND FAMILY ROOM. How large are the living room and the family or recreation room (if any)? Will the shape of each room and the available wall space accommodate the furniture that will probably be placed in it?

DINING ROOM OR DINING AREA. Is the dining area convenient to the kitchen and large enough for the number of people who will be eating there?

KITCHEN. Is the kitchen convenient to an outside entrance and to the garage or carport? Is there adequate counter and cabinet space?

BEDROOMS. How large are the bedrooms? Is there a master bedroom that's significantly larger than the other bedrooms? Are the bedroom closets big enough? Where are the bedrooms located in the house? It's better for the bedrooms to be located apart from the living room, family room, kitchen, and other work or recreational spaces.

BATHROOMS. There should be at least two bathrooms if the house has more than two bedrooms. In many areas, particularly in newer houses, a private bathroom off the master bedroom is standard. Are there windows or ceiling fans in the bathrooms to provide adequate ventilation?

DESIGN DEFICIENCIES. Here is a brief list of some of the most common design deficiencies to watch out for:

- The front door opens directly into the living room.
- There's no front hall closet.

- The back door is difficult to reach from the kitchen, or from the driveway or garage.
- There's no comfortable area in or near the kitchen where the family can eat informally.
- The dining room is not easily accessible from the kitchen.
- The stairway leading to the second story is off of a room rather than in a hallway or foyer.
- A bathroom or some of the bedrooms are visible from the living room or foyer.
- The family room or recreation room is not visible from the kitchen.
- There is no direct access to the basement from outside the house.
- The bedrooms are not separated by a bathroom or closet wall (for soundproofing).
- It's necessary to pass through one of the bedrooms to reach another bedroom.
- Outdoor living areas (such as a patio or deck) are not accessible from the kitchen.

CHOOSING COMPARABLE PROPERTIES

You now know a great deal of information about the seller's property. The next step in your CMA is to choose comparable properties that have recently sold and others that are now for sale. (These properties are called **comparables** because they have the same or nearly the same characteristics as the seller's property.) By evaluating the sales prices or listing prices of these comparable properties, you will be able to estimate a reasonable listing price for the seller's property.

As you choose your comparables, you will refer to various sources of information. You will need to obtain comprehensive market data, which includes the listing and sales prices of properties in the seller's neighborhood, the financing terms of the sales transactions, and the physical characteristics of the properties. You may want to maintain your own history file of real estate activity in your area so you can have the information you need at your fingertips. The most reliable source of sales information is the multiple listing service. An MLS usually requires active members to assemble and share complete records of transactions, showing not only listing prices but also other useful data such as consummated sales, financing terms, and length of time on the market. Other sources of information include:

- your broker's previous listings;
- real estate advertisements in the local newspapers (this provides listing prices only);
- other brokers and salespersons, loan officers, escrow officers, or anyone else actively involved with the local real estate market; and
- practical, everyday experience gained from previewing properties in a neighborhood over time.

Comparable properties must be truly comparable to the subject property in the areas of greatest importance, which are listed below. In choosing your comparables, these are the areas you should focus on. Whether a potential comparable is a currently listed property, a recently expired listing, or a property that has recently sold, you will be concerned with two key factors:

1. **LOCATION OF COMPARABLE.** We already mentioned how important location is to the value of a home. Ideally, a comparable property should be in the same neighborhood as the seller's property. If you can't find enough comparables in the seller's neighborhood, you can choose comparables from similar neighborhoods nearby.

   Even if your comparable is located in the same neighborhood as the seller's home, you may have to take into account differences in value due to location *within* a neighborhood.

   EXAMPLE: Two basically identical properties located one block apart in the same neighborhood may have very different values if one of the properties has lake frontage and the other does not. The values of the properties could also differ if one is located on a busy main avenue, while the other is on a quiet side street.

   If a comparable is in an inferior neighborhood, it is probably less valuable than the subject property, even if it's structurally identical. The opposite is true of a comparable from a superior neighborhood.

2. **PHYSICAL CHARACTERISTICS.** To qualify as a comparable, a property should have physical characteristics that are similar to the subject property, including size, style, layout and design, construction materials, and condition of the building.

If the comparable has recently sold, you will also be concerned with the following factors, in addition to location and physical characteristics:

3. **DATE OF COMPARABLE SALE.** The sale should be recent. The comparison is more reliable if the sale occurred within the last six months, and sales more than one year old should not be used at all. Older sales aren't reliable enough because market conditions (such as sales prices, interest rates, and construction costs) change over time. If the comparable you're considering sold between six months and one year ago, you may have to make adjustments for the time factor, allowing for inflationary or deflationary trends or other changes in the market since the sale of the comparable.

4. **TERMS OF SALE.** How was the sale financed? If the financing terms did not affect the price paid for the property, the financing is referred to as **cash equivalent**. If the buyer used a standard conventional loan to finance the sale of the home, the financing would be considered cash equivalent. But if the financing terms were unusual, they may have affected the sales price of the comparable.

Nonstandard financing can take a variety of forms, from seller financing to an interest rate buydown. (See Chapter 9.) In some cases, the effect of a special financing arrangement may be fairly obvious.

EXAMPLE: The buyer's lender is charging $3,000 in discount points. The seller is going to pay the points to help the buyer qualify for the loan. The purchase price the buyer has agreed to pay is about $3,000 more than he would otherwise have paid, to compensate the seller for paying the points. In this case, the effect on the sales price equals the amount paid by the seller.

Other cases are not so clear-cut. In a sale that involves seller financing, for instance, the buyer may benefit in any of several ways. A below-market interest rate, a small downpayment, reduced (or zero) loan fees, and easier loan qualification are some of the possible benefits of seller financing.

Calculating the effect of nonstandard financing on price is rarely a simple task. If you don't feel comfortable making those calculations, it may be best to find another comparable with cash equivalent financing terms.

5. **CONDITIONS OF SALE.** This factor concerns the motivations of the buyer and seller in a particular transaction. If the buyer and/or seller had some unusual motivation, the sale was probably not an **arm's length transaction**. An arm's length transaction is one in which both parties are fully informed of the property's merits and shortcomings, neither is acting under unusual pressure, and the property has been exposed on the open market for a reasonable length of time. Sales that were not arm's length transactions should not be used as comparables; the price paid is not a reliable indicator of market value, because the buyer and seller were acting under the influence of forces that do not affect the market in general.

EXAMPLE: Morgan has been transferred to another city, and she's due to begin her new job in four weeks. Her employer is paying for her moving expenses and has also offered to make up the difference between the market value of her house and any reasonable offer that is made in the first three weeks. Morgan can accept a low offer just to make a quick sale, since she won't personally lose any money on the transaction. This seller is not typically motivated, so this transaction should not be used as a comparable.

MAKING ADJUSTMENTS TO THE COMPARABLES

Now that you have chosen your comparable properties, you must compare each one to the seller's property. The comparison is made on the basis of the same elements you used to choose the comparables in the first place: 1) location, 2) physical characteristics, 3) date of sale, and 4) terms of sale. (The conditions of sale have already been taken into account, because the comparables are all arm's length transactions.) Before, you used these elements to weed out noncomparable properties. Now you'll use them to make minor adjustments in the sales prices or listing prices of the comparables.

Of course, the more similar the comparable, the easier the comparison. A comparable that was identical in design, neighborhood, site characteristics, and condition that sold under typical financing terms the previous month would give you an excellent indication of the market value of the subject property with no adjustments necessary. However, except in some new housing developments, you're not likely to find comparables that similar to the seller's property. Instead, there will nearly always be at least a few significant differences between the comparables and the seller's property. So you'll have to make the proper adjustments to the value of the comparables.

EXAMPLE: You've found a comparable that's very similar to the subject property, except that it has three bedrooms and the subject property has only two. The comparable recently sold for $335,000. If you know that a third bedroom is worth approximately $9,000, you'll subtract $9,000 from the sales price of the comparable. This adjusted price reflects the difference in the number of bedrooms.

One of the greatest challenges of completing a CMA is determining the value of the differences between the comparables and the subject property. How do you know how much an extra bedroom or bathroom, or proximity to a good elementary school, is really worth?

When you begin your real estate career, placing a value on individual features will be a matter of careful research and comparison.

EXAMPLE: You have two properties, A and B. They are virtually identical except that A has two bathrooms and B has three. Property A sold for $347,000 and B sold for $353,500. Since the number of the bathrooms is the only real difference between the two properties, the value of the third bathroom is about $6,500.

By comparing many different properties in this way, you will be able to place a particular value on several different features. Of course, in the real world you may not find properties with only one distinguishing feature, like the one in our example. But with time and experience you will able to place a value on each of the many features that differ from one property to another.

The chart in Figure 4.4 illustrates how you can estimate the value of individual features. As you examine the chart, note that a few of the properties had no variables, so they were used as the standard against which the value of each distinguishing feature was measured.

FIG. 4.4 FINDING THE ADJUSTMENT VALUE FOR INDIVIDUAL FEATURES

Features	Comparables							
	A	**B**	**C**	**D**	**E**	**F**	**G**	**H**
Sales price	$332,500	$326,000	$332,500	$342,500	$341,000	$332,500	$324,500	$322,500
Location	Riverbend	Riverbend	Riverbend	Riverbend	Riverbend	Riverbend	Riverbend	Wood Hill
Age	8 yrs	7 yrs	8 yrs	6 yrs	8 yrs	7 yrs	6 yrs	7 yrs
Lot size	75 x 200	80 x 200	75 x 200	75 x 200	100 x 200	75 x 200	75 x 200	80 x 200
Construction	frame	frame	frame	frame	frame	frame	frame	frame
Style	ranch	ranch	ranch	ranch	ranch	ranch	ranch	ranch
No. of rooms	7	7	7	8	7	7	6	7
No. of bedrooms	3	3	3	4	3	3	2	3
No. of baths	2	1	2	2	2	2	2	2
Square feet	1,300	1,300	1,300	1,425	1,300	1,300	1,250	1,300
Exterior	good	good	good	good	good	good	good	good
Interior	good	good	good	good	good	good	good	good
Garage	2-car, att.	2-car, att.	2-car, att.	2-car, att.	2-car, att.	2-car, att.	2-car, att.	2-car, att.
Other	basement	basement	basement	basement	basement	basement	basement	basement
Financing	80% S/L	80% S/L	90% S/L	90% S/L	80% S/L	90% S/L	90% S/L	90% S/L
Date of sale	8 wk.	7 wk.	6 wk.	8 wk.	5 wk.	7 wk.	6 wk.	9 wk.
Typical house value	$332,500	$332,500	$332,500	$332,500	$332,500	$332,500	$332,500	$332,500
Variable feature		1 bath		4 bdrm.	larger lot		2 bdrm.	poor loc.
Adjustment value for variable		$6,500		$10,000	$8,500		$8,000	$10,000

Remember that it's the sales or listing price of the comparable that is adjusted to indicate the probable market value of the subject property. Never try to make the adjustments to the value of the subject property. If a comparable lacks a feature that the subject property has, *add* the value of the missing feature to the comparable's price. If a comparable has a feature that the subject property lacks, *subtract* the value of the feature from the comparable's price. The completed comparison chart shown in Figure 4.6 illustrates this process.

ESTIMATING MARKET VALUE

After making all the required adjustments for varying features, you will have an adjusted market value figure for each comparable. You'll use these figures to estimate the market value of the seller's property. To do this, you have to evaluate the reliability of each comparable. The comparables that are most like the subject property (and consequently have the fewest adjustments) offer the most reliable indication of market value.

EXAMPLE: You have found three comparables with the values shown in Figure 4.5. Obviously, Comparable C has a significant number of variables (differences between the comparable and the subject property), which makes it less reliable as a comparable. Comparables A and B are much more similar to the subject property, with A being most like it. Therefore, the market value of A should be given the most weight and C the least. In this situation, you might estimate the market value of the seller's property to be about $339,000.

FIG. 4.5   COMPARABLES FOR EXAMPLE ABOVE

	Comparables		
	A	**B**	**C**
Selling price	$346,500	$353,150	$370,050
Extra bedroom	– 8,000	– 8,000	– 8,000
Two-car garage			– 6,300
Large lot			– 8,750
Aluminum siding		– 4,750	
Final value	$338,500	$340,400	$347,000

FIG. 4.6   COMPARABLE SALES COMPARISON CHART

Comparable Sales Comparison Chart					
Features	**Subject Property**	**Comparables**			
		1	**2**	**3**	**4**
Sales price		$341,750	$346,500	$332,000	$336,500
Location	quiet street				
Age	7 yrs.				
Lot size	80 x 200				
Construction	frame			+$7,000	
Style	ranch				
Number of rooms	7		− $7,500		
Number of bedrooms	3			+$8,500	+$8,500
Number of baths	2	+$6,500			
Square feet	1,400				
Exterior	good				
Interior	good				
Garage	2-car att.				
Other improvements		− $3,000			
Financing					
Date of sale			+$3,000		
Net adjustments		+$3,500	− $4,500	+$15,500	+$8,500
Adjusted value		$345,250	$342,000	$347,500	$345,000

Of course, when you're estimating market value to help the seller set a realistic listing price, you don't need to provide an exact figure. You can give the seller a range of figures, such as "between $338,000 and $341,000." It's then up to the seller to choose the listing price he wants.

COMPLETING A CMA

Let's walk through the process of doing a competitive market analysis for a hypothetical property. Although the steps we will follow are the same ones you'll use when preparing CMAs in real life, the data we'll be using is simplified. The actual CMAs you'll prepare will usually involve more complex data and a greater number of variables.

Some prospective sellers have asked you for advice on how much their house could sell for on the current market. They'll give you the listing if they're happy with the suggested price.

Your first step is to gather information about the sellers' house, the subject property. You walk through the house with the sellers, taking notes. You observe the property's amenities and defects; you also discuss the sellers' motivation for selling and their time parameters. When you leave, you drive through the neighborhood, noting the benefits and drawbacks of the area. You look for other properties that are on the market or that have recently sold.

After viewing the property, talking with the sellers, and studying the neighborhood, you have the following information: The house is located in Cedar Hills, which is a small, stable, middle-income neighborhood three miles north of the business district of Jeffersville. The house has three bedrooms, two full bathrooms, a dining room, and a large, well-landscaped back yard. It's a two-story house with a double garage. The house is four years old and in excellent condition.

The next step is to select comparable properties and gather information about them. You refer to your own files, talk to some other sales agents in your office, and browse the computer database of your MLS. You find several potential comparable properties, walk through the ones that are currently for sale, and drive by the properties that have sold or that have expired listings. After analyzing them as to date of sale, location, physical characteristics, and terms and conditions of sale, you

---

FIG. 4.7   COMPARABLES FOR CEDAR HILLS CMA

- **COMPARABLE A:** 3 BEDROOMS, 2 BATHS, DINING ROOM, 3-CAR GARAGE, LARGE BACK YARD, 3½ YRS OLD. SOLD 5 MONTHS AGO FOR $445,500.

- **COMPARABLE B:** 4 BEDROOMS, 2 BATHS, DINING ROOM, 2-CAR GARAGE, LARGE SIDE YARD, 4 YRS OLD. SOLD 2 MONTHS AGO FOR $447,700.

- **COMPARABLE C:** 3 BEDROOMS, 2 BATHS, LARGE BACK YARD, 3-CAR GARAGE, 3½ YRS OLD. NO DINING ROOM. SOLD 7 MONTHS AGO FOR $441,000.

- **COMPARABLE D:** 3 BEDROOMS, 3 BATHS, 2-CAR GARAGE, LARGE BACK YARD, 5 YRS OLD. NO DINING ROOM. CURRENTLY LISTED FOR $449,500.

- **COMPARABLE E:** 4 BEDROOMS, 2 BATHS, DINING ROOM, 3-CAR GARAGE, LARGE BACK YARD, 4 YRS OLD. LISTING EXPIRED 2 WEEKS AGO; PRICE WAS $473,500.

---

choose the comparables listed in Figure 4.7. Like the sellers' property, all of them are located in the Cedar Hills neighborhood, have two stories, and are in excellent condition.

In preparing a CMA, remember that sales prices are better indications of value than listing prices. Sales prices represent what buyers were actually willing to pay in this marketplace. Listing prices are more likely to represent the ceiling of values in the area, since buyers rarely pay more for a property than the asking price, unless the market is exceptionally competitive.

Next, you compare the comparables you've chosen to your sellers' property. Of course, there are differences between the subject property and the comparables that will require some adjustments, including:

1. a double garage versus a three-car garage;
2. three bedrooms versus four bedrooms;
3. two bathrooms versus three bathrooms; and
4. the presence or absence of a dining room.

Before you can make the appropriate adjustments for these differences, you must determine the adjustment value of each distinguishing feature. By referring to your history file and some other sources, you find four pairs of properties that provide the information you need.

1. Two houses are nearly identical to one another, except that one has a double garage and the other has a three-car garage. One sold for $478,700 and the other for $485,500. From this you conclude that a three-car garage is worth approximately $6,800 more than a double garage.

2. Two other houses are nearly identical except that one has three bedrooms and the other has four. The first sold for $453,000 and the other for $464,500. So you conclude that a fourth bedroom is worth about $11,500.

3. Two more houses are nearly identical except that one has three bathrooms and the other has only two. The first sold for $474,750 and the other sold for $461,550. The third bathroom is apparently worth about $13,200.

4. Finally, two other houses are nearly identical except that one has a dining room and the other does not. The one with the dining room sold for $427,000 and the other for $420,800. Thus, the dining room is worth about $6,200.

Based on these other sales, you have a general idea of how each of the variables in question should be valued. Now you make the adjustments for each of these features, as shown in Figure 4.8.

FIG. 4.8   ADJUSTED VALUES FOR COMPARABLES

	Comparables				
	A	B	C	D	E
Market value	$445,500	$447,700	$441,000	$449,500	$473,500
Three-car garage	– $6,800		– $6,800		– $6,800
Fourth bedroom		– $11,500			– $11,500
Third bathroom			– $13,200	– $13,200	
Dining room			+ $6,200	+ $6,200	
Total adjustments	– $6,800	– $11,500	– $13,800	– $7,000	– $18,300
Total adjusted value	$438,700	$436,200	$427,200	$442,500	$455,200

You now have the adjusted market values for the five comparables and can formulate an opinion of the subject property's market value. First you consider the reliability of each comparable. Comparable C has the most distinguishing features and thus the most adjustments, so it is the least reliable. Comparables A and B each have only one adjustment, but the variable between Comparable A and the subject property (the three-car garage) is less important to the property's overall value. Comparable A is probably the most reliable; but note how close the market values of A and B are anyway. Comparable D has not yet sold, so its listing price can be considered the ceiling of value. The listing on Comparable E expired, so its price was evidently unreasonable in current market conditions. Overall, you decide that a reasonable estimate of market value for the subject property is $438,000.

You present your estimate of value and give the sellers a range of reasonable listing prices—from $436,000 to $439,000. You explain the supporting data to them, discussing each comparable and how it affected your estimated price range. Impressed with your professional competence, the sellers give you their listing. They decide on a listing price of $438,500, a price you all feel comfortable with.

THE CMA FORM

When you prepare a CMA and present it to the seller, it is helpful to use a CMA form such as the one shown in Figure 4.9.

This form is easy to use and to explain. A major advantage is that it shows the seller what buyers can pay, will pay, and will not pay for a home in her neighborhood. The form also helps you plan your presentation in a logical sequence. Of course, as with any form, it is only useful if the information contained in it is accurate and up to date.

The form has spaces for up to 15 homes that are comparable to the seller's property. Of course, the more similar they are to the seller's property, the more likely the seller is to accept your estimate of value.

The first section of the form calls for homes that are for sale now. Their prices represent what a buyer could pay for a similar home today on the open market. From your current listing file, select the homes (up to five) that are the most comparable to the seller's home. For each one, list the address, age, style, number of rooms, number of bedrooms and baths, condition, financing terms, date listed, and other characteristics.

FIG. 4.9 COMPETITIVE MARKET ANALYSIS FORM

Competitive Market Analysis

Subject Property Address: 458 Maple

Address	Price	Age	Lot Size	Style	Exterior	No. of Rooms	Sq. Ft.	No. of Bedrms	Baths	Garage	Condition	Other Impr.	Terms	$ per sq. ft.	List Date	Date Sold
Subject	$322,500	7 yrs	80 x 150	ranch	wood	7	1,350	3	2	1-car, att	excellent	—	cash	$239		
Current Listings																
291 Maple	$320,000	8 yrs	70 x 140	ranch	wood	6	1,250	3	1	1-car, att	excellent	basemnt	cash	$256	July	
175 Main	$318,700	12 yrs	70 x 140	ranch	brick	7	1,350	3	2	1-car, att	good		cash	$236	Aug.	
389 - 5th	$323,000	10 yrs	80 x 150	ranch	brick	7	1,420	3	2	2-car, att	good	basemnt	cash	$227	Aug.	
995 Merrit	$314,500	5 yrs	80 x 150	rance	wood	6	1,415	2	2	1-car, att	good		cash	$222	June	
Recently Sold																
256 Oak	$315,400	10 yrs	80 x 140	ranch	wood	7	1,270	3	2	2-car, att	good		cash	$248	March	May
1156 Larch	$312,000	6 yrs	80 x 150	ranch	brick	6	1,400	3	1	1-car, att	excellent		cash	$223	Feb.	April
1052 - 8th	$305,250	7 yrs	80 x 140	ranch	brick	7	1,300	3	2	1-car, att	good		cash	$235	April	June
Expired Listings																
2782 Cherry	$333,600	6 yrs	80 x 150	ranch	wood	6	1,150	2	2	1-car, att	good		cash	$290	Jan.	
10012 - 7th	$338,800	4 yrs	80 x 140	ranch	brick	7	1,300	3	2	2-car, att	excellent		cash	$261	March	

Location: centrally located, convenient to business center and public transportation

Assets: excellent condition, professionally landscaped yard

Drawbacks: no basement

Market Conditions: market is very competitive, sales price within 2% of market value

Financing Terms: cash

Probable Market Value: $322,500

General Comments:

Company: Smith Realty

Agent: Susan James

Phone: 555-8811

The next section is for homes that have sold in the past 12 months. These show what buyers have actually paid for similar homes. You should choose the five homes in your history file that are the most recent and most comparable to the seller's property, and fill in the pertinent information. Of course, the most important information is how much the comparable sold for and the terms under which it sold.

The next section deals with listings that have expired in the past 12 months. These represent what buyers would not pay for a similar home in this market. List all of the information called for on the form.

Other items to be filled in on the form include the subject property's location, strong points, and drawbacks; market conditions; financing; and general comments.

As an alternative to filling out a form such as the one shown here, you can use a computer program to generate a CMA. These programs simplify the task considerably. Ask whether such a program is available in your office.

All the information you have gathered and analyzed about the seller's property and the comparable properties should be presented to the seller during your listing presentation, along with your explanation of how this information indicates market value. The information presented in the form can correct any misconceptions the seller has regarding the current market conditions in his neighborhood. It should help the seller take a realistic approach to pricing.

THE PROBLEM OF A LOW APPRAISAL

In spite of your best efforts to help sellers choose a listing price based on the market value of their home, you're likely to run into the problem of a low appraisal from time to time.

A low appraisal is an appraiser's estimate of value that is significantly lower than the price a seller and a buyer have agreed on. They've entered into a contract at a sales price that both of them are pleased with. But when the property is formally appraised for the buyer's lender, the appraiser concludes that the property is not worth as much as the buyer has agreed to pay.

A low appraisal puts the sale in serious jeopardy. If the transaction is contingent on financing, the buyer doesn't have to complete the sale if the appraised value turns out to be less than the agreed price. Not surprisingly, buyers are reluctant to pay more for a home than a professional appraiser says it is worth. And even when a buyer would like to go ahead with the purchase in spite of the low appraisal, she may not be able to afford to do so. The purchase loan is based on the sales price or the appraised value, whichever is less, so a low appraisal means a smaller loan—and a bigger downpayment.

EXAMPLE:

1. Buyer is prepared to make a 10% downpayment and obtain a 90% loan.

2. Sales price is $310,000.

3. Appraisal is issued at $300,000.

4. Maximum loan amount is 90% of $300,000.

$300,000 Appraised value
×   90% Loan-to-value ratio
$270,000 Maximum loan amount

Because of the low appraisal ($10,000 less than the sales price), the loan amount is limited to $270,000. The buyer expected to make a $31,000 downpayment ($310,000 sales price × 90% = $279,000 loan). But the buyer would now have to make a $40,000 downpayment ($310,000 − $270,000 loan = $40,000) to pay the $310,000 price.

The easy solution to the problem of a low appraisal is for the seller to lower the sales price to the appraised value. But the seller may not be willing to do this; once a seller has become accustomed to a certain sales price, he'll be very reluctant to give it up.

Sometimes the buyer and seller will agree to a compromise price between the appraised value and the original sales price. More often, this solution runs up against both the seller's reluctance to lower the price and the buyer's reluctance (or inability) to pay any more than the appraised value.

Because of these problems, when there's a significant gap between the sales price and the appraised value, the most likely result is termination of the sale. It's the real estate agent's job to help the parties avoid this outcome whenever possible.

In some cases the agent should ask the lender to reconsider the appraised value, in the hope that it will be increased to a figure more acceptable to the buyer and seller. This is called a request for reconsideration of value.

REQUEST FOR RECONSIDERATION OF VALUE

Although appraisers try to be objective, subjective considerations are a part of every appraisal. In the end, the appraiser's conclusions are only an opinion of value. When you get a low appraisal and you genuinely believe the appraiser is mistaken, you can appeal the appraisal by submitting a request for reconsideration of value to the lender. With the proper documentation, you may be able to get the appraised value increased, possibly to the figure the buyer and seller originally agreed on.

EVALUATING A LOW APPRAISAL. The sooner you find out about a low appraisal, the better. After the appraiser has inspected the seller's property, ask a representative of the lender (for example, the loan officer) to call you with the results of the appraisal as soon as they are received. Don't try to get the results directly from the appraiser; she has a fiduciary relationship with the lender and is not allowed to divulge information about the appraisal to others without the lender's permission.

If the appraisal comes in low, ask the loan officer for the following information:

1. the final value estimate,
2. the value indicated by the sales comparison method, and
3. the addresses of the three comparables the appraiser used.

This is the essential information, because the sales comparison analysis is the heart of a residential appraisal, the part that the lender really relies on in deciding whether to approve a loan.

Evaluate the appraiser's comparables and update your competitive market analysis. Then decide if a request for reconsideration of value is a realistic option. You will have to support your request with at least three comparable sales (not listings) that indicate a higher value estimate is in order. If you're going to persuade the lender to accept your comparables over the appraiser's, yours must be at least as similar to the subject property as the appraiser's are.

If you believe the lender is likely to grant a request for reconsideration, your next step is to prepare the request and a cover letter.

PREPARING A RECONSIDERATION REQUEST. Some lenders have their own form for requests for reconsideration of value. If so, you should use their form (in fact, you may even be required to). Otherwise, you can prepare your own. It makes sense to present your information in the same format as the Sales Comparison Analysis section of the Uniform Residential Appraisal Report form. Make four columns for the properties, with the subject property in the first column and the three comparables to the right.

Write a cover letter making your request and attach your competitive market analysis to it. The cover letter should be simple and very polite; do not criticize the appraiser.

Sometimes appraisers don't use the best information available, and when they don't, their findings can be successfully challenged. If your request for reconsideration of value contains well-researched, properly documented information and is presented in a professional manner, your chances of success are good.

CHAPTER SUMMARY

1. It is the seller's responsibility to establish a listing price. However, your sellers will rely on you for advice about the listing price. Your advice should usually take the form of a competitive market analysis, which presents information about similar properties that are currently for sale or that have sold recently in the seller's neighborhood.

2. While there are many different types of value, you will be most concerned with market value, which should be the basis for the seller's listing price. Market value is defined as the most probable price that a property should bring in an arm's length transaction. (Remember to distinguish value from price and cost. Price is what a buyer actually paid for a property, and cost is what was paid to purchase a property and build the improvements on it.)

3. When you estimate the value of a seller's property, your first step is to collect and study information about the property. Your information will come from a neighborhood analysis, a site analysis, and a building analysis. As you study the house itself, you should pay particular attention to its design and layout. Once you have a clear picture of all the features, amenities, and drawbacks of the seller's property, you can choose your comparables.

4. Comparables are properties in the seller's neighborhood (or a similar neighborhood) that are similar to the seller's property and that are currently for sale or have sold recently. Once you've picked your comparables, you'll note the differences between the comparables and the seller's property and adjust the value of the comparables accordingly. Features that a comparable property lacks are taken into account by adding the value of the missing feature to the comparable's price. Features that a comparable property has that the seller's property lacks are taken into account by deducting the value of the feature from the comparable's price. You'll then use the adjusted prices of the comparables as the basis for a reasonable price range for the seller's property.

5. You may present your CMA to the seller by filling out a CMA form or using a CMA computer program. Giving the seller a worksheet that provides all the key information will enable the seller to understand your presentation more easily.

6. A low appraisal is one that concludes the property is worth less than the buyer has agreed to pay for it. If the sale is contingent on financing, the buyer won't be required to complete it. In some cases, you can appeal a low appraisal by submitting a request for reconsideration of value to the lender.

CHAPTER QUIZ

1. The value of an item comes primarily from the:

    a. average of its cost and its market price

    b. intrinsic qualities of the item

    c. perceptions and attitudes people have about the item

    d. rarity of the item

2. A competitive market analysis (CMA) is an effective way to estimate value because:

    a. an informed buyer acting free of pressure will not pay more for a property than she could pay for another property that is equally desirable

    b. a buyer will never pay more than market value for a property

    c. it takes more neighborhoods into account in evaluating the property

    d. the income method of appraisal is the most reliable way to value residential property

3. Which of the following is true about neighborhood characteristics?

    a. The boundaries are defined by the county planning board

    b. Neighborhood characteristics set the upper limit of value for the properties located there

    c. Neighborhood characteristics do not affect the value of vacant lots located there

    d. A neighborhood's effect on property values is determined by the most expensive properties located there

4. What kind of topography is considered most desirable for a residential neighborhood?

    a. Level

    b. Sloping

    c. Gently subsiding

    d. Mildly rolling

5. A bathroom with a wash basin, toilet, and bathtub, but no shower, is a:

   a. half bath

   b. three-quarter bath

   c. full bath

   d. design deficiency

6. Which of the following is a common design deficiency?

   a. More bathrooms than bedrooms

   b. Front door opens directly into living room

   c. Bedrooms are not visible from living room

   d. Kitchen too close to garage

7. Which of the following is an example of an arm's length transaction?

   a. The seller of the property is the buyer's uncle, but both the buyer and the seller are being advised by attorneys

   b. The seller of the property is the buyer's aunt, but the buyer and the seller are represented by different brokers

   c. The seller is relocating to take a new job, so she lets her employer take care of selling the house for her

   d. The seller finds a buyer after the property has been on the market for two months and the buyer has been looking in this area for some time

8. In a CMA, which of the following elements may make it necessary to adjust the prices of the comparables?

   a. Date of sale

   b. Value in use

   c. Cost

   d. Conditions of sale

9. To prepare a CMA for your seller's property, you choose three properties as comparables. You make all the necessary adjustments to reflect how the comparables differ from the subject property. Comparable A has an adjusted value of $311,000. Comparable B has an adjusted value of $327,500. Comparable C has an adjusted value of $314,000. How do you arrive at an estimate of the value of the subject property?

   a. Take the average of the adjusted values of the comparables

   b. Let the seller choose between the three values to set a listing price

   c. Evaluate the reliability of each comparable and use that as a basis for deciding on a suggested price

   d. Choose the value of the comparable property with the fewest adjustments

10. To have the best chance of succeeding with a request for reconsideration of value, you should use:

   a. exactly the same comparables as the appraiser

   b. the income approach to value method of appraisal

   c. only currently listed properties as comparables

   d. comparable sales that are at least as similar to the subject property as the appraiser's comparables

ANSWER KEY

1. **c.** Value is created by people. Our perceptions and attitudes do more to determine the value of an item than the characteristics of the item itself.

2. **a.** Competitive market analysis is a modified form of the sales comparison method of appraisal. It is based on the assumption that a buyer will not want to pay more for a property than she could pay for a similar comparable property.

3. **b.** Neighborhood characteristics set both the upper and lower limits of a property's value.

4. **d.** Mildly rolling terrain is usually considered preferable, both as a neighborhood characteristic and for the property site itself.

5. **c.** A bathroom with a wash basin, toilet, and bathtub is considered a full bath, regardless of whether or not it has a shower.

6. **b.** It's considered a design deficiency when the front door of a house opens directly into the living room, without any sort of front hall or entryway.

7. **d.** An arm's length transaction is one in which both parties are fully informed of the property's merits and shortcomings, neither is acting under unusual pressure, and the property has been exposed on the open market for a reasonable length of time.

8. **a.** If a comparable did not sell recently, it may be necessary to make an adjustment to take into account changes in the market since the date of sale. Sales more than one year old should not be used as comparables.

9. **c.** You have to evaluate the reliability of each comparable to estimate the market value of the subject property. The comparables that are most like the subject property offer the most reliable indication of market value.

10. **d.** To persuade the lender to accept your estimate of value over the appraiser's, you need to select comparable sales that are at least as similar to the subject property as the appraiser's comparables.

5

PREPARING AND NEGOTIATING OFFERS

MAKING AN OFFER TO PURCHASE
- Preparing an offer
- How offers are presented
- Multiple offers
- Backup offers
- Revoking an offer

COUNTEROFFERS AND NEGOTIATIONS
- Making a counteroffer
- Multiple counteroffers
- The negotiation process

ACCEPTING AN OFFER
- Communicating acceptance
- Manner of acceptance

CONTRACT AMENDMENTS

CONTRACT CANCELLATION

GOOD FAITH DEPOSITS
- Size of the deposit
- Form of the deposit
- Handling the deposit

FAIR HOUSING CONSIDERATIONS

INTRODUCTION

After a buyer finds a house he wants and decides to make an offer on it, what happens next? How and when are offers presented to a seller? What is your role as negotiator? What if you're representing the seller instead of the buyer?

In this chapter, we will discuss preparing and presenting an offer to purchase, negotiating terms, and the point at which an offer becomes a binding contract. We will also explain the procedures for handling the good faith deposit that customarily accompanies an offer.

MAKING AN OFFER TO PURCHASE

You're helping your buyers—a married couple—look for a house that meets their needs: at least 1,800 square feet, three bedrooms, two baths, a large kitchen, and a double garage, in the $380,000 price range. After you've shown them several houses that fulfill these requirements, the buyers find one they are really interested in. You can tell, because they linger there a little longer, ask specific questions ("How old is the roof?" "How far is it to the elementary school?"), and mentally "move in" to the house, visualizing where their own furniture would go. They may make plans to come back and see the house again, perhaps bringing a third party—such as a parent or a more experienced friend—to examine the property with them.

After the buyers have had a chance to look at the property on their own and discuss it between themselves, you review the property's features and benefits and how well it meets their housing needs. If any initial objections they raise can be overcome, they are now ready to make an offer to purchase the house. They ask you to write up their offer for them and present it to the seller.

PREPARING AN OFFER

Under the statute of frauds, an offer to purchase real property must be in writing and signed by the offeror (the buyer). The statute of frauds is the law that requires certain types of contracts to be in writing.

An offer to purchase residential property is usually written up on a standard purchase agreement form (see Chapter 6). It must set forth all of the essential terms of the buyer's offer, including the purchase price, the deposit the buyer is willing to provide as an indication of good faith, how he will pay the purchase price, and the proposed closing date. It's important to include all of the terms on which the buyer is willing to purchase the property, because once the document is signed by both the buyer and the seller, it becomes a binding contract—their purchase agreement. Since the purchase agreement also serves as a receipt for the buyer's deposit, in California it is commonly referred to as the **deposit receipt**.

WHO CAN PREPARE AN OFFER. Whose job is it to prepare the offer to purchase? A buyer could write her own offer; it is always legal (although generally not advisable) for the parties to a transaction to draw up their own contract. Or an attorney at law could draft the buyer's offer for her. What about you, the real estate agent? Can you prepare the buyer's offer?

When someone draws up a contract on behalf of others, he or she is considered to be practicing law. As a general rule, only a licensed attorney is permitted to practice law. However, there is an exception to this rule: Real estate agents may prepare routine deposit receipts using standard forms that were originally written and approved by attorneys with expertise in real estate law. But even this exception is limited. As a real estate agent, you may only fill out a deposit receipt form in connection with a transaction that you are handling. And you cannot charge a separate fee (in addition to your share of the brokerage commission) for completing the forms.

Note that when you fill out a contract form, you will be held to the same standard of care that is required of a lawyer. If, through negligence, you make a mistake, you (or your broker) may be liable for any harm suffered by the buyer or the seller because of that mistake.

Also, remember that you are only allowed to fill in the blanks on a standard form. Writing special clauses to insert into the preprinted form or advising the parties on the legal effect of certain provisions may constitute the unauthorized practice of law, which is a criminal offense.

REVIEWING THE OFFER. After filling out the deposit receipt form, check it over to see if it's complete and accurate. Then go over the form with the buyer, to make sure he understands and is satisfied with all of the terms. If the buyer has questions about the legal consequences of particular provisions, refer him to a real estate lawyer.

When you review the financial aspects of the offer, it is helpful to use a "Buyer's Estimated Net Cost" worksheet to calculate the buyer's closing costs and explain approximately how much cash will be needed to close the transaction if the seller accepts the offer. (See Figure 10.4 in Chapter 10.)

After going through the offer with the buyer, have him sign it, and then immediately give him a copy of the signed form. At this point, the buyer will usually give you a good faith deposit (discussed later in this chapter), which you will turn over to your broker. Of course, the deposit receipt form serves as the buyer's receipt.

LEGAL REQUIREMENTS. In addition to being in writing and signed, a buyer's offer must meet certain other basic legal requirements to serve as the basis for a binding contract. To be valid, the offer must be definite and certain in its terms, not vague or incomplete. If you fill out the deposit receipt form properly, including the price, the closing date, and all of the other important terms, the buyer's offer will meet this requirement.

A valid offer must also clearly express a willingness to enter into a contract. Again, a standard deposit receipt will fulfill this requirement.

WHEN TO SEEK ADVICE. In filling out a deposit receipt form, there are three key areas where problems most often occur:

- **PROPERTY DESCRIPTION.** The property must be correctly described for the offer (and the subsequent purchase contract) to be enforceable. A full legal description is not required, but one should be used whenever possible.

- **METHOD OF PAYMENT.** The offer must state how the buyer intends to pay the purchase price. Will the buyer obtain institutional financing, pay cash, or take advantage of seller financing?

- **CONTINGENCIES OR SPECIAL ARRANGEMENTS.** If the offer is contingent (on loan approval, on inspection results, or on the sale of the buyer's current residence, for example), the contingency provision must clearly state the circumstances under which the contingency will be considered fulfilled. And any special arrangements that the buyer wants to make, such as taking possession before the closing date, need to be spelled out in the offer.

These are areas you should pay extra attention to, but of course all of the terms of the offer are important. When you feel there may be a problem with one of the terms of the buyer's offer, or if you think you may have made a mistake, ask your broker for advice right away. Remember, you are preparing the offer as your broker's agent, so your broker wants it to be problem-free.

Occasionally your broker will instruct you to get in touch with a real estate attorney. (Larger brokerages often have a legal staff of their own.) You should also consult an attorney in any of these situations:

- You have a question and your broker is not available.
- Because of special terms in the offer, you can't use a preprinted deposit receipt or addendum. (Remember, you may not draft an agreement or even a complicated clause.)
- You need legal documents, such as an easement or a road maintenance agreement, to be prepared.

HOW OFFERS ARE PRESENTED

It's usually the listing agent who presents an offer to the seller. But the selling agent can also play an important role. We'll look at the presentation of a buyer's offer to a seller first from the selling agent's point of view and then from the listing agent's.

SELLING AGENT'S ROLE. If you are the selling agent and the listing agent is going to present the offer to the seller, you should thoroughly explain it to the listing agent first. You may also want to go along when the listing agent meets with the seller, so that you can answer questions about the buyer or the offer.

> **EXAMPLE:** The terms of your buyers' offer include paying cash for the seller's home—without any financing—and closing the transaction within 15 days. Because a cash sale is so unusual, you want to be there when the listing agent presents the offer to the seller. The seller might be suspicious of the buyers and want to know who they are, where they got their money, and why they want to close the transaction so quickly. You can relieve the seller's concerns by explaining the situation: the buyers recently received a large inheritance, and they want to move

into a new house quickly because they are expecting their first baby soon. Making this explanation in person may be more effective than simply asking the listing agent to relay the information.

If the buyer is especially likable, or in a situation that could evoke sympathy, it may be a good idea to bring the buyer along to meet the seller. Though financial considerations will be the primary basis for the seller's decision, he may view the offer more favorably if he thinks about the buyer as a real person rather than in the abstract.

Note that if you go along when the offer is presented to the seller, you must disclose your agency status to the seller.

Naturally, you should give the seller the opportunity to discuss the offer privately with the listing agent. Whatever the seller decides to do about the offer, it is your job to convey that decision to the buyer.

Listing Agent's Role. If you are the listing agent and receive a written offer to purchase, you should arrange to meet with the seller to discuss the offer right away. Any and all offers you receive must be presented to the seller as soon as possible.

When you meet with the seller, you should go over all of the terms and conditions of the offer and make sure the seller understands them. When there is more than one seller, it's a good idea to give each of them a copy of the offer. For instance, if the sellers are a married couple, make a photocopy of the offer so that each spouse can have a copy to look at as you discuss it. Then go through the offer line by line, answering the sellers' questions. It's especially important to discuss the following provisions:

- the proposed closing date and date of possession;
- the list of included items (any personal property that would be transferred to the buyers along with the real property);
- any contingencies (such as whether the buyers need to sell their own house first); and
- any obligations the sellers would have to fulfill before closing, such as completing repairs or cleanup.

If the sellers have legal questions, recommend that they consult an attorney. Do not try to answer legal questions yourself.

The sellers may ask questions about the buyers—who they are, whether they can afford the home, and how motivated they are to buy. When you describe the buyers, take care to avoid doing so in terms that might lead to a violation of the fair housing laws. Certain characteristics—race, national origin, religion, and so on—should not be mentioned.

When you review the financial aspects of the sale, it's helpful to use a "Seller's Estimated Net Proceeds" worksheet, which will make it easier to calculate the selling costs and the amount of cash the sellers can expect to receive at closing. (See Figure 10.5 in Chapter 10.)

MULTIPLE OFFERS

Sometimes a seller has more than one offer to consider at the same time. Two or more offers may come in simultaneously, or an additional offer may come in while the seller is considering an earlier one. You must present every offer you receive to your seller, even if the seller has already decided to accept another offer.

> **EXAMPLE:** You presented an offer to the sellers two days ago. They've been considering it very seriously, and this morning they told you that they're almost sure they will accept it. They just want a little more time to think it over.
>
> A few minutes ago, a selling agent faxed you another offer on the sellers' house. This offer is not nearly as attractive as the first one. Even so, you are required to present the new offer to the sellers right away. You can't wait around to see whether they accept or reject the first offer.

When faced with multiple offers, a seller has a number of options. The seller may decide to:

- reject all of the offers;
- accept one of the offers and reject the others;
- make a counteroffer on one offer and reject the others;
- make multiple counteroffers; or
- accept one offer and make a contingent counteroffer on another.

The last of these alternatives, the contingent counteroffer, brings us to the subject of backup offers.

Backup Offers

Some buyers are so interested in a particular house that they are willing to make a backup offer—an offer that's contingent on the failure of a previous sales contract.

> **Example:** You showed Clark's house to Lenihan a week ago, and this morning Lenihan called to say he wants to make an offer on it. You contact the listing agent and learn that the seller has already signed a purchase agreement. Your client, Lenihan, is extremely disappointed. You explain that he can make a backup offer that is contingent on the failure of the first contract. He agrees to this, and you submit Lenihan's backup offer to the listing agent.

A listing agent is not only required to present additional offers received while the seller is already considering an offer, he must also present offers that come in after the seller has signed a contract, up until that sale actually closes. However, when an offer is submitted after the seller has signed a contract, it should be made contingent on the first sale's failure to close. You may use a purchase agreement addendum such as the one shown in Figure 5.1 to add a backup contingency clause to the second buyer's offer.

Contingent Counteroffer. Suppose you're representing a seller who has already signed a deposit receipt, and another buyer makes an offer. The seller is interested in accepting this as a backup offer, but it isn't contingent on the failure of the first contract. You should advise the seller to make a contingent counteroffer. The counteroffer will repeat the buyer's offer but add a contingency clause regarding the first contract.

> **Example:** Your sellers have accepted an offer from the Browns. The Browns' offer is for the full listing price, but it's by no means certain that the Browns will qualify for the financing they need to complete the purchase. So when you present an offer from Finney, the sellers are very interested. Finney's offer is for $4,000 less than the Browns' offer, but Finney will undoubtedly qualify for the necessary loan.
>
> The sellers want to accept Finney's offer as a backup offer. However, Finney's offer does not include a clause that makes it contingent on the failure of the first agreement. So you advise the sellers to make a counteroffer. They offer Finney the same terms set forth in his

FIG. 5.1 PURCHASE AGREEMENT ADDENDUM

CALIFORNIA ASSOCIATION OF REALTORS®

PURCHASE AGREEMENT ADDENDUM
May Also Be Used With Counter Offer
(C.A.R. Form PAA, Revised 10/02)

This is an addendum to the ☐ California Residential Purchase Agreement, ☐ Counter Offer No._____, ☐ Other _____
_____, ("Agreement"), dated _____,
on property known as _____ ("Property"),
between _____ ("Buyer"),
and _____ ("Seller").
(The definitions in the California Residential Purchase Agreement are applicable to this Purchase Agreement Addendum.)

1. ☐ **CANCELLATION OF PRIOR SALE; BACK-UP OFFER** (If checked): This Agreement is in back-up position number _____, and is contingent upon written cancellation of any prior contracts and related escrows ("Prior Contracts") between Seller and other buyers. Seller and other buyers may mutually agree to modify or amend the terms of Prior Contracts. Buyer may cancel this Agreement in writing at any time before Seller provides Buyer Copies of written cancellations of Prior Contracts Signed by all parties to those contracts. If Seller is unable to provide such written Signed cancellations to Buyer by _____ (date), then either Buyer or Seller may cancel the Agreement in writing.
   A. **BUYER'S DEPOSIT CHECK** shall be: **(i)** held uncashed until Copies of the written cancellations Signed by all parties to the Prior Contracts are provided to Buyer; OR **(ii)** (if checked) ☐ immediately handled as provided in the Agreement.
   B. **TIME PERIODS** in the Agreement for Investigations, contingencies, covenants and other obligations **(i)** shall begin on the Day After Seller provides Buyer Copies of Signed cancellations of Prior Contracts; OR **(ii)** (if checked) ☐ all time periods shall begin as provided in this Agreement. However, if the date for Close Of Escrow is a specific calendar date, that date shall NOT be extended, unless agreed to in writing by Buyer and Seller.

2. ☐ **SELLER TO REMAIN IN POSSESSION AFTER CLOSE OF ESCROW** (If checked): This provision is intended for short-term occupancy (i.e. less than 30 Days). If occupancy is intended to be for 30 Days or longer, use Residential Lease After Sale (C.A.R. Form RLAS). **Note: Local rent control or other Law regarding tenant's rights may impact Buyer's and Seller's rights and obligations.**
   A. **TERM:** Seller to remain in possession of Property for _____ Days After Close Of Escrow (or ☐ _____).
   B. **COMPENSATION:** Seller agrees to pay Buyer $_____ per Day (or ☐ _____), which **(i)** Seller shall deposit with escrow holder prior to Close Of Escrow; or **(ii)** shall be withheld from Seller's proceeds. Seller agrees to pay $_____ per Day for any holding over.
   C. **LATE CHARGE/NSF CHECKS:** If any payment from Seller to Buyer is required outside of escrow, and any such payment is not received by Buyer within 5 (or _____) Days After date due, Seller shall pay to Buyer an additional sum of $_____ as a Late Charge. If a check is returned for non-sufficient fund ("NSF"), Seller shall pay to Buyer $25.00 as an NSF charge. Seller and Buyer agree that these charges represent a fair and reasonable estimate of the costs Buyer may incur by reason of Seller's late or NSF payment. Buyer's acceptance of any Late Charge or NSF fee shall not constitute a waiver as to any default by Seller.
   D. **UTILITIES:** Seller agrees to pay for all utilities and services, and the following charges: _____
   _____ except _____ which shall be paid for by Buyer.
   E. **ENTRY:** Seller shall make Property available to Buyer for the purpose of entering to make necessary or agreed repairs, or to supply necessary or agreed services, or to show Property to prospective or actual purchasers, tenants, mortgagees, lenders, appraisers or contractors. Buyer and Seller agree that 24 hours notice (oral or written) shall be reasonable and sufficient notice. In an emergency, Buyer may enter Property at any time without prior notice.
   F. **MAINTENANCE:** Seller shall maintain the Property, including pool, spa, landscaping and grounds, and all personal property included in the sale in substantially the same condition as on the date of Acceptance of the Agreement. Except as provided in the Agreement, Seller shall not make alterations to the Property without Buyer's written consent.
   G. **ASSIGNMENT; SUBLETTING:** Seller shall not assign or sublet all or any part of the Property, or assign or transfer the right to occupy the Property. Any assignment, subletting or transfer of the Property by voluntary act of Seller, by operation of Law or otherwise, without Buyer's prior written consent shall give Buyer the right to terminate Seller's right to possession.
   H. **SELLER'S OBLIGATIONS UPON DELIVERY OF POSSESSION:** Upon delivery of possession to Buyer, Seller shall deliver the Property in the condition and on the terms provided in the Agreement.
   I. **INSURANCE:** Seller's personal property (including vehicles) is not insured by Buyer, and, if applicable, owner's association, against loss or damage due to fire, theft, vandalism, rain, water, criminal or negligent acts of others, or any other cause. Seller is to carry Seller's own insurance to protect Seller from such loss.
   J. **WAIVER:** The waiver of any breach shall not be construed as a continuing waiver of the same or any subsequent breach.
   K. **OTHER TERMS AND CONDITIONS/SUPPLEMENTS:** _____
   _____
   _____

PAA REVISED 10/02 (PAGE 1 OF 2) Print Date

Buyer's Initials (_____)(_____)
Seller's Initials (_____)(_____)

Reviewed by _____ Date _____

EQUAL HOUSING OPPORTUNITY

PURCHASE AGREEMENT ADDENDUM (PAA PAGE 1 OF 2)

Reprinted with permission, California Association of Realtors®. No endorsement implied.

Property Address: _____ Date: _____

3. ☐ **TENANT TO REMAIN IN POSSESSION** (If checked): Buyer shall take Property subject to the rights of existing tenants. Seller shall, within **7 (or** ☐ _____**) Days** After Acceptance, deliver to Buyer Copies of all: estoppel certificates sent to and received back from tenants; leases; rental agreements; and current income and expense statements ("Rental Documents"). Seller shall give Buyer written notice of any changes to existing leases or tenancies or new agreements to lease or rent ("Proposed Changes") at least **7 (or** ☐ _____**) Days** prior to any Proposed Changes. Buyer's approval of the Rental Documents and Proposed Changes is a contingency of the Agreement. Buyer shall, within **5 (or** ☐ _____**) Days** After receipt of Rental Documents or Proposed Changes remove the applicable contingency or cancel the Agreement. Seller shall transfer to Buyer, through escrow, all unused tenant deposits. No warranty is made concerning compliance with governmental restrictions, if any, limiting the amount of rent that can lawfully be charged, and/or the maximum number of persons who can lawfully occupy the Property, unless otherwise agreed in writing.

4. ☐ **SECONDARY OR ASSUMED LOAN** (If checked): Obtaining the secondary loan or assumption below and approval of such financing is a contingency of this Agreement. Buyer shall act diligently and in good faith to obtain the designated financing.

   A. ☐ **SECONDARY LOAN:**
      (1) New second deed of trust in favor of LENDER encumbering the Property, securing a note payable at maximum interest of _____% fixed rate or _____% initial adjustable rate, with a maximum interest rate of _____%, balance due in _____ years. Buyer shall pay loan fees/points not to exceed _____. (These terms apply whether the designated loan is conventional, FHA or VA.)
      (2) Within **17 (or** ☐ _____ **Days)** After Acceptance, Buyer shall, as specified in the Agreement, remove this contingency or cancel this Agreement; OR (if checked) ☐ secondary loan contingency shall remain in effect until the loan is funded.

   B. ☐ **ASSUMPTION OF EXISTING LOAN:**
      (1) Assumption of existing deed of trust encumbering the Property, securing a note payable at maximum interest of _____% fixed rate or _____% initial adjustable rate, with a maximum interest rate of _____%, balance due in _____ years. Buyer shall pay loan fees/points not to exceed _____. Seller shall, within **5 (or** ☐ _____**) Days** After Acceptance, request from Lender, and upon receipt provide to Buyer, Copies of all applicable notes and deeds of trust, loan balances and current interest rates. Differences between estimated and actual loan balances shall be adjusted at Close Of Escrow by cash down payment. Impound accounts, if any, shall be assigned and charged to Buyer and credited to Seller. If this is an assumption of a VA Loan, the sale is contingent upon Seller being provided a release of liability and substitution of eligibility, unless otherwise agreed in writing.
      (2) Within **17 (or** ☐ _____ **Days)** After Acceptance, Buyer shall, as specified in the Agreement, remove this contingency or cancel this Agreement. However, if the assumed loan documents are not provided to Buyer within 7 Days After Acceptance, Buyer has **5 (or** ☐ _____**) Days** after receipt of these documents, or the time fixed specified in 4B(2), whichever occurs last, to remove this contingency or cancel the Agreement; OR (if checked) ☐ assumed loan contingency shall remain in effect until the assumption is approved.

5. ☐ **SHORT PAY** (If checked): This Agreement is contingent upon Seller's receipt of written consent from all existing secured lenders and lienholders ("Short-Pay Lenders"), no later than 5:00 P.M. on _____ (date) ("Short-Pay Contingency Date"), to reduce their respective loan balances by an amount sufficient to permit the proceeds from the sale of the Property, without additional funds from Seller, to pay the existing balances on loans, real property taxes, brokerage commissions, closing costs, and other monetary obligations the Agreement requires Seller to pay at Close Of Escrow (including, but not limited to, escrow charges, title charges, documentary transfer taxes, prorations, retrofit costs and Repairs). If Seller fails to give Buyer written notice of all existing Short-Pay Lenders' consent by the Short-Pay Contingency Date, either Seller or Buyer may cancel the Agreement in writing. Seller shall reasonably cooperate with existing Short-Pay lenders in the short-pay off process. Buyer and Seller understand that Lenders are not obligated to accept a short-pay off and may accept other offers, and that Seller, Buyer and Brokers do not have control over whether Short-Pay Lenders will consent to a short-pay off, or any act, omission, or decision by any Short-Pay Lender in the short-pay off process. Seller is informed that a short-pay may create credit or legal problems, or may result in taxable income to Seller. Seller may present to Short-Pay Lender any additional offers that are received on the Property. **Seller is advised to seek advice from an attorney, certified public accountant or other expert regarding such potential consequences of a short-pay off.**

6. ☐ **COURT CONFIRMATION** (If checked): This Agreement is contingent upon court confirmation on or before _____ (date). If court confirmation is not obtained by that date, Buyer may cancel this Agreement in writing. Court confirmation may be required in probate, conservatorship, guardianship, receivership, bankruptcy, or other proceedings. The court may allow open, competitive bidding, resulting in Property being sold to the highest bidder. Broker recommends that Buyer appear at court confirmation hearing. Buyer understands that **(i)** Broker and others may continue to market the Property and **(ii)** Broker may represent other competitive bidders prior to and at the court confirmation.

Date _____   Date _____

Buyer _____   Seller _____

Buyer _____   Seller _____

SURE TRAC The System for Success™   Published by the California Association of REALTORS®

PAA REVISED 10/02 (PAGE 2 OF 2)   Reviewed by _____ Date _____

PURCHASE AGREEMENT ADDENDUM (PAA PAGE 2 OF 2)

original offer, but they include a purchase agreement addendum making the sale to Finney contingent on the failure of the sale to the Browns. Finney accepts the sellers' counteroffer. Now if the Browns fail to qualify for financing, the sellers will have a binding contract with Finney.

BACKUP OFFERS AND BREACH OF CONTRACT. If a seller were to accept a second offer without a backup contingency clause, she would end up obligated to sell the house under two different contracts. Because one contract couldn't be fulfilled without breaching the other, the seller would be liable for breach of contract to the potential buyer who didn't get the property.

EXAMPLE: Returning to the previous example, suppose your sellers accepted Finney's offer without adding the contingency provision. They would then be obligated to sell the property both to Finney and to the Browns. Obviously, the sellers can only transfer the property to one of the buyers. So if the sale to the Browns closed, Finney could sue the sellers for breach of his contract.

Never try to convince a seller to break an existing agreement in order to accept another offer, even if the second offer is much better. If you were to do that, you could be found guilty of a tort (a civil wrong) called "tortious interference with a contractual relationship." You could be held liable for damages caused by the breach of contract.

EXAMPLE: Now suppose that Finney's offer is substantially better than the Browns' offer. Finney is offering $5,000 more than the listing price, will pay all of the closing costs, and is sure to qualify for the necessary financing. The sellers would be better off with this offer, and so would you (your commission would be larger because of the higher purchase price). But you should not suggest that the sellers breach their contract with the Browns in order to accept Finney's offer. If you did, the Browns could sue you for damages, and you could also lose your real estate license.

If your clients express an interest in breaching a contract in favor of another offer, you should strongly recommend that they talk to a real estate attorney before taking any action.

NOTICE TO BACKUP BUYER. When a seller has accepted a backup offer and the first sale fails to close, the seller needs to notify the backup buyer that their contingent agreement is now a binding contract. Depending on how the backup offer was worded, the seller may also need to provide the backup buyer with a copy of the written cancellation of the first purchase agreement.

REVOKING AN OFFER

A buyer can revoke an offer to purchase at any time until she is notified that the seller is accepting the offer. At that point, the offer becomes a binding contract, and the buyer can't back out without breaching it.

Even if an offer gives the seller a specific length of time to consider it, the buyer can revoke the offer sooner than that, as long as she acts before the seller sends his acceptance.

EXAMPLE: Grant offers to buy Rush's house for $515,000. The offer states that it will terminate in 48 hours. If the 48 hours pass without an acceptance, Grant's offer will terminate automatically. But if Grant changes her mind about buying the house before that (for example, 30 hours after making the offer) and Rush has not yet accepted it, Grant is free to revoke the offer. Rush cannot force her to keep the offer open for the full 48 hours.

If a time limit is not stated in the offer, it will terminate after a reasonable amount of time.

EXAMPLE: Now suppose that Grant's offer to Rush doesn't have a termination date. Rush doesn't respond to the offer for weeks. Finally, six weeks after receiving the offer, Rush notifies Grant that he's accepting it. It's too late, however. It's not reasonable to expect that an offer to purchase a house will be kept open for six weeks. If Grant has changed her mind about buying, she's no longer bound by her offer.

COUNTEROFFERS AND NEGOTIATIONS

Unless a buyer has made an offer that matches all of the seller's terms, there is likely to be some negotiation. In fact, negotiation is the norm rather than the exception. Sellers don't generally expect full-price offers, and buyers aren't surprised when the seller rejects their first offer and counters with another offer. The most common objections to initial offers concern these matters:

- the price offered,
- the size of the good faith deposit,
- the proposed closing date and date of possession,
- which furnishings or fixtures are included in the sale, and
- financing terms.

MAKING A COUNTEROFFER

If the seller decides to counter the buyer's offer with another offer, you may be able to make the seller's changes on the original deposit receipt form.

> **EXAMPLE:** Gordon has offered Lamont $275,000 for her house, with a closing date of June 16. He is making a good faith deposit of $2,500. Lamont is pleased with nearly all of the terms of Gordon's offer, but she wants a larger deposit—$5,000. Lamont's agent simply crosses out the $2,500 deposit figure on the form submitted by Gordon and writes in $5,000. Lamont initials the change, and her agent presents the counteroffer (the revised deposit receipt form) to Gordon.

For simple changes such as the one in the example, this might work just fine. But it's usually better to use a separate counteroffer form, such as the one shown in Figure 5.2, especially when the changes are numerous or complicated. Otherwise the deposit receipt may become confusing and, as a result, unenforceable.

On the counteroffer form in Figure 5.2, you identify the original offer by filling in the date it was signed by the buyer, the property description, and the names of the buyer and seller.

The counteroffer states that all of the terms of the original offer are accepted by the seller, except for the changes noted. There is space on the form for the seller's proposed changes, or an addendum may be attached, if necessary. There's a provision for setting a deadline, to indicate how long the buyer has to consider the counteroffer before it will terminate. The counteroffer is then signed by the seller and presented to the buyer for approval or rejection.

FIG. 5.2. COUNTEROFFER FORM

CALIFORNIA ASSOCIATION OF REALTORS®

COUNTER OFFER No. _____
For use by Seller or Buyer. May be used for Multiple Counter Offer.
(C.A.R. Form CO, Revised 10/02)

Date _____, at _____, California.
This is a counter offer to the: ☐ California Residential Purchase Agreement, ☐ Counter Offer, or ☐ Other _____ ("Offer"),
dated _____, on property known as _____ ("Property"),
between _____ ("Buyer") and _____ ("Seller").

1. **TERMS:** The terms and conditions of the above referenced document are **accepted subject to the following:**
   A. **Paragraphs in the Offer that require initials by all parties, but are not initialed by all parties, are excluded from the final agreement unless specifically referenced for inclusion in paragraph 1C of this or another Counter Offer.**
   B. **Unless otherwise agreed in writing, down payment and loan amount(s) will be adjusted in the same proportion as in the original Offer.**
   C. _____
   _____
   _____
   _____
   _____
   _____
   _____
   _____
   D. **The following attached supplements are incorporated in this Counter Offer:** ☐ Addendum No. _____
      ☐

2. **RIGHT TO ACCEPT OTHER OFFERS:** Seller has the right to continue to offer the Property for sale or for other transaction, and to accept any other offer at any time prior to notification of acceptance, as described in paragraph 3. If this is a Seller Counter Offer, Seller's acceptance of another offer prior to Buyer's acceptance and communication of notification of this Counter Offer, shall revoke this Counter Offer.

3. **EXPIRATION:** This Counter Offer shall be deemed revoked and the deposits, if any, shall be returned unless this Counter Offer is Signed by the Buyer or Seller to whom it is sent and a Copy of the Signed Counter Offer is personally received by the person making this Counter Offer or _____,
   who is authorized to receive it, by 5:00 PM on the third Day After this Counter Offer is made or, (if checked)
   by ☐ _____ (date), at _____ AM/PM. This Counter Offer may be executed in counterparts.

4. ☐ **(If checked:) MULTIPLE COUNTER OFFER:** Seller is making a Counter Offer(s) to another prospective buyer(s) on terms that may or may not be the same as in this Counter Offer. Acceptance of this Counter Offer by Buyer shall **not** be binding unless and until it is subsequently re-Signed by Seller in paragraph 7 below and a Copy of the Counter Offer Signed in paragraph 7 is personally received by Buyer or by _____, who is authorized to receive it. Prior to the completion of all of these events, Buyer and Seller shall have no duties or obligations for the purchase or sale of the Property.

5. **OFFER: BUYER OR SELLER MAKES THIS COUNTER OFFER ON THE TERMS ABOVE AND ACKNOWLEDGES RECEIPT OF A COPY.**
   _____ Date _____
   _____ Date _____

6. **ACCEPTANCE: I/WE** accept the above Counter Offer **(If checked ☐ SUBJECT TO THE ATTACHED COUNTER OFFER)** and acknowledge receipt of a Copy.
   _____ Date _____ Time _____ AM/PM
   _____ Date _____ Time _____ AM/PM

7. **MULTIPLE COUNTER OFFER SIGNATURE LINE: By signing below, Seller accepts this Multiple Counter Offer.**
   NOTE TO SELLER: Do NOT sign in this box until after Buyer signs in paragraph 6. (Paragraph 7 applies only if paragraph 4 is checked.)
   _____ Date _____ Time _____ AM/PM
   _____ Date _____ Time _____ AM/PM

8. (_____/_____) (Initials) **Confirmation of Acceptance:** A Copy of Signed Acceptance was personally received by the maker of the Counter Offer, or that person's authorized agent as specified in paragraph 3 (or, if this is a Multiple Counter Offer, the Buyer or Buyer's authorized agent as specified in paragraph 4) on (date) _____, at _____ AM/PM. A binding Agreement is created when a Copy of Signed Acceptance is personally received by the maker of the Counter Offer, or that person's authorized agent (or, if this is a Multiple Counter Offer, the Buyer or Buyer's authorized agent) whether or not confirmed in this document. Completion of this confirmation is not legally required in order to create a binding Agreement; it is solely intended to evidence the date that Confirmation of Acceptance has occurred.

SURE TRAC
The System for Success™

Published by the
California Association of REALTORS®

CO REVISED 10/02 (PAGE 1 OF 1) Print Date

Reviewed by _____ Date _____

EQUAL HOUSING OPPORTUNITY

COUNTER OFFER (CO PAGE 1 OF 1)

Reprinted with permission, California Association of Realtors®. No endorsement implied.

When your seller decides to make a counteroffer, be sure to explain that the counteroffer will terminate the original offer and all of the buyer's obligations under that offer.

EXAMPLE: Returning to the previous example, suppose that Gordon rejects Lamont's counteroffer. He doesn't want to make a $5,000 good faith deposit. In that case, Gordon has no further obligation to Lamont. That's because Lamont's counteroffer had the same effect as a rejection of Gordon's original offer would have had: it terminated the offer. So when Gordon refuses to pay a larger deposit, Lamont can't simply change her mind and decide to accept Gordon's original offer. His offer has already been terminated by rejection. If Gordon still wants to buy the property, he can renew his offer to Lamont; but if he no longer wants to buy it (or buy it on the terms he originally offered), he is not obligated to do so.

If you are presenting a counteroffer to a buyer, review every term the seller has altered. You may want to prepare another "Buyer's Estimated Costs" worksheet if the counteroffer changes the buyer's costs.

If the buyer decides to accept the counteroffer, have her sign the counteroffer form and then notify the seller that the counteroffer has been accepted. Alternatively, the buyer may choose to respond with a counteroffer of her own. Each counteroffer may be made using a new copy of the counteroffer form, which is designed for use by either the buyer or the seller.

MULTIPLE COUNTEROFFERS

Sometimes a seller receives more than one attractive offer, but the seller still wants to negotiate some additional terms. One option is for the seller to make a counteroffer to the buyer who's made the most attractive offer and reject the other offers, but this limits the seller to negotiating with only one buyer. If the buyer rejected the counteroffer and no longer wanted to buy the property, the seller would no longer have the other offers to fall back on.

So in this situation, the seller might choose to make multiple counter-offers—in other words, counteroffers to more than one of the potential buyers. The seller must inform each buyer that she is making multiple counteroffers. The counteroffer form in Figure 5.2 can be used for this purpose.

To protect the seller from becoming obligated under more than one contract, the multiple counteroffer paragraph provides that the buyer's acceptance of the counteroffer won't automatically create a binding contract. Instead, the contract will be formed if the seller re-signs the counteroffer after the buyer has accepted it. That way, if more than one buyer accepts a counteroffer from the seller, the seller can choose which one to go with.

THE NEGOTIATION PROCESS

In some cases, the parties will trade counteroffers back and forth a number of times. The negotiation process can be frustrating or even nerve-wracking. Remember to maintain your professionalism and do what you can to keep the parties from becoming hostile. Refrain from making negative comments about either party. It's your responsibility to serve the best interests of your client, and a transaction that satisfies both parties is in your client's best interests, whether you're representing the buyer or the seller.

Don't forget to give the parties copies of any documents they sign when they sign them. Each party who makes a counteroffer should get a copy of it immediately after signing it, and both parties should get a copy of the final agreement as soon as it is signed.

Like any offer, a counteroffer can be revoked at any time until the other party accepts it. You should notify the other party as quickly as possible that the offer is being withdrawn.

ACCEPTING AN OFFER

When an offer (or a counteroffer) is accepted, a contract is formed and the parties are legally bound by it. There are three rules to keep in mind concerning the acceptance of an offer.

The acceptance:

1. must be communicated to the person who made the offer;
2. must be made in the specified manner; and
3. cannot change any of the terms of the offer.

COMMUNICATING ACCEPTANCE

To be effective and create a valid contract, the offeree's acceptance must be communicated to the offeror. (The offeree is the person to whom the offer was made, and the offeror is the person who made it.) A seller may have decided to accept a buyer's offer, but until the seller notifies the buyer that the offer has been accepted, the buyer can still revoke it.

EXAMPLE: White is selling his home. Hathaway makes an offer to buy it, and White's agent presents the offer to White.

In the meantime, Hathaway finds another house she likes better. She immediately notifies White that she's revoking her offer.

White protests, claiming that he had already signed Hathaway's offer before she revoked it. But since White hadn't given the signed contract to Hathaway yet, the acceptance was not communicated. As a result, Hathaway still had the right to revoke the offer.

MAILBOX RULE. Acceptance of an offer may be communicated in a number of ways. When the seller's acceptance is delivered to the buyer in person, acceptance is deemed to take place at the time of delivery. But there are times when a seller may use the mail to notify the buyer of an acceptance. In this situation, the "mailbox rule" applies: the acceptance creates a binding contract when the seller drops it in the mailbox, even though the buyer will not receive it right away. The mailbox rule has been extended to other similar methods of communication, such as telegrams or faxed messages.

COMMUNICATION TO AGENT. Acceptance is also considered to be communicated when the seller delivers it to the buyer's agent, even before the buyer's agent relays the acceptance to the buyer.

MANNER OF ACCEPTANCE

Because a contract to purchase real estate must be in writing, an offer to purchase real estate must be accepted in writing. A spoken acceptance does not create an enforceable contract.

EXAMPLE: Adams submits a written offer to purchase Baker's property. Baker finds the offer very attractive, so she immediately calls Adams and accepts the offer over the phone. Two hours later, Baker receives an even better offer. Baker can still withdraw her acceptance of the offer because the acceptance wasn't in writing.

Sometimes an offer calls for a particular manner of acceptance. If so, the acceptance must be made in the specified manner to be binding.

> **EXAMPLE:** Wallace offers to buy Sanchez's property. But Wallace is leaving town shortly, so he includes the following provision in the offer: "This offer shall become a binding contract when written acceptance is hand-delivered to my attorney at 437 First Avenue, Suite 312." Sanchez can only accept the offer by having the acceptance hand-delivered to Wallace's attorney at the specified address.

If the offer does not call for a particular manner of acceptance, it may be accepted by any reasonable medium of communication. A medium is considered reasonable if it is the same one that was used by the buyer, if it is one that is customarily used in similar transactions, or if it has been used by the parties in previous transactions. For instance, if the buyer sent the offer to the seller by fax, it's reasonable for the seller to send the acceptance to the buyer by fax. (Note that if you fax offers and acceptances, it's a good idea to get signed originals from both parties.)

To create a contract, the seller must accept the buyer's terms exactly as offered. The seller can't modify the terms of the offer or add any new terms. An acceptance with modifications is actually a counteroffer, not an acceptance.

CONTRACT AMENDMENTS

When an offer to purchase (or a counteroffer) is accepted in the proper manner, a contract is created. The terms of the contract can't be changed without the consent of both parties.

If the buyer and seller agree to modify their contract, you should use a separate form instead of writing the changes on the original purchase agreement. For example, amendments to the California Association of Realtors® deposit receipt form may be made using the addendum form shown in Chapter 6 (Figure 6.4).

The form used for an amendment should identify the original contract, provide space to write in the changes, and require the signatures of both parties. The signed amendment form should be attached to the original agreement. Each party should be given a copy of the amendment as soon as he or she signs it.

When you're filling out a form to amend a contract, remember that writing a special provision for the parties would be considered the unauthorized practice of law. When a transaction requires a special provision, ask your broker. She is likely to have one or more standard clauses drafted by lawyers that are appropriate for your transaction.

CONTRACT CANCELLATION

Sometimes both the buyer and the seller change their minds, and they agree to rescind or cancel their contract. The parties are always free to terminate their contract by mutual agreement. To do this, the buyer and the seller should sign a cancellation agreement, which officially terminates the purchase agreement. An example of a cancellation form is shown in Figure 5.3.

A cancellation agreement should describe how the good faith deposit will be handled. When a purchase agreement is canceled by mutual agreement, the buyer and the seller typically agree to let the listing and selling brokers split the deposit in lieu of receiving the commission. Technically, the seller is still liable for the brokerage commission, but the brokers are usually willing to share the good faith deposit instead.

For the brokers' protection, a cancellation form may have a safety clause similar to the ones that appear in listing agreements. Under this type of provision, if the seller enters into a new purchase agreement with this same buyer within a specified period (such as six months) after canceling their original agreement, the seller will be required to pay the brokers their full commission.

A cancellation agreement may also be used when a purchase agreement terminates because a contingency has not been fulfilled. This is discussed in Chapter 7.

GOOD FAITH DEPOSITS

An important part of helping a buyer make an offer to purchase a home is handling the deposit. It's traditional for the buyer to give the seller a good faith deposit (sometimes called earnest money) as evidence

FIG. 5.3 CANCELLATION OF CONTRACT FORM

CALIFORNIA ASSOCIATION OF REALTORS®

CANCELLATION OF CONTRACT, RELEASE OF DEPOSIT AND JOINT ESCROW INSTRUCTIONS
(C.A.R. Form CC, 10/03)

In accordance with the terms and conditions of the: ☐ California Residential Purchase Agreement; or ☐ Other _____ ("Agreement"), dated _____, including all amendments and related documents, on property known as _____ ("Property"), between _____ ("Buyer") and _____ ("Seller").

Paragraphs 1 and 2 below constitute escrow instructions to Escrow Holder. Release of funds (pursuant to paragraph 2) requires mutual Signed release instructions from Buyer and Seller, judicial decision or arbitration award. A party may be subject to a civil penalty of up to $1,000 for refusal to sign such instructions if no good faith dispute exists as to who is entitled to the deposited funds (Civil Code §1057.3).

1. **CANCELLATION OF CONTRACT:** ☐ Buyer or ☐ Seller cancels the Agreement and ☐ (if applicable), escrow # _____ with _____, Escrow Holder, for the following reason:

   A. ☐ Seller has failed to take the following applicable contractual action as required by the Agreement: _____

   OR B. ☐ Seller has failed to remove the applicable contingency after being given a Notice to Seller to Perform (C.A.R. Form NSP).

   OR C. ☐ Buyer has failed to remove the applicable contingency after being given a Notice to Buyer to Perform (C.A.R. Form NBP).

   OR D. ☐ Buyer has failed to take the applicable contractual action after being given a Notice to Buyer to Perform (C.A.R. Form NBP).

   OR E. ☐ As otherwise permitted by paragraph _____ of the Agreement.

   Buyer's or Seller's Signature (party cancelling the contract) _____ Date _____

   Buyer's or Seller's Signature (party cancelling the contract) _____ Date _____

2. **RELEASE OF DEPOSIT**

   A. ☐ Seller authorizes release of deposit, less fees and costs, to Buyer.

   OR B. ☐ Buyer authorizes release of deposit, less fees and costs, to Seller. (☐ A liquidated damages clause was properly included as part of the Agreement, and the Property contains no more than four residential units, one of which the Buyer intended to occupy. Buyer's authorization of release of deposit to Seller is limited to no more than 3% of the purchase price. Any additional deposit to be returned to Buyer.)

   OR C. ☐ Other: _____

   Buyer and Seller mutually release each other from all obligation to buy, sell, or exchange the Property under the Agreement, and from all claims, actions and demands that each may have against the other(s) by reason of the Agreement. Buyer and Seller intend that all rights and obligations arising out of the Agreement are null and void.

   Date _____ Date _____
   Buyer _____ Seller _____
   Buyer _____ Seller _____

SURE TRAC
The System for Success™

Published by the
California Association of REALTORS®

CC 10/03 (PAGE 1 OF 1) Print Date

Reviewed by _____ Date _____

EQUAL HOUSING OPPORTUNITY

CANCELLATION OF CONTRACT, RELEASE OF DEPOSIT AND JOINT ESCROW INSTRUCTIONS (CC PAGE 1 OF 1)

Reprinted with permission, California Association of Realtors®. No endorsement implied.

of the buyer's good faith intention to buy the property on the terms he has offered.

There's no law that requires a buyer to give the seller a good faith deposit, but nearly every seller will expect one. A seller doesn't want to take her home off the market, possibly for several weeks, unless the buyer is actually going to follow through on his promise to buy the property. Since the buyer will usually forfeit the deposit if he backs out, the deposit gives the seller some assurance that the buyer really is ready, willing, and able to buy the property.

THE SIZE OF THE DEPOSIT

There is no "standard" deposit amount or percentage. In fact, the size of the good faith deposit usually depends on the buyer's circumstances. A buyer who is planning on making a large cash downpayment generally won't have any trouble making a substantial deposit; the deposit will simply be applied toward the downpayment when the sale closes. On the other hand, if the buyer is planning to finance the purchase with a no-downpayment VA loan, he may not have enough cash for a big deposit.

As a general rule, the deposit should be large enough to give the buyer an economic incentive to complete the transaction. It should also be large enough to compensate the seller for the time and expense involved in taking the house off the market if the buyer fails to complete the transaction.

EXAMPLE: Bernhardt offers to buy Warren's property for $250,000. He makes a $250 deposit. Two weeks later, Bernhardt finds another property he likes more than Warren's for only $240,000. He decides to walk away from his contract with Warren, forfeit the $250 deposit, and purchase the other property.

Even though Bernhardt is legally obligated to purchase Warren's home, Warren is unlikely to go to the trouble and expense of suing Bernhardt for breach of contract. Instead, like most sellers, Warren will just keep the deposit as payment for his time and trouble. But in this case, the deposit was too small to serve its purpose. The $250 deposit was not enough money to convince Bernhardt to honor his contract, nor was it enough to compensate Warren for taking his property off the market for two weeks.

THE FORM OF THE DEPOSIT

A real estate agent who accepts a good faith deposit from a buyer is required to tell the seller—before the seller accepts the buyer's offer—the amount of the deposit and what form it is in. Is it cash, a money order, a personal check, a cashier's check, a postdated check, or a promissory note? You could face disciplinary action if you knowingly misrepresent the form or amount of the deposit to the seller.

> **EXAMPLE:** You're the listing agent for Peterson's house. When Thompson makes an offer, he tells you that he'll give Peterson a $5,000 good faith deposit. However, he explains that he can't write the deposit check until he has transferred funds into his checking account. He assures you that he'll bring you a check tomorrow. He asks you to present the offer to Peterson right away.
>
> When you present the offer, you tell Peterson that Thompson is making a $5,000 deposit, but neglect to mention that he hasn't given you the check yet. You could be subject to disciplinary action for failing to disclose this information.
>
> Peterson accepts Thompson's offer without asking to see the check. She assumes that you already have it and will give it to your broker, in the usual way. The next day, Thompson puts you off for one more day. The day after that, he refuses to give you the check and tells you he's decided to back out of his contract with Peterson. Now, not only are you subject to disciplinary action, but Peterson could sue your broker for the money she should have received as compensation for Thompson's breach of contract.

Now let's consider the advantages and disadvantages of the different forms a good faith deposit can take.

PERSONAL CHECKS. Most buyers make their good faith deposit with a personal check. The check should be made payable to the brokerage that will actually deposit the check if the buyer's offer is accepted.

> **EXAMPLE:** You work for Hadley Realty. Your customer, Morris, is making an offer and writing a personal check for the deposit. The check should be made payable to Hadley Realty, not to you or the seller.

Some brokers require a cashier's check or a money order instead of a personal check. You should ask your broker whether it is company policy to accept personal checks.

Sometimes a buyer will want to use a postdated check, which can't be deposited until the date on the check. Before you accept it, you should check your broker's policies. Some brokers won't accept postdated checks. If you do accept a postdated check, you must tell the seller. It's wise to make this disclosure in writing.

As an alternative to using a postdated check, the buyer may choose to make a small good faith deposit with the offer and include a provision in the offer that she will make an additional deposit within a certain period of time.

> **EXAMPLE:** Hassam wants to make an offer on a home. She has a certificate of deposit that will mature in ten days, and she's planning on using those funds for the downpayment. Right now, however, she only has enough cash available to make a $300 good faith deposit. She doesn't want to cash in her certificate of deposit before it matures, because she would have to pay a penalty for early withdrawal. Instead, she gives you a $300 check with her offer and agrees in writing to make an additional good faith deposit in the amount of $1,500 in ten days.

CASH. Sometimes a buyer will offer to make the good faith deposit in cash. But accepting a deposit in cash may increase the chance of loss or improper handling.

> **EXAMPLE:** A buyer wants to make an offer for a property on Friday evening. He gives you a cash deposit of $1,200. You can't turn the cash over to your broker until Monday. What do you do with the cash over the weekend? You can't deposit it in your own account (that would be commingling trust funds with personal funds), but you will be responsible if the cash is lost or stolen.

Your broker may have a policy against accepting cash deposits. Once you explain some of the problems with a cash deposit, most buyers are willing to use a money order or a check instead of cash.

If you do take a cash deposit, you must turn it over to the broker in its original cash form. You may not deposit it into your account and then write a check against the deposit. Nor may you purchase a money order or a cashier's check with the cash.

PROMISSORY NOTES. Although it's risky to accept a promissory note as a good faith deposit, sometimes a seller is willing to do so. When you tell the seller that the deposit is in the form of a note, be sure he understands the risk. If the buyer refuses to pay the note when it comes due, a lawsuit would be the only way to collect the money owed.

PERSONAL PROPERTY. In unusual cases, a buyer may want to use an item of personal property as a good faith deposit. For instance, you might encounter a buyer who wants to use stock certificates, bonds, or a boat as part or all of the deposit. It is up to the seller to decide whether to accept such an item as a deposit. The parties and your broker will have to arrange an appropriate method of safekeeping for the item in question.

HANDLING THE DEPOSIT

How the broker handles a good faith deposit is governed partly by the trust fund procedures set forth by state law, and partly by the terms of the deposit receipt (the buyer's offer). By law, when the broker receives trust funds, he or she has three business days to deposit them:

1. with the principal,
2. into a neutral escrow account, or
3. into the broker's trust account.

If trust funds are given to a salesperson, instead of directly to the broker, the salesperson must turn the funds over to the broker immediately, or else (if directed to do so by the broker) deposit the funds as listed above.

However, there is an exception to these rules that allows a broker to hold a deposit check uncashed, provided that:

1. the check is not negotiable by the broker, or the buyer has given written instructions to hold the check uncashed until the offer is accepted; and
2. the seller is informed, before or when the offer is presented, that the check is being held uncashed.

Once the offer is accepted, the broker has three business days to deposit the check as listed above, unless the seller gives written authorization to continue to hold the check uncashed.

Some deposit receipts specifically provide that the broker may hold the check for the good faith deposit uncashed until the seller accepts the offer. The broker is directed to deposit the check into his trust account within a specified number of days after the seller's acceptance. If the seller rejects the offer, the check is returned to the buyer. If the seller makes a counteroffer that the buyer rejects, the buyer may ask for his check back. If the buyer accepts the seller's counteroffer, the broker must then deposit the check into his trust account within the specified number of days. If the buyer decides to reject the counteroffer and make another counteroffer, the broker should continue to hold the check until there is an acceptance or a final rejection.

BROKER'S RESPONSIBILITIES. Generally, the broker who receives the good faith deposit is the one responsible for handling the funds properly. Thus, the selling broker is usually the one who is required to deposit the funds, deliver them to the designated third party, or hold them until the seller accepts the offer. Usually, the deposit is first given to the selling salesperson, who is supposed to turn the deposit over to her broker immediately. Every broker is responsible for setting up office procedures for handling deposits. For example, a broker should give his sales agents instructions on what to do if they receive a good faith deposit when the broker is out of the office or when the office is closed.

The listing agreement typically gives the listing broker the authority to hold a good faith deposit on behalf of the seller. In the rare case where the listing agreement does not give that authority to the listing broker, the listing broker may still hold the deposit, but acts as the buyer's agent only in regard to the deposit. In this way, the seller would not be liable to the buyer if the broker lost or misappropriated the deposit.

BOUNCED OR STOPPED CHECKS. After the broker deposits a good faith check into the appropriate trust account, problems can still arise. The check may fail to clear, or the buyer may stop payment for some reason.

> **EXAMPLE:** On Tuesday, Green made an offer on Bowen's property. He gave you a $1,000 personal check for the deposit, and you immediately turned it over to your broker.
>
> Wednesday morning, your broker deposited the check into her trust account. Wednesday evening, Bowen rejected Green's offer, so Green asked for a refund of his deposit. Thursday morning, your broker wrote Green a $1,000 check from her trust account.

On Friday morning, the bank calls your broker to inform her that Green's check failed to clear his bank due to insufficient funds. Now Green has your broker's $1,000, your broker's trust account is overdrawn, and your broker may face disciplinary action for the shortfall.

To prevent this type of problem, the deposit receipt can include a provision that requires the buyer to wait until his check clears before requesting a refund of the good faith deposit. Of course, if the agreement provides that the broker will hold the deposit until the seller accepts the offer, this problem is avoided altogether.

REFUND OR FORFEITURE OF DEPOSIT. If the buyer and seller have signed a purchase agreement, but the sale fails to close, the deposit will either be returned to the buyer or forfeited to the seller. The circumstances under which it will be refunded or forfeited should be stated clearly in the purchase agreement. This is the best way to prevent a dispute between the buyer and the seller over who is entitled to the deposit.

Typically, the buyer is entitled to a refund of the deposit if:

- the seller rejects the offer;
- the buyer withdraws the offer before it is accepted; or
- the seller accepts the offer, but a contingency provision is not fulfilled, so the contract is terminated.

> **EXAMPLE:** Lindor and Jones have a purchase agreement that's contingent on Lindor obtaining a conventional loan to finance the purchase. Lindor applies to three lenders, but they all reject his loan application. The contingency hasn't been fulfilled, so the contract is terminated, and Lindor is entitled to a refund of the deposit.

On the other hand, the deposit will generally be forfeited to the seller if the buyer simply changes her mind and backs out of the sale. Most deposit receipts provide that the deposit will be treated as **liquidated damages** in the event of a breach of contract. If the buyer defaults, the seller will keep the deposit as liquidated damages rather than suing the buyer for actual damages.

LIQUIDATED DAMAGES. There are some statutory restrictions on using a good faith deposit as liquidated damages. In a sale of one- to four-unit, owner-occupied residential property, the buyer's deposit may be treated as liquidated damages only if these two requirements are met:

1. The total amount to be forfeited does not exceed 3% of the purchase price. Any excess must be refunded to the buyer.
2. The contract has a liquidated damages provision in either 10-point bold type or 8-point red type that is separately signed and initialed by both buyer and seller.

Before the good faith deposit is disbursed to either the seller or the buyer, the broker should get the parties to agree to the disbursement in writing. If they disagree as to which of them is entitled to the deposit, the broker may have to submit the matter to arbitration or to a court proceeding.

Remember, it is the broker or the escrow agent—not the salesperson—who is responsible for disbursing a good faith deposit. If a buyer or seller has questions about how the deposit will be handled, always refer him or her to your broker or the escrow agent. Never try to answer these questions yourself.

Some deposit receipts provide that any expenses already incurred that were to be paid at closing will be deducted from the good faith deposit before it's forfeited to the seller. Also, listing agreements typically provide that the seller will pay half of the remainder of the deposit to the listing broker and selling broker in place of their commission.

FAIR HOUSING CONSIDERATIONS

As you prepare offers and negotiate counteroffers, you must be sure to avoid discrimination based on race, color, religion, ancestry, national origin, sex, disability, medical condition, age, sexual orientation, familial status, or marital status. The potential for discriminating against a buyer begins with your first meeting. Even before you show the buyer a house, prepare an offer, or negotiate a sale, you could engage in discriminatory conduct.

It's important to remember that you do not have to intend to discriminate in order to violate a state or federal fair housing law. Acting in a discriminatory manner, or with a discriminatory effect, is enough. (See Chapter 3.)

Federal and state fair housing laws make a wide array of discriminatory actions toward home buyers illegal. It violates these laws when any of the following actions is based on race, religion, or one of the other protected characteristics:

- refusing to receive or failing to transmit a bona fide offer;
- refusing to negotiate for the sale of property, or otherwise making it unavailable;
- changing the terms of the sale for different potential buyers;
- discriminating in providing services or facilities in connection with a real estate transaction;
- representing that a property is not available for inspection or sale when it is in fact available;
- failing to advise a prospect about a property listing;
- using any application form or making any record or inquiry which indicates, directly or indirectly, an intent to discriminate; and
- discriminating in negotiating or executing any service or item (such as title insurance or mortgage insurance) in connection with a real estate transaction.

These actions involving discrimination against buyers can generally be categorized into three groups: refusing to show a property based on discriminatory considerations, steering, and treating certain types of buyers less favorably than others.

You should never refuse to show a buyer a particular house because of the buyer's race or another characteristic protected under the fair housing laws. Any buyer who asks to see a particular property should be shown the property.

EXAMPLE: You have shown Hernandez, a Hispanic buyer, several houses. Hernandez looks over the entries in your multiple listing book and asks to be shown a particular house. He thinks it might be just the place he's looking for. From office rumors, you know that the seller will probably refuse to accept an offer from any minority buyer. You are anxious to avoid a confrontation, so you tell Hernandez that the seller has already accepted an offer and the house is no longer available. You have just discriminated against Hernandez by representing that the property is not available when in fact it is.

As explained in Chapter 3, steering refers to channeling prospective buyers or tenants toward or away from specific neighborhoods based on their race (or national origin, religion, etc.) in order to maintain or change the character of those neighborhoods.

EXAMPLE: There are thirteen white agents and four African-American agents in your office. African-American buyers are directed to the African-American agents, who are "encouraged" to show them homes only in the one neighborhood in the city that's mainly African-American. This is done on the principle that these buyers would be more comfortable living there. Your real estate office is guilty of steering.

You must also be sure to treat all buyers the same in terms of client and customer services. It would obviously be discriminatory to ignore minority prospects when they enter your office, or to refuse to drive them to see the listed houses that interest them (if that's a service you ordinarily provide). A more subtle form of discrimination involves changing the questions you ask during the financial prequalifying process.

EXAMPLE: When you prequalify most buyers, you ask them general financial questions. What is their annual income? How large a down-payment can they make? Do they have any credit problems? However, your broker believes that minority prospects usually fail to qualify for financing. To avoid wasting company time, your broker requires you to ask minority prospects detailed financial and personal questions, such as: How many charge cards do they have? Have they ever paid any bills late? Has their phone ever been disconnected? Have they ever been fired from a job? Have they ever been on unemployment? Have they ever been on welfare? These extra questions are discriminatory and illegal.

Because so many actions could be considered discriminatory, it's important to develop sales practices that will ensure your compliance with fair housing laws. Here are a few guidelines to follow when interviewing buyers, showing homes, and presenting and negotiating offers:

- Use consistent prequalifying techniques with all buyers. Using a standard prequalifying form will help you ask each prospect the same questions. Keep records that demonstrate that all buyers are asked the same questions and given equal treatment.

- Never imply that a person of a particular race, color, religion, national origin, etc., will have a harder time getting financing.
- Always offer to show your prospects all the listed properties in your market area that meet their objective criteria. Don't make assumptions about a buyer's housing needs or neighborhood preferences based on stereotypes.
- Be sure to treat all prospects equally when setting up showings, making keys available, setting appointments to present offers, or conducting negotiations.
- Report any suspected discriminatory act or statement on the part of a seller to your broker immediately. Check with your broker (or a lawyer, if necessary) on what you should do about a rejection that seemed to be based on discriminatory reasons.

CHAPTER SUMMARY

1. As a real estate agent, you may fill out a standard deposit receipt form, but only for a transaction you are handling, and you cannot charge a separate fee for the service. You may not draft special clauses or give advice about the legal effect of provisions in the form. If you have any questions or concerns when filling out a form, you should talk to your broker or a real estate attorney.

2. All offers, regardless of their merit, must be presented to the seller. You must even present offers received after the seller has already accepted another offer. (These backup offers should be made contingent on the failure of the first sales contract.) Offers are usually presented by the listing agent. You must disclose your agency status before presenting an offer to purchase.

3. When a seller "accepts" an offer with a few modifications, the seller is actually rejecting the offer and making a counteroffer. When a party wants to make a counteroffer, it is best to use a separate form. When you present a counteroffer, be sure to explain each term that has been changed and discuss the financial ramifications of the changes.

4. If an offer does not have a time limit, it will terminate after a reasonable period of time. An offer can be revoked at any time up until it is accepted. To be effective, the acceptance must be communicated to the person who made the offer. If the offer is mailed, it is deemed to be communicated when it is put into a mailbox. An offer to purchase real property must be in writing. The acceptance also must be in writing, and any other stipulations about the manner of acceptance must be complied with.

5. When an offer is properly accepted, a binding contract is created. It can't be modified without the written consent of both parties. The parties may mutually agree to terminate the contract, although the seller may still owe the broker the sales commission. If the contract is terminated, the parties should sign a cancellation agreement.

6. You must disclose the amount and the form of the buyer's good faith deposit to the seller and also disclose any problems with the deposit. Most deposits are personal checks, but they may also be in the form of cash, a money order, a cashier's check, a promissory note, or personal property.

7. Good faith deposits generally must be delivered to the seller, deposited in the broker's trust account, or deposited into escrow within three business days of receipt. However, a deposit check may be held uncashed if: (1) the check is not negotiable by the broker, or the buyer has given written instructions not to cash the check until the buyer accepts the offer; and (2) the seller is informed that the check is being held. If the sale closes, the good faith deposit will be credited against the buyer's downpayment. If the sale fails to close, the deposit will either be returned to the buyer or forfeited to the seller, depending on the circumstances.

8. In showing homes, preparing offers, and negotiating sales, be sure you do not discriminate against the buyers you're working with. Discrimination does not have to be intentional to violate fair housing laws.

CHAPTER QUIZ

1. Which of the following statements about an offer to purchase real property is true?

    a. The offer needs to be in writing, but the acceptance does not

    b. Both the offer and the acceptance must be in writing

    c. Neither the offer nor the acceptance needs to be in writing, but the deed to transfer title must be in writing

    d. The offer does not have to be in writing, but the acceptance must include all of the terms of the offer

2. Which of the following statements about preparing an offer to purchase is true?

    a. The buyer cannot write her own offer without engaging in the unauthorized practice of law

    b. A real estate agent may write special clauses for the parties as long as they are inserted into a preprinted form written and approved by attorneys

    c. A real estate agent may not prepare an offer if he is also representing one of the parties

    d. A real estate agent is held to the same standard of care as a lawyer when preparing an offer

3. A contingent counteroffer would be appropriate when:

    a. the seller has already signed a purchase agreement, and then receives an attractive offer from another buyer

    b. the seller wants to accept the buyer's offer, but modify some of the terms

    c. the buyer wants to accept the seller's counteroffer, but isn't sure if he'll qualify for financing

    d. the seller has received multiple offers and wants to withdraw her previous counteroffer to one buyer and accept another buyer's offer

4. The seller's acceptance would be effective (so that the buyer could no longer withdraw his offer) in all of the following situations, except:

   a. The seller accepts the buyer's offer over the phone

   b. The seller uses a fax machine to transmit her acceptance

   c. The seller sends her acceptance in the mail, but with delivery confirmation

   d. The seller sends her acceptance via telegram

5. Once it has been signed by both the buyer and the seller, a purchase agreement can be modified only if:

   a. a contingency clause is not fulfilled

   b. the buyer accepts the seller's counteroffer in writing

   c. both parties agree to the modifications in writing

   d. the seller failed to disclose certain information he was legally required to disclose

6. Which of the following is least likely to be found in a cancellation agreement?

   a. A safety clause

   b. A notice to the backup buyer

   c. An agreement to allow the listing and selling brokers to share the good faith deposit in lieu of a commission

   d. The signatures of both parties

7. After accepting a good faith deposit from a buyer, you are required to tell the seller:

   a. what form the deposit is in

   b. if the deposit is a postdated check

   c. the amount of the deposit

   d. All of the above

8. If you accept cash as a good faith deposit, you:

    a. must turn the deposit over to the broker in its original cash form

    b. should use the cash to purchase a certified check, to prevent the funds from being lost or stolen

    c. should have the buyer's receipt notarized

    d. may face disciplinary action for violating the Real Estate Law

a

9. Many deposit receipt forms have a provision allowing the broker to hold a check for the good faith deposit for a specified period without depositing it in a trust account. One advantage of this is that:

    a. it gives the seller more time to consider the offer

    b. the broker can simply return the check to the buyer if the offer is rejected

    c. it ensures that the buyer has sufficient funds in her account

    d. the check can be postdated by a week or more

b

10. A buyer signs a purchase agreement for a duplex that she intends to occupy. If she forfeits the good faith deposit as liquidated damages for breach of the purchase agreement:

    a. the full amount of the deposit will be split between the selling broker and the listing broker in lieu of a commission

    b. any amount in excess of 3% of the purchase price must be refunded to the buyer

    c. any amount in excess of $10,000 must be refunded to the buyer

    d. the seller will be entitled to keep the entire amount, less any expenses incurred by the listing broker

b

ANSWER KEY

1. b. The statute of frauds requires both an offer to purchase real property and the acceptance of the offer to be in writing.

2. d. When filling out a contract form, a real estate agent is held to the same standard of care that is required of a lawyer.

3. a. A contingent counteroffer allows a seller to accept a second offer, contingent on the failure of the first contract.

4. a. In order to form a contract to purchase real estate, the acceptance must be made in writing. Telephone communication is not a valid form of acceptance. The mailbox rule would apply to all of the other situations listed.

5. c. Once a contract has been formed, the terms of the contract can't be changed without the written consent of both parties. The parties may agree to amend the contract for any reason.

6. b. A contract cancellation agreement should be signed by both parties and describe how the good faith deposit will be handled. It may include a safety clause for the brokers' protection. If the seller has accepted a backup offer, the notice to the backup buyer will be handled separately.

7. d. A real estate agent who accepts a good faith deposit is required to disclose the amount and form of the deposit to the seller. The agent should follow office policies regarding the form and handling of the deposit, and also inform the seller of anything unusual about the deposit, such as the fact that the buyer's check is postdated.

8. a. If you accept a good faith deposit in cash, you must turn the cash over to your broker so that it can be placed in the trust account in cash. Although accepting a good faith deposit in cash increases the chance of loss or improper handling, it is not in itself grounds for disciplinary action.

9. b. Deposit receipts often allow the broker to hold the good faith deposit check without depositing it until the seller accepts the offer. This makes it easier to return the good faith deposit to the buyer if the offer is rejected.

10. b. If the buyer breaches the purchase agreement, no more than 3% of the purchase price can be retained as liquidated damages. After expenses incurred by the brokers have been deducted, the seller usually keeps half of the remainder and gives the listing broker the other half. The listing broker will usually split this portion with the selling broker.

6

DEPOSIT RECEIPTS

REQUIREMENTS FOR A VALID PURCHASE AGREEMENT

TYPICAL PROVISIONS IN A RESIDENTIAL DEPOSIT RECEIPT

- Identifying the parties
- Property description
- Purchase price and method of payment
- Receipt for good faith deposit
- Closing date
- Transfer of possession
- Closing agent
- Allocation of costs
- Lead-based paint disclosures
- Included items
- Buyer's investigation and repairs
- Conveyance and title
- Sale of buyer's property
- Agency disclosure
- Default
- Dispute resolution
- Time is of the essence
- Addenda
- Offer and acceptance
- Signatures

Introduction

There are a variety of techniques you can learn that will help you find potential buyers, show properties, and negotiate offers. Your broker will undoubtedly give you training in these matters. However, learning the functions of a deposit receipt—a purchase agreement between a buyer and a seller—and understanding its provisions may be just as important to your career. If you make a mistake in filling out a deposit receipt form, you could face the loss of your commission, a lawsuit by the buyer or the seller, and disciplinary action. This chapter describes the requirements for a valid purchase agreement, the provisions typically found in a residential deposit receipt form, and some of the addenda commonly used in residential transactions.

Requirements for a Valid Purchase Agreement

When a buyer is ready to make an offer, he may not understand why it's necessary to fill out a deposit receipt form. After all, the buyer figures, it's just an offer. Why not just jot down the important part—the sales price—on a piece of paper? If the seller's interested, they can agree on the details later.

There are two main problems with that approach. First, the seller can't decide whether the buyer's offer is acceptable unless all of the material terms of the proposed transaction have been set forth. Anything from the amount of the good faith deposit to the date set for closing—not just the sales price—could affect the seller's decision.

Second, when the seller signs the buyer's written offer, agreeing to the buyer's terms, a contract is formed. The purpose of the contract is to hold the buyer and seller to their agreement until the sale is ready to close. But the contract won't be enforceable unless it includes all of the terms that are legally required for a valid purchase agreement.

A purchase agreement must meet the basic legal requirements for any contract. The parties must be competent, and there must be mutual consent (offer and acceptance), a lawful objective, and consideration (the seller's promise to sell and the buyer's promise to buy).

In addition, a purchase agreement must:

1. be in writing;
2. identify the parties and describe the property;

3. state the price and method of payment;
4. list the liens or other encumbrances the buyer will assume or take title subject to;
5. specify the financing amount and terms, if any, to be obtained by the buyer; and
6. describe any conditions of the sale.

While these are the minimum requirements for validity, most deposit receipt forms are quite detailed. It is important for the agreement between the parties to be stated fully and accurately; anything that isn't made clear at the outset can give rise to a dispute later on, and might prevent the transaction from closing.

TYPICAL PROVISIONS IN A RESIDENTIAL DEPOSIT RECEIPT

There is no standard deposit receipt form that all real estate agents must use. A variety of forms are available from multiple listing services, other professional organizations, and legal form publishers. As an example, Figure 6.1 shows the residential deposit receipt form that the California Association of Realtors® (C.A.R.) uses. Of course, you need to become familiar with the terms of the deposit receipt form that is used in your office. Our discussion will be an overview of the provisions found in most deposit receipt forms.

To fill out a deposit receipt form, you need to be able to answer these questions:

1. What information needs to be filled in?
2. Which provisions are pertinent to this transaction?
3. Which provisions should be crossed out?
4. What other provisions need to be attached to the form as addenda?

Remember that contract forms should always be filled in completely. If an entry doesn't apply to the transaction, write in "N/A" (for "not applicable") instead of leaving the space blank.

Also, a form must be used only for its intended purpose. For instance, the form in Figure 6.1 is intended for residential sales only. It shouldn't be used for any other type of transaction.

FIG. 6.1   RESIDENTIAL PURCHASE AGREEMENT (DEPOSIT RECEIPT)

(handwritten, top right) → most important → RE to make $$

CALIFORNIA ASSOCIATION OF REALTORS®

CALIFORNIA RESIDENTIAL PURCHASE AGREEMENT AND JOINT ESCROW INSTRUCTIONS
For Use With Single Family Residential Property — Attached or Detached
(C.A.R. Form RPA-CA, Revised 10/02)

Date __10/12/05__, at __Vallejo__ *(where property is)*, California.

1. **OFFER:**
   A. **THIS IS AN OFFER FROM** __(legal names)__ ("Buyer").
   B. **THE REAL PROPERTY TO BE ACQUIRED** is described as __address__, Assessor's Parcel No. _____, situated in _____, County of _____, California, ("Property").
   C. **THE PURCHASE PRICE** offered is __five hundred fifty thousand__ Dollars $ __550,000__.
   D. **CLOSE OF ESCROW** shall occur on _____ (date)(or ☐ _____ **Days** After Acceptance).

2. **FINANCE TERMS:** Obtaining the loans below **is a contingency** of this Agreement unless: **(i)** either 2K or 2L is checked below; or **(ii)** otherwise agreed in writing. Buyer shall act diligently and in good faith to obtain the designated loans. Obtaining deposit, down payment and closing costs **is not a contingency.** Buyer represents that funds will be good when deposited with Escrow Holder.
   A. **INITIAL DEPOSIT:** Buyer has given a deposit in the amount of .... $ _____
   to the agent submitting the offer (or to ☐ _____), by personal check
   (or ☐ _____), made payable to _____,
   which shall be held uncashed until Acceptance and then deposited within 3 business days after
   Acceptance (or ☐ _____), with
   Escrow Holder, (or ☐ into Broker's trust account).
   B. **INCREASED DEPOSIT:** Buyer shall deposit with Escrow Holder an increased deposit in the amount of ...$ _____
   within _____ **Days** After Acceptance, or _____.
   C. **FIRST LOAN IN THE AMOUNT OF** .... $ _____
   (1) NEW First Deed of Trust in favor of lender, encumbering the Property, securing a note payable at
   maximum interest of _____ % fixed rate, or _____ % initial adjustable rate with a maximum
   interest rate of _____%, balance due in _____ years, amortized over _____ years. Buyer
   shall pay loan fees/points not to exceed _____ (These terms apply whether the designated loan
   is conventional, FHA or VA.)
   (2) ☐ FHA ☐ VA: (The following terms only apply to the FHA or VA loan that is checked.)
   Seller shall pay _____% discount points. Seller shall pay other fees not allowed to be paid by
   Buyer, ☐ not to exceed $ _____. Seller shall pay the cost of lender required Repairs
   (including those for wood destroying pest) not otherwise provided for in this Agreement, ☐ not to
   exceed $ _____. (Actual loan amount may increase if mortgage insurance premiums,
   funding fees or closing costs are financed.)
   D. **ADDITIONAL FINANCING TERMS:** ☐ Seller financing (C.A.R. Form SFA); ☐ secondary financing, ...$ _____
   (C.A.R. Form PAA, paragraph 4A); ☐ assumed financing (C.A.R. Form PAA, paragraph 4B)
   _____
   E. **BALANCE OF PURCHASE PRICE** (not including costs of obtaining loans and other closing costs) in the amount of ...$ _____
   to be deposited with Escrow Holder within sufficient time to close escrow.
   F. **PURCHASE PRICE (TOTAL):** .... $ _____
   G. **LOAN APPLICATIONS:** Within 7 (or ☐ _____) After Acceptance, Buyer shall provide Seller a letter from lender or mortgage loan broker stating that, based on a review of Buyer's written application and credit report, Buyer is prequalified or preapproved for the NEW loan specified in 2C above.
   H. **VERIFICATION OF DOWN PAYMENT AND CLOSING COSTS:** Buyer (or Buyer's lender or loan broker pursuant to 2G) shall, within 7 (or ☐ _____) Days After Acceptance, provide Seller written verification of Buyer's down payment and closing costs.
   I. **LOAN CONTINGENCY REMOVAL:** (i) Within 17 (or ☐ _____) **Days** After Acceptance, Buyer shall, as specified in paragraph 14, remove the loan contingency or cancel this Agreement; **OR (ii)** (if checked) ☐ the loan contingency shall remain in effect until the designated loans are funded.
   J. **APPRAISAL CONTINGENCY AND REMOVAL:** This Agreement is (OR, if checked, ☐ is NOT) contingent upon the Property appraising at no less than the specified purchase price. If there is a loan contingency, at the time the loan contingency is removed (or, if checked, ☐ within 17 (or ☐ _____) Days After Acceptance), Buyer shall, as specified in paragraph 14B(3), remove the appraisal contingency or cancel this Agreement. If there is no loan contingency, Buyer shall, as specified in paragraph 14B(3), remove the appraisal contingency within 17 (or _____) Days After Acceptance.
   K. ☐ **NO LOAN CONTINGENCY** (If checked): Obtaining any loan in paragraphs 2C, 2D or elsewhere in this Agreement is NOT a contingency of this Agreement. If Buyer does not obtain the loan and as a result Buyer does not purchase the Property, Seller may be entitled to Buyer's deposit or other legal remedies.
   L. ☐ **ALL CASH OFFER** (If checked): No loan is needed to purchase the Property. Buyer shall, within 7 (or ☐ _____) Days After Acceptance, provide Seller written verification of sufficient funds to close this transaction.

3. **CLOSING AND OCCUPANCY:**
   A. Buyer intends (or ☐ does not intend) to occupy the Property as Buyer's primary residence.
   B. **Seller-occupied or vacant property:** Occupancy shall be delivered to Buyer at _____ AM/PM, ☐ on the date of Close Of Escrow; ☐ on _____; or ☐ no later than _____ Days After Close Of Escrow. (C.A.R. Form PAA, paragraph 2.) If transfer of title and occupancy do not occur at the same time, Buyer and Seller are advised to: (i) enter into a written occupancy agreement; and (ii) consult with their insurance and legal advisors.

The copyright laws of the United States (Title 17 U.S. Code) forbid the unauthorized reproduction of this form, or any portion thereof, by photocopy machine or any other means, including facsimile or computerized formats. Copyright © 1991-2003, CALIFORNIA ASSOCIATION OF REALTORS®, INC. ALL RIGHTS RESERVED.
RPA-CA REVISED 10/02 (PAGE 1 OF 8)   Print Date

Buyer's Initials (_____)(_____)
Seller's Initials (_____)(_____)
Reviewed by _____ Date _____

EQUAL HOUSING OPPORTUNITY

CALIFORNIA RESIDENTIAL PURCHASE AGREEMENT   (RPA-CA PAGE 1 OF 8)

Reprinted with permission, California Association of Realtors®. No endorsement implied.

(handwritten margin notes)

40 - 45 days (reasonable) seller can withdraw the contract if escrow goes beyond the date

should work w/ lender first

try to get as much $ down

include letter pre qual

if it does not appraise the contract is voidable

no time frame may decide not to sell — doing into negative change of job of occupancy will be at close of Escrow

★ Fill it out completely

(handwritten bottom) If buyer moves in before close of Escrow, fill out a rental agreement

[handwritten margin notes, top left: "find out when lease ends / lease's / if new buyer needs to honor lease / give 30 day notice"]

Property Address: _____ Date: _____

C. **Tenant-occupied property: (i) Property shall be vacant** at least 5 (**or** ☐ _____) **Days** Prior to Close Of Escrow, unless otherwise agreed in writing. **Note to Seller: If you are unable to deliver Property vacant in accordance with rent control and other applicable Law, you may be in breach of this Agreement.**

OR (ii) (if checked) ☐ **Tenant to remain in possession.** The attached addendum is incorporated into this Agreement (C.A.R. Form PAA, paragraph 3.);

OR (iii) (if checked) ☐ **This Agreement is contingent** upon Buyer and Seller entering into a written agreement regarding occupancy of the Property within the time specified in paragraph 14B(1). If no written agreement is reached within this time, either Buyer or Seller may cancel this Agreement in writing.

D. At Close Of Escrow, Seller assigns to Buyer any assignable warranty rights for items included in the sale and shall provide any available Copies of such warranties. Brokers cannot and will not determine the assignability of any warranties.

E. At Close Of Escrow, unless otherwise agreed in writing, Seller shall provide keys and/or means to operate all locks, mailboxes, security systems, alarms and garage door openers. If Property is a condominium or located in a common interest subdivision, Buyer may be required to pay a deposit to the Homeowners' Association ("HOA") to obtain keys to accessible HOA facilities.

4. **ALLOCATION OF COSTS** (If checked): Unless otherwise specified here, this paragraph only determines who is to pay for the report, inspection, test or service mentioned. If not specified here or elsewhere in this Agreement, the determination of who is to pay for any work recommended or identified by any such report, inspection, test or service shall be by the method specified in paragraph 14B(2).

[handwritten margin note, left: "negotiable"]

A. **WOOD DESTROYING PEST INSPECTION:**
   (1) ☐ Buyer ☐ Seller shall pay for an inspection and report for wood destroying pests and organisms ("Report") which shall be prepared by _____, a registered structural pest control company. The Report shall cover the accessible areas of the main building and attached structures and, if checked: ☐ detached garages and carports, ☐ detached decks, ☐ the following other structures or areas _____. The Report shall not include roof coverings. If Property is a condominium or located in a common interest subdivision, the Report shall include only the separate interest and any exclusive-use areas being transferred and shall not include common areas, unless otherwise agreed. Water tests of shower pans on upper level units may not be performed without consent of the owners of property below the shower.

   OR (2) ☐ **(If checked)** The attached addendum (C.A.R. Form WPA) regarding wood destroying pest inspection and allocation of cost is incorporated into this Agreement.

[handwritten margin note, right: "Buyer usually pays for inspect"]

B. **OTHER INSPECTIONS AND REPORTS:**
   (1) ☐ Buyer ☐ Seller shall pay to have septic or private sewage disposal systems inspected _____
   (2) ☐ Buyer ☐ Seller shall pay to have domestic wells tested for water potability and productivity _____
   (3) ☐ Buyer ☐ Seller shall pay for a natural hazard zone disclosure report prepared by _____
   (4) ☐ Buyer ☐ Seller shall pay for the following inspection or report _____
   (5) ☐ Buyer ☐ Seller shall pay for the following inspection or report _____

[handwritten margin notes, right: "roof / pest / considerable contact if something wrong + have home warranty"]

C. **GOVERNMENT REQUIREMENTS AND RETROFIT:**
   (1) ☐ Buyer ☐ Seller shall pay for smoke detector installation and/or water heater bracing, if required by Law. Prior to Close Of Escrow, Seller shall provide Buyer a written statement of compliance in accordance with state and local Law, unless exempt.
   (2) ☐ Buyer ☐ Seller shall pay the cost of compliance with any other minimum mandatory government retrofit standards, inspections and reports if required as a condition of closing escrow under any Law. _____

D. **ESCROW AND TITLE:**
   (1) ☐ Buyer ☐ Seller shall pay escrow fee _____
       Escrow Holder shall be _____
   (2) ☐ Buyer ☐ Seller shall pay for **owner's** title insurance policy specified in paragraph 12E _____
       Owner's title policy to be issued by _____
       (Buyer shall pay for any title insurance policy insuring Buyer's **lender**, unless otherwise agreed in writing.)

E. **OTHER COSTS:**
   (1) ☐ Buyer ☐ Seller shall pay County transfer tax or transfer fee _____
   (2) ☐ Buyer ☐ Seller shall pay City transfer tax or transfer fee _____
   (3) ☐ Buyer ☐ Seller shall pay HOA transfer fee _____
   (4) ☐ Buyer ☐ Seller shall pay HOA document preparation fees _____
   (5) ☐ Buyer ☐ Seller shall pay the cost, not to exceed $ _____, of a one-year home warranty plan, issued by _____
       with the following optional coverage: _____
   (6) ☐ Buyer ☐ Seller shall pay for _____
   (7) ☐ Buyer ☐ Seller shall pay for _____

5. **STATUTORY DISCLOSURES (INCLUDING LEAD-BASED PAINT HAZARD DISCLOSURES) AND CANCELLATION RIGHTS:**
   A. (1) Seller shall, within the time specified in paragraph 14A, deliver to Buyer, if required by Law: **(i)** Federal Lead-Based Paint Disclosures and pamphlet ("Lead Disclosures"); and **(ii)** disclosures or notices required by sections 1102 et. seq. and 1103 et. seq. of the California Civil Code ("Statutory Disclosures"). Statutory Disclosures include, but are not limited to, a Real Estate Transfer Disclosure Statement ("TDS"), Natural Hazard Disclosure Statement ("NHD"), notice or actual knowledge of release of illegal controlled substance, notice of special tax and/or assessments (or, if allowed, substantially equivalent notice regarding the Mello-Roos Community Facilities Act and Improvement Bond Act of 1915) and, if Seller has actual knowledge, an industrial use and military ordnance location disclosure (C.A.R. Form SSD).
      (2) Buyer shall, within the time specified in paragraph 14B(1), return Signed Copies of the Statutory and Lead Disclosures to Seller.
      (3) In the event Seller, prior to Close Of Escrow, becomes aware of adverse conditions materially affecting the Property, or any material inaccuracy in disclosures, information or representations previously provided to Buyer of which Buyer is otherwise unaware, Seller shall promptly provide a subsequent or amended disclosure or notice, in writing, covering those items. **However, a subsequent or amended disclosure shall not be required for conditions and material inaccuracies disclosed in reports ordered and paid for by Buyer.**

[handwritten margin note, right: "1978 or older → ? lead based paint"]

Buyer's Initials (_____)(_____)
Seller's Initials (_____)(_____)

Copyright © 1991-2003, CALIFORNIA ASSOCIATION OF REALTORS®, INC.
RPA-CA REVISED 10/02 (PAGE 2 OF 8)

Reviewed by _____ Date _____

CALIFORNIA RESIDENTIAL PURCHASE AGREEMENT (RPA-CA PAGE 2 OF 8)

[handwritten note, bottom center: "if older home do whole house inspect"]

Property Address: _____ Date: _____

(4) If any disclosure or notice specified in 5A(1), or subsequent or amended disclosure or notice is delivered to Buyer after the offer is Signed, Buyer shall have the right to cancel this Agreement within **3 Days** After delivery in person, or **5 Days** After delivery by deposit in the mail, by giving written notice of cancellation to Seller or Seller's agent. (Lead Disclosures sent by mail must be sent certified mail or better.)

(5) Note to Buyer and Seller: Waiver of Statutory and Lead Disclosures is prohibited by Law.

B. NATURAL AND ENVIRONMENTAL HAZARDS: Within the time specified in paragraph 14A, Seller shall, if required by Law: **(i)** deliver to Buyer earthquake guides (and questionnaire) and environmental hazards booklet; **(ii)** even if exempt from the obligation to provide a NHD, disclose if the Property is located in a Special Flood Hazard Area; Potential Flooding (Inundation) Area; Very High Fire Hazard Zone; State Fire Responsibility Area; Earthquake Fault Zone; Seismic Hazard Zone; and **(iii)** disclose any other zone as required by Law and provide any other information required for those zones.

C. DATA BASE DISCLOSURE: NOTICE: The California Department of Justice, sheriff's departments, police departments serving jurisdictions of 200,000 or more and many other local law enforcement authorities maintain for public access a data base of the locations of persons required to register pursuant to paragraph (1) of subdivision (a) of Section 290.4 of the Penal Code. The data base is updated on a quarterly basis and a source of information about the presence of these individuals in any neighborhood. The Department of Justice also maintains a Sex Offender Identification Line through which inquiries about individuals may be made. This is a "900" telephone service. Callers must have specific information about individuals they are checking. Information regarding neighborhoods is not available through the "900" telephone service.

6. CONDOMINIUM/PLANNED UNIT DEVELOPMENT DISCLOSURES:

A. SELLER HAS: 7 (or ☐ ____) Days After Acceptance to disclose to Buyer whether the Property is a condominium, or is located in a planned unit development or other common interest subdivision (C.A.R. Form SSD).

B. If the Property is a condominium or is located in a planned unit development or other common interest subdivision, Seller has **3 (or ☐ ____) Days** After Acceptance to request from the HOA (C.A.R. Form HOA): **(i)** Copies of any documents required by Law; **(ii)** disclosure of any pending or anticipated claim or litigation by or against the HOA; **(iii)** a statement containing the location and number of designated parking and storage spaces; **(iv)** Copies of the most recent 12 months of HOA minutes for regular and special meetings; and **(v)** the names and contact information of all HOAs governing the Property (collectively, "CI Disclosures"). Seller shall itemize and deliver to Buyer all CI Disclosures received from the HOA and any CI Disclosures in Seller's possession. Buyer's approval of CI Disclosures is a contingency of this Agreement as specified in paragraph 14B(3).

7. CONDITIONS AFFECTING PROPERTY:

A. Unless otherwise agreed: **(i)** the Property is sold **(a)** in its PRESENT physical condition as of the date of Acceptance and **(b) subject to Buyer's Investigation rights; (ii)** the Property, including pool, spa, landscaping and grounds, is to be maintained in substantially the same condition as on the date of Acceptance; and **(iii)** all debris and personal property not included in the sale shall be removed by Close Of Escrow.

B. SELLER SHALL, within the time specified in paragraph 14A, DISCLOSE KNOWN MATERIAL FACTS AND DEFECTS affecting the Property, including known insurance claims within the past five years, AND MAKE OTHER DISCLOSURES REQUIRED BY LAW (C.A.R. Form SSD).

C. NOTE TO BUYER: You are strongly advised to conduct investigations of the entire Property in order to determine its present condition since Seller may not be aware of all defects affecting the Property or other factors that you consider important. Property improvements may not be built according to code, in compliance with current Law, or have had permits issued.

D. NOTE TO SELLER: Buyer has the right to inspect the Property and, as specified in paragraph 14B, based upon information discovered in those inspections: **(i)** cancel this Agreement; or **(ii)** request that you make Repairs or take other action.

8. ITEMS INCLUDED AND EXCLUDED:

A. NOTE TO BUYER AND SELLER: Items listed as included or excluded in the MLS, flyers or marketing materials are **not** included in the purchase price or excluded from the sale unless specified in 8B or C.

B. ITEMS INCLUDED IN SALE:
(1) All EXISTING fixtures and fittings that are attached to the Property;
(2) Existing electrical, mechanical, lighting, plumbing and heating fixtures, ceiling fans, fireplace inserts, gas logs and grates, solar systems, built-in appliances, window and door screens, awnings, shutters, window coverings, attached floor coverings, television antennas, satellite dishes, private integrated telephone systems, air coolers/conditioners, pool/spa equipment, garage door openers/remote controls, mailbox, in-ground landscaping, trees/shrubs, water softeners, water purifiers, security systems/alarms; and
(3) The following items: _____
(4) Seller represents that all items included in the purchase price, unless otherwise specified, are owned by Seller.
(5) All items included shall be transferred free of liens and without Seller warranty.

C. ITEMS EXCLUDED FROM SALE: _____

9. BUYER'S INVESTIGATION OF PROPERTY AND MATTERS AFFECTING PROPERTY:

A. Buyer's acceptance of the condition of, and any other matter affecting the Property, is a contingency of this Agreement as specified in this paragraph and paragraph 14B. Within the time specified in paragraph 14B(1), Buyer shall have the right, at Buyer's expense unless otherwise agreed, to conduct inspections, investigations, tests, surveys and other studies ("Buyer Investigations"), including, but not limited to, the right to: **(i)** inspect for lead-based paint and other lead-based paint hazards; **(ii)** inspect for wood destroying pests and organisms; **(iii)** review the registered sex offender database; **(iv)** confirm the insurability of Buyer and the Property; and **(v)** satisfy Buyer as to any matter specified in the attached Buyer's Inspection Advisory (C.A.R. Form BIA). Without Seller's prior written consent, Buyer shall neither make nor cause to be made: **(i)** invasive or destructive Buyer Investigations; or **(ii)** inspections by any governmental building or zoning inspector or government employee, unless required by Law.

B. Buyer shall complete Buyer Investigations and, as specified in paragraph 14B, remove the contingency or cancel this Agreement. Buyer shall give Seller, at no cost, complete Copies of all Buyer Investigation reports obtained by Buyer. Seller shall make the Property available for all Buyer Investigations. Seller shall have water, gas, electricity and all operable pilot lights on for Buyer's Investigations and through the date possession is made available to Buyer.

Buyer's Initials (_____)(_____)
Seller's Initials (_____)(_____)

Reviewed by _____ Date _____

CALIFORNIA RESIDENTIAL PURCHASE AGREEMENT (RPA-CA PAGE 3 OF 8)

Property Address: _____ Date: _____

10. REPAIRS: Repairs shall be completed prior to final verification of condition unless otherwise agreed in writing. Repairs to be performed at Seller's expense may be performed by Seller or through others, provided that the work complies with applicable Law, including governmental permit, inspection and approval requirements. Repairs shall be performed in a good, skillful manner with materials of quality and appearance comparable to existing materials. It is understood that exact restoration of appearance or cosmetic items following all Repairs may not be possible. Seller shall: **(i)** obtain receipts for Repairs performed by others; **(ii)** prepare a written statement indicating the Repairs performed by Seller and the date of such Repairs; and **(iii)** provide Copies of receipts and statements to Buyer prior to final verification of condition.

11. BUYER INDEMNITY AND SELLER PROTECTION FOR ENTRY UPON PROPERTY: Buyer shall: **(i)** keep the Property free and clear of liens; **(ii)** Repair all damage arising from Buyer Investigations; and **(iii)** indemnify and hold Seller harmless from all resulting liability, claims, demands, damages and costs. Buyer shall carry, or Buyer shall require anyone acting on Buyer's behalf to carry, policies of liability, workers' compensation and other applicable insurance, defending and protecting Seller from liability for any injuries to persons or property occurring during any Buyer Investigations or work done on the Property at Buyer's direction prior to Close Of Escrow. Seller is advised that certain protections may be afforded Seller by recording a "Notice of Non-responsibility" (C.A.R. Form NNR) for Buyer Investigations and work done on the Property at Buyer's direction. Buyer's obligations under this paragraph shall survive the termination of this Agreement.

12. TITLE AND VESTING:
   A. Within the time specified in paragraph 14, Buyer shall be provided a current preliminary (title) report, which is only an offer by the title insurer to issue a policy of title insurance and may not contain every item affecting title. Buyer's review of the preliminary report and any other matters which may affect title are a contingency of this Agreement as specified in paragraph 14B.
   B. Title is taken in its present condition subject to all encumbrances, easements, covenants, conditions, restrictions, rights and other matters, whether of record or not, as of the date of Acceptance except: **(i)** monetary liens of record unless Buyer is assuming those obligations or taking the Property subject to those obligations; and **(ii)** those matters which Seller has agreed to remove in writing.
   C. Within the time specified in paragraph 14A, Seller has a duty to disclose to Buyer all matters known to Seller affecting title, whether of record or not.
   D. At Close Of Escrow, Buyer shall receive a grant deed conveying title (or, for stock cooperative or long-term lease, an assignment of stock certificate or of Seller's leasehold interest), including oil, mineral and water rights if currently owned by Seller. Title shall vest as designated in Buyer's supplemental escrow instructions. THE MANNER OF TAKING TITLE MAY HAVE SIGNIFICANT LEGAL AND TAX CONSEQUENCES. CONSULT AN APPROPRIATE PROFESSIONAL.
   E. Buyer shall receive a CLTA/ALTA Homeowner's Policy of Title Insurance. A title company, at Buyer's request, can provide information about the availability, desirability, coverage, and cost of various title insurance coverages and endorsements. If Buyer desires title coverage other than that required by this paragraph, Buyer shall instruct Escrow Holder in writing and pay any increase in cost.

13. SALE OF BUYER'S PROPERTY:
   A. This Agreement is NOT contingent upon the sale of any property owned by Buyer.
   OR B. ☐ (If checked): The attached addendum (C.A.R. Form COP) regarding the contingency for the sale of property owned by Buyer is incorporated into this Agreement.

14. TIME PERIODS; REMOVAL OF CONTINGENCIES; CANCELLATION RIGHTS: The following time periods may only be extended, altered, modified or changed by mutual written agreement. Any removal of contingencies or cancellation under this paragraph must be in writing (C.A.R. Form CR).
   A. SELLER HAS: 7 (or ☐ _____) Days After Acceptance to deliver to Buyer all reports, disclosures and information for which Seller is responsible under paragraphs 4, 5A and B, 6A, 7B and 12.
   B. (1) BUYER HAS: 17 (or ☐ _____) Days After Acceptance, unless otherwise agreed in writing, to:
      (i) complete all Buyer Investigations; approve all disclosures, reports and other applicable information, which Buyer receives from Seller; and approve all matters affecting the Property (including lead-based paint and lead-based paint hazards as well as other information specified in paragraph 5 and insurability of Buyer and the Property); and
      (ii) return to Seller Signed Copies of Statutory and Lead Disclosures delivered by Seller in accordance with paragraph 5A.
      (2) Within the time specified in 14B(1), Buyer may request that Seller make repairs or take any other action regarding the Property (C.A.R. Form RR). Seller has no obligation to agree to or respond to Buyer's requests.
      (3) By the end of the time specified in 14B(1) (or 2I for loan contingency or 2J for appraisal contingency), Buyer shall, in writing, remove the applicable contingency (C.A.R. Form CR) or cancel this Agreement. However, if the following inspections, reports or disclosures are not made within the time specified in 14A, then Buyer has **5 (or ☐ _____) Days** after receipt of any such items, or the time specified in 14B(1), whichever is later, to remove the applicable contingency or cancel this Agreement in writing: **(i)** government-mandated inspections or reports required as a condition of closing; or **(ii)** Common Interest Disclosures pursuant to paragraph 6B.
   C. CONTINUATION OF CONTINGENCY OR CONTRACTUAL OBLIGATION; SELLER RIGHT TO CANCEL:
      (1) Seller right to Cancel; Buyer Contingencies: Seller, after first giving Buyer a Notice to Buyer to Perform (as specified below), may cancel this Agreement in writing and authorize return of Buyer's deposit if, by the time specified in this Agreement, Buyer does not remove in writing the applicable contingency or cancel this Agreement. Once all contingencies have been removed, failure of either Buyer or Seller to close escrow on time may be a breach of this Agreement.
      (2) Continuation of Contingency: Even after the expiration of the time specified in 14B(1), Buyer retains the right to make requests to Seller, remove in writing the applicable contingency or cancel this Agreement until Seller cancels this Agreement pursuant to 14C(1). Once Seller receives Buyer's written removal of all contingencies, Seller may not cancel this Agreement pursuant to 14C(1).
      (3) Seller right to Cancel; Buyer Contract Obligations: Seller, after first giving Buyer a Notice to Buyer to Perform (as specified below), may cancel this Agreement in writing and authorize return of Buyer's deposit for any of the following reasons: **(i)** if Buyer fails to deposit funds as required by 2A or 2B; **(ii)** if the funds deposited pursuant to 2A or 2B are not good when deposited; **(iii)** if Buyer fails to provide a letter as required by 2G; **(iv)** if Buyer fails to provide verification as required by 2H or 2L; **(v)** if Seller reasonably disapproves of the verification provided by 2H or 2L; **(vi)** if Buyer fails to return Statutory and Lead Disclosures as required by paragraph 5A(2); or **(vii)** if Buyer fails to sign or initial a separate liquidated damage form for an increased deposit as required by paragraph 16. **Seller is not required to give Buyer a Notice to Perform regarding Close of Escrow.**
      (4) Notice To Buyer To Perform: The Notice to Buyer to Perform (C.A.R. Form NBP) shall: **(i)** be in writing; **(ii)** be signed by Seller; and **(iii)** give Buyer at least **24 (or ☐ _____) hours** (or until the time specified in the applicable paragraph, whichever occurs last) to take the applicable action. A Notice to Buyer to Perform may not be given any earlier than **2 Days** Prior to the expiration of the applicable time for Buyer to remove a contingency or cancel this Agreement or meet a 14C(3) obligation.

Buyer's Initials (_____)(_____)
Seller's Initials (_____)(_____)

Reviewed by _____ Date _____

CALIFORNIA RESIDENTIAL PURCHASE AGREEMENT (RPA-CA PAGE 4 OF 8)

Property Address: _____   Date: _____

D. EFFECT OF BUYER'S REMOVAL OF CONTINGENCIES : If Buyer removes, in writing, any contingency or cancellation rights, unless otherwise specified in a separate written agreement between Buyer and Seller, Buyer shall conclusively be deemed to have: **(i)** completed all Buyer Investigations, and review of reports and other applicable information and disclosures pertaining to that contingency or cancellation right; **(ii)** elected to proceed with the transaction; and **(iii)** assumed all liability, responsibility and expense for Repairs or corrections pertaining to that contingency or cancellation right, or for inability to obtain financing.

E. EFFECT OF CANCELLATION ON DEPOSITS: If Buyer or Seller gives written notice of cancellation pursuant to rights duly exercised under the terms of this Agreement, Buyer and Seller agree to Sign mutual instructions to cancel the sale and escrow and release deposits, less fees and costs, to the party entitled to the funds. Fees and costs may be payable to service providers and vendors for services and products provided during escrow. **Release of funds will require mutual Signed release instructions from Buyer and Seller, judicial decision or arbitration award. A party may be subject to a civil penalty of up to $1,000 for refusal to sign such instructions if no good faith dispute exists as to who is entitled to the deposited funds (Civil Code §1057.3).**

15. FINAL VERIFICATION OF CONDITION: Buyer shall have the right to make a final inspection of the Property within 5 **(or _____) Days** Prior to Close Of Escrow, NOT AS A CONTINGENCY OF THE SALE, but solely to confirm: **(i)** the Property is maintained pursuant to paragraph 7A; **(ii)** Repairs have been completed as agreed; and **(iii)** Seller has complied with Seller's other obligations under this Agreement.

16. LIQUIDATED DAMAGES: If Buyer fails to complete this purchase because of Buyer's default, Seller shall retain, as liquidated damages, the deposit actually paid. If the Property is a dwelling with no more than four units, one of which Buyer intends to occupy, then the amount retained shall be no more than 3% of the purchase price. Any excess shall be returned to Buyer. Release of funds will require mutual, Signed release instructions from both Buyer and Seller, judicial decision or arbitration award. BUYER AND SELLER SHALL SIGN A SEPARATE LIQUIDATED DAMAGES PROVISION FOR ANY INCREASED DEPOSIT. (C.A.R. FORM RID)

| Buyer's Initials _____ / _____ | Seller's Initials _____ / _____ |

17. DISPUTE RESOLUTION:

A. MEDIATION: Buyer and Seller agree to mediate any dispute or claim arising between them out of this Agreement, or any resulting transaction, before resorting to arbitration or court action. Paragraphs 17B(2) and (3) below apply whether or not the Arbitration provision is initialed. Mediation fees, if any, shall be divided equally among the parties involved. If, for any dispute or claim to which this paragraph applies, any party commences an action without first attempting to resolve the matter through mediation, or refuses to mediate after a request has been made, then that party shall not be entitled to recover attorney fees, even if they would otherwise be available to that party in any such action. THIS MEDIATION PROVISION APPLIES WHETHER OR NOT THE ARBITRATION PROVISION IS INITIALED.

B. ARBITRATION OF DISPUTES: (1) Buyer and Seller agree that any dispute or claim in Law or equity arising between them out of this Agreement or any resulting transaction, which is not settled through mediation, shall be decided by neutral, binding arbitration, including and subject to paragraphs 17B(2) and (3) below. The arbitrator shall be a retired judge or justice, or an attorney with at least 5 years of residential real estate Law experience, unless the parties mutually agree to a different arbitrator, who shall render an award in accordance with substantive California Law. The parties shall have the right to discovery in accordance with California Code of Civil Procedure §1283.05. In all other respects, the arbitration shall be conducted in accordance with Title 9 of Part III of the California Code of Civil Procedure. Judgment upon the award of the arbitrator(s) may be entered into any court having jurisdiction. Interpretation of this agreement to arbitrate shall be governed by the Federal Arbitration Act.

(2) EXCLUSIONS FROM MEDIATION AND ARBITRATION: The following matters are excluded from mediation and arbitration: **(i)** a judicial or non-judicial foreclosure or other action or proceeding to enforce a deed of trust, mortgage or installment land sale contract as defined in California Civil Code §2985; **(ii)** an unlawful detainer action; **(iii)** the filing or enforcement of a mechanic's lien; and **(iv)** any matter that is within the jurisdiction of a probate, small claims or bankruptcy court. The filing of a court action to enable the recording of a notice of pending action, for order of attachment, receivership, injunction, or other provisional remedies, shall not constitute a waiver of the mediation and arbitration provisions.

(3) BROKERS: Buyer and Seller agree to mediate and arbitrate disputes or claims involving either or both Brokers, consistent with 17A and B, provided either or both Brokers shall have agreed to such mediation or arbitration prior to, or within a reasonable time after, the dispute or claim is presented to Brokers. Any election by either or both Brokers to participate in mediation or arbitration shall not result in Brokers being deemed parties to the Agreement.

"NOTICE: BY INITIALING IN THE SPACE BELOW YOU ARE AGREEING TO HAVE ANY DISPUTE ARISING OUT OF THE MATTERS INCLUDED IN THE 'ARBITRATION OF DISPUTES' PROVISION DECIDED BY NEUTRAL ARBITRATION AS PROVIDED BY CALIFORNIA LAW AND YOU ARE GIVING UP ANY RIGHTS YOU MIGHT POSSESS TO HAVE THE DISPUTE LITIGATED IN A COURT OR JURY TRIAL. BY INITIALING IN THE SPACE BELOW YOU ARE GIVING UP YOUR JUDICIAL RIGHTS TO DISCOVERY AND APPEAL, UNLESS THOSE RIGHTS ARE SPECIFICALLY INCLUDED IN THE 'ARBITRATION OF DISPUTES' PROVISION. IF YOU REFUSE TO SUBMIT TO ARBITRATION AFTER AGREEING TO THIS PROVISION, YOU MAY BE COMPELLED TO ARBITRATE UNDER THE AUTHORITY OF THE CALIFORNIA CODE OF CIVIL PROCEDURE. YOUR AGREEMENT TO THIS ARBITRATION PROVISION IS VOLUNTARY."

"WE HAVE READ AND UNDERSTAND THE FOREGOING AND AGREE TO SUBMIT DISPUTES ARISING OUT OF THE MATTERS INCLUDED IN THE 'ARBITRATION OF DISPUTES' PROVISION TO NEUTRAL ARBITRATION."

| Buyer's Initials _____ / _____ | Seller's Initials _____ / _____ |

RPA-CA REVISED 10/02 (PAGE 5 OF 8)

Buyer's Initials (_____)(_____)
Seller's Initials (_____)(_____)
Reviewed by _____ Date _____

CALIFORNIA RESIDENTIAL PURCHASE AGREEMENT (RPA-CA PAGE 5 OF 8)

Property Address: _____   Date: _____

18. **PRORATIONS OF PROPERTY TAXES AND OTHER ITEMS:** Unless otherwise agreed in writing, the following items shall be PAID CURRENT and prorated between Buyer and Seller as of Close Of Escrow: real property taxes and assessments, interest, rents, HOA regular, special, and emergency dues and assessments imposed prior to Close Of Escrow, premiums on insurance assumed by Buyer, payments on bonds and assessments assumed by Buyer, and payments on Mello-Roos and other Special Assessment District bonds and assessments that are now a lien. The following items shall be assumed by Buyer WITHOUT CREDIT toward the purchase price: prorated payments on Mello-Roos and other Special Assessment District bonds and assessments and HOA special assessments that are now a lien but not yet due. Property will be reassessed upon change of ownership. Any supplemental tax bills shall be paid as follows: **(i)** for periods after Close Of Escrow, by Buyer; and **(ii)** for periods prior to Close Of Escrow, by Seller. TAX BILLS ISSUED AFTER CLOSE OF ESCROW SHALL BE HANDLED DIRECTLY BETWEEN BUYER AND SELLER. Prorations shall be made based on a 30-day month.

19. **WITHHOLDING TAXES:** Seller and Buyer agree to execute any instrument, affidavit, statement or instruction reasonably necessary to comply with federal (FIRPTA) and California withholding Law, if required (C.A.R. Forms AS and AB).

20. **MULTIPLE LISTING SERVICE ("MLS"):** Brokers are authorized to report to the MLS a pending sale and, upon Close Of Escrow, the terms of this transaction to be published and disseminated to persons and entities authorized to use the information on terms approved by the MLS.

21. **EQUAL HOUSING OPPORTUNITY:** The Property is sold in compliance with federal, state and local anti-discrimination Laws.

22. **ATTORNEY FEES:** In any action, proceeding, or arbitration between Buyer and Seller arising out of this Agreement, the prevailing Buyer or Seller shall be entitled to reasonable attorney fees and costs from the non-prevailing Buyer or Seller, except as provided in paragraph 17A.

23. **SELECTION OF SERVICE PROVIDERS:** If Brokers refer Buyer or Seller to persons, vendors, or service or product providers ("Providers"), Brokers do not guarantee the performance of any Providers. Buyer and Seller may select ANY Providers of their own choosing.

24. **TIME OF ESSENCE; ENTIRE CONTRACT; CHANGES:** Time is of the essence. All understandings between the parties are incorporated in this Agreement. Its terms are intended by the parties as a final, complete and exclusive expression of their Agreement with respect to its subject matter, and may not be contradicted by evidence of any prior agreement or contemporaneous oral agreement. If any provision of this Agreement is held to be ineffective or invalid, the remaining provisions will nevertheless be given full force and effect. **Neither this Agreement nor any provision in it may be extended, amended, modified, altered or changed, except in writing Signed by Buyer and Seller.**

25. **OTHER TERMS AND CONDITIONS,** including attached supplements:
    A. ☒ Buyer's Inspection Advisory (C.A.R. Form BIA)
    B. ☐ Purchase Agreement Addendum (C.A.R. Form PAA paragraph numbers: _____)
    C. _____
       _____
       _____

26. **DEFINITIONS:** As used in this Agreement:
    A. **"Acceptance"** means the time the offer or final counter offer is accepted in writing by a party and is delivered to and personally received by the other party or that party's authorized agent in accordance with the terms of this offer or a final counter offer.
    B. **"Agreement"** means the terms and conditions of this accepted California Residential Purchase Agreement and any accepted counter offers and addenda.
    C. **"C.A.R. Form"** means the specific form referenced or another comparable form agreed to by the parties.
    D. **"Close Of Escrow"** means the date the grant deed, or other evidence of transfer of title, is recorded. If the scheduled close of escrow falls on a Saturday, Sunday or legal holiday, then close of escrow shall be the next business day after the scheduled close of escrow date.
    E. **"Copy"** means copy by any means including photocopy, NCR, facsimile and electronic.
    F. **"Days"** means calendar days, unless otherwise required by Law.
    G. **"Days After"** means the specified number of calendar days after the occurrence of the event specified, not counting the calendar date on which the specified event occurs, and ending at 11:59PM on the final day.
    H. **"Days Prior"** means the specified number of calendar days before the occurrence of the event specified, not counting the calendar date on which the specified event is scheduled to occur.
    I. **"Electronic Copy" or "Electronic Signature"** means, as applicable, an electronic copy or signature complying with California Law. Buyer and Seller agree that electronic means will not be used by either party to modify or alter the content or integrity of this Agreement without the knowledge and consent of the other.
    J. **"Law"** means any law, code, statute, ordinance, regulation, rule or order, which is adopted by a controlling city, county, state or federal legislative, judicial or executive body or agency.
    K. **"Notice to Buyer to Perform"** means a document (C.A.R. Form NBP), which shall be in writing and Signed by Seller and shall give Buyer at least 24 hours **(or as otherwise specified in paragraph 14C(4))** to remove a contingency or perform as applicable.
    L. **"Repairs"** means any repairs (including pest control), alterations, replacements, modifications or retrofitting of the Property provided for under this Agreement.
    M. **"Signed"** means either a handwritten or electronic signature on an original document, Copy or any counterpart.
    N. **Singular and Plural** terms each include the other, when appropriate.

Buyer's Initials (_____)(_____)
Seller's Initials (_____)(_____)

RPA-CA REVISED 10/02 (PAGE 6 OF 8)

Reviewed by _____ Date _____

CALIFORNIA RESIDENTIAL PURCHASE AGREEMENT (RPA-CA PAGE 6 OF 8)

Property Address: _____ Date: _____

27. AGENCY:

A. DISCLOSURE: Buyer and Seller each acknowledge prior receipt of C.A.R. Form AD "Disclosure Regarding Real Estate Agency Relationships."

B. POTENTIALLY COMPETING BUYERS AND SELLERS: Buyer and Seller each acknowledge receipt of a disclosure of the possibility of multiple representation by the Broker representing that principal. This disclosure may be part of a listing agreement, buyer-broker agreement or separate document (C.A.R. Form DA). Buyer understands that Broker representing Buyer may also represent other potential buyers, who may consider, make offers on or ultimately acquire the Property. Seller understands that Broker representing Seller may also represent other sellers with competing properties of interest to this Buyer.

C. CONFIRMATION: The following agency relationships are hereby confirmed for this transaction:
Listing Agent _____ (Print Firm Name) is the agent of (check one): ☐ the Seller exclusively; or ☐ both the Buyer and Seller.
Selling Agent _____ (Print Firm Name) (if not same as Listing Agent) is the agent of (check one): ☐ the Buyer exclusively; or ☐ the Seller exclusively; or ☐ both the Buyer and Seller. Real Estate Brokers are not parties to the Agreement between Buyer and Seller.

28. JOINT ESCROW INSTRUCTIONS TO ESCROW HOLDER:

A. The following paragraphs, or applicable portions thereof, of this Agreement constitute the joint escrow instructions of Buyer and Seller to Escrow Holder, which Escrow Holder is to use along with any related counter offers and addenda, and any additional mutual instructions to close the escrow: 1, 2, 4, 12, 13B, 14E, 18, 19, 24, 25B and C, 26, 28, 29, 32A, 33 and paragraph D of the section titled Real Estate Brokers on page 8. If a Copy of the separate compensation agreement(s) provided for in paragraph 29 or 32A, or paragraph D of the section titled Real Estate Brokers on page 8 is deposited with Escrow Holder by Broker, Escrow Holder shall accept such agreement(s) and pay out from Buyer's or Seller's funds, or both, as applicable, the Broker's compensation provided for in such agreement(s). The terms and conditions of this Agreement not set forth in the specified paragraphs are additional matters for the information of Escrow Holder, but about which Escrow Holder need not be concerned. Buyer and Seller will receive Escrow Holder's general provisions directly from Escrow Holder and will execute such provisions upon Escrow Holder's request. To the extent the general provisions are inconsistent or conflict with this Agreement, the general provisions will control as to the duties and obligations of Escrow Holder only. Buyer and Seller will execute additional instructions, documents and forms provided by Escrow Holder that are reasonably necessary to close the escrow.

B. A Copy of this Agreement shall be delivered to Escrow Holder within **3** business days after Acceptance (or ☐ _____). Buyer and Seller authorize Escrow Holder to accept and rely on Copies and Signatures as defined in this Agreement as originals, to open escrow and for other purposes of escrow. The validity of this Agreement as between Buyer and Seller is not affected by whether or when Escrow Holder Signs this Agreement.

C. Brokers are a party to the escrow for the sole purpose of compensation pursuant to paragraphs 29, 32A and paragraph D of the section titled Real Estate Brokers on page 8. Buyer and Seller irrevocably assign to Brokers compensation specified in paragraphs 29 and 32A, respectively, and irrevocably instruct Escrow Holder to disburse those funds to Brokers at Close Of Escrow or pursuant to any other mutually executed cancellation agreement. Compensation instructions can be amended or revoked only with the written consent of Brokers. Escrow Holder shall immediately notify Brokers: **(i)** if Buyer's initial or any additional deposit is not made pursuant to this Agreement, or is not good at time of deposit with Escrow Holder; or **(ii)** if Buyer and Seller instruct Escrow Holder to cancel escrow.

D. A Copy of any amendment that affects any paragraph of this Agreement for which Escrow Holder is responsible shall be delivered to Escrow Holder within **2** business days after mutual execution of the amendment.

29. BROKER COMPENSATION FROM BUYER: If applicable, upon Close Of Escrow, **Buyer** agrees to pay compensation to Broker as specified in a separate written agreement between Buyer and Broker.

30. TERMS AND CONDITIONS OF OFFER:

This is an offer to purchase the Property on the above terms and conditions. All paragraphs with spaces for initials by Buyer and Seller are incorporated in this Agreement only if initialed by all parties. If at least one but not all parties initial, a counter offer is required until agreement is reached. Seller has the right to continue to offer the Property for sale and to accept any other offer at any time prior to notification of Acceptance. Buyer has read and acknowledges receipt of a Copy of the offer and agrees to the above confirmation of agency relationships. If this offer is accepted and Buyer subsequently defaults, Buyer may be responsible for payment of Brokers' compensation. This Agreement and any supplement, addendum or modification, including any Copy, may be Signed in two or more counterparts, all of which shall constitute one and the same writing.

Buyer's Initials (_____)(_____)
Seller's Initials (_____)(_____)

RPA-CA REVISED 10/02 (PAGE 7 OF 8)

Reviewed by _____ Date _____

CALIFORNIA RESIDENTIAL PURCHASE AGREEMENT (RPA-CA PAGE 7 OF 8)

addendum needs to be signed by seller & buyer

Property Address: _____ Date: _____

31. EXPIRATION OF OFFER: This offer shall be deemed revoked and the deposit shall be returned unless the offer is Signed by Seller and a Copy of the Signed offer is personally received by Buyer, or by _____, who is authorized to receive it by 5:00 PM on the third calendar day after this offer is signed by Buyer (or, if checked, ☐ by _____ (date), at _____ AM/PM).

Date _____   Date _____
BUYER _____   BUYER _____

(Print name) _____   **(Print name)** _____

(Address) _____

32. BROKER COMPENSATION FROM SELLER:
   A. Upon Close Of Escrow, **Seller** agrees to pay compensation to Broker as specified in a separate written agreement between Seller and Broker.
   B. If escrow does not close, compensation is payable as specified in that separate written agreement.

33. ACCEPTANCE OF OFFER: Seller warrants that Seller is the owner of the Property, or has the authority to execute this Agreement. Seller accepts the above offer, agrees to sell the Property on the above terms and conditions, and agrees to the above confirmation of agency relationships. Seller has read and acknowledges receipt of a Copy of this Agreement, and authorizes Broker to deliver a Signed Copy to Buyer.
   ☐ (If checked) **SUBJECT TO ATTACHED COUNTER OFFER, DATED** _____.

Date _____   Date _____
SELLER _____   SELLER _____

(Print name) _____   **(Print name)** _____

(Address)

(_____/_____)   **CONFIRMATION OF ACCEPTANCE:** A Copy of Signed Acceptance was personally received by Buyer or Buyer's authorized **(Initials)** agent on (date) _____ at _____ AM/PM. **A binding Agreement is created when a Copy of Signed Acceptance is personally received by Buyer or Buyer's authorized agent whether or not confirmed in this document. Completion of this confirmation is not legally required In order to create a binding Agreement; it is solely intended to evidence the date that Confirmation of Acceptance has occurred.**

REAL ESTATE BROKERS:
A. **Real Estate Brokers are not parties to the Agreement between Buyer and Seller.**
B. Agency relationships are confirmed as stated in paragraph 27.
C. If specified in paragraph 2A, Agent who submitted the offer for Buyer acknowledges receipt of deposit.
D. **COOPERATING BROKER COMPENSATION:** Listing Broker agrees to pay Cooperating Broker (**Selling Firm**) and Cooperating Broker agrees to accept, out of Listing Broker's proceeds in escrow: **(i)** the amount specified in the MLS, provided Cooperating Broker is a Participant of the MLS in which the Property is offered for sale or a reciprocal MLS; or **(ii)** ☐ (if checked) the amount specified in a separate written agreement (C.A.R. Form CBC) between Listing Broker and Cooperating Broker.

Real Estate Broker (Selling Firm) _____
By _____   Date _____
Address _____ City _____ State _____ Zip _____
Telephone _____ Fax _____ E-mail _____

Real Estate Broker (Listing Firm) _____
By _____   Date _____
Address _____ City _____ State _____ Zip _____
Telephone _____ Fax _____ E-mail _____

ESCROW HOLDER ACKNOWLEDGMENT:
Escrow Holder acknowledges receipt of a Copy of this Agreement, (if checked. ☐ a deposit in the amount of $ _____), counter offer numbers _____ and _____, and agrees to act as Escrow Holder subject to paragraph 28 of this Agreement, any supplemental escrow instructions and the terms of Escrow Holder's general provisions.

Escrow Holder is advised that the date of Confirmation of Acceptance of the Agreement as between Buyer and Seller is _____

Escrow Holder _____   Escrow # _____
By _____   Date _____
Address _____
Phone/Fax/E-mail _____
Escrow Holder is licensed by the California Department of ☐ Corporations, ☐ Insurance, ☐ Real Estate. License # _____

(_____/_____)   **REJECTION OF OFFER:** No counter offer is being made. This offer was reviewed and rejected by Seller on **(Seller's Initials)** _____ (Date)

THIS FORM HAS BEEN APPROVED BY THE CALIFORNIA ASSOCIATION OF REALTORS® (C.A.R.). NO REPRESENTATION IS MADE AS TO THE LEGAL VALIDITY OR ADEQUACY OF ANY PROVISION IN ANY SPECIFIC TRANSACTION. A REAL ESTATE BROKER IS THE PERSON QUALIFIED TO ADVISE ON REAL ESTATE TRANSACTIONS. IF YOU DESIRE LEGAL OR TAX ADVICE, CONSULT AN APPROPRIATE PROFESSIONAL.

This form is available for use by the entire real estate industry. It is not intended to identify the user as a REALTOR®. REALTOR® is a registered collective membership mark which may be used only by members of the NATIONAL ASSOCIATION OF REALTORS® who subscribe to its Code of Ethics.

SURE TRAC
The System for Success™

Published by the
California Association of REALTORS®

Reviewed by _____ Date _____

EQUAL HOUSING OPPORTUNITY

RPA-CA REVISED 10/02 (PAGE 8 OF 8)
CALIFORNIA RESIDENTIAL PURCHASE AGREEMENT (RPA-CA PAGE 8 OF 8)

IDENTIFYING THE PARTIES

We generally refer to the parties to a purchase agreement as the buyer and the seller. But in many transactions there's more than one buyer and/ or more than one seller.

You must make sure that everyone who has an ownership interest in the property signs the contract. If any owner fails to sign it, the buyer may only be able to enforce the sale of a partial interest in the property, or the contract may not be enforceable at all.

EXAMPLE: A property is owned by three cousins who inherited it from their grandfather. One of the cousins has lived in South America for several years, and the other two cousins have managed the property. When they ask you to handle the sale of the property, you must be sure that the third cousin will be available to sign the sales contract, either in person or through a representative (such as an attorney in fact). Otherwise, a buyer would only be able to purchase a partial interest in the property. (Note that the absent cousin must also sign the listing agreement.)

You should also consider whether everyone who is signing the contract has contractual capacity. If one of the parties is a minor (younger than 18) or mentally incompetent, the contract should be signed by that party's legal guardian. Otherwise, the purchase agreement will be void.

MARITAL PROPERTY. Find out whether or not each buyer or seller who is going to sign the deposit receipt is married, and make sure each married party's spouse is going to sign the agreement too. In California, when community property is bought or sold, both the husband and the wife must join in the contract.

EXAMPLE: Henry and Deborah's house is community property. They've been talking about selling it for some time. While Deborah's out of town, Henry decides to surprise her. He signs a deposit receipt with the Bentleys, agreeing to sell their house for $325,000. When Deborah comes home and hears the news, she's aghast. She believes their house is worth much more than $325,000, and she isn't ready to move so soon. Deborah can call off the sale, because the house is community property and she didn't sign the contract.

Although a married person can sell his or her separate property without the spouse's consent, it's often difficult to know when property owned by a married person is community property or separate property. It's not your job to determine the status of the property, so it's always best to get both spouses to sign all documents related to the transaction. If they have questions about the separate or community status of their property, they should consult an attorney.

When filling in the names of a married couple, state each name separately. For example, you would write "Edward K. Hardy and Joanna T. Hardy," not "Mr. and Mrs. Edward K. Hardy." You may want to identify married sellers; for example, "Edward K. Hardy and Joanna T. Hardy, a married couple." However, to avoid any claims of discrimination, you should not identify buyers in terms related to marital status (e.g., an unmarried woman, husband and wife, etc.).

OTHER FORMS OF CO-OWNERSHIP. When property is owned as a tenancy in common or in joint tenancy, all of the owners must sign the deposit receipt in order to convey full ownership to the buyer. However, an individual tenant in common or joint tenant can convey his or her own interest without the consent of the other owner(s).

BUSINESS ASSOCIATIONS AS PARTIES. When one of the parties to the contract is a partnership, the names of all of the general partners (and their spouses) and the name of the partnership itself should appear in the contract. For both partnerships and corporations, the company's address and the state in which it is organized or incorporated should also be shown.

For partnerships, corporations, and other types of associations, legal authority to enter into the transaction must be established. Before closing, the escrow agent (or other closing agent) will require documentation proving that a partner or a corporate officer has authority to sign on behalf of the association. The documentation could be in the form of a power of attorney (see below) or a resolution of the board of directors. If there's any doubt about who needs to sign the documents, it's best to get the advice of a lawyer.

ESTATES AND TRUSTS. When property that is part of an estate is sold, the personal representative or executor of the estate must sign the deposit receipt and other documents. To sell property that is part of a trust, the trustee must sign the documents.

ATTORNEYS IN FACT. If a party to a contract is unavailable or unable to sign the contract documents, a personal representative may be authorized to sign on his behalf. Authorization to sign for someone else is granted by a written document called a **power of attorney**. The authorized person is referred to as an **attorney in fact**. The power of attorney is valid only while the person who granted it is still alive and mentally competent. A power of attorney pertaining to real property must be recorded in the county where the property is located.

When an attorney in fact signs for another person, she usually signs that person's name and then writes her own name beneath it:

Michelle H. Plunkett
by Sarah R. Johnson, her Attorney in Fact

In a sale you're involved in, if an attorney in fact is going to sign any of the documents, ask to see a copy of the power of attorney.

PROPERTY DESCRIPTION

To be enforceable, a purchase agreement must have an unambiguous description of the property. A complete legal description should always be used. Don't assume that either the street address or the property tax identification number will be enough. Tax numbers are subject to change, and the description in the tax statement might be incomplete.

When there isn't enough room for the property's legal description on the form, an addendum containing the description should be attached. Put a reference to the addendum in the space provided for the property description (for example, "See Addendum A"). If the legal description is complicated, photocopy it from the seller's deed or get a photocopy from a title company. That way, you'll avoid the transcription mistakes that commonly occur when a complicated description is copied by hand.

PURCHASE PRICE AND METHOD OF PAYMENT

The full purchase price, including any mortgages or other liens that the buyer is going to assume, should be stated in the agreement. For example, if the buyer is going to assume the seller's mortgage, which has a remaining principal balance of $297,000, and also give the seller $55,000 in cash at closing, then you should fill in $352,000 as the purchase price on the deposit receipt form.

Most residential deposit receipts are contingent on financing; in other words, the agreement will not be binding unless the buyer is able to obtain a loan. This requires a contingency provision, which is typically set forth in the agreement itself. The financing contingency provision may specify the downpayment the buyer is willing to make and the loan amount and terms he will apply for. The provision may also state the buyer's duty to make a good faith effort to obtain financing. Financing contingencies are discussed in Chapter 7, and an example is shown in Figure 7.1.

Some transactions are financed completely or partially by the seller. The seller may accept a cash downpayment with a real estate contract or a deed of trust for all or part of the remainder of the purchase price. In that case, the interest rate, payment amount, and other terms for the seller financing must be included in the deposit receipt. The parties can use a form such as the seller financing addendum shown in Figure 6.2 to include the additional financing terms. (For more information about seller financing, see Chapter 9. Seller financing disclosure requirements are discussed in Chapter 8.)

RECEIPT FOR GOOD FAITH DEPOSIT

As you know, the purchase agreement serves as the buyer's receipt for the good faith deposit. The agreement should state the amount of the deposit and how it will be held. As we explained in Chapter 5, the agreement should also state whether the deposit is in the form of cash, a money order, a check, or a promissory note.

In most cases, the buyer gives the selling agent a personal check for the deposit, and the deposit receipt provides that the selling broker will hold the check undeposited until the seller has accepted the buyer's offer. That makes it easy to return the deposit to the buyer if the seller rejects the offer. (See Chapter 5.)

CLOSING DATE

The closing date is the date when the proceeds of the sale are disbursed to the seller, the deed is delivered to the buyer, and all the appropriate

FIG. 6.2   SELLER FINANCING ADDENDUM

CALIFORNIA ASSOCIATION OF REALTORS®

SELLER FINANCING ADDENDUM AND DISCLOSURE
(California Civil Code §§2956-2967)

(C.A.R. Form SFA, Revised 10/02)

This is an addendum to the ☐ California Residential Purchase Agreement, ☐ Counter Offer, or ☐ Other _____
_____, ("Agreement"), dated _____
On property known as _____ ("Property"),
between _____ ("Buyer"),
and _____ ("Seller").
Seller agrees to extend credit to Buyer as follows:

1. **PRINCIPAL; INTEREST; PAYMENT; MATURITY TERMS:** ☐ Principal amount $ _____, interest at _____%
   per annum, payable at approximately $ _____ per ☐ month, ☐ year, or ☐ other _____,
   remaining principal balance due in _____ years.

2. **LOAN APPLICATION; CREDIT REPORT:** Within **5 (or** ☐ _____**) Days** After Acceptance: **(a)** Buyer shall provide Seller a completed
   loan application on a form acceptable to Seller (such as a FNMA/FHLMC Uniform Residential Loan Application for residential one to four
   unit properties); and **(b)** Buyer authorizes Seller and/or Agent to obtain, at Buyer's expense, a copy of Buyer's credit report. Buyer shall
   provide any supporting documentation reasonably requested by Seller. Seller, after first giving Buyer a Notice to Buyer to Perform, may
   cancel this Agreement in writing and authorize return of Buyer's deposit if Buyer fails to provide such documents within that time, or if
   Seller disapproves any above item within **5 (or** ☐ _____**) Days** After receipt of each item.

3. **CREDIT DOCUMENTS:** This extension of credit by Seller will be evidenced by: ☐ Note and deed of trust; ☐ All-inclusive
   note and deed of trust; ☐ Installment land sale contract; ☐ Lease/option (when parties intend transfer of equitable title);
   OR ☐ Other (specify) _____

**THE FOLLOWING TERMS APPLY ONLY IF CHECKED. SELLER IS ADVISED TO READ ALL TERMS, EVEN THOSE NOT
CHECKED, TO UNDERSTAND WHAT IS OR IS NOT INCLUDED, AND, IF NOT INCLUDED, THE CONSEQUENCES THEREOF.**

4. ☐ **LATE CHARGE:** If any payment is not made within _____ **Days** After it is due, a late charge of either $ _____
   or _____% of the installment due, may be charged to Buyer. **NOTE:** On single family residences that Buyer intends to occupy,
   California Civil Code §2954.4(a) limits the late charge to no more than 6% of the total installment payment due and requires a
   grace period of no less than 10 days.

5. ☐ **BALLOON PAYMENT:** The extension of credit will provide for a balloon payment, in the amount of $ _____,
   plus any accrued interest, which is due on _____ (date).

6. ☐ **PREPAYMENT:** If all or part of this extension of credit is paid early, Seller may charge a prepayment penalty as follows (if
   applicable): _____. Caution: California Civil Code
   §2954.9 contains limitations on prepayment penalties for residential one-to-four unit properties.

7. ☐ **DUE ON SALE:** If any interest in the Property is sold or otherwise transferred, Seller has the option to require immediate
   payment of the entire unpaid principal balance, plus any accrued interest.

8.* ☐ **REQUEST FOR COPY OF NOTICE OF DEFAULT:** A request for a copy of Notice of Default as defined in California Civil
   Code §2924b will be recorded. **If Not,** Seller is advised to consider recording a Request for Notice of Default.

9.* ☐ **REQUEST FOR NOTICE OF DELINQUENCY:** A request for Notice of Delinquency, as defined in California Civil Code §2924e,
   to be signed and paid for by Buyer, will be made to senior lienholders. **If not,** Seller is advised to consider making a Request for
   Notice of Delinquency. Seller is advised to check with senior lienholders to verify whether they will honor this request.

10.* ☐ **TAX SERVICE:**
   A. If property taxes on the Property become delinquent, tax service will be arranged to report to Seller. **If not,** Seller is
   advised to consider retaining a tax service, or to otherwise determine that property taxes are paid.
   B. ☐ Buyer, ☐ Seller, shall be responsible for the initial and continued retention of, and payment for, such tax service.

11. ☐ **TITLE INSURANCE:** Title insurance coverage will be provided to **both** Seller and Buyer, insuring their respective interests
   in the Property. **If not,** Buyer and Seller are advised to consider securing such title insurance coverage.

12. ☐ **HAZARD INSURANCE:**
   A. The parties' escrow holder or insurance carrier will be directed to include a loss payee endorsement, adding Seller to
   the Property insurance policy. **If not,** Seller is advised to secure such an endorsement, or acquire a separate
   insurance policy.
   B. Property insurance **does not** include earthquake or flood insurance coverage, unless checked:
   ☐ Earthquake insurance will be obtained; ☐ Flood insurance will be obtained.

13. ☐ **PROCEEDS TO BUYER:** Buyer will receive cash proceeds at the close of the sale transaction. The amount received will be
   approximately $ _____, from _____ (indicate source of
   proceeds). Buyer represents that the purpose of such disbursement is as follows: _____.

14. ☐ **NEGATIVE AMORTIZATION; DEFERRED INTEREST:** Negative amortization results when Buyer's periodic payments are
   less than the amount of interest earned on the obligation. Deferred interest also results when the obligation does not
   require periodic payments for a period of time. In either case, interest is not payable as it accrues. This accrued interest
   will have to be paid by Buyer at a later time, and may result in Buyer owing more on the obligation than at its origination.
   The credit being extended to Buyer by Seller will provide for negative amortization or deferred interest as indicated below.
   (Check A, B, or C. CHECK ONE ONLY.)
   ☐ **A.** All negative amortization or deferred interest shall be added to the principal _____
   (e.g., annually, monthly, etc.), and thereafter shall bear interest at the rate specified in the credit documents (compound interest);
   OR ☐ **B.** All deferred interest shall be due and payable, along with principal, at maturity;
   OR ☐ **C.** Other _____

*(For Paragraphs 8-10) In order to receive timely and continued notification, Seller is advised to record appropriate notices and/or to
notify appropriate parties of any change in Seller's address.

Buyer's Initials (_____)(_____)
Seller's Initials (_____)(_____)

Reviewed by _____ Date _____

SFA REVISED 10/02 (PAGE 1 OF 3) Print Date

SELLER FINANCING ADDENDUM AND DISCLOSURE (SFA PAGE 1 OF 3)

Reprinted with permission, California Association of Realtors®. No endorsement implied.

Property Address: _____ Date: _____

15. ☐ ALL-INCLUSIVE DEED OF TRUST; INSTALLMENT LAND SALE CONTRACT: This transaction involves the use of an all-inclusive (or wraparound) deed of trust or an installment land sale contract. That deed of trust or contract shall provide as follows:
A. In the event of an acceleration of any senior encumbrance, the responsibility for payment, or for legal defense is: _____ ; OR ☐ **Is not** specified in the credit or security documents.
B. In the event of the prepayment of a senior encumbrance, the responsibilities and rights of Buyer and Seller regarding refinancing, prepayment penalties, and any prepayment discounts are: _____ ; OR ☐ **Are not** specified in the documents evidencing credit.
C. Buyer will make periodic payments to _____ (Seller, collection agent, or any neutral third party), who will be responsible for disbursing payments to the payee(s) on the senior encumbrance(s) and to Seller. **NOTE:** The Parties are advised to designate a neutral third party for these purposes.

16. ☐ TAX IDENTIFICATION NUMBERS: Buyer and Seller shall each provide to each other their Social Security Numbers or Taxpayer Identification Numbers.

17. ☐ OTHER CREDIT TERMS _____

18. ☐ RECORDING: The documents evidencing credit (paragraph 3) will be recorded with the county recorder where the Property is located. **If not**, Buyer and Seller are advised that their respective interests in the Property may be jeopardized by intervening liens, judgments, encumbrances, or subsequent transfers.

19. ☐ JUNIOR FINANCING: There will be additional financing, secured by the Property, junior to this Seller financing. Explain: _____

20. SENIOR LOANS AND ENCUMBRANCES: The following information is provided on loans and/or encumbrances that will be **senior** to Seller financing. **NOTE:** The following are estimates, unless otherwise marked with an asterisk (*). If checked: ☐ A separate sheet with information on additional senior loans/encumbrances is attached

		1st	2nd
A.	Original Balance	$ _____	$ _____
B.	Current Balance	$ _____	$ _____
C.	Periodic Payment (e.g. $100/month):	$ _____	$ _____ /
	Including Impounds of:	$ _____	$ _____ /
D.	Interest Rate (per annum)	_____ %	_____ %
E.	Fixed or Variable Rate:	_____	_____
	If Variable Rate: Lifetime Cap (Ceiling)	_____	_____
	Indicator (Underlying Index)	_____	_____
	Margins	_____	_____
F.	Maturity Date	_____	_____
G.	Amount of Balloon Payment	$ _____	$ _____
H.	Date Balloon Payment Due	_____	_____
I.	Potential for Negative Amortization? (Yes, No, or Unknown)	_____	_____
J.	Due on Sale? (Yes, No, or Unknown)	_____	_____
K.	Pre-payment penalty? (Yes, No, or Unknown)	_____	_____
L.	Are payments current? (Yes, No, or Unknown)	_____	_____

21. BUYER'S CREDITWORTHINESS: (CHECK EITHER A OR B. Do not check both.) In addition to the loan application, credit report and other information requested under paragraph 2:
A. ☐ No other disclosure concerning Buyer's creditworthiness has been made to Seller;
OR B. ☐ The following representations concerning Buyer's creditworthiness are made by Buyer(s) to Seller:

Borrower	**Co-Borrower**
1. Occupation _____	1. Occupation _____
2. Employer _____	2. Employer _____
3. Length of Employment _____	3. Length of Employment _____
4. Monthly Gross Income _____	4. Monthly Gross Income _____
5. Other _____	5. Other _____

22. ADDED, DELETED OR SUBSTITUTED BUYERS: The addition, deletion or substitution of any person or entity under this Agreement or to title prior to close of escrow shall require Seller's written consent. Seller may grant or withhold consent in Seller's sole discretion. Any additional or substituted person or entity shall, if requested by Seller, submit to Seller the same documentation as required for the original named Buyer. Seller and/or Brokers may obtain a credit report, at Buyer's expense, on any such person or entity.

Buyer's Initials (_____)(_____)
Seller's Initials (_____)(_____)

Reviewed by _____ Date _____

SFA REVISED 10/02 (PAGE 2 OF 3)

SELLER FINANCING ADDENDUM AND DISCLOSURE (SFA PAGE 2 OF 3)

Property Address: _____   Date: _____

23. CAUTION:

A. If the Seller financing requires a balloon payment, Seller shall give Buyer written notice, according to the terms of Civil Code §2966, at least 90 and not more than 150 days before the balloon payment is due if the transaction is for the purchase of a dwelling for not more than four families.

B. If **any** obligation secured by the Property calls for a balloon payment, Seller and Buyer are aware that refinancing of the balloon payment at maturity may be difficult or impossible, depending on conditions in the conventional mortgage marketplace at that time. There are no assurances that new financing or a loan extension will be available when the balloon prepayment, or any prepayment, is due.

C. If **any** of the existing or proposed loans or extensions of credit would require refinancing as a result of a lack of full amortization, such refinancing might be difficult or impossible in the conventional mortgage marketplace.

D. In the event of default by Buyer: (1) Seller may have to reinstate and/or make monthly payments on any and all senior encumbrances (including real property taxes) in order to protect Seller's secured interest; (2) Seller's rights are generally limited to foreclosure on the Property, pursuant to California Code of Civil Procedure §580b; and (3) the Property may lack sufficient equity to protect Seller's interests if the Property decreases in value.

If this three-page Addendum and Disclosure is used in a transaction for the purchase of a dwelling for not more than four families, it shall be prepared by an Arranger of Credit as defined in California Civil Code §2957(a). (The Arranger of Credit is usually the agent who obtained the offer.)

Arranger of Credit - (Print Firm Name) _____   By _____   Date _____

Address _____   City _____   State _____   Zip _____

Phone _____   Fax _____

> BUYER AND SELLER ACKNOWLEDGE AND AGREE THAT BROKERS: (A) WILL NOT PROVIDE LEGAL OR TAX ADVICE; (B) WILL NOT PROVIDE OTHER ADVICE OR INFORMATION THAT EXCEEDS THE KNOWLEDGE, EDUCATION AND EXPERIENCE REQUIRED TO OBTAIN A REAL ESTATE LICENSE; OR (C) HAVE NOT AND WILL NOT VERIFY ANY INFORMATION PROVIDED BY EITHER BUYER OR SELLER. BUYER AND SELLER AGREE THAT THEY WILL SEEK LEGAL, TAX AND OTHER DESIRED ASSISTANCE FROM APPROPRIATE PROFESSIONALS. BUYER AND SELLER ACKNOWLEDGE THAT THE INFORMATION EACH HAS PROVIDED TO THE ARRANGER OF CREDIT FOR INCLUSION IN THIS DISCLOSURE FORM IS ACCURATE. BUYER AND SELLER FURTHER ACKNOWLEDGE THAT EACH HAS RECEIVED A COMPLETED COPY OF THIS DISCLOSURE FORM.

Buyer _____   Date _____
        (signature)
Address _____   City _____   State _____   Zip _____
Phone _____   Fax _____   E-mail _____

Buyer _____   Date _____
        (signature)
Address _____   City _____   State _____   Zip _____
Phone _____   Fax _____   E-mail _____

Seller _____   Date _____
        (signature)
Address _____   City _____   State _____   Zip _____
Phone _____   Fax _____   E-mail _____

Seller _____   Date _____
        (signature)
Address _____   City _____   State _____   Zip _____
Phone _____   Fax _____   E-mail _____

THIS FORM HAS BEEN APPROVED BY THE CALIFORNIA ASSOCIATION OF REALTORS® (C.A.R.). NO REPRESENTATION IS MADE AS TO THE LEGAL VALIDITY OR ADEQUACY OF ANY PROVISION IN ANY SPECIFIC TRANSACTION. A REAL ESTATE BROKER IS THE PERSON QUALIFIED TO ADVISE ON REAL ESTATE TRANSACTIONS. IF YOU DESIRE LEGAL OR TAX ADVICE, CONSULT AN APPROPRIATE PROFESSIONAL.

This form is available for use by the entire real estate industry. It is not intended to identify the user as a REALTOR®. REALTOR® is a registered collective membership mark which may be used only by members of the NATIONAL ASSOCIATION OF REALTORS® who subscribe to its Code of Ethics.

SURE TRAC
The System for Success™

Published by the
California Association of REALTORS®

SFA REVISED 10/02 (PAGE 3 OF 3)

Reviewed by _____ Date _____

EQUAL HOUSING OPPORTUNITY

SELLER FINANCING ADDENDUM AND DISCLOSURE (SFA PAGE 3 OF 3)

documents are recorded. The deposit receipt usually sets a specific date for closing. A lender will be able to recommend a suitable date, based on conditions in the local finance market.

In setting a closing date, it's important to consider how long it will take to meet any conditions that the deposit receipt is contingent on (see Chapter 7) and any obligations it imposes. For example, the buyer may have to apply for a loan, which will involve an appraisal and a complete credit check. The seller may have to arrange to clear away liens and could be required to make some repairs. The chosen closing date must allow enough time for the parties to fulfill these conditions and obligations.

If the closing date is approaching and repairs have not been completed, a loan approval has not been obtained, or some other contingency has not yet been satisfied, the parties may want to change the closing date by executing a written extension agreement. The purchase agreement will terminate on the date set for closing, so try to get an extension agreement signed as soon as possible. Failure to extend the closing date may result in an unenforceable agreement. A special form may be used for an extension agreement, or it may simply be an amendment addendum in which the parties agree to defer the closing to some later date.

On the other hand, if all conditions and obligations have been fulfilled well before the date set for closing, the buyer and seller may agree to move the closing date up. This amendment should also be in writing and signed by both parties.

TRANSFER OF POSSESSION

Most deposit receipt forms have a space for filling in the date of possession, when the seller will relinquish possession of the property to the buyer. The seller usually agrees that the property will be maintained in its present condition until the buyer takes possession.

Possession is normally transferred to the buyer at closing. Sometimes the buyer wants to take possession a few days or even a few weeks earlier, or the seller wants a few extra days to vacate the property.

EXAMPLE: Jenkins is buying Hahn's home. The sale will close on October 17. However, the sale of Jenkins's current home will close on October 10. Jenkins wants to move into Hahn's home on October 7 to avoid the nuisance of moving twice. Hahn agrees to move out by October 6.

If possession is transferred before (or after) the closing date, the parties should execute a separate rental agreement. An example of a rental agreement that can be used for this purpose is shown in Figure 6.3. This agreement sets forth the dates of occupancy, the rental rate, and other terms that will govern possession during the rental period.

Transfer of possession to the buyer before closing may cause trouble for the seller if the sale fails to close. If the buyer/tenant refuses to vacate the property in accordance with the terms of the rental agreement, the seller might have to take legal action to evict him. Note that the C.A.R. deposit receipt form advises both buyers and sellers to consult their lawyers and insurance advisors before entering into such an arrangement.

CLOSING AGENT

The buyer should designate an escrow agent or other closing agent on the deposit receipt form. In many cases, the escrow department of the buyer's lender serves as the closing agent.

Closing agents may perform a wide variety of tasks, such as ordering title insurance, arranging for liens to be paid off and released, and preparing documents on behalf of both the buyer and the seller. They also hold funds and documents in escrow for the parties, distributing them only when specified conditions have been fulfilled. All of these conditions are set forth in the escrow instructions for the transaction. While the escrow instructions may be a separate document, the C.A.R. deposit receipt form incorporates the escrow instructions into the purchase agreement. (See paragraph 28 in Figure 6.1. Escrow instructions and the closing process are discussed in Chapter 10.)

A federal law called the Foreign Investment in Real Property Tax Act (FIRPTA) applies to some transactions in which the seller is not a U.S. citizen. FIRPTA requires the buyer to withhold a certain percentage of the price from the seller and turn that money over to the Internal Revenue Service. (Many residential transactions are exempt from FIRPTA. See Chapter 10.) In addition, California state law requires 3.33% of the sales price to be withheld from the seller as a prepayment of state income tax in some transactions. These withholdings are ordinarily handled by the closing agent on behalf of the parties. The deposit receipt may include a provision concerning compliance with these laws.

FIG. 6.3 INTERIM OCCUPANCY AGREEMENT

CALIFORNIA ASSOCIATION OF REALTORS®

INTERIM OCCUPANCY AGREEMENT
Buyer in Possession Prior to Close of Escrow
(C.A.R. Form IOA, Revised 4/03)

_____ ("Seller/Landlord")
and _____ ("Buyer/Tenant")
have entered into a purchase agreement for the real property described below. Close of escrow for the purchase agreement is scheduled
to occur on _____ (date). Seller, as Landlord, and Buyer, as Tenant, agree as follows:

1. **PROPERTY:**
   A. Landlord rents to Tenant and Tenant rents from Landlord, the real property and improvements described as: _____
   _____ ("Premises").
   B. The Premises are for the sole use as a personal residence by the following named persons **only:** _____
   _____
   C. The personal property listed in the purchase agreement, maintained pursuant to paragraph 11, is included.

2. **TERM:** The term begins on (date) _____ ("Commencement Date") and shall terminate
   at _____ ☐AM/☐PM on the earliest: of **(a)** the date scheduled for close of escrow of the purchase agreement as specified above,
   or as modified in writing; or **(b)** mutual cancellation of the purchase agreement. Tenant shall vacate the Premises upon termination
   of this Agreement, unless **(i)** landlord and tenant have signed a new agreement, **(ii)** mandated by local rent control law, or **(iii)**
   Landlord accepts Rent from Tenant (other than past due Rent), in which case a month-to-month tenancy shall be created which either
   party may terminate pursuant to California Civil Code § 1946.1. Rent shall be at a rate agreed to by Landlord and Tenant, or as
   allowed by law. All other terms and conditions of this Agreement shall remain in full force and effect.

3. **RENT:** "Rent" shall mean all monetary obligations of Tenant to Landlord under the terms of this Agreement, except security deposit.
   A. Tenant agrees to pay $ _____ per month for the term of this Agreement.
   B. Rent is payable in advance on the **1st (or ☐ ____) day** of each calendar week, and is delinquent on the next day; or ☐ in full at
   close of escrow; or ☐ _____ .
   C. PAYMENT: The Rent shall be paid by ☐ cash, ☐ personal check, ☐ money order, ☐ cashier check, ☐ through escrow (per
   escrow instructions), ☐ other _____ to (name) _____
   (phone) _____ at (address) _____ ,
   (or at any other location specified by Landlord in writing to Tenant) between the hours of _____ and _____ on the following
   days: _____. If any payment is returned for non-sufficient
   funds ("NSF") or other reason then all future Rent shall be paid by ☐ cash, ☐ money order, ☐ cashier check.

4. **SECURITY DEPOSIT:**
   A. Tenant agrees to pay $ _____ as a security deposit. Security deposit will be
   ☐ transferred to and held by Seller; ☐ held in Seller's Broker's trust account; or ☐ held in escrow (per escrow instructions).
   B. **(1)** If the tenancy is terminated due to the close of escrow by Buyer under the purchase agreement, the full amount of the security
   deposit, less any deductions below, shall be credited to Buyer's down payment on the purchase (or, if checked ☐ returned to
   Buyer from Seller's proceeds in escrow). If required by lender for closing, Seller shall place the security deposit into escrow
   prior to the signing of loan documents by Buyer.
   (2) All or any portion of the security deposit may be used, as reasonably necessary, to: **(i)** cure Tenant's default in payment of Rent
   (which includes Late Charges, NSF fees or other sums due); **(ii)** repair damage, excluding ordinary wear and tear, caused by Tenant
   or by a guest or licensee of Tenant; **(iii)** clean Premises, if necessary, upon termination of the tenancy; and **(iv)** replace or return
   personal property or appurtenances. **SECURITY DEPOSIT SHALL NOT BE USED BY TENANT IN LIEU OF PAYMENT OF
   LAST MONTH'S RENT.** If all or any portion of the security deposit is used during the tenancy, Tenant agrees to reinstate
   the total security deposit within 5 days after written notice is delivered to Tenant.
   (3) Within three weeks after Tenant vacates the Premises, Landlord shall: **(i)** furnish Tenant an itemized statement indicating
   the amount of any security deposit received and the basis for its disposition; and **(ii)** return any remaining portion of the
   security deposit to Tenant.
   C. Except when escrow closes, security deposit will not be returned until all Tenants have vacated the Premises. Any security
   deposit returned by check shall be made out to all Tenants named on this Agreement, or as subsequently modified.
   D. No interest will be paid on security deposit unless required by local ordinance.
   E. If the security deposit is held by Seller, Tenant agrees not to hold Seller responsible for its return. If the security deposit is held in
   Seller's Broker's trust account, **and** Broker's authority is terminated before expiration of this Agreement, **and** security deposit is
   released to someone other than Tenant, **then** Broker shall notify Tenant, in writing, where and to whom security deposit has been
   released. Once Tenant has been provided such notice, Tenant agrees not to hold Broker responsible for the security deposit.

5. **MOVE-IN COSTS RECEIVED/DUE:** Move-in funds made payable to _____ shall be
   paid by ☐ cash, ☐ personal check, ☐ money order, ☐ cashier check, ☐ through escrow (per escrow instructions)

Category	Total Due	Payment Received	Balance Due	Date Due
Rent from _____ to _____ (date)				
*Security Deposit				
Other _____				
Other _____				
Total				

*The maximum amount Landlord may receive as security deposit, however designated, cannot exceed two months' Rent for
unfurnished premises, or three months' Rent for furnished premises.

IOA REVISED 4/03 (PAGE 1 OF 6) Print Date

Tenant's Initials (_____)(_____)
Landlord's Initials (_____)(_____)
Reviewed by _____ Date _____

INTERIM OCCUPANCY AGREEMENT (IOA PAGE 1 OF 6)

Reprinted with permission, California Association of Realtors®. No endorsement implied.

Premises: _____   Date: _____

6. LATE CHARGE;RETURNED CHECKS:
   A. Tenant acknowledges either late payment of Rent or issuance of a returned check may cause Landlord to incur costs and expenses, the exact amounts of which are extremely difficult and impractical to determine. These costs may include, but are not limited to, processing, enforcement and accounting expenses, and late charges imposed on Landlord. If any installment of Rent due from Tenant is not received by Landlord within **5 (or ☐ _____)** **calendar days** after the date due, or if a check is returned, Tenant shall pay to Landlord, respectively, an additional sum of $ _____ or _____% of the Rent due as a Late Charge and $25.00 as a NSF fee for the first returned check and $35.00 as a NSF fee for each additional returned check, either or both of which shall be deemed additional Rent.
   B. Landlord and Tenant agree these charges represent a fair and reasonable estimate of the costs Landlord may incur by reason of Tenant's late or NSF payment. Any Late Charge or NSF fee due shall be paid with the current installment of Rent. Landlord's acceptance of any Late Charge or NSF fee shall not constitute a waiver as to any default of Tenant. Landlord's right to collect a Late Charge or NSF fee shall not be deemed an extension of the date Rent is due under paragraph 3 or prevent Landlord from exercising any other rights and remedies under this Agreement and as provided by law.

7. PARKING: (Check A or B)
   ☐ **A.** Parking is permitted as follows: _____
   _____
   The right to parking ☐ is ☐ is not included in the Rent charged pursuant to paragraph 3. If not included in the Rent, the parking rental fee shall be an additional $ _____ per month. Parking space(s) are to be used for parking properly licensed and operable motor vehicles, except for trailers, boats, campers, buses or trucks (other than pick-up trucks). Tenant shall park in assigned space(s) only. Parking space(s) are to be kept clean. Vehicles leaking oil, gas or other motor vehicle fluids shall not be parked on the Premises. Mechanical work or storage of inoperable vehicles is not permitted in parking space(s) or elsewhere on the Premises.
   OR ☐ **B.** Parking is not permitted on the Premises.

8. STORAGE: (Check A or B)
   ☐ **A.** Storage is permitted as follows:
   The right to storage space ☐ is ☐ is not included in the Rent charged pursuant to paragraph 3. If not included in the Rent, storage space fee shall be an additional $ _____ per month. Tenant shall store only personal property Tenant owns, and shall not store property claimed by another or in which another has any right, title or interest. Tenant shall not store any improperly packaged food or perishable goods, flammable materials, explosives, hazardous waste or other inherently dangerous material, or illegal substances.
   OR ☐ **B.** Storage is not permitted on the Premises.

9. UTILITIES: Tenant agrees to pay for all utilities and services, and the following charges: _____ except _____, which shall be paid for by Landlord. If any utilities are not separately metered, Tenant shall pay Tenant's proportional share, as reasonably determined and directed by Landlord. If utilities are separately metered, Tenant shall place utilities in Tenant's name as of the Commencement Date. Landlord is only responsible for installing and maintaining one usable telephone jack and one telephone line to the Premises. Tenant shall pay any cost for conversion from existing utilities service provider.

10. CONDITION OF PREMISES: Tenant has examined Premises, all furniture, furnishings, appliances, landscaping, if any, and fixtures, including smoke detector(s).
   (Check all that apply:)
   ☐ **A.** Tenant acknowledges these items are clean and in operable condition, with the following exceptions: _____
   ☐ **B.** Tenant's acknowledgment of the condition of these items is contained in an attached statement of condition (C.A.R. Form MIMO).
   ☐ **C.** Tenant will provide Landlord a list of items that are damaged or not in operable condition within **3 (or ☐ _____) days** after Commencement Date, not as a contingency of the Agreement but rather as an acknowledgment of the condition of the Premises.
   ☐ **D.** Other: _____

11. MAINTENANCE:
   A. Tenant shall properly use, operate and safeguard Premises, including if applicable, any landscaping, furniture, furnishings and appliances, and all mechanical, electrical, gas and plumbing fixtures, and keep them and the Premises clean, sanitary and well ventilated. Tenant shall be responsible for checking and maintaining all smoke detectors and any additional phone lines beyond the one line and jack that Landlord shall provide and maintain. Tenant shall immediately notify Landlord, in writing, of any problem, malfunction or damage. Tenant shall be charged for all repairs or replacements caused by Tenant, pets, guests or licensees of Tenant, excluding ordinary wear and tear. Tenant shall be charged for all damage to Premises as a result of failure to report a problem in a timely manner. Tenant shall be charged for repair of drain blockages or stoppages, unless caused by defective plumbing parts or tree roots invading sewer lines.
   B. ☐ Landlord ☐ Tenant shall water the garden, landscaping, trees and shrubs, except: _____
   C. ☐ Landlord ☐ Tenant shall maintain the garden, landscaping, trees and shrubs, except: _____
   D. ☐ Landlord ☐ Tenant shall maintain _____
   E. Tenant's failure to maintain any item for which Tenant is responsible shall give Landlord the right to hire someone to perform such maintenance and charge Tenant to cover the cost of such maintenance.
   F. The following items of personal property are included in the Premises without warranty and Landlord will not maintain, repair or replace them: _____

Copyright © 1995-2003, CALIFORNIA ASSOCIATION OF REALTORS®, INC.
IOA REVISED 4/03 (PAGE 2 OF 6)

Tenant's Initials (_____)(_____)
Landlord's Initials (_____)(_____)
Reviewed by _____ Date _____

INTERIM OCCUPANCY AGREEMENT   (IOA PAGE 2 OF 6)

Premises: _____ Date: _____

12. NEIGHBORHOOD CONDITIONS: Tenant is advised to satisfy him or herself as to neighborhood or area conditions, including schools, proximity and adequacy of law enforcement, crime statistics, proximity of registered felons or offenders, fire protection, other governmental services, availability, adequacy and cost of any speed-wired, wireless internet connections or other telecommunications or other technology services and installations, proximity to commercial, industrial or agricultural activities, existing and proposed transportation, construction and development that may affect noise, view, or traffic, airport noise, noise or odor from any source, wild and domestic animals, other nuisances, hazards, or circumstances, cemeteries, facilities and condition of common areas, conditions and influences of significance to certain cultures and/or religions, and personal needs, requirements and preferences of Tenant.

13. PETS: Unless otherwise provided in California Civil Code § 54.2, no animal or pet shall be kept on or about the Premises without Landlord's prior written consent, except: _____

14. RULES;REGULATIONS:
A. Tenant agrees to comply with all Landlord rules and regulations that are at any time posted on the Premises or delivered to Tenant. Tenant shall not, and shall ensure that guests and licensees of Tenant shall not, disturb, annoy, endanger or interfere with other tenants of the building or neighbors, or use the Premises for any unlawful purposes, including, but not limited to, using, manufacturing, selling, storing, or transporting illicit drugs or other contraband, or violate any law or ordinance, or commit a waste or nuisance on or about the Premises.
B. (If applicable, check one:)
  ☐ **(1)** Landlord shall provide Tenant with a copy of the rules and regulations within _____ days or _____.
OR ☐ **(2)** Tenant has been provided with and acknowledges receipt of, a copy of the rules and regulations.

15. ☐ (If checked) **CONDOMINIUM;PLANNED UNIT DEVELOPMENT:**
A. The Premises is a unit in a condominium, planned unit, development or other common interest subdivision governed by a homeowners' association ("HOA"). The name of the HOA is _____.
Tenant agrees to comply with all HOA covenants, conditions and restrictions, bylaws, rules and regulations and decisions. Tenant shall reimburse Landlord for any fines or charges imposed by HOA or other authorities, due to any violation by Tenant, or the guests or licensees of Tenant.
B. (Check one:)
  ☐ **(1)** Landlord shall provide Tenant with a copy of the HOA rules and regulations within _____ days or _____.
OR ☐ **(2)** Tenant has been provided with, and acknowledges receipt of, a copy of the HOA rules and regulations.

16. ALTERATIONS;REPAIRS: Unless otherwise specified by law or paragraph 27C or pursuant to the purchase agreement, without Landlord's prior written consent, **(i)** Tenant shall not make any repairs, alterations or improvements in or about the Premises including: painting, wallpapering, adding or changing locks, installing antenna or satellite dish(es), placing signs, displays or exhibits, or using screws, fastening devices, large nails or adhesive materials; **(ii)** Landlord shall not be responsible for the costs of repairs, alterations or improvements made by Tenant; **(iii)** Tenant shall not deduct from Rent the costs of any repairs, alterations or improvements; and **(iv)** any deduction made by Tenant shall be considered unpaid Rent. Tenant shall immediately notify Landlord if Tenant, individually or by or through others, commences any work on the Premises. Tenant shall be charged for any costs Landlord incurs to post and record a Notice of NonResponsibility for any such work. Upon completion of any such work, Tenant shall notify Landlord. Tenant shall be charged for any costs Landlord incurs to post and record a Notice of Completion relating to any such work. Tenant agrees to indemnify, defend and hold harmless Landlord for any mechanic's lien attaching to the Premises or other claim resulting from any work ordered by Tenant.

17. KEYS;LOCKS:
A. Tenant acknowledges receipt of (or Tenant will receive ☐ prior to the Commencement Date, or ☐ _____);
  ☐ _____ key(s) to Premises,   ☐ _____ remote control device(s) for garage door/gate opener(s),
  ☐ _____ key(s) to mailbox,   ☐ _____
  ☐ _____ key(s) to common area(s),   ☐ _____
B. Tenant acknowledges that locks to the Premises ☐ have, ☐ have not, been re-keyed.
C. If Tenant re-keys existing locks or opening devices, Tenant shall immediately deliver copies of all keys to Landlord. Tenant shall pay all costs and charges related to loss of any keys or opening devices. Tenant may not remove locks, even if installed by Tenant.

18. ENTRY:
A. Tenant shall make Premises available to Landlord or Landlord's representative for the purpose of entering to make necessary or agreed repairs, decorations, alterations, or improvements, or to supply necessary or agreed services, or to show Premises to prospective or actual purchasers, tenants, mortgagees, lenders, appraisers, or contractors.
B. Landlord and Tenant agree that 24-hour written notice shall be reasonable and sufficient notice. However, if the purpose of the entry is to: **(i)** show the Premises to actual or prospective purchasers, the notice may be given orally provided Tenant has been notified in writing within 120 days preceding the oral notice that the Premises are for sale and that oral notice may be given to show the Premises; or **(ii)** conduct an inspection of the Premises prior to the Tenant moving out, 48-hour written notice is required unless the Tenant waives the right to such notice; or **(iii)** enter in case of an emergency, Landlord or Landlord's representative may enter Premises at any time without prior notice.
C. ☐ (If checked) Tenant authorizes the use of a keysafe/lockbox to allow entry into the Premises and agrees to sign a keysafe/lockbox addendum (C.A.R. Form KLA).

19. SIGNS: Tenant authorizes Landlord to place FOR SALE/LEASE signs on the Premises.

20. ASSIGNMENT;SUBLETTING: Tenant shall not sublet all or any part of Premises, or assign or transfer the Agreement or any interest herein, without Landlord's prior written consent. Unless such consent is obtained, any assignment, transfer or subletting of Premises or the Agreement or tenancy, by voluntary act of Tenant, operation of law or otherwise, shall be null and void and, at the option of Landlord, terminate the Agreement. Any proposed assignee, transferee or sublessee shall submit to Landlord an application and credit information for Landlord's approval and, if approved, sign a separate written agreement with Landlord and Tenant. Landlord's consent to any one assignment, transfer or sublease, shall not be construed as consent to any subsequent assignment, transfer or sublease and does not release Tenant of Tenant's obligations under the Agreement.

21. JOINT AND INDIVIDUAL OBLIGATIONS: If there is more than one Tenant, each one shall be individually and completely responsible for the performance of all obligations of Tenant under the Agreement, jointly with every other Tenant, and individually, whether or not in possession.

Tenant's Initials (_____)(_____)
Landlord's Initials (_____)(_____)

IOA REVISED 4/03 (PAGE 3 OF 6)

Reviewed by _____ Date _____

INTERIM OCCUPANCY AGREEMENT (IOA PAGE 3 OF 6)

Premises: _____   Date: _____

22. ☐ **LEAD-BASED PAINT (If Checked):** Premises was constructed prior to 1978. In accordance with federal law, Landlord gives and Tenant acknowledges receipt of the disclosures on the attached form (C.A.R. Form FLD) and a federally approved lead pamphlet.

23. ☐ **MILITARY ORDNANCE DISCLOSURE:** (If applicable and known to Landlord) Premises is located within one mile of an area once used for military training, and may contain potentially explosive munitions.

24. ☐ **PERIODIC PEST CONTROL:** Landlord has entered into a contract for periodic pest control treatment of the Premises and shall give Tenant a copy of the notice originally given to Landlord by the pest control company.

25. **DATABASE DISCLOSURE: NOTICE:** The California Department of Justice, sheriff's departments, police departments serving jurisdictions of 200,000 or more, and many other local law enforcement authorities maintain for public access a database of the locations of persons required to register pursuant to paragraph (1) of subdivision (a) of Section 290.4 of the Penal Code. The data base is updated on a quarterly basis and a source of information about the presence of these individuals in any neighborhood. The Department of Justice also maintains a Sex Offender Identification Line through which inquiries about individuals may be made. This is a "900" telephone service. Callers must have specific information about individuals they are checking. Information regarding neighborhoods is not available through the "900" telephone service.

26. **POSSESSION:** If Landlord is unable to deliver possession of Premises on Commencement Date, such Date shall be extended to the date on which possession is made available to Tenant. If Landlord is unable to deliver possession within **5 (or ☐ _____) calendar days** after agreed Commencement Date, Tenant may terminate the Agreement by giving written notice to Landlord, and shall be refunded all Rent and security deposit paid. Possession is deemed terminated when Tenant has returned all keys to the Premises to Landlord. ☐ Tenant is already in possession of the Premises.

27. **TENANT'S OBLIGATIONS UPON VACATING PREMISES:** If the tenancy is terminated due to any reason other than close of escrow by Buyer under the purchase agreement, upon termination of the Agreement:
   A. Tenant shall: **(i)** give Landlord all copies of all keys or opening devices to Premises, including any common areas; **(ii)** vacate and surrender Premises to Landlord, empty of all persons; **(iii)** vacate any/all parking and/or storage space; **(iv)** clean and deliver Premises, as specified in paragraph C below, to Landlord in the same condition as referenced in paragraph 10; **(v)** remove all debris; **(vi)** give written notice to Landlord of Tenant's forwarding address; and **(vii)** _____.
   B. All alterations/improvements made by or caused to be made by Tenant, with or without Landlord's consent, become the property of Landlord upon termination. Landlord may charge Tenant for restoration of the Premises to the condition it was in prior to any alterations/improvements.
   C. **Right to Pre-Move Out Inspection and Repairs as follows: (i)** After giving or receiving notice of termination of a tenancy (C.A.R. Form NTT), or before the end of a lease, Tenant has the right to request that an inspection of the Premises take place prior to termination of the lease or rental (C.A.R. Form NRI). If Tenant requests such an inspection, Tenant shall be given an opportunity to remedy identified deficiencies prior to termination, consistent with the terms of the Agreement. **(ii)** Any repairs or alterations made to the Premises as a result of this inspection (collectively, "Repairs") shall be made at Tenant's expense. Repairs may be performed by Tenant or through others, who have adequate insurance and licenses and are approved by Landlord. The work shall comply with applicable law, including governmental permit, inspection and approval requirements. Repairs shall be performed in a good, skillful manner with materials of quality and appearance comparable to existing materials. It is understood that exact restoration of appearance or cosmetic items following all Repairs may not be possible. **(iii)** Tenant shall: **(a)** obtain receipts for Repairs performed by others; **(b)** prepare a written statement indicating the Repairs performed by Tenant and the date of such Repairs; and **(c)** provide copies of receipts and statements to Landlord prior to termination.

28. **BREACH OF CONTRACT;EARLY TERMINATION:** In addition to any obligations established by paragraph 27, in event of termination by Tenant prior to completion of the original term of the Agreement, Tenant shall also be responsible for lost Rent, rental commissions, advertising expenses and painting costs necessary to ready Premises for re-rental. Landlord may withhold any such amounts from Tenant's security deposit.

29. **TEMPORARY RELOCATION:** Subject to local law, Tenant agrees, upon demand of Landlord, to temporarily vacate Premises for a reasonable period, to allow for fumigation (or other methods) to control wood destroying pests or organisms, or other repairs to Premises. Tenant agrees to comply with all instructions and requirements necessary to prepare Premises to accommodate pest control, fumigation or other work, including bagging or storage of food and medicine, and removal of perishables and valuables. Tenant shall only be entitled to a credit of Rent equal to the per diem Rent for the period of time Tenant is required to vacate Premises.

30. **DAMAGE TO PREMISES:** If, by no fault of Tenant, Premises are totally or partially damaged or destroyed by fire, earthquake, accident or other casualty that render Premises totally or partially uninhabitable, either Landlord or Tenant may terminate the Agreement by giving the other written notice. Rent shall be abated as of the date Premises become totally or partially uninhabitable. The abated amount shall be the current monthly Rent prorated on a 30-day period. If the Agreement is not terminated, Landlord shall promptly repair the damage, and Rent shall be reduced based on the extent to which the damage interferes with Tenant's reasonable use of Premises. If damage occurs as a result of an act of Tenant or Tenant's guests, only Landlord shall have the right of termination, and no reduction in Rent shall be made.

31. **INSURANCE:** Tenant's or guest's personal property and vehicles are not insured by Landlord, manager or, if applicable, HOA, against loss or damage due to fire, theft, vandalism, rain, water, criminal or negligent acts of others, or any other cause. **Tenant is advised to carry Tenant's own insurance (renter's insurance) to protect Tenant from any such loss or damage.** Tenant shall comply with any requirement imposed on Tenant by Landlord's insurer to avoid: **(i)** an increase in Landlord's insurance premium (or Tenant shall pay for the increase in premium); or **(ii)** loss of insurance.

32. **WATERBEDS:** Tenant shall not use or have waterbeds on the Premises unless: **(i)** Tenant obtains a valid waterbed insurance policy; **(ii)** Tenant increases the security deposit in an amount equal to one-half of one month's Rent; and **(iii)** the bed conforms to the floor load capacity of Premises.

Tenant's Initials (_____)(_____)
Landlord's Initials (_____)(_____)

Reviewed by _____ Date _____

EQUAL HOUSING OPPORTUNITY

INTERIM OCCUPANCY AGREEMENT (IOA PAGE 4 OF 6)

Premises: _____ Date: _____

33. WAIVER: The waiver of any breach shall not be construed as a continuing waiver of the same or any subsequent breach.

34. NOTICE: Notices may be served at the following address, or at any other location subsequently designated:
Landlord: _____ Tenant: _____
_____ _____
_____ _____

35. TENANT ESTOPPEL CERTIFICATE: Tenant shall execute and return a tenant estoppel certificate delivered to Tenant by Landlord or Landlord's agent within 3 days after its receipt. Failure to comply with this requirement shall be deemed Tenant's acknowledgment that the tenant estoppel certificate is true and correct, and may be relied upon by a lender or purchaser.

36. TENANT REPRESENTATIONS; CREDIT: Tenant warrants that all statements in Tenant's rental application are accurate. Tenant authorizes Landlord and Broker(s) to obtain Tenant's credit report periodically during the tenancy in connection with modification or enforcement of the Agreement. Landlord may cancel the Agreement: **(i)** before occupancy begins; **(ii)** upon disapproval of the credit report(s); or **(iii)** at any time, upon discovering that information in Tenant's application is false. A negative credit report reflecting on Tenant's record may be submitted to a credit reporting agency if Tenant fails to fulfill the terms of payment and other obligations under the Agreement.

37. MEDIATION:
  A. Consistent with paragraphs B and C below, Landlord and Tenant agree to mediate any dispute or claim arising between them out of the Agreement, or any resulting transaction, before resorting to court action. Mediation fees, if any, shall be divided equally among the parties involved. If, for any dispute or claim to which this paragraph applies, any party commences an action without first attempting to resolve the matter through mediation, or refuses to mediate after a request has been made, then that party shall not be entitled to recover attorney fees, even if they would otherwise be available to that party in any such action.
  B. The following matters are excluded from mediation: **(i)** an unlawful detainer action; **(ii)** the filing or enforcement of a mechanic's lien; and **(iii)** any matter within the jurisdiction of a probate, small claims or bankruptcy court. The filing of a court action to enable the recording of a notice of pending action, for order of attachment, receivership, injunction, or other provisional remedies, shall not constitute a waiver of the mediation provision.
  C. Landlord and Tenant agree to mediate disputes or claims involving Listing Agent, Leasing Agent or property manager ("Broker"), provided Broker shall have agreed to such mediation prior to, or within a reasonable time after, the dispute or claim is presented to such Broker. Any election by Broker to participate in mediation shall not result in Broker being deemed a party to the Agreement.

38. ATTORNEY FEES: In any action or proceeding arising out of the Agreement, the prevailing party between Landlord and Tenant shall be entitled to reasonable attorney fees and costs, except as provided in paragraph 37A.

39. C.A.R. FORM: C.A.R. Form means the specific form referenced.

40. OTHER TERMS AND CONDITIONS;SUPPLEMENTS: _____
_____
The following ATTACHED supplements are incorporated in the Agreement: ☐ Keysafe/Lockbox Addendum (C.A.R. Form KLA); ☐ Interpreter/Translator Agreement (C.A.R. Form ITA); ☐ Lead-Based Paint and Lead-Based Paint Hazards Disclosure (C.A.R. Form FLD)

41. TIME OF ESSENCE; ENTIRE CONTRACT; CHANGES: Time is of the essence. All understandings between the parties are incorporated in the Agreement. Its terms are intended by the parties as a final, complete and exclusive expression of their Agreement with respect to its subject matter, and may not be contradicted by evidence of any prior agreement or contemporaneous oral agreement. If any provision of the Agreement is held to be ineffective or invalid, the remaining provisions will nevertheless be given full force and effect. Neither the Agreement nor any provision in it may be extended, amended, modified, altered or changed except in writing. The Agreement and any supplement, addendum or modification, including any copy, may be signed in two or more counterparts, all of which shall constitute one and the same writing.

42. AGENCY:
  A. **CONFIRMATION:** The following agency relationship(s) are hereby confirmed for this transaction:
  Listing Agent: (Agent representing the Seller in the purchase agreement)
  (Print firm name) _____
  is the agent of (check one): ☐ the Landlord exclusively; or ☐ both the Landlord and Tenant.
  Selling Agent: (Agent representing the Buyer in the purchase agreement)
  (Print firm name) _____
  (if not same as Listing Agent) is the agent of (check one): ☐ the Tenant exclusively; or ☐ the Landlord exclusively; or ☐ both the Tenant and Landlord.
  B. **DISCLOSURE:** ☐ (If checked): The term of this lease exceeds one year. A disclosure regarding real estate agency relationships (C.A.R. Form AD) has been provided to Landlord and Tenant, who each acknowledge its receipt.

Tenant's Initials (_____)(_____)
Landlord's Initials (_____)(_____)

IOA REVISED 4/03 (PAGE 5 OF 6)

Reviewed by _____ Date _____

INTERIM OCCUPANCY AGREEMENT (IOA PAGE 5 OF 6)

Premises: _____ Date: _____

43. ☐ **INTERPRETER/TRANSLATOR:** The terms of the Agreement have been interpreted/translated for Tenant into the following language: _____. Landlord and Tenant acknowledge receipt of the attached interpretation/translation agreement, (C.A.R. Form ITA).

44. **FOREIGN LANGUAGE NEGOTIATION:** If the Agreement has been negotiated primarily in Spanish, Tenant shall be provided a Spanish language translation of the Agreement pursuant to the California Civil Code.

45. **RECEIPT:** If specified in paragraph 5, Landlord or Broker, acknowledges receipt of move-in funds.

Landlord and Tenant acknowledge and agree Brokers: **(a)** do not guarantee the condition of the Premises; **(b)** cannot verify representations made by others; **(c)** cannot provide legal or tax advice; **(d)** will not provide other advice or information that exceeds the knowledge, education or experience required to obtain a real estate license. Furthermore, Brokers: **(e)** do not decide what rental rate a Tenant should pay or Landlord should accept; and **(f)** do not decide upon the length or other terms of tenancy. Landlord and Tenant agree they will seek legal, tax, insurance and other desired assistance from appropriate professionals.

Tenant/Buyer _____ Date _____
Address _____ City _____ State ____ Zip _____
Telephone _____ Fax _____ E-mail _____

Tenant/Buyer _____ Date _____
Address _____ City _____ State ____ Zip _____
Telephone _____ Fax _____ E-mail _____

Landlord /Seller _____ Date _____
Landlord /Seller _____ Date _____
Landlord Address _____ City _____ State ____ Zip _____
Telephone _____ Fax _____ E-mail _____

REAL ESTATE BROKERS:
A. Brokers are not a party to the Agreement between Landlord and Tenant.
B. Agency relationships are confirmed as above.

Real Estate Broker _____
(Agent representing the Buyer in the purchase agreement)
By (Agent) _____ Date _____
Address _____ City _____ State ____ Zip _____
Telephone _____ Fax _____ E-mail _____

Real Estate Broker _____
(Agent representing the Seller in the purchase agreement)
By (Agent) _____ Date _____
Address _____ City _____ State ____ Zip _____
Telephone _____ Fax _____ E-mail _____

THIS FORM HAS BEEN APPROVED BY THE CALIFORNIA ASSOCIATION OF REALTORS® (C.A.R.). NO REPRESENTATION IS MADE AS TO THE LEGAL VALIDITY OR ADEQUACY OF ANY PROVISION IN ANY SPECIFIC TRANSACTION. A REAL ESTATE BROKER IS THE PERSON QUALIFIED TO ADVISE ON REAL ESTATE TRANSACTIONS. IF YOU DESIRE LEGAL OR TAX ADVICE, CONSULT AN APPROPRIATE PROFESSIONAL.
This form is available for use by the entire real estate industry. It is not intended to identify the user as a REALTOR®. REALTOR® is a registered collective membership mark which may be used only by members of the NATIONAL ASSOCIATION OF REALTORS® who subscribe to its Code of Ethics.

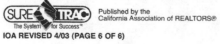

Published by the
California Association of REALTORS®

IOA REVISED 4/03 (PAGE 6 OF 6)

Reviewed by _____ Date _____

INTERIM OCCUPANCY AGREEMENT (IOA PAGE 6 OF 6)

ALLOCATION OF COSTS

A residential real estate transaction may involve a wide variety of closing costs (see Chapter 10). Whether a particular closing cost will be paid by the seller or the buyer usually depends on what's customary in your area, but the parties can allocate most costs however they wish in their contract. Provisions concerning inspection fees, the cost of compliance with certain regulations, and the escrow fee are commonly included in the deposit receipt.

INSPECTIONS. In California, lenders typically require a structural pest control inspection, performed by a licensed pest control inspector. Usually a seller will order an inspection at the time the house is listed. In the deposit receipt, you can indicate the inspection company used and which party will be responsible for the inspection cost.

A buyer may want to order inspections of certain other aspects of the property. (See the discussion of inspection contingencies in Chapter 7.) Which party will pay for these other inspections and for any necessary repairs can also be specified in the deposit receipt.

MEETING GOVERNMENT REQUIREMENTS. Residential properties are required by law to have smoke detectors installed and water heaters properly braced. In addition, some communities require certain retrofit repairs, such as the installation of low-flow toilets and the use of tempered glass in sliding doors. The parties can designate who pays for smoke detector installation, water heater bracing, or retrofit work in the deposit receipt.

ESCROW FEE AND PRORATED EXPENSES. The deposit receipt should also state which party is responsible for paying the escrow agent's fee; it is typically split between the parties. In addition, the agreement should set forth how certain property expenses (property taxes, homeowners' association dues, etc.) will be shared. These are ordinarily prorated as of the closing date, unless otherwise agreed. We will discuss closing costs in more detail and explain how to do prorations in Chapter 10.

LEAD-BASED PAINT DISCLOSURES

To comply with the federal disclosure law discussed in Chapter 2, a residential deposit receipt may have a provision and/or an addendum concerning lead-based paint. In transactions that involve housing built before 1978, the federal law requires the seller to disclose information about lead-based paint on the property to potential buyers. Specific warnings must be included in the deposit receipt, along with signed statements from the parties acknowledging that the requirements of the law have been fulfilled. The signed acknowledgments must be kept for at least three years as proof of compliance.

Included Items

An "included items" paragraph states that certain items are included in the sale unless otherwise noted in the deposit receipt. The list usually includes carpeting, built-in appliances, window coverings, air conditioning equipment, shrubs, and so forth. Even without this provision in the contract, many of the items listed would be considered fixtures or attachments and included in the sale, but the provision helps prevent disputes over this issue.

If the seller wants to remove an item listed in the provision or exclude an item that would normally be considered real property, you can specify that the item is excluded from the sale. Similarly, if an item that is not listed in the provision will be included in the sale, you can state that the item is included. Some deposit receipt forms have blank lines in the included items paragraph for this purpose; otherwise, you can use an addendum.

Buyer's Investigation and Repairs

It's always best for a buyer to inspect a property thoroughly before purchasing it. And most buyers don't want to be obligated to go through with the transaction if an inspection reveals serious flaws. For this reason, the deposit receipt form typically gives the buyer the right to investigate the property, and makes the buyer's offer contingent on her approval of the property's condition. The buyer has a set period of time to complete her inspections and then either remove the contingency or cancel the agreement.

If the inspections reveal any problems, the buyer must decide whether she wants those problems corrected before she purchases the property. If the buyer does want corrective work completed before the sale, the parties must negotiate who will complete and pay for the repair work. (Inspection contingencies are also discussed in Chapter 7.)

CONVEYANCE AND TITLE

A deposit receipt form includes provisions pertaining to the conveyance of the property and the condition of title. The type of deed that the seller will execute in favor of the buyer (ordinarily a grant deed) is specified. Typically, the seller agrees to provide the buyer with a preliminary title report listing liens and other encumbrances. The buyer usually agrees to take title subject to existing non-financial encumbrances (easements and restrictive covenants), with a standard coverage title insurance policy. The seller agrees to pay off any liens at closing (if not before), unless the buyer is assuming or taking title subject to an existing lien.

The seller is required to disclose to the buyer any information he has about matters affecting the title, whether or not they appear in the title report. If the seller is a party to a legal action—such as a bankruptcy, a divorce, or a foreclosure action—the seller may not be able to convey clear title. This is a material fact and should be disclosed to the buyer. If the buyer has questions about the legal ramifications of the seller's court proceedings, the buyer should consult an attorney.

SALE OF BUYER'S PROPERTY

Often, a buyer needs to sell her current home in order to have the money to purchase a new home. The buyer does not want to be obligated to go through with the purchase if she is unable to sell her current home. This problem can be solved by making the purchase agreement contingent on the sale of the buyer's current home. The contingency should be listed in the deposit receipt, and the appropriate contingency addendum form must be filled out and attached to the contract. We'll discuss this type of contingency in more detail in the next chapter.

AGENCY DISCLOSURE

As we discussed in Chapter 1, the real estate agents involved in a transaction must inform both the buyer and the seller which party (or parties) they are representing. An agency disclosure must be made to the buyer before the buyer signs the offer to purchase, and to the seller before the seller signs the offer. The disclosures must be confirmed in writing, either in the deposit receipt or in a separate agency confirmation form.

DEFAULT PROVISIONS

A deposit receipt usually states the remedies available to the buyer or the seller if the other party defaults, and explains how the good faith deposit will be handled in case of default.

SELLER'S REMEDIES. In California, most residential deposit receipts have a liquidated damages provision similar to Paragraph 16 in the C.A.R. form shown in Figure 6.1. If both parties to the contract initial and date this provision, the good faith deposit will be treated as liquidated damages. If they choose this option, the parties are defining what the seller's only remedy will be in the event that the buyer defaults. The seller will keep the good faith deposit as compensation for the buyer's breach of contract, but the seller will not be allowed to seek any additional compensation.

California has a special law concerning liquidated damages that applies to real estate transactions involving residential property with up to four dwelling units, if the buyer intends to occupy one of the units. This law requires a liquidated damages provision in the deposit receipt to be in bold or red type and separately initialed by both the buyer and the seller, to show that each of them was aware of the provision and specifically consented to it. Otherwise, the provision is unenforceable, which means that the seller will be allowed to choose what legal remedy to pursue if the buyer defaults. (Typically, the seller would file a lawsuit against the buyer in this situation.)

Also under this state law—again, in a residential transaction with up to four units, if the buyer intends to occupy one of the units—no more than 3% of the property's sales price can be treated as liquidated damages. So if the buyer's good faith deposit was more than 3% of the price, the seller will be required to return the excess if the buyer forfeits the deposit. (The law concerning liquidated damages is also covered in Chapter 5.)

DISPOSITION OF GOOD FAITH DEPOSIT. A deposit receipt may provide that if the buyer is entitled to have the good faith deposit returned, the broker or closing agent who is holding the deposit may first deduct expenses that have already been incurred on the buyer's behalf.

If the buyer forfeits the good faith deposit to the seller, the listing broker is usually entitled to half of the money the seller receives (but not more than the broker would have been paid as a commission if the sale had closed). This is usually provided for in the listing agreement rather than the deposit receipt (see Chapter 2). In practical terms, this usually means that the seller gets 50% of the deposit, the listing broker gets 25% of the deposit, and the selling broker gets 25% of the deposit.

> **EXAMPLE:** Bowen agreed to sell her house to Wilder for $275,000. The good faith deposit was $10,000. Wilder defaulted on the purchase agreement, and under the terms of the agreement Bowen is entitled to keep the good faith deposit as liquidated damages. However, the law allows her to keep no more than 3% of the sales price, which is $8,250, so she must return $1,750 to Wilder.
>
> When she listed her property, Bowen agreed to give 50% of any forfeited deposit to the listing broker. As a result, Bowen and the listing broker each get $4,125. Under the terms of a commission split agreement, the listing broker is then required to split his share with the selling broker. Thus, each broker ends up with $2,062.50.

DISPUTE RESOLUTION

Unfortunately, disputes arising out of a real estate transaction are sometimes unavoidable. The deposit receipt form can be used to establish the procedures that will be used to resolve disputes between the buyer and seller. By agreeing in advance how they will handle any disagreements that arise, the parties can streamline the dispute resolution process. The alternatives to a lawsuit include mediation and arbitration.

MEDIATION. As we explained in Chapter 2, in mediation a neutral third party (the mediator) helps the parties involved in a dispute reach a mutually satisfactory solution. The C.A.R. deposit receipt form contains a mediation clause. In this provision, the buyer and seller agree that they will try to mediate any disputes before turning to arbitration or filing a lawsuit. If one of them resorts to arbitration or a lawsuit without attempting mediation first, he will not be entitled to have his attorneys' fees paid by the other party if he wins. (See the discussion of attorneys' fees later in this section of the chapter.) The buyer and seller also agree to split the cost of the mediation.

ARBITRATION. The C.A.R. deposit receipt form also contains an arbitration clause. This provision, unlike the mediation clause, applies only if it's initialed by both the buyer and the seller. By initialing the arbitration clause, the parties agree in advance to arbitrate any disputes that haven't been resolved through mediation. They give up the right to file a lawsuit and the right to appeal the arbitrator's decision to a court. It's important that both parties understand these consequences before deciding to initial the arbitration clause.

Arbitration proceedings are conducted according to California state law. Both parties are entitled to discovery, which means they may request documents and interview witnesses. The arbitrator will be a retired judge or an experienced real estate attorney, unless the buyer and seller agree to a different arbitrator. The arbitrator's decision may be filed with the court and made into an enforceable court order. By contrast, a mediator's decision is not legally binding on the parties.

ATTORNEYS' FEES. A deposit receipt typically includes an attorneys' fees provision. Under this type of provision, if a dispute ends up in arbitration or in court, the attorneys' fees of the winning party must be paid by the losing party. Remember that the C.A.R. deposit receipt form provides that if a party takes legal action without attempting to mediate the dispute first, that party will not be entitled to attorneys' fees even if she prevails in the legal proceeding.

TIME IS OF THE ESSENCE

A deposit receipt usually states that "time is of the essence." This phrase doesn't simply mean that the parties hope the sale progresses as quickly as possible; it means they are legally required to meet all deadlines set in the agreement. Performance on or before the specified dates (not just within a reasonable time thereafter) is considered one of the essential terms of the agreement. Failure to meet any of the deadlines is a breach of contract.

ADDENDA

Often, a deposit receipt has a number of addenda attached to it and made part of the contract between the buyer and the seller. We've already mentioned various addendum forms, such as the seller financing addendum and the sale of buyer's property contingency addendum. To incorporate the addenda into the agreement, they should be listed in the space provided on the deposit receipt and then attached to the main document. The parties must sign or initial and date each page of the attachments.

In some cases the buyer and seller may want to add other contract terms that are not covered in a specific addendum form. If the additional terms are simple, you can use a general addendum form, such as the one shown in Figure 6.4, for this purpose. But if the additional terms are at all complicated or unusual, an attorney should draft them. As we've discussed, real estate agents are not allowed to write complicated clauses to include in a deposit receipt.

OFFER AND ACCEPTANCE

A deposit receipt form will typically have space for the buyer to set a deadline for acceptance of the offer. The manner in which the seller is required to communicate acceptance may also be specified. The C.A.R. form, for example, provides that the seller's acceptance will not be effective until a copy of the agreement signed by the seller is received by the buyer or the buyer's agent. An offer that is not accepted in this manner expires when the deadline passes, and the good faith deposit will be refunded to the buyer.

A deposit receipt may also set a deadline for the buyer's acceptance of a counteroffer. Remember that a counteroffer isn't an acceptance, so the buyer isn't contractually bound unless he accepts the seller's counteroffer.

SIGNATURES

Of course, space is provided at the end of a deposit receipt for each party's signature. The buyer's signature makes the form an offer to purchase, and the seller's signature turns it into a binding contract. On many forms, the listing and selling agents are also supposed to sign and fill in the names of their brokerages.

With some deposit receipt forms, when the seller signs the form to accept the buyer's offer, the seller is also agreeing to pay the real estate

FIG. 6.4 ADDENDUM

CALIFORNIA ASSOCIATION OF REALTORS®

ADDENDUM
(C.A.R. Form ADM, Revised 10/01)

No. _____

The following terms and conditions are hereby incorporated in and made a part of the: ☐ Residential Purchase Agreement, ☐ Manufactured Home Purchase Agreement, ☐ Business Purchase Agreement, ☐ Residential Lease or Month-to-Month Rental Agreement, ☐ Vacant Land Purchase Agreement, ☐ Residential Income Property Purchase Agreement, ☐ Commercial Property Purchase Agreement, ☐ other_____

dated _____, on property known as _____,

in which _____ is referred to as ("Buyer/Tenant")

and _____ is referred to as ("Seller/Landlord").

_____
_____
_____
_____
_____

The foregoing terms and conditions are hereby agreed to, and the undersigned acknowledge receipt of a copy of this document.

Date _____   Date _____

Buyer/Tenant _____   Seller/Landlord _____

Buyer/Tenant _____   Seller/Landlord _____

Published and Distributed by:
REAL ESTATE BUSINESS SERVICES, INC.
a subsidiary of the CALIFORNIA ASSOCIATION OF REALTORS®
525 South Virgil Avenue, Los Angeles, California 90020

Reviewed by _____
Broker or Designee _____ Date _____

EQUAL HOUSING OPPORTUNITY

ADM-11 REVISED 10/01 (PAGE 1 OF 1) **Print Date**

ADDENDUM (ADM-11 PAGE 1 OF 1)

Reprinted with permission, California Association of Realtors®. No endorsement implied.

broker's commission. If a form contains this type of clause, it's often printed right above the space for the seller's signature. This gives the broker a safety net, in case the listing agreement was invalid for some reason (or even if there was no written listing agreement). The clause in the deposit receipt satisfies the statute of frauds and allows the broker to sue the seller for the commission, if necessary.

Chapter Summary

1. A properly executed purchase agreement, or deposit receipt, is a binding contract that holds the parties to the terms of their agreement until all conditions have been fulfilled and the transaction is ready to close.

2. The parties to a purchase agreement are the buyer(s) and the seller(s). All parties must have contractual capacity. Everyone with an interest in the property must sign the agreement. The spouse of any married seller or buyer should also sign.

3. Every deposit receipt must have an adequate description of the property, specify the total purchase price and the method of payment, list the liens and encumbrances the buyer will assume, specify the amount and terms of the buyer's financing, and describe the conditions of sale.

4. Deposit receipts almost always contain a "time is of the essence" clause, which makes the dates agreed to a material term of the contract. Closing must take place on or before the date stated in the agreement, unless the parties agree in writing to an extension.

5. In California, a deposit receipt should include an agency disclosure paragraph, stating that the real estate agents involved in the transaction made the required disclosures concerning which party or parties they were representing.

6. The deposit receipt form also serves as the buyer's receipt for the good faith deposit. In most residential deposit receipts, the selling broker is directed to hold the buyer's good faith deposit check uncashed until the seller has accepted the buyer's offer.

CHAPTER QUIZ

1. If the seller is a minor, the deposit receipt should be signed by:

    a. the seller's husband or wife

    b. both the seller and the seller's spouse

    c. the seller's legal guardian

    d. both the seller and the seller's attorney in fact

2. The purchase price stated in the deposit receipt should include any:

    a. mortgages or other liens being assumed by the buyer

    b. seller financing

    c. new loan to be obtained by the buyer

    d. All of the above

3. The buyer usually gives the good faith deposit to the:

    a. selling agent

    b. seller

    c. listing broker

    d. listing agent

4. The "included items" paragraph is used to:

    a. disclose the encumbrances on the property

    b. list the documents that are being attached to the agreement

    c. determine how closing costs will be allocated

    d. specify fixtures and personal property that will be part of the sale

5. In setting a closing date, you should take into account all of the following except:

    a. when the next installment of the property taxes will be due

    b. how long the seller needs to make any necessary repairs

    c. whether the buyer needs to sell her current home

    d. the time needed for all of the inspections that will be required

6. The parties are required to initial the liquidated damages clause in a damage receipt:

    a. if the buyer's deposit exceeds 3% of the sales price

    b. to show that they were aware of the provision and specifically consented to it

    c. to provide that the selling broker can hold the good faith deposit check uncashed until the seller accepts the offer

    d. to allow the seller to choose what remedy to pursue in the event that the buyer defaults

7. Because a purchase agreement has a "time is of the essence" clause:

    a. a check for the good faith deposit can be held for no more than three days

    b. the seller must accept the buyer's offer within five days, or the offer will terminate

    c. failure to meet a deadline set in the agreement is a breach of contract

    d. the closing must take place within 45 days after the agreement is signed

8. To be enforceable, an arbitration clause in a deposit receipt must be:

    a. in a separate addendum

    b. initialed by the buyer and seller

    c. initialed by the selling agent and the listing agent

    d. All of the above

9. The Foreign Investment in Real Property Tax Act (FIRPTA) applies to certain transactions when:

    a. the broker is not a U.S. citizen

    b. the buyer is not a U.S. citizen

    c. the closing agent is not a U.S. citizen

    d. the seller is not a U.S. citizen

10. If a buyer defaults on a purchase agreement, the good faith deposit is typically:

    a. returned to the buyer

    b. split between the buyer and seller

    c. forfeited to the listing broker

    d. forfeited to the seller

ANSWER KEY

1. c. If one of the parties to a contract is a minor (under 18 years of age), the contract should be signed by that party's legal guardian.

2. d. The purchase price stated in the agreement should be the full price being paid for the property, including the downpayment, any mortgages or liens the buyer is assuming, and any financing, whether the financing is provided by the seller or by a lender.

3. a. In most cases, the buyer will give the good faith deposit to the selling agent (and the deposit will be held in trust or delivered to an escrow agent by the selling broker).

4. d. The "included items" paragraph lists items that are included in the sale unless otherwise noted. (Many of the items listed would be considered fixtures or attachments to the real property and included in the sale even without this provision.)

5. a. In setting a closing date, it's important to consider how long it will take the parties to fulfill their obligations and satisfy any contingencies in the deposit receipt. The due date for the property taxes is irrelevant, since the taxes will be prorated.

6. b. The liquidated damages clause must be initialed by the buyer and the seller to show that they were aware of the provision and specifically consented to it. (If the clause is initialed, liquidated damages are the seller's only remedy for breach of contract.)

7. c. The purpose of a "time is of the essence" clause is to make the dates and deadlines specified in the agreement material terms of the contract. As a result, one party's failure to meet a deadline may be treated as a breach of contract by the other party.

8. b. An arbitration clause in a deposit receipt is enforceable only if it has been initialed by both the buyer and the seller.

9. d. FIRPTA applies to certain transactions in which the seller is not a U.S. citizen.

10. d. When a buyer defaults on a purchase agreement, her good faith deposit is forfeited to the seller. In many cases, the seller will split the deposit with the listing broker, who will then split his share with the selling broker.

CHAPTER 7

CONTINGENT TRANSACTIONS

How Contingencies Work
- Termination or removal
- Good faith effort required
- Basic elements of a contingency clause

Types of Contingencies
- Financing contingencies
- Inspection contingencies
- Sale of buyer's home contingencies
- Purchase of replacement property contingencies
- Other types of contingencies

Unfulfilled Contingencies
- Notices to perform
- Canceling the purchase agreement

INTRODUCTION

In many cases a buyer wants to make an offer on a house, but does not want to become bound by a contract with the seller unless a particular event occurs first. For instance, the buyer may need to get a purchase loan approved, or she may want to have the house inspected by an expert. However, the buyer doesn't want to wait until that event occurs before making an offer on the house—by that time, the seller might have sold the property to someone else. In this situation, the buyer needs to make her offer conditional or contingent on the occurrence of the event in question.

To help a buyer prepare a contingent offer, you need to know how contingency clauses work, the essential elements of a contingency, the common types of contingencies, and the various preprinted forms you can use to establish a contingency.

HOW CONTINGENCIES WORK

Many purchase agreements are enforceable only if a certain event occurs. The event is called a **contingency**, or a **condition** of the sale. If the specified event occurs, then both the buyer and the seller are bound to carry out the terms of their contract. If the specified event does not occur, the agreement may be terminated and, in most cases, the buyer is entitled to a refund of the good faith deposit.

TERMINATION OR REMOVAL

A contingency provision is typically included in a contract for the benefit of one of the parties rather than both of them. If the contingency is not fulfilled—if the specified event does not happen—the benefiting party has two choices. He may:

1. terminate the contract without penalty, or
2. remove the condition and proceed with the contract.

Only the benefiting party has the right to choose between terminating the contract or removing the condition. By removing the condition, the party waives the option to terminate the contract and gives up the rights associated with the contingency. If the benefiting party is willing to remove the condition, the other party cannot refuse to go through with the sale because the condition has not been met.

> **EXAMPLE:** Suppose a deposit receipt is contingent on the buyer obtaining a fixed-rate conventional loan with a $20,000 downpayment within 30 days of the seller's acceptance of the offer. This contingency benefits the buyer. It protects the buyer from being forced to complete the purchase if he can't get the financing he needs.
>
> If the buyer gets the loan within the 30-day period, he is obligated to buy the seller's property. If the buyer got the loan but refused to purchase the property anyway, the seller would be able to keep the buyer's good faith deposit as liquidated damages or (depending on the terms of their agreement) sue the buyer.
>
> On the other hand, if he doesn't get the loan, the buyer can take one of two courses of action. He can give the seller notice that the condition has not been met, terminate the agreement, and get the deposit back. Alternatively, he can remove the financing contingency and go ahead with the transaction. This would mean that he would have to come up with the purchase price from some other source by the closing date, or else forfeit his deposit.
>
> If the buyer decides to go ahead with the purchase, the seller cannot then refuse to complete the transaction because the condition was not met. Since the condition was included in the purchase agreement for the benefit of the buyer, only the buyer can choose whether to remove the condition or terminate the sale.

In the unusual case when a contingency clause benefits both parties to a contract, the condition can only be removed with the consent of both parties. In other words, if the condition were not met, either party would have the option of terminating the contract.

FOR THE BUYER'S BENEFIT. Contingency provisions in a deposit receipt are usually for the benefit of the buyer. They protect the buyer from becoming obligated to go through with the purchase if something doesn't work out in her own situation, or if it turns out that the property is unsuitable in some way—for instance, because it can't be subdivided, or it's infested with termites, or the well water is contaminated. Common contingency provisions in real estate transactions concern the buyer's financing (as in the example above); the sale of property the buyer currently owns; a satisfactory pest, soil, septic, well, or structural inspection; obtaining approval for a rezone, variance, or subdivision from the local planning commission; or the issuance of some sort of license needed to operate an establishment (such as a liquor license).

Good Faith Effort Required

Whenever a contract contains a contingency clause, the benefited party has an implied legal obligation to make a reasonable, good faith effort to fulfill the contingency.

> **Example:** Hanson's agreement to purchase Moore's house is contingent on Hanson getting a 90% fixed-rate loan at 6% interest. Three days after signing the agreement, Hanson decides she doesn't want to buy Moore's property after all. So she doesn't even bother to apply for a loan. Hanson then tells Moore that she's terminating the contract because the contingency hasn't been fulfilled, and she demands the return of her good faith deposit.
>
> However, Hanson had a legal obligation to make a reasonable effort to get a loan. Because she didn't fulfill that obligation, she has breached the purchase agreement and is not entitled to a refund of her deposit.

If the responsible party does not make a good faith effort to satisfy the contingency, then it is dropped from the contract. That party is bound by the contract even though the condition has not been met. Under these circumstances, as in the example above, the seller could keep the deposit if the buyer failed to go through with the purchase.

If an effort to fulfill a contingency were not required, the parties wouldn't really have a contract at all. The fulfillment of the contingency would be discretionary, and the contract would be "illusory." A contract is illusory when one party is not actually obligated to perform any duties under the contract.

> **Example:** Englewood agrees to purchase Foley's property on the condition "that Buyer accepts his company's early retirement offer." This clause gives Englewood the discretion to accept early retirement or not, so Englewood has complete control over whether a sale will take place. Foley cannot force Englewood to accept the early retirement offer, so any rights Foley has under this agreement are illusory. The purchase agreement is void.

Although the obligation to make a good faith effort to fulfill a condition is always implied in the contract, the contingency clause should spell out that obligation. For example, the financing contingency contained in the C.A.R. deposit receipt form (see Figure 6.1) includes the following language:

> *Buyer shall act diligently and in good faith to obtain the designated loans.*

BASIC ELEMENTS OF A CONTINGENCY CLAUSE

Any type of contingency provision, whether it's a financing contingency, an inspection contingency, or some other type, should contain all of the following elements:

1. A clear statement of exactly what the condition is and what has to be done to fulfill it.
2. The procedure for notifying the other party of either satisfaction or removal of the condition.
3. A deadline by which the condition must be met or removed.
4. The rights of the parties if the condition is not met or removed by the specified date.

While it's important to know the elements a contingency clause should have, you shouldn't try to draft one yourself. When necessary, you can use a preprinted, attorney-approved contingency form that can be attached as an addendum to the deposit receipt. In the case of the C.A.R. deposit receipt form, a number of contingency clauses, including a financing contingency and an inspection contingency, are already included in the form itself. If you were to write your own provision instead of using a preprinted contingency clause or form, that could be considered the unauthorized practice of law.

TYPES OF CONTINGENCIES

In deposit receipts for residential transactions, three types of contingency clauses are very common. These are financing contingencies, inspection contingencies, and contingencies concerning the sale of the buyer's home.

FINANCING CONTINGENCIES

Most residential purchase agreements are contingent on whether the buyer can obtain the financing needed in order to be able to pay the seller the agreed price. Standard contract forms may either include a financing contingency clause in the deposit receipt itself, or require an addendum that sets forth the terms of the financing contingency.

The primary purpose of a financing contingency is to allow the buyer to be released from the agreement and get the deposit back if she can't get the necessary financing.

A financing contingency usually states the type of financing the buyer will apply for, sets deadlines for the loan application and fulfillment or removal of the contingency, specifies the notice periods, and describes how lender-required inspections and repairs will be handled.

FINANCING TERMS. The financing terms set forth in the contingency clause may be general or specific. In this regard, the parties have conflicting interests. The buyer may want the contract to be contingent on a specific and very favorable financing arrangement, one that is as affordable as possible. On the other hand, the seller—who wants to hold the buyer to the agreement, or to keep the deposit if the buyer backs out—would prefer a financing contingency that simply calls for a typical institutional loan in the current marketplace. The seller probably won't agree to a financing contingency that specifies a below-market interest rate or unusually low loan fees, because it's much less likely that the buyer will be able to obtain that type of financing.

Figure 7.1 shows the financing contingency provisions in the C.A.R. deposit receipt form. Unless otherwise noted, this deposit receipt is automatically contingent on financing. If the buyer doesn't want her offer to include a financing contingency, she must specify this by checking Paragraph 2K.

This financing contingency allows you to set forth quite specific financing terms. You're given space to state the amount of the buyer's loan, the interest rate and whether the rate is fixed or variable, the loan term, and whether the loan will be fully or partially amortized. You'll need to fill in additional information if the buyer plans to seek FHA or VA financing. Again, a very specific financing contingency is ordinarily to the buyer's advantage and the seller's disadvantage.

FIG. 7.1   FINANCING CONTINGENCY CLAUSE IN RESIDENTIAL PURCHASE AGREEMENT

CALIFORNIA ASSOCIATION OF REALTORS®

CALIFORNIA
RESIDENTIAL PURCHASE AGREEMENT
AND JOINT ESCROW INSTRUCTIONS
For Use With Single Family Residential Property — Attached or Detached
(C.A.R. Form RPA-CA, Revised 10/02)

Date _____, at _____, California.

1. **OFFER:**
   A. **THIS IS AN OFFER FROM** _____ ("Buyer").
   B. **THE REAL PROPERTY TO BE ACQUIRED** is described as _____
      _____, Assessor's Parcel No. _____, situated in
      _____, County of _____, California, ("Property").
   C. **THE PURCHASE PRICE** offered is _____
      _____ Dollars $ _____.
   D. **CLOSE OF ESCROW** shall occur on _____ (date)(or ☐ _____ **Days** After Acceptance).

2. **FINANCE TERMS:** Obtaining the loans below **is a contingency** of this Agreement unless: **(i)** either 2K or 2L is checked below; or **(ii)** otherwise agreed in writing. Buyer shall act diligently and in good faith to obtain the designated loans. Obtaining deposit, down payment and closing costs **is not a contingency.** Buyer represents that funds will be good when deposited with Escrow Holder.
   A. **INITIAL DEPOSIT:** Buyer has given a deposit in the amount of . . . .$ _____
      to the agent submitting the offer (or to ☐ _____), by personal check
      (or ☐ _____), made payable to _____
      which shall be held uncashed until Acceptance and then deposited within **3** business days after
      Acceptance (or ☐ _____), with
      Escrow Holder, (or ☐ into Broker's trust account).
   B. **INCREASED DEPOSIT:** Buyer shall deposit with Escrow Holder an increased deposit in the amount of . . .$ _____
      within _____ **Days** After Acceptance, or _____.
   C. **FIRST LOAN IN THE AMOUNT OF** . . . .$ _____
      (1) NEW First Deed of Trust in favor of lender, encumbering the Property, securing a note payable at
      maximum interest of _____ % fixed rate, or _____ % initial adjustable rate with a maximum
      interest rate of _____ %, balance due in _____ years, amortized over _____ years. Buyer
      shall pay loan fees/points not to exceed _____ (These terms apply whether the designated loan
      is conventional, FHA or VA.)
      (2) ☐ FHA ☐ VA: (The following terms only apply to the FHA or VA loan that is checked.)
      Seller shall pay _____ % discount points. Seller shall pay other fees not allowed to be paid by
      Buyer, ☐ not to exceed $ _____. Seller shall pay the cost of lender required Repairs
      (including those for wood destroying pest) not otherwise provided for in this Agreement, ☐ not to
      exceed $ _____. (Actual loan amount may increase if mortgage insurance premiums,
      funding fees or closing costs are financed.)
   D. **ADDITIONAL FINANCING TERMS:** ☐ Seller financing, (C.A.R. Form SFA); ☐ secondary financing, ...$ _____
      (C.A.R. Form PAA, paragraph 4A); ☐ assumed financing (C.A.R. Form PAA, paragraph 4B)
      _____
      _____
   E. **BALANCE OF PURCHASE PRICE** (not including costs of obtaining loans and other closing costs) in the amount of . . .$ _____
      to be deposited with Escrow Holder within sufficient time to close escrow.
   F. **PURCHASE PRICE (TOTAL):** . . . .$ _____
   G. **LOAN APPLICATIONS:** Within **7 (or** ☐ _____ **) Days** After Acceptance, Buyer shall provide Seller a letter from lender or
      mortgage loan broker stating that, based on a review of Buyer's written application and credit report, Buyer is prequalified or
      preapproved for the NEW loan specified in 2C above.
   H. **VERIFICATION OF DOWN PAYMENT AND CLOSING COSTS:** Buyer (or Buyer's lender or loan broker pursuant to 2G) shall, within
      7 (or ☐ _____ **) Days** After Acceptance, provide Seller written verification of Buyer's down payment and closing costs.
   I. **LOAN CONTINGENCY REMOVAL: (i)** Within **17 (or** ☐ _____ **) Days** After Acceptance, Buyer shall, as specified in paragraph
      14, remove the loan contingency or cancel this Agreement; **OR (ii)** (if checked) ☐ the loan contingency shall remain in effect
      until the designated loans are funded.
   J. **APPRAISAL CONTINGENCY AND REMOVAL:** This Agreement is **(OR,** if checked, ☐ is **NOT)** contingent upon the Property
      appraising at no less than the specified purchase price. If there is a loan contingency, at the time the loan contingency is
      removed (or, if checked, ☐ within **17 (or** _____ **) Days** After Acceptance), Buyer shall, as specified in paragraph 14B(3), remove
      the appraisal contingency or cancel this Agreement. If there is no loan contingency, Buyer shall, as specified in paragraph
      14B(3), remove the appraisal contingency within **17 (or** _____ **) Days** After Acceptance.
   K. ☐ **NO LOAN CONTINGENCY** (If checked): Obtaining any loan in paragraphs 2C, 2D or elsewhere in this Agreement is NOT
      a contingency of this Agreement. If Buyer does not obtain the loan and as a result Buyer does not purchase the Property, Seller
      may be entitled to Buyer's deposit or other legal remedies.
   L. ☐ **ALL CASH OFFER** (If checked): No loan is needed to purchase the Property. Buyer shall, within **7 (or** ☐ _____ **) Days** After Acceptance,
      provide Seller written verification of sufficient funds to close this transaction.

3. **CLOSING AND OCCUPANCY:**
   A. Buyer intends (or ☐ does not intend) to occupy the Property as Buyer's primary residence.
   B. **Seller-occupied or vacant property:** Occupancy shall be delivered to Buyer at _____ AM/PM, ☐ on the date of Close Of
      Escrow; ☐ on _____; or ☐ no later than _____ **Days** After Close Of Escrow. (C.A.R. Form PAA, paragraph 2.) If
      transfer of title and occupancy do not occur at the same time, Buyer and Seller are advised to: **(i)** enter into a written occupancy
      agreement; and **(ii)** consult with their insurance and legal advisors.

RPA-CA REVISED 10/02 (PAGE 1 OF 8)   Print Date

Buyer's Initials (_____)(_____)
Seller's Initials (_____)(_____)

Reviewed by _____ Date _____

EQUAL HOUSING OPPORTUNITY

CALIFORNIA RESIDENTIAL PURCHASE AGREEMENT   (RPA-CA PAGE 1 OF 8)

Reprinted with permission, California Association of Realtors®. No endorsement implied.

If the seller has agreed to pay discount points or other closing costs to help the buyer get the loan, the contingency clause may indicate the maximum amount the seller is willing to pay. (See Chapter 9 for information about discount points.)

DEADLINES. A financing contingency usually states that the buyer must apply for the loan within a certain number of days. In addition, the provision will set a deadline for fulfilling the contingency or notifying the seller that the contingency is removed. If the buyer has not notified the seller that the contingency has been fulfilled or removed by that deadline, the seller can terminate their agreement.

The seller must first notify the buyer that she intends to terminate the agreement, by sending the buyer a notice to perform (discussed at the end of this chapter). The buyer gets a final chance to remove the contingency after receiving this notice. The required notice period will be stated in the contingency provision in the deposit receipt. It will also state the seller's obligation to return the good faith deposit to the buyer if the purchase agreement is terminated.

FHA AND VA PROVISIONS. A financing contingency often includes special provisions concerning FHA and VA financing. The regulations that govern the FHA and VA programs prevent the buyer from paying certain loan and closing costs, so the seller agrees to pay these costs if the buyer is applying for an FHA or VA loan.

APPRAISAL PROVISIONS. Because the buyer's loan amount depends in part on the appraised value of the property, the financing contingency may include an appraisal contingency. This makes the agreement contingent on whether the property is appraised at the agreed sales price (or a higher value). If the appraisal indicates that the property isn't worth at least as much as the buyer agreed to pay, the buyer may cancel the agreement without forfeiting the good faith deposit.

If the appraisal is low, it may be possible to get a reappraisal. If the buyer is getting an FHA loan, the reappraisal must be made by the same appraiser who initially submitted the low appraisal. See Chapter 4 for a more general discussion of the low appraisal problem.

LENDER-REQUIRED INSPECTIONS. Before approving a loan application, many lenders require the property to be inspected, and a financing contingency may describe how a lender-required inspection will be handled. If so, the contingency will state that the seller agrees to allow this type of inspection. It will also state whether the seller will pay for the inspection (usually not).

If the inspection report says that repairs are needed, the lender may require the repairs to be completed as a condition of loan approval. The financing contingency may set a limit on how much the seller can be required to spend on repairs. If the repairs cost more than the seller agreed to pay and the parties cannot resolve the issue of payment, the agreement will terminate and the good faith deposit will be refunded to the buyer.

HOMEOWNER'S INSURANCE. Some financing contingencies make the transaction depend not only on whether the buyer can get a loan, but also on whether the buyer can get homeowner's insurance. At one time a buyer who could qualify for a loan would have no problem obtaining a homeowner's policy, but that isn't always the case now. Because of an increase in large claims in recent years, many insurance companies are imposing stricter standards.

An insurer might deny a buyer's application for a homeowner's policy because of the buyer's credit history or insurance claims history. Or the application might be denied because of the condition of the property or a history of insurance claims connected with the property. If the contingency provision covers insurance as well as financing and the buyer can't obtain a policy, she will be able to withdraw from the purchase agreement without forfeiting the good faith deposit.

INSPECTION CONTINGENCIES

Another very common type of contingency in residential deposit receipts is an inspection contingency. The contract may be made contingent on one or more expert inspections of the property: for example, a general home inspection, a geological inspection, a hazardous substances inspection, and/or a structural pest control inspection.

An inspection contingency should establish:

- which party is responsible for ordering and paying for the inspection;
- a deadline for the buyer to review inspection results and either remove the contingency or cancel the agreement;

• an opportunity for reinspection by the buyer if the seller needs to make repairs.

BUYER'S INSPECTIONS. Most inspection contingencies provide a deadline for the buyer to complete inspections and either remove the contingency or cancel the purchase agreement. The inspections must be ordered and completed, and the buyer must decide whether she approves or disapproves of the inspection report, before the contingency deadline. The seller is required to make the property available for the inspections.

Unless the property is brand-new, the inspections will almost certainly reveal at least a few issues with the property. Depending on the number and seriousness of the issues, the buyer may:

• ask the seller to make repairs to the property,
• negotiate a lower purchase price,
• remove the inspection contingency, or
• cancel the purchase agreement.

REQUEST FOR REPAIR. If the buyer wants the seller to make repairs, she can give the seller a request for repair form, such as the one shown in Figure 7.2. Each problem the buyer wants corrected should be listed on the form. It's a good idea to attach copies of any inspection reports or other documents describing the problems to help clarify the requested repair work.

If the seller is willing to make the repairs, the repairs are generally subject to reinspection and approval. If the seller refuses to make the requested repairs, the buyer then must decide whether to remove the condition and proceed with the transaction, or else terminate the purchase agreement.

Sometimes a seller responds to the buyer by offering to make only some of the requested repairs, or by offering to modify their contract in some way (for example, by lowering the purchase price). It is then up to the buyer to accept or reject the seller's offer. The parties may go back and forth in this way several times before a compromise is reached or the buyer decides to give up and terminate the contract.

EXAMPLE: A deposit receipt with an inspection contingency is signed on January 1. The deposit receipt gives the buyer, Ellen, fifteen days to

FIG. 7.2 REQUEST FOR REPAIR

Reprinted with permission, California Association of Realtors®. No endorsement implied.

have her inspections completed and notify the seller, Ralph, whether she will remove the contingency or cancel the agreement.

Ellen has the house inspected on January 4. On January 6, Ellen gives Ralph her request for repairs. She objects to the condition of the roof, attaches the portion of the written inspection report that describes the roof's condition, and asks Ralph to have the roof repaired. Ralph now must decide whether or not he wants to correct the roof's condition. Ellen and Ralph discuss lowering the sales price as an alternative to making repairs, but they can't agree on the amount of the price reduction and no written agreement is ever signed. On January 11, Ralph gives Ellen his response to the request for repairs, stating that he rejects the request to repair the roof.

Ellen now has five days to decide whether to remove the contingency or cancel the agreement. Ellen decides she does not want to purchase a house with roof problems, and she gives notice of cancellation on the 15th. The purchase agreement is now canceled, and the good faith deposit must be returned to Ellen.

By requesting and agreeing to make repairs, the parties are changing the terms of their contract. Because of this, you should always handle negotiations over repairs in writing. The form shown in Figure 7.2 provides space for the seller to respond to the buyer's request, and additional forms can be used if necessary.

Code Violations. Sellers should be aware that if an inspection reveals violations of the building code or other laws, public authorities could order them to correct the violations, whether or not the sale to the buyer proceeds.

Sale of Buyer's Home Contingencies

Unless you're helping them buy their first home, your buyers will usually have to sell their current home before buying a new one. For one thing, they probably need to sell their current home to generate the cash for the downpayment on the new home. Also, few buyers can afford the mortgage payments on two houses at the same time. For both of these reasons, it's very common to make the sale of the buyer's current home a condition of the contract for the purchase of the new home.

Depending on the terms of the deposit receipt, this condition may actually be a "hidden contingency." In other words, the agreement may be contingent on the sale of the buyer's home even though that contingency is not expressly stated in the agreement.

EXAMPLE: Wilder has agreed to purchase Greenbaum's home. The sale is contingent on financing: unless Wilder obtains a purchase loan from an institutional lender, the contract will not be binding.

When Wilder applies for a loan, she doesn't have enough cash for the downpayment she'll be required to make. She plans to sell her current home to get the necessary cash. The lender processes the application and approves the loan on the condition that Wilder obtain the necessary cash before closing. If Wilder is unable to sell her home before the closing date set in her contract with Greenbaum, she won't have the cash for the downpayment and the lender will refuse to fund the loan. Thus, the sale of Greenbaum's home is actually contingent on the sale of Wilder's home, even though this contingency was not stated in their deposit receipt.

Naturally, it's better to state the terms of any contingency clearly rather than leave it unstated or hidden behind another contingency. The seller needs to be aware of all the contingencies of the sale before he can make an informed decision about whether or not to accept the buyer's offer. This is particularly important when the buyer must sell her own property before completing the purchase. If this contingency is not made clear to the seller, the seller may believe that the buyer has a much better chance of getting a loan than she actually does. If the transaction doesn't close because the buyer is unable to sell her home (and thus get the loan), the seller could claim that by failing to disclose the hidden contingency, you misrepresented the buyer's financial ability to complete the purchase.

The C.A.R. deposit receipt form is designed to prevent this particular hidden contingency: the form specifically states that obtaining the good faith deposit, downpayment, and closing costs is *not* a contingency of the purchase agreement. If you use a different deposit receipt form, it may not have similar language, and this type of hidden contingency could be an issue.

ELEMENTS. Some deposit receipts have preprinted clauses to fill out in order to make the offer contingent on the sale of the buyer's home. Or an addendum may be used, such as the one shown in Figure 7.3. In any case, the contingency provision should be explicit about:

- the circumstances under which the condition will be considered fulfilled;
- the deadline for meeting the condition;
- what will happen if the condition isn't met or removed by the buyer; and
- what will happen if the seller gets another offer during the contingency period.

ACCEPTANCE OR CLOSING. There are two ways to set up this type of contingency provision. The sale can be made contingent on the buyer's *acceptance of an offer* to buy his current home, or on the *closing of the sale* of his current home. The seller will usually prefer to base fulfillment of the contingency on the buyer's acceptance of an offer. That way, the seller doesn't have to wait until the buyer's sale closes to know whether she and the buyer have a binding contract. If the buyer doesn't get an acceptable offer for his house within a specified period—for example, 30 days—then his agreement with the seller can be terminated.

From the buyer's point of view, it's preferable to base fulfillment of the contingency on the actual closing of his sale and the receipt of enough cash from that sale to close the transaction with the seller.

> **EXAMPLE:** Whitfield is offering to buy Mayer's home for $329,000, with a $33,000 downpayment. The deposit receipt will be contingent on the sale of Whitfield's current home.
>
> Whitfield wants the contingency clause to be written so that the condition will be fulfilled only if the sale of his home actually closes within 90 days and he nets enough cash to make his $33,000 downpayment. He's afraid of what would happen if the condition were fulfilled when he accepted an offer for his home, but that sale failed to close for some reason. He wouldn't be able to go through with his purchase of Mayer's home (because he wouldn't have the money for the downpayment). As a result, Whitfield would be in default on the purchase agreement, and he would forfeit his good faith deposit to Mayer.

FIG. 7.3   SALE OF BUYER'S HOME CONTINGENCY ADDENDUM

CALIFORNIA ASSOCIATION OF REALTORS®

CONTINGENCY FOR SALE OR PURCHASE OF OTHER PROPERTY
(C.A.R. Form COP, Revised 10/03)

This is an addendum to the ☐ California Residential Purchase Agreement, ☐ Counter Offer, ☐ Other _____
_____ ("Agreement"), dated _____
on property known as _____ ("Seller's Property"),
between _____ ("Buyer")
and _____ ("Seller").

A. ☐ (If checked) **SALE OF BUYER'S PROPERTY:**

1. **(a)** The Agreement is contingent on the close of escrow of Buyer's property, described as: _____
    _____ ("Buyer's Property").
    (b) If Buyer's Property does not close escrow by the earliest of: **(i)** the scheduled close of escrow of Seller's Property;
    (ii) the date specified in paragraph A3; or **(iii)** Other ☐ _____, then either Seller,
    after first giving Buyer a Notice to Buyer to Perform (C.A.R. Form NBP), or Buyer may cancel the Agreement in writing.

2. ☐ (If checked) Buyer's Property is **not** now in escrow and (check boxes as applicable):
    (a) ☐ is not yet listed for sale.
    (b) ☐ is listed for sale with _____ company and
    is offered for sale in the _____ MLS, # _____.
    (c) Buyer shall, within **17 (or** ☐ _____**) Days** After Acceptance, provide Seller with Copies of the contract,
    escrow instructions and all related documents ("Escrow Evidence") for the sale of Buyer's Property showing that
    Buyer's Property has entered escrow.

3. ☐ (If checked) Buyer's Property **is in escrow** with _____
    escrow holder, (escrow # _____) scheduled to close escrow on _____ (date).
    Buyer shall, within **5 Days** After Acceptance, deliver to Seller Escrow Evidence that Buyer's Property is in escrow.

4. If Buyer fails to provide to Seller Escrow Evidence within the time specified in A2(c) or A3, Seller, after first giving Buyer
    a Notice to Buyer to Perform, may cancel the Agreement in writing.

5. If Buyer's Property is in or enters escrow, Buyer shall give Seller written notice if either party to that escrow gives notice
    to the other of intent to cancel. In such event, either Buyer or Seller may cancel the Agreement in writing.

6. After Acceptance, Seller shall have the right to continue to offer the Property for sale:
    (a) Removal of Sale and Loan Contingency: If Seller accepts another written offer, Seller shall give written notice to
    Buyer to, in writing : **(i)** remove this contingency; **(ii)** remove the loan contingency, if any; **(iii)** provide verification of
    sufficient funds to close escrow without the sale of Buyer's Property; and **(iv)** comply with the following additional
    requirement(s): _____.
    If Buyer fails to complete these actions within **72 (or** ☐ _____**) hours** after receipt of such notice, Seller
    may immediately cancel the Agreement in writing.
    OR (b) ☐ (If checked) **Backup Offers Only:** Seller shall have the right to continue to offer the Property for sale for
    backup offers only and shall not invoke the notice provisions in paragraph A6(a): **(i)** within the first
    17 (or ☐ _____**) Days** After Acceptance; or **(ii)** (if checked) ☐ during the term of the Agreement.

B. ☐ (If checked) **SELLER'S PURCHASE OF REPLACEMENT PROPERTY:**

1. The Agreement is contingent on Seller entering a contract to acquire replacement property.

2. Seller shall, within **17 (or** ☐ _____**) Days** After Acceptance, remove this contingency or cancel the Agreement.
    If Seller does not remove this contingency in writing within that time, Buyer, after first giving Seller a Notice to Seller to
    Perform (C.A.R. Form NSP), may cancel the Agreement in writing.

3. **(a)** Time periods in the Agreement for inspections, contingencies, covenants and other obligations shall begin: **(i)** as
    specified in the Agreement; **(ii)** (if checked) ☐ the day after Seller delivers to Buyer a written notice removing this
    contingency; or **(iii)** (if checked) ☐ Other _____.
    (b) Buyer and Seller agree that Seller may, by providing Buyer written notice at the time Seller removes this contingency,
    extend the Close Of Escrow date for a maximum of _____ additional Days or until ☐ _____ (date).

4. Even after the expiration of the time specified in B2, Seller retains, until Buyer cancels pursuant to B2, the right to
    remove in writing this contingency or cancel the Agreement. Once Buyer receives Seller's written removal of this
    contingency, Buyer may not cancel pursuant to B2.

By signing below, Buyer and Seller each acknowledge that they have read, understand, accept and have received a copy of this Addendum.

Date _____   Date _____

Buyer _____   Seller _____

Buyer _____   Seller _____

SURE TRAC
The System for Success™

Published by the
California Association of REALTORS®

COP REVISED 10/03 (PAGE 1 OF 1) Print Date

Reviewed by _____ Date _____

CONTINGENCY FOR SALE OR PURCHASE OF OTHER PROPERTY (COP PAGE 1 OF 1)

Reprinted with permission, California Association of Realtors®. No endorsement implied.

On the other hand, Mayer wants the contingency clause to be written so that the condition will be fulfilled if Whitfield accepts an offer on his current home within 30 days of signing the deposit receipt with Mayer. Mayer doesn't want to wait up to 90 days to see whether Whitfield's sale is actually going to close. He wants to know that they have an enforceable contract much sooner than that. Otherwise, he would rather wait for another offer.

One way the buyer can handle this problem is by applying to a lender for a **swing loan** (also called a bridge loan or gap loan). This loan will provide the buyer with the funds to close the purchase of the new house. It creates a lien against the old house, and the buyer will pay it off when the sale of the old house eventually closes.

DEADLINES. The conflicting interests of the buyer and the seller are also apparent when you fill in the time periods in this type of contingency clause or addendum. The buyer will want as much time as possible to fulfill the contingency, so that her house can be sold for the highest possible price. The seller, on the other hand, will usually want the present transaction to close as soon as possible, so that he'll have the money from the sale more quickly. So the parties must agree on a compromise that will give the buyer a reasonable length of time to market her house without delaying the resolution of the present transaction (either a successful closing or the failure of the condition) for too long.

It's extremely important to make sure that the dates in the contingency clause agree with the other dates in the deposit receipt. For example, the contingency should not give the buyer 120 days to sell her home if the current sale is supposed to close within 90 days.

RELEASE CLAUSES. When a deposit receipt is contingent on the sale of the buyer's home, it's common to include a provision that gives the seller the right to keep the house on the market and accept another offer. This provision, known as a "release clause" or a "72-hour clause," may be used with any type of contingency, but is most commonly used with offers that are contingent on the sale of the buyer's home. That's because this contingency tends to involve greater uncertainty and a longer wait than other types. While you can usually predict whether a buyer will be able to get a loan or whether a pest inspection will be satisfactory, it's harder to predict whether a buyer will be able to sell his home by a certain date on terms that will generate a certain amount of cash.

A release clause helps reconcile the buyer's need for time to sell his current home with the seller's need for a timely resolution of her contingent contract with the buyer. It may also solve the problem of whether to make the contract contingent on the buyer's acceptance of an offer or on the closing of the sale of the buyer's home. Essentially, a release clause allows the seller to accept an uncertain offer without having to take her property off the market.

The contingency addendum in Figure 7.3 includes a release clause. It provides that the seller will have the right to continue to market her property until the buyer notifies the seller that the contingency has been satisfied or removed. If the seller receives and accepts a second offer during this period, the seller will notify the buyer of this acceptance. The buyer is given a short period of time—the default period is 72 hours—to notify the seller that the sale of buyer's home contingency and the financing contingency have both been either satisfied or removed. Otherwise, the seller may cancel the transaction and the deposit will be returned to the buyer.

PURCHASE OF REPLACEMENT PROPERTY CONTINGENCIES

Just like buyers who are selling their current home to buy a new one, sellers often want to buy another home when they sell their current property. Occasionally a seller will want to make the deposit receipt contingent on whether she's able to find a new home to buy. This is known as a contingency for the purchase of replacement property.

This type of contingency is much less common than a sale of buyer's home contingency. While a purchase agreement may fall apart if the buyer isn't able to sell his current home, a delay in finding a new home usually won't prevent the seller from going through with the sale.

The contingency form in Figure 7.3 can be used to make a sale contingent either on the sale of the buyer's current home or on the seller's purchase of a replacement property.

OTHER TYPES OF CONTINGENCIES

The financing contingency, inspection contingency, and sale of buyer's home contingency are the types of contingencies you will encounter most often. But the parties can agree to make their contract contingent on almost any condition that might affect whether one or both of them want to go through with the transaction. If the buyer or seller wants to make the purchase agreement contingent on a specific event, check with your broker about what forms to use.

UNFULFILLED CONTINGENCIES

As we discussed at the beginning of this chapter, the party that benefits from a contingency provision must make a good faith effort to fulfill it. Naturally, your job as a real estate agent is to help the parties satisfy any contingencies so that they can successfully complete the transaction. But sometimes, despite your best efforts, a contingency can't be fulfilled, and the benefiting party will decide to cancel the purchase agreement.

NOTICES TO PERFORM

A contingency provision should always set a deadline for the benefiting party (usually the buyer) to fulfill or remove the condition. If the buyer doesn't meet this deadline, the seller may terminate the purchase agreement. Before doing this, however, the contingency clause usually requires the seller to give the buyer a notice to perform. This lets the buyer know that the deadline has passed and gives her one last chance to decide if she wants to remove the contingency and proceed with the transaction.

The C.A.R. Notice to Buyer to Perform is shown in Figure 7.4. It can be used if the buyer misses the deadline to remove a contingency, or if the buyer is late in meeting an obligation set forth in the deposit receipt. Similarly, the buyer can give the seller a notice to perform if the seller has not satisfied some of his obligations under the purchase agreement.

CANCELING THE PURCHASE AGREEMENT

When a purchase agreement is terminated because a contingency was neither satisfied nor removed, the seller usually still wants to sell the property. In some cases, the seller has already entered into a backup agreement that is conditioned on the termination of the first agreement. But uncertainties about the rights and obligations of the buyer and seller under the first agreement may cause problems for a subsequent sale.

FIG. 7.4   NOTICE TO BUYER TO PERFORM

CALIFORNIA ASSOCIATION OF REALTORS®

NOTICE TO BUYER TO PERFORM
No. _____
(C.A.R. Form NBP, Revised 10/02)

In accordance with the terms and conditions of the: ☐ California Residential Purchase Agreement or ☐ Other _____
_____ ("Agreement"), dated _____,
on property known as _____ ("Property"),
between _____ ("Buyer"),
and _____ ("Seller").

SELLER hereby gives Buyer notice to remove the following contingencies or take the specified contractual action:

Contingency

☐ **ALL CONTINGENCIES**
A. ☐ Loan (Paragraph 2I)
B. ☐ Appraisal (Paragraph 2J)
C. ☐ Tenant-Occupied Property (Paragraph 3C(iii))
D. ☐ Disclosures/Reports (Paragraphs 4 and 5)
E. ☐ Common Interest (HOA) Disclosures (Paragraph 6B)
F. ☐ Buyer Investigation, including insurability (Paragraph 9)
G. ☐ Title: Preliminary Report (Paragraph 12)
H. ☐ Sale of Buyer's Property (Paragraph 13)
I. ☐ _____
J. ☐ _____
K. ☐ _____

Contractual Action

L. ☐ Initial Deposit (Paragraph 2A)
M. ☐ Increased Deposit (Paragraph 2B)
N. ☐ Loan Application Letter (Paragraph 2G)
O. ☐ Down Payment Verification (Paragraph 2H)
P. ☐ All Cash Verification (Paragraph 2L)
Q. ☐ Return of Statutory Disclosures (Paragraph 5A(2))
R. ☐ Return of Lead Disclosures (Paragraph 5A(2))
S. ☐ Receipt for Increased Deposit (Paragraph 16)
T. ☐ Escrow Evidence, Sale of Buyer's Property (C.A.R. Form COP, Paragraph A2 or A3)
U. ☐ _____
V. ☐ _____

NOTE: Paragraph numbers refer to the California Residential Purchase Agreement (C.A.R. Form RPA-CA)

BUYER: If you do not remove the contingency(ies) (C.A.R. Form CR) or take the contractual actions specified above within 24 (or ☐ _____) hours (but no less than the time specified in the Agreement) of receipt of this Notice to Buyer to Perform, Seller may cancel the Agreement.

_____   _____   _____ AM/PM
Seller   Date   Time

_____   _____   _____ AM/PM
Seller   Date   Time

(____/____) (Initials) **CONFIRMATION OF RECEIPT:** A Copy of this Signed Notice to Buyer to Perform was personally received by Buyer or authorized agent on _____ (date), at _____ AM/PM.

SURE TRAC The System for Success™
Published by the California Association of REALTORS®

Reviewed by _____ Date _____

EQUAL HOUSING OPPORTUNITY

NBP REVISED 10/02 (PAGE 1 OF 1) Print Date

NOTICE TO BUYER TO PERFORM (NBP PAGE 1 OF 1)

Reprinted with permission, California Association of Realtors®. No endorsement implied.

Thus, a second sale should not proceed until the first agreement has been officially terminated and it is clearly established that the first buyer has no right to enforce that earlier agreement. This is done by having the first buyer and the seller sign a cancellation agreement.

As explained in Chapter 5, a cancellation agreement formally terminates a purchase agreement. It should authorize the party who is holding the good faith deposit—either the broker or the closing agent—to disburse it to the appropriate party. Remember, if the parties disagree about how the good faith deposit should be handled, the broker should not disburse the funds to either of them. Instead, mediation, arbitration, or a court proceeding will be necessary to determine who is entitled to the funds. An example of a cancellation agreement is shown in Chapter 5 (Figure 5.3).

CHAPTER SUMMARY

1. Most deposit receipts are contingent on the occurrence of a specified event (or events). Unless the event occurs, the party benefiting from the contingency (usually the buyer) is not obligated to follow through with the transaction. The party benefiting from the contingency has an obligation to make a good faith effort to fulfill it.

2. A contingency provision should state what the condition is and what has to occur to fulfill it, the time limit for fulfilling or removing the condition, and what happens if the condition is not fulfilled or removed.

3. The three most common types of contingencies in residential deposit receipts are financing contingencies, inspection contingencies, and sale of the buyer's home contingencies.

4. A financing contingency gives the buyer the right to be released from the agreement without forfeiting her deposit if she can't get the financing she needs. The financing contingency may be specific or general about the terms of the loan the buyer will apply for.

5. An inspection contingency conditions the sale on a satisfactory structural, pest, soil, geological, or hazardous substances inspection. The inspection contingency should state who is responsible for ordering and paying for the inspection and set a deadline for reviewing results and either removing the contingency or canceling the agreement.

6. An offer may be conditioned on the sale of the buyer's current home. The contingency provision should state whether the condition will be fulfilled by the acceptance of an offer or when the sale of the buyer's home closes; the deadline for fulfillment or removal of the contingency; and what happens if the seller gets another offer during the contingency period.

7. A release clause allows the seller to continue actively marketing her property during the contingency period. If the seller accepts another offer, the seller notifies the first buyer and gives the first buyer a short time to either meet or remove the contingency, or the first contract will terminate.

8. If a contingent transaction fails, the buyer and seller should sign a cancellation agreement. A cancellation agreement formally terminates the purchase agreement and authorizes the disbursement of the good faith deposit. Once a cancellation agreement has been signed by the first buyer and the seller, the seller can safely enter into a purchase agreement with another buyer.

CHAPTER QUIZ

1. If a contingency clause benefits both parties to a contract, it:
   a. can only be removed with the consent of both parties
   b. cannot be removed by either party
   c. can be removed by either party
   d. can be removed by the buyer, but not by the seller

2. A contract is considered illusory if:
   a. the contract has not been signed
   b. one party is not actually obligated to perform any duties under the contract
   c. one party does not have discretion over whether or not to fulfill the contract
   d. the contract contains a contingency that hasn't been satisfied

3. Which of the following is least likely to be included in a financing contingency provision?
   a. The parties' options in case of a low appraisal
   b. The amount of the buyer's downpayment
   c. The terms of the seller financing arrangement
   d. A deadline for applying for the loan

4. If an inspection reveals building code violations, which of the following is true?
   a. The buyer's lender may require the seller to correct the violations as a condition of loan approval
   b. The buyer may require the seller to correct the violations before proceeding with the contract
   c. Public authorities may order the seller to correct the violations whether or not the transaction closes
   d. All of the above

5. An inspection contingency provision will often contain a:
   a. hidden contingency
   b. clause providing for a reinspection of the property after any repairs are made
   c. schedule of adjustments in the purchase price for different problems that may be found during the inspection
   d. release clause allowing the seller to keep the property on the market and accept other offers

6. After an inspection, the buyer requests that the seller make certain repairs. Which of the following is not one of the ways in which the seller can respond?
   a. Removing the inspection contingency
   b. Refusing to make the requested repairs
   c. Offering to modify the contract
   d. Offering to make only some of the requested repairs

7. A sale of buyer's home contingency will usually state:
   a. a price at which the buyer will be required to accept an offer on his current home
   b. that the seller may continue to market her property until the contingency is removed or fulfilled
   c. that all contingencies must be waived on any offer on the buyer's current home
   d. a deadline for applying for a swing loan

8. With a sale of buyer's home contingency, the common approaches to resolving the conflicting needs of the buyer and seller do not include:
   a. having the buyer get the funds to close the purchase of the seller's home with a swing loan
   b. allowing the seller to keep his property on the market and accept other offers
   c. a release clause
   d. a cancellation agreement

9. Which of the following is true of most contingencies?

   a. The seller wants the contingency resolved quickly so that he knows whether the transaction will go through

   b. The benefiting party is not required to make any effort to fulfill the contingency

   c. Before the buyer removes the contingency, she must give the seller a notice to perform

   d. The seller is usually the party that benefits from the contingency

10. Which of the following ways of including a contingency in a deposit receipt would *not* be advisable?

    a. Using a preprinted contingency addendum form

    b. Checking a contingency clause in the deposit receipt form itself

    c. Having an attorney draft a special contingency clause

    d. Writing a special contingency clause yourself on an addendum form

ANSWER KEY

1. a. When a contingency clause benefits both parties to a contract, the condition can only be removed with the consent of both parties. If the condition isn't satisfied, either party can terminate the contract.

2. b. A contract is considered illusory when one party has complete discretion over whether a contingency will be fulfilled. In effect, that party is not obligated to perform any duties under the contract. An illusory contract is not enforceable.

3. c. If the seller is going to provide financing for the buyer, the terms should be set forth in another addendum, and the financing forms that will be used must be attached. (Seller financing is not ordinarily treated as a contingency.)

4. d. Either the buyer or the buyer's lender may require repairs based on an inspection report. And if an inspection reveals violations of the building code or other laws, public authorities could order the seller to correct the violations, regardless of whether the sale to the buyer proceeds.

5. b. If the seller makes repairs to address problems revealed by an inspection, the seller typically must allow the property to be reinspected once the repairs have been completed.

6. a. The inspection contingency is for the benefit of the buyer, so only the buyer has the ability to remove it.

7. b. A typical sale of buyer's home contingency will include a release clause, which allows the seller to keep her property on the market and consider other offers.

8. d. A cancellation agreement terminates a purchase agreement, so it would only be used if the contingency was not fulfilled.

9. a. Most contingencies benefit the buyer, and the seller wants the contingency to be resolved as soon as possible. The seller doesn't want to take the property off the market for long if the transaction is not certain to go through.

10. d. You should never try to draft a contingency clause yourself, since that might be considered the unauthorized practice of law.

8

LOAN QUALIFYING

PREQUALIFYING BUYERS
- Prequalifying vs. preapproval
- How to prequalify buyers

THE UNDERWRITING PROCESS
- Income analysis
  - Stable monthly income
  - Income verification
  - Income ratios
- Net worth
- Credit history
- Low documentation loans

CHOOSING A LOAN
- Truth in Lending Act
- Other finance disclosure laws
- Locking in the interest rate
- Other considerations

INTRODUCTION

Many buyers, especially first-time buyers, have only a vague idea of what they can afford to pay for a home. Other buyers think they know exactly how much they can afford to pay for housing on a monthly basis, but they don't realize that the percentage of income they're prepared to spend on a mortgage payment would be unacceptably high to a lender.

While financing the sale is the buyer's responsibility, and judging the creditworthiness of the buyer is the lender's responsibility, you should be prepared to help your buyers assess their financial qualifications and show them houses that are in the right price range. In this chapter, we will explain loan prequalifying and preapproval. We'll also review the underwriting process lenders use to evaluate the creditworthiness of mortgage loan applicants, and how a loan applicant can compare different loans.

PREQUALIFYING BUYERS

A couple finds a house that they are thrilled with. It costs more than they planned to spend, but it's perfect for them. They immediately make a full-price offer, and the seller accepts it. The buyers apply for a loan and happily make arrangements to move into the house. Unfortunately, their loan application is rejected. The sale, which was contingent on financing, is terminated, and the seller is very upset. The buyers are mortified. In fact, they feel so bad that they postpone looking for another house indefinitely.

Could you have helped the buyers avoid the disappointment of a rejected loan application? Would you have advised them to make an offer on that particular house? Would you even have shown them that house in the first place?

This scenario could have been prevented if the buyers had found out how large a mortgage loan they could qualify for before they started house-hunting. Their maximum loan amount, together with the money they have available for a downpayment and closing costs, determines the upper limit of their price range. If they'd known their maximum loan amount, they would have focused their search on homes that they could afford.

PREQUALIFYING VS. PREAPPROVAL

There are two ways homebuyers can find out in advance how large a mortgage loan they'll be able to obtain: they can get prequalified for a loan, or they can get preapproved for one.

Prequalifying is an informal process that can be done by a real estate agent or by a lender. You prequalify buyers when you sit down with them, ask them a variety of questions about their income, assets, debts, and credit history, and then use that information to determine a range of affordable home prices.

Preapproval, by contrast, is a formal process that can only be done by a lender. To get preapproved, buyers must complete a loan application and provide the required supporting documentation, just as if they were applying for a loan after finding a house. The lender evaluates an application for preapproval in the same way as an ordinary loan application, with this exception: there's no property appraisal or title report at this point, since the buyers have not yet chosen a home to buy. If the buyers are creditworthy, the lender uses their income and net worth information to set a maximum loan amount. The lender gives the buyers a **preapproval letter**, agreeing to loan them up to the specified amount when they find the home they want to buy, as long as the property meets the lender's standards. The preapproval letter will expire at the end of a specified period—for example, after three or four months. If the buyers haven't found the house they want yet, the lender may agree to an extension.

The basic point of prequalifying and preapproval is the same. Both let buyers know in advance how expensive a home they can afford. But preapproval has some distinct advantages over prequalifying.

For one thing, a preapproval letter can be an extremely useful tool in negotiating with a seller. It gives the seller confidence that if he accepts the buyers' offer, the financing contingency won't be a problem; the buyers are ready, willing, and able to buy. In an active market, a listing agent might advise her sellers to consider offers only from preapproved buyers. Certainly, a seller weighing two or more offers should always take into account whether each buyer has been preapproved or not.

In addition to its value in negotiations, preapproval helps streamline the closing process. The lender has already fully evaluated the buyers, and only the appraisal and title report remain to be done. For buyers who are sure that they're ready to buy, preapproval can be terrific. Getting preapproved for a loan has become a very popular choice.

On the other hand, many buyers aren't ready to take the formal step of applying for a loan before they've even started looking for a house. They may want to get a better idea of what's available on the market and what they can afford before they go any further. For them, prequalifying is a better choice, at least initially. But if they will be competing with many other buyers in an active market, they should probably get preapproved at some point before they start making offers.

PREQUALIFICATION AND PREAPPROVAL LETTERS. A buyer who has been prequalified by a lender will usually be given a **prequalification letter**. It's important to distinguish between a prequalification letter and a preapproval letter. Unlike a preapproval letter, a prequalification letter does not commit the lender to making a loan. The lender will still have to fully analyze and verify the buyer's financial information before a loan is approved. For this reason, a prequalification letter doesn't wield the same clout in negotiations with a seller that a preapproval letter does.

Buyers and sellers should beware of mislabeling. A lender might refer to its letter as a preapproval letter, but indicate in the body of the letter that loan approval is subject to verification of the buyer's income and credit information. This is really only a prequalification letter and should be treated as such.

USING A LENDER'S LETTER IN NEGOTIATIONS. In negotiations with sellers, there's one potential disadvantage to a letter from a lender, whether it's a preapproval letter or a prequalification letter. The lender's letter will ordinarily state the *maximum* amount that the buyer is preapproved or prequalified for. This is fine if the buyer is looking for a home near the upper limit of her price range, but it can be a drawback if she is making an offer on a home that's well within the limit.

EXAMPLE: The buyer has a preapproval letter that says she's financially qualified to purchase property worth up to $350,000. But the buyer is interested in a home that's listed for only $320,000, and she wants to make a starting offer of $310,000. The seller will be able to tell from the buyer's preapproval letter that the buyer could easily afford to pay the full listing price for his home. That's likely to make the seller much less inclined to accept a lower offer than he might otherwise be.

There is a way around this problem. To make an offer on this property, the buyer could ask her lender for a special version of the preapproval letter indicating that the buyer is preapproved to purchase a $325,000 home. This would assure the seller that the buyer is financially qualified to buy his home, without revealing the buyer's full purchasing power.

Your broker may have a specific policy or general guidelines about prequalifying and preapproval. Some brokers encourage their agents to prequalify buyers themselves, as part of the process of getting to know their buyers. Other brokers have their agents refer buyers to a lender to be prequalified; this puts the buyers in expert hands and allows agents to focus on finding suitable homes. Still other brokers want their agents to work only with buyers who have been formally preapproved for a loan. But whatever your broker's policy, you should understand how prequalifying works.

HOW TO PREQUALIFY BUYERS

The prequalifying process is essentially an informal version of a lender's underwriting procedures. Let's suppose some first-time buyers, a young couple, have come into your office for help in finding a home. You're going to prequalify them yourself rather than sending them to a lender. You will ask the buyers about their income, assets, debts, and credit history, and then calculate a loan amount for them, using the underwriting standards that lenders generally apply. That loan amount will be the basis for setting a realistic price range for the buyers.

Your first step should be to choose a quiet, private place to talk with the buyers. Many buyers are uncomfortable discussing their financial situation when they feel their conversation is being overheard by strangers. Most people consider their financial information confidential.

For the same reason, you need to explain the importance of the prequalifying process. Although at first you might feel awkward asking people you've just met for financial information, they usually won't hesitate to provide it if they understand why you need it to help them find the right house.

Make sure that your conversation is free from interruptions. Give your full attention to the buyers. Don't interrupt them to take phone calls, and don't browse through listings while they are talking.

FIG. 8.1   PREQUALIFYING INTERVIEW QUESTIONS

- How long have you lived where you live now?
- How soon do you want to move?
- Do you own your current home or are you renting?
- Do you have to sell your current home to buy a new one?
- How much do you expect to get from the sale of your current home?
- Will you have to convert any other assets (such as stocks or bonds) into cash to buy a new home?
- What price range are you considering for your new home?
- How big a downpayment do you want to make?
- How much do you feel you can spend for housing on a monthly basis?
- Where are you employed?
- How long have you worked there?
- What is your monthly income from your employment?
- Do you have any other sources of income?
- What kind of monthly expenses do you have?
- Have you had any credit problems in the past?

A good prequalifier asks the buyers for more than just their basic financial information. The prequalification interview should also reveal their motives for buying, how prepared they are to buy, and their time frame for buying. Some of the questions you may want to ask your buyers are listed in Figure 8.1.

Once you have the answers to your questions, you're ready to do the prequalifying calculations. For this step, your broker may have a prequalifying worksheet for you to use along with a handheld financial calculator. Or you could use prequalifying software provided by your broker or a lender, or a prequalifying calculator offered online. (If you use an online prequalifying calculator, make sure it's on a reliable website, such as the website of an established, reputable lender, or Fannie Mae or Freddie Mac's website.)

Whatever tool you use, this is the underlying process:

1. Income ratios are applied to the buyers' monthly income and debt payments to calculate the approximate maximum monthly mortgage payment they will qualify for. This payment amount must cover principal, interest, taxes, and insurance (PITI).
2. The payment amount is reduced by a certain percentage that represents the taxes and insurance, to arrive at an estimate of the maximum principal and interest payment.
3. This maximum principal and interest payment, along with the interest rate that would probably apply in the current market, is used to calculate the maximum loan amount.
4. The maximum loan amount is divided by an appropriate loan-to-value ratio to determine the most the buyers can pay for a home.

EXAMPLE: Applying standard income ratios to your buyers' income and expenses, you calculate that they can qualify for a monthly mortgage payment of $1,941. You subtract 15% as an estimate of the portion of the payment that will have to cover property taxes, hazard insurance, and mortgage insurance. The result is $1,650. That's the principal and interest payment they qualify for.

You know that in the current market they should be able to get a 30-year fixed-rate loan at 6.25% annual interest. By entering the payment amount, loan term, and interest rate into your calculator, you determine that the original principal amount of a 30-year mortgage at 6.25% with a monthly principal and interest payment of $1,650 would be about $268,000. This is the buyers' maximum loan amount. The next step is to divide the loan amount by a loan-to-value ratio. You decide to use a 90% LTV in this case. The answer is approximately $298,000, and that's the buyers' maximum purchase price. They can qualify for a $268,000 loan to buy a $298,000 home, paying $30,000 down.

This example is just intended to give you a sense of the basic process. In real life, prequalifying is more complicated. For instance, maybe the buyers don't have $30,000 for a downpayment. In that case, they'll need to consider alternatives such as a smaller loan amount, a 95% loan, gift funds, or a special financing program. A lender's qualifying standards interact with factors such as the loan-to-value ratio, the loan term, the loan program, the interest rate, and discount points to create affordable

---

FIG. 8.2   PREQUALIFYING A PROSPECTIVE HOME BUYER

- APPLY INCOME RATIOS TO BUYER'S INCOME AND EXPENSES TO DETERMINE MAXIMUM MONTHLY MORTGAGE PAYMENT (PITI)

- SUBTRACT TAXES AND INSURANCE TO FIND MAXIMUM PRINCIPAL AND INTEREST PAYMENT

- CALCULATE MAXIMUM LOAN AMOUNT BASED ON MAXIMUM PRINCIPAL AND INTEREST PAYMENT AND MARKET INTEREST RATE

- DIVIDE MAXIMUM LOAN AMOUNT BY LOAN-TO-VALUE RATIO TO DETERMINE CEILING OF PRICE RANGE

---

financing options for a particular buyer. The more you know about the alternatives, the better your prequalifying will be. We'll cover loan features and loan programs in the next chapter.

BUYERS WHO HAVE ALREADY FOUND A HOUSE. It's ideal when buyers get prequalified or preapproved before they begin house-hunting, but that won't always be the case. Sometimes buyers come to you after they have already found their dream home. For instance, they may have found the home they want by going to various open houses. Now they want you to show them that home again, give them additional information about the property, and help them make an offer. Even though these buyers don't want you to show them any other homes, they should still be prequalified. You may discover that they can't afford the home they've chosen. It will save them time, disappointment, and embarrassment if you can steer them to a more affordable home.

EXAMPLE: The Langleys went to an open house and immediately decided to make an offer. The house has everything they want, including four bedrooms, a formal dining room, a fireplace in the master suite, and a swimming pool. They got your name from a neighbor and want you to set up an appointment so they can see the home one more time and gather some additional information about the property. They are especially interested in finding out about local schools for their children.

When you meet the Langleys, you tell them that to better serve them, you need some preliminary information. You begin the prequalifying process and discover that the house costs a lot more than they can afford. You know they will be disappointed, and you break the news gently. "I know you really want this house," you say. "But lenders are just going to look at your current income and your current savings. And the numbers simply don't work for this house. But there are several attractive properties that you could easily finance. I know of one in particular that's only a few blocks away from the best elementary school in the district."

By prequalifying the Langleys (or sending them to a lender for prequalification or preapproval), you save them from a loan rejection and are able to steer them to more affordable housing.

BUYERS WHO HAVE PREQUALIFIED THEMSELVES. It's increasingly likely that you'll meet buyers who tell you that they've already prequalified themselves for a loan using an online calculator at a lender's website. There is a lot of good homebuyer education information on the Internet, and buyers who are so inclined should be encouraged to make use of it. But it isn't safe to assume that your buyers have been able to use the online information and prequalifying tools well.

For example, a buyer might calculate his stable monthly income incorrectly, either by failing to count a source of income that a lender would consider acceptable (such as regular seasonal work), or by counting a type of income that a lender would ignore (such as recent unusual overtime). Or the buyer might not understand that there are limits on the amount of gift funds that a lender will allow him to use toward the required downpayment. These and similar mistakes could make the conclusion reached with an online prequalifying calculator very misleading. It might lead the buyer to believe that he can qualify for a much bigger loan—or a much smaller one—than he actually can.

Whenever possible, you should persuade your buyers to go through the prequalifying process with a professional (either with you or with a lender) to assess their buying power more accurately.

THE UNDERWRITING PROCESS

Before you can prequalify buyers or discuss financing options with them, you must understand the criteria a lender will use to qualify a buyer for a loan. These criteria are referred to as **qualifying standards** or **loan underwriting standards**.

Loan underwriting is the process a lender goes through to evaluate the buyer and the property to determine whether the proposed loan would be a good risk. The lender has employees called loan underwriters (or credit underwriters) who carry out the underwriting process and decide whether to accept or reject the loan application.

Every loan carries some degree of risk. In fact, every time a lender makes a loan, the lender assumes two risks:

1. the risk that the borrower will not pay off the loan as agreed; and
2. the risk that, if the borrower does default, the property will be worth less than what the borrower owes the lender.

If a loan underwriter feels that these events are likely to occur, the loan is considered too risky, and the application will be rejected.

To evaluate the lender's risk, the underwriter tries to answer two questions during the underwriting process:

1. Can the borrower be expected to make the monthly loan payments on time, based on his or her overall financial situation?
2. If the borrower defaults, will the security property generate enough money in a foreclosure sale to pay off the loan balance?

To help answer these two questions, the underwriter applies underwriting standards to both the buyer and the property. The underwriter's evaluation of the property is based on an appraisal. The appraisal process is similar to the process you go through when you price property (discussed in Chapter 4), but it is more rigorous. In this chapter, we will focus on the standards that are applied to the buyer.

Many years ago, individual lenders established their own qualifying standards. Today, most lenders use the qualifying standards set by the major secondary market agencies (Fannie Mae and Freddie Mac), or by the FHA or the VA. Secondary market agencies purchase loans from lenders as an investment. If a conventional loan doesn't meet the standards set by these agencies, it is considered **nonconforming**, and it generally can't be sold on the secondary market. And a loan that doesn't meet the standards set by the FHA or the VA isn't eligible for FHA insurance or the VA guaranty.

Each loan program has its own set of qualifying standards, but the underwriting process is basically the same no matter what type of loan the buyer has applied for. This section will focus on the basic underwriting process. The specific qualifying standards for the major loan programs will be discussed in the next chapter.

Nowadays, a lender may handle many aspects of the underwriting process by computer. For example, Fannie Mae and Freddie Mac provide special underwriting software for lenders who sell loans to them. And some large lenders have their own underwriting software.

While computer programs can speed up the underwriting process, the analysis of a loan application can't be entirely automated. As a general rule, the ultimate decision—whether or not to approve the loan—is still made by human beings, not computers.

When qualifying a buyer, a lender examines the information included in the loan application, plus additional information acquired from a credit report and verification forms. The lender uses all this information to evaluate the buyer's complete financial situation. This information can be broken down into three basic categories:

1. income,
2. net worth, and
3. credit history.

INCOME ANALYSIS

An underwriter carefully analyzes a loan applicant's income to see if he or she can really afford the monthly payment that would be required to pay off the requested loan. Once you know how an underwriter analyzes income, you can do the same computations yourself to prequalify your buyers. This is the key information you'll rely on to determine the price range of homes they should be looking at, or whether they can afford the payments on the particular home they've already chosen.

When an underwriter looks at a loan applicant's income, she goes through a two-step process. First, the underwriter will decide how much of the applicant's income is acceptable income, generally referred to as **stable monthly income**. Next, the underwriter will decide if the loan applicant has enough stable monthly income to make the monthly mortgage payment reliably.

CHARACTERISTICS OF STABLE MONTHLY INCOME. To be counted as stable monthly income, a loan applicant's income must be of a high quality, and it must also be durable.

QUALITY. To evaluate the quality of an applicant's income, the underwriter looks at the source. High-quality income comes from a dependable source. For example, if the income is salary income, the more established the employer, the higher the quality of the income.

EXAMPLE: Your buyer, Hathaway, has applied for a loan. She works for the U.S. Postal Service. Because the Postal Service is a government agency, it is considered a very dependable source of income. Therefore, Hathaway's salary will be considered high-quality income.

The less dependable the source of the income, the lower the quality of that income.

EXAMPLE: Suppose instead that Hathaway works for a new construction company that is struggling to make ends meet. The underwriter might decide that the company is not a very dependable source of income, and therefore consider Hathaway's salary low-quality income.

DURABILITY. Income is considered durable if it can be expected to continue for a long period of time. Durable income typically includes wages from permanent employment, disability benefits, and interest on established investments. An example of a type of income that isn't considered durable is income from unemployment benefits. Unemployment benefits, by their very nature, are not expected to continue for a long period of time.

ACCEPTABLE TYPES OF INCOME. Lenders have general rules of thumb that they follow when determining what is or is not stable monthly income. Let's take a look at some of those general rules.

PERMANENT EMPLOYMENT. Lenders will accept a loan applicant's income from permanent employment as stable monthly income only if he has a history of continuous, stable employment. As a general rule, a loan applicant should have continuous employment for at least two years in the same field. However, each of your buyers is unique. Even without a two-year work history, there may be extenuating circumstances that would warrant loan approval; for example, having recently finished college or left the armed services. Special training or education can also make up for minor weaknesses in job history.

Another point to keep in mind: if your buyer has changed jobs once or twice within the last few years to advance within the same line of work, this is a good sign. However, if she has changed jobs persistently without any advancement, the lender will probably see this as a problem.

SELF-EMPLOYMENT. Special rules apply if the loan applicant's primary income source is self-employment. Self-employment income is considered less durable and dependable than other types of employment income, so lenders are more reluctant to count it as stable monthly income.

A self-employed buyer will have to meet rigorous qualifying standards. If he has been self-employed for less than two years, he may have a hard time qualifying for a loan. And if he has been in business for less than one year, it will be even more difficult. A lender will only count the income of a self-employed buyer who has been in business for a short time if the buyer has a history of employment in the same field and can document a reasonable chance for success based on market feasibility studies and pro forma financial statements. This is difficult to do, but not impossible.

OTHER EMPLOYMENT INCOME. In addition to a salary or wages from a full-time job, a buyer can use other types of employment income to qualify for a loan. Bonuses, commissions, and part-time earnings can be considered stable monthly income if they've been a regular part of a loan applicant's overall earnings pattern for at least one, but preferably two, years. Lenders prefer not to consider overtime stable income, but they will if overtime is clearly a regular part of the applicant's earnings.

EXAMPLE: Schwinn's salary is $2,500 a month. Over the last three months, she worked many hours of overtime. She averaged an additional $500 a month in overtime during those three months. A lender will not count that additional $500 a month as stable income, because Schwinn only earned it for three months.

If, however, Schwinn could show that she earned an average of $500 a month in overtime over the previous 14 months, the lender would probably consider that part of her stable monthly income. Or if Schwinn could show that she earned an average of $1,500 a year in seasonal overtime from September to November every year for the past three years, and that this pattern is likely to continue, the lender would probably be willing to count the overtime as stable income.

SECONDARY INCOME SOURCES. There are other acceptable income sources besides employment income. For example, **pension and social security payments** are also considered part of a loan applicant's stable monthly income.

Alimony or spousal support payments are only considered stable monthly income if the payments are reliable. So the underwriter will look to see whether the payments are required by a court decree, how long the loan applicant has been receiving the payments, the financial status of the ex-spouse, and the applicant's ability to compel payment.

Child support payments are accepted as stable monthly income under the same conditions: if they are required by a court decree and there is proof of regular payment. If payments are missed, or regularly late, the underwriter may decide to exclude the child support from the loan applicant's stable monthly income. Also, child support payments typically stop when the child turns 18. So the closer the child is to age 18, the less durable the child support income is. If the child is over 15, the underwriter probably won't count the support payments as part of the loan applicant's stable monthly income.

> **EXAMPLE:** Martinez gets court-ordered child support for her daughter, who is 16, and for her son, who is 13. Martinez has received the child support regularly for three years. The lender will probably consider only the child support for her son as part of her stable monthly income. The child support for the daughter will only last another two years, so it isn't durable.

Income from **public assistance programs** may also be acceptable income. The Equal Credit Opportunity Act prohibits lenders from discriminating against loan applicants just because all or part of their income is from a public assistance program, such as welfare, food stamps, or Temporary Assistance to Needy Families. Public assistance payments are considered stable monthly income if they are durable—that is, if they are expected to continue for a long period of time. If the loan applicant's eligibility for the program will terminate shortly, the lender is unlikely to consider the income as part of the loan applicant's stable monthly income.

> **EXAMPLE:** A loan applicant receives monthly income from a public assistance program. Although the lender generally will consider public

assistance payments as stable monthly income, the loan applicant's eligibility for this particular program is expected to run out in a year and a half. From the lender's point of view, the payments are not durable enough to be counted in calculating the applicant's stable monthly income.

Dividends or interest on investments are also part of stable monthly income, unless the loan applicant will need to cash in the investment to have enough funds for a downpayment or to pay for closing costs.

Lenders will accept **rental income** as stable monthly income if the loan applicant can prove that the rental payments are made regularly. Since rental income is unpredictable, lenders typically consider only a certain percentage of the rental income as stable monthly income. In this way, they can make allowances for vacancies or uncollected rent.

> **EXAMPLE:** Your buyer regularly receives $1,800 a month in rental income. The lender is only willing to consider 75% of that income as stable monthly income. Thus, the buyer can add $1,350 of rental income to her other stable income sources.

Sometimes it's very clear that a buyer won't have enough income to support the loan application. In that case, a **co-mortgagor** can be used. A co-mortgagor is simply a co-borrower—someone who signs the mortgage and note and is obligated to pay off the loan along with the primary borrower. For instance, parents often use their income history and financial status to help their children qualify for a loan.

Like the primary borrower, a co-mortgagor must have an income, net worth, and credit history that are acceptable to the lender. To help the borrower, the co-mortgagor must be able to support both his own housing expense and a proportionate share of the borrower's new housing expense.

UNACCEPTABLE TYPES OF INCOME. Some types of income are not considered to be stable monthly income. As mentioned earlier, **unemployment benefits** last only for a limited period of time, so they are virtually never considered stable monthly income.

Also, lenders are generally not interested in the **earnings of family members** other than the loan applicants themselves. For instance, if a married couple is applying for a loan, the lender will take into account the income of both the husband and the wife. However, income that the couple's teenage children earn will not be considered, because the children won't necessarily be sharing their parents' home for much longer.

Income from full- or part-time **temporary work** is not considered stable monthly income. Income from a temporary job does not pass the test of durability. Note that a job does not have to have a termination date for the lender to consider it temporary. Other factors can be taken into account, such as the nature of the work itself.

> **EXAMPLE:** A recent flood has damaged a large portion of an industrial complex. The property manager has hired several full-time workers to help clean up the mess left by the flood and repair the damage. These jobs have no termination date, but are by their nature temporary. The income generated by these jobs wouldn't be considered stable monthly income.

However, income from temporary work may be accepted if the loan applicant has supported herself through a particular type of temporary work for years. The income from temporary work is then considered self-employment income.

> **EXAMPLE:** Ingraham works in the computer industry as a temporary employee. She goes from job to job, helping to set up databases. Each job is temporary. However, Ingraham has supported herself for four years with this kind of temporary work. At this point, a lender might regard these temporary jobs as a form of self-employment and consider Ingraham's earnings to be stable monthly income.

VERIFYING INCOME. Naturally, lenders need to verify the income information given to them by loan applicants. A lender may send an income verification form directly to the applicant's employer. The employer fills out the form and then sends it directly back to the lender. The verification form is never handled by the loan applicant at all.

In some cases a lender will use an alternative income verification method. The loan applicant gives the lender W-2 forms for the previous two years, and payroll stubs or vouchers for the previous 30-day period. The lender then confirms the employment and income information with a phone call to the employer.

The lender will also verify other types of income. For example, if the applicant is relying on commission income, the lender will require copies of the applicant's federal income tax returns for the previous two years.

A self-employed loan applicant will have to give the lender audited financial statements and federal income tax statements for the two years prior to the loan application.

For alimony or child support income, the lender will require a copy of the court decree and proof that the payments are received. A bank statement showing that the checks have been deposited into the applicant's account may be good enough. However, some lenders may require photocopies of the deposited checks.

To verify rental income, the loan applicant will have to submit authenticated copies of the rental property's books, along with his income tax returns for the previous two years.

Under certain conditions a lender may be willing to approve a loan application without verifying the buyer's employment and income. Low-documentation loans are discussed later in this chapter.

CALCULATING MONTHLY INCOME. The lender will want to know the amount of the loan applicant's income in monthly terms. Likewise, when you prequalify buyers, you should always translate their income into monthly income. If a buyer works full-time (40 hours per week) for an hourly wage, you can calculate monthly income by multiplying the hourly wage by 173.33.

> **EXAMPLE:** Your buyer makes $11.50 an hour. To find her monthly earnings, multiply $11.50 by 173.33. $11.50 × 173.33 = $1,993.30. Her monthly earnings are $1,993.30.

If a buyer gets paid twice a month, simply multiply the amount of the paycheck by two.

> **EXAMPLE:** Your buyer gets paid $2,350 twice a month. $2,350 × 2 = $4,700. His monthly income is $4,700.

It's a little more complicated if the buyer gets paid every two weeks. First, you must multiply the payment by 26 to get the annual income figure, and then you must divide that figure by 12 to get the monthly income figure.

> **EXAMPLE:** Your buyer gets paid $2,350 every two weeks. $2,350 × 26 = $61,100. Her annual income is $61,100. Now divide $61,100 by 12. $61,100 ÷ 12 = $5,092. Her monthly income is $5,092.

USING INCOME RATIOS. Now you have a rough idea of how much stable monthly income your buyer has. Next comes the second part of the income analysis—determining if that income is enough.

The lender will usually use two numbers, called **income ratios** or **qualifying ratios**, to measure the buyer's income. The rationale behind income ratios is that if a loan applicant's regular monthly expenses exceed a certain percentage of his monthly income, the applicant may have a difficult time making loan payments. The lender wants to be sure that the applicant can make the mortgage payment and still have enough income left over for other expenses, such as food, clothing, doctor bills, car payments, and other necessities.

There are two types of income ratios:

1. a debt to income ratio, and
2. a housing expense to income ratio.

A debt to income ratio measures the monthly mortgage payment plus any other regular installment debt payments against the monthly income. A housing expense to income ratio measures the monthly mortgage payment alone against the monthly income. For the purposes of income ratios, the monthly mortgage payment includes principal, interest, taxes, and insurance (PITI).

Each ratio is expressed as a percentage. For instance, a loan applicant's housing expense to income ratio would be 29% if her proposed mortgage payment represented 29% of her monthly income.

Each loan program has its own income ratio requirements. For example, the maximum acceptable debt to income ratio might be 36% or 41%, depending on the loan program. We will discuss the specific income ratio limits used for various loan programs in the next chapter. Once you learn those ratios, you will able to tailor your prequalifying process to the type of loan program the buyer is interested in. For now, so you can learn how to apply income ratios, we will use the common rule of thumb that the monthly mortgage payment (PITI) should not exceed 28% of the loan applicant's income.

EXAMPLE: Robinson's annual salary is $42,000. During the last four months, she made an extra $300 per month in overtime. For the past three years, she has received an annual bonus of $600. She owns a rental house that rents for $1,100 a month.

First determine which portions of Robinson's employment income would be considered stable. Her salary is stable monthly income, but you should exclude the overtime, because it hasn't been a regular part of her earnings history. You can include her annual bonuses, because she has received them for the past three years. So add $600 to her annual income of $42,000.

$$\$42,000 + \$600 = \$42,600$$

To calculate Robinson's stable monthly income from employment, divide this annual figure by 12 to arrive at a monthly figure.

$$\$42,600 \div 12 = \$3,550$$

Now take 75% of her regular rental income (to allow for vacancies and uncollected rents) and add that to her monthly employment income.

$$\$1,100 \times .75 = \$825$$
$$\$825 + \$3,550 = \$4,375$$

All together, Robinson's stable monthly income is about $4,375. To get a rough idea of the maximum loan payment she would qualify for, multiply her stable monthly income by 28%.

$$\$4,375 \times .28 = \$1,225$$

Robinson could probably qualify for a monthly housing payment of $1,225. About 15% of that ($185) would go to taxes and insurance; the rest ($1,040) is her maximum principal and interest payment.

NET WORTH

Along with income, a lender will also analyze the buyer's net worth. Net worth is the buyer's "bottom line"—the value of his total financial holdings, in dollars and cents. To calculate his net worth, you simply subtract his liabilities (debts) from his assets.

EXAMPLE: Brown owns a house, a car, and some furniture, and he has $2,900 in savings. The total value of all of these items (or assets) is $177,000. Brown owes $5,000 on the car and $143,000 on the house; he owns the furniture free and clear.

To determine Brown's net worth, subtract the money he owes (his liabilities) from the value of his assets. $177,000 − $148,000 = $29,000. Brown has a net worth of $29,000.

Net worth is important to lenders for a number of reasons. First, lenders feel that if a loan applicant has accumulated a significant amount of net worth, that's a sign that she will be a good credit risk. A healthy net worth is especially important if the loan application is weak in another area. For instance, if a loan applicant's income is marginal, an above-average net worth can mean the difference between loan approval and rejection.

> **EXAMPLE:** Carter has been out of college for three years. She makes $3,300 a month. She paid cash for her car; it's worth about $6,000. She has $4,258 in an IRA account, $1,500 in mutual funds, and $7,500 in a savings account set aside for the downpayment and closing expenses. Her monthly bills consist of a credit card payment of $35 and a college loan payment of $55. She's applied for a loan that would require monthly payments of $1,050.
>
> Using the lender's income ratios, the highest payment Carter can qualify for is $924. However, because Carter has managed to accumulate a significant amount of assets in a short period of time, the lender may approve the loan anyway. Carter's accumulation of assets shows that she's an able money manager and a good credit risk.

Significant net worth—particularly cash—also tells the lender that the loan applicant will have sufficient funds to complete the purchase. The applicant will need enough cash to cover the downpayment, the closing costs, and any other expenses involved in buying the property.

Also, lenders often require a loan applicant to have **reserves** left over after making the downpayment and paying the closing costs. Typically, the reserves must be enough to cover two or three months' mortgage payments. Reserves give the lender confidence that the applicant could handle a temporary financial emergency without defaulting on the loan.

Thus, a significant net worth tells the lender that the loan applicant:

1. knows how to manage money;
2. has enough cash to close the transaction; and
3. can weather a financial emergency without missing a loan payment.

TYPES OF ASSETS. A buyer should list all of his assets on the loan application. An asset is anything of value, including real estate, cars, furniture, jewelry, stocks, bonds, or the cash value in a life insurance policy.

LIQUID ASSETS. Liquid assets are generally more important to an underwriter than non-liquid assets. Liquid assets include cash and any other assets that can be quickly converted to cash. For example, stocks (which can easily be sold) are preferred over real estate. And cash in the bank is best of all.

A loan applicant will be required to give the lender all the pertinent information about her bank accounts, including the name of the bank, the account number, and the balance. This information enables the lender to verify the applicant's cash deposits.

VERIFYING ACCOUNT INFORMATION. The lender may use a "Request for Verification of Deposit" form to verify that the loan applicant actually has the money in his bank accounts that he claims to have. This form is sent directly to the bank and returned directly to the lender. In many cases lenders are willing to accept a faster, alternative method of verification: the loan applicant is asked to submit original bank statements for the previous three months.

The lender looks for four things when it verifies deposits:

1. Does the verified information agree with the amounts claimed in the loan application?
2. Does the loan applicant have enough money in the bank to meet the expenses of purchasing the property?
3. Has the bank account been opened only recently (within the last couple of months)?
4. Is the present balance significantly higher than the average balance?

If the account was opened recently or has a higher balance than normal, the lender may become suspicious. These are strong indications that the loan applicant borrowed the funds for the downpayment and closing costs, which generally is not allowed. However, if the funds are a gift, the lender may find this acceptable. (See the discussion of gift funds, below.)

REAL ESTATE. Often, a buyer is selling one home in order to buy another (usually more expensive) home. In that case, the buyer can use her **net equity** in the first home as a liquid asset. Net equity is the difference between the market value of the property and the sum of the liens against the property, plus the selling expenses. In other words, net equity is the money the buyer expects to receive from the sale of her current home.

To estimate the amount of equity your buyer can apply toward the new purchase, take the appraised value of the current home (or the sales price, if a sale is already pending), subtract any outstanding mortgages or other liens, and then subtract the estimated selling costs (which are commonly between 10% and 13% of the sales price).

EXAMPLE: The market value of the buyer's current home is $350,000. There's a mortgage with a $294,000 balance to be paid off when the home is sold. To calculate the buyer's gross equity, subtract the mortgage balance from the market value.

$$\$350,000 - \$294,000 = \$56,000$$

The gross equity is $56,000. From the gross equity, deduct the estimated selling expenses, which come to $38,500.

$$\$56,000 - \$38,500 = \$17,500$$

Your buyer will have approximately $17,500 in net equity to apply to the purchase of a new home.

Sometimes equity in other property is the primary source of the cash that the buyer will use to purchase the new property. In this situation, the lender will require proof that the property has been sold and that the buyer has received the sale proceeds before it will make the new loan.

If it looks as though the buyer will not be able to sell his other property right away, then he may be able to arrange a swing loan, as we explained in Chapter 7. The swing loan provides the cash to close the buyer's purchase transaction, and when the other property eventually sells, the buyer will pay the swing loan off out of the sale proceeds.

Your buyer may also own real estate that she is not planning to sell. The property may be a rental house, a small apartment building, or vacant land. In any case, the property must be included in the loan application. Again, it is the equity in this other real estate that is important, not just the appraised value. If the buyer has little or no equity in the property, the lender will view it as a liability rather than an asset.

LIABILITIES. As we explained earlier, to determine net worth, the lender subtracts liabilities from assets. So after listing all his assets on the loan application, a buyer must then list all his liabilities.

Liabilities include balances owing on credit cards, charge accounts, student loans, car loans, and other installment debts. Other types of debts, such as income taxes that are currently payable, are also considered liabilities.

GIFT FUNDS. Sometimes a buyer has enough income to qualify for a loan, but lacks the liquid assets necessary to close the loan. In that case, the buyer's family may be willing to make up the deficit. This is acceptable to most lenders, as long as the money supplied by the family is a gift and not a loan.

A gift of money from a relative must be confirmed with a **gift letter**. The letter should clearly state that the money is a gift to the buyer and does not have to be repaid, and it must be signed by the donor. Lenders often have their own form for gift letters and may require the donor to use their form.

The lender will have to verify the gift funds, so the donor should give them to the buyer as soon as possible. It's best if the lender can verify the gift funds when it verifies the buyer's other bank deposits.

Many loan programs have limits on the amount of gift funds that can be used in a transaction. These limits are intended to ensure that the buyer invests at least a small amount of his own money in the property he's buying.

CREDIT HISTORY

The third part of the qualifying process is analyzing the loan applicant's credit history. The lender does this by obtaining a credit report from a credit reporting agency. The applicant (the buyer) normally pays the fee for the credit report.

A personal credit report includes information about an individual's debts and repayment history for the preceding seven years. A credit report primarily covers credit cards and loans. Other bills, such as utility bills, usually aren't listed unless they were turned over to a collection agency.

DEROGATORY CREDIT INFORMATION. If a loan applicant's credit report shows a history of slow payment or other credit problems, the loan application could be declined. Derogatory credit information includes all of the following.

- **SLOW PAYMENTS.** If the loan applicant is chronically late in paying bills, this will show up on the credit report. Slow payments may be a sign that the applicant is unable to pay on time, perhaps because she is already financially overextended. Or they may be a sign that she does not take debt repayment seriously.

- **DEBT CONSOLIDATION AND REFINANCING.** A pattern of continually increasing liabilities and periodic "bailouts" through refinancing and debt consolidation is a red flag to a lender. It suggests that the loan applicant has a tendency to live beyond a prudent level.

- **COLLECTIONS.** After several attempts to get a debtor to pay a bill, a frustrated creditor may turn the bill over to a collection agency. Collections show up on the debtor's credit report for seven years.

- **REPOSSESSIONS.** If someone purchases an item on credit and fails to make the payments, the creditor may be able to repossess the item. Repossessions stay on the debtor's credit report for seven years.

- **FORECLOSURE.** A real estate foreclosure stays on the debtor's credit report for seven years.

- **JUDGMENTS.** If someone successfully sued the loan applicant, that, too, will show up on the credit report. A judgment is listed on a credit report for seven years after it is entered in the public record.

- **BANKRUPTCY.** Not surprisingly, lenders look at bankruptcy with disfavor. A bankruptcy stays on the debtor's credit report longer than other credit problems—for ten years instead of seven.

CREDIT SCORES. Many underwriters now use **credit scores** to help evaluate a loan applicant's credit history. A credit reporting agency calculates an individual's credit score using the information that appears in his credit report and a quantitative model developed by a national credit scoring company. Credit scoring models, which are based on statistical analysis of large numbers of mortgages, are designed to predict the likelihood of successful repayment of or default on a mortgage. In general, someone with a poor credit score is much more likely to default than someone with a good credit score.

FIG. 8.3   MORTGAGE LOAN UNDERWRITING

INCOME ANALYSIS
- STABLE MONTHLY INCOME: QUALITY AND DURABILITY
- INCOME VERIFICATION
- INCOME RATIOS MEASURE ADEQUACY OF STABLE MONTHLY INCOME

NET WORTH
- ASSETS MINUS LIABILITIES
- LIQUID VS. NON-LIQUID ASSETS
- ASSET VERIFICATION
- RESERVES REQUIRED AFTER CLOSING
- GIFT FUND LIMITS

CREDIT HISTORY
- CREDIT REPORT (COVERS SEVEN YEARS)
- CREDIT SCORES
- MITIGATING CIRCUMSTANCES FOR PAST PROBLEMS

There are a variety of credit scoring models in use. The two most widely used types of credit scores are FICO bureau scores (also called Fair Isaac scores) and MDS bankruptcy scores. FICO scores range from around 300 to 850. A high FICO score (for example, over 660) is a positive sign. MDS bankruptcy scores, which range from around 150 to 1,000, work the opposite way: a high MDS score (over 550) indicates an increased likelihood of bankruptcy, so it is a negative sign.

HOW CREDIT SCORES ARE USED. In some cases, underwriters use credit scores to decide what level of review to apply to a loan applicant's credit history. For example, if an applicant has a very good credit score, the underwriter might perform a basic review, simply confirming that the information in the credit report is complete and accurate without investigating further. Aside from a foreclosure or a bankruptcy, the underwriter probably won't question the applicant about derogatory information in the report, because it's already been taken into account in calculating the credit score. On the other hand, if the applicant has a mediocre or poor credit score, the underwriter will perform a more complete review, looking into the circumstances that led to credit problems.

A loan applicant's credit score may also be a factor in determining the interest rate that will apply if the loan is approved. If the credit score is mediocre, instead of rejecting the application altogether, the lender may approve the loan but charge a higher interest rate to make up for the increased risk of default.

MAINTAINING A GOOD CREDIT SCORE. Any information that appears on a person's credit report may affect his credit score, but credit activity within the last two years has the greatest impact.

While most people would expect chronically late payments and collection problems to hurt someone's credit rating, they might be surprised at some of the other factors that can. For example, with a revolving credit card, maintaining a balance near the credit limit ("maxing out" the card) will have a negative impact on the cardholder's credit score, even if she always makes the minimum monthly payment on time.

Applying for too much credit can also have a negative effect. Each time a person applies for credit (a store charge card, a car loan, a home equity loan, and so on), the creditor makes a "credit inquiry" that becomes part of the applicant's credit history. Occasional inquiries are fine, but more than a few inquiries within the past year can detract from the applicant's credit score. From a lender's point of view, too many credit inquiries may be an indication that the applicant is becoming overextended.

A special rule applies when a number of credit inquiries are made within a two-week period. This could happen, for example, if someone were applying for a car loan or mortgage loan from various different lenders, intending to compare loan offers and accept the best one. To allow for that type of situation, all of the credit inquiries within a 14-day period are treated as a single inquiry when the applicant's credit score is calculated.

OBTAINING CREDIT INFORMATION. It's a good idea for prospective home-buyers to obtain their credit reports and find out their credit scores well before they apply for a mortgage. (Obtaining a copy of your own credit report does not count as a credit inquiry.) A credit report may contain incorrect information, and the Fair Credit Reporting Act, a federal law, requires credit reporting agencies to investigate complaints and make corrections. This process can take a month or more.

There are three major credit reporting agencies: Equifax, Experian, and TransUnion. A buyer should obtain a credit report from each of the three agencies. Credit scores should also be requested; they are not automatically part of the credit report.

EXPLAINING CREDIT PROBLEMS. A negative credit report or a poor credit score won't necessarily prevent a buyer from getting a loan at a reasonable interest rate. Credit problems can often be explained. If the lender is convinced that the past problems don't reflect the buyer's overall attitude toward credit and that the circumstances leading to the problems were temporary and are unlikely to recur, the loan application may well be approved. By obtaining her credit report before applying for a mortgage loan, the buyer can be prepared to discuss any problems with the lender.

Most people try to meet their credit obligations on time; when they don't, there's usually a reason. Loss of a job, divorce, hospitalization, prolonged illness, or a death in the family can create extraordinary financial pressures and adversely affect bill-paying habits. If a buyer has a poor credit score, it may be possible to show that the credit problems occurred during a specific period for an understandable reason, and that the buyer has handled credit well both before and since that period. The buyer should put this explanation in writing and be prepared to provide supporting documentation (such as hospital records) from a third party.

When a buyer explains a credit problem to a lender, it's a mistake to blame the problem on the creditor. Lenders hear too many excuses from loan applicants who refuse to accept responsibility for their own actions. The lender's reaction is predictable: skepticism and rejection of the loan application. The lender will reason that someone who won't take responsibility for previous credit problems won't take responsibility for future ones, either.

It's important to remember that even serious credit problems can be resolved with time. When buyers tell you they have had credit problems in the past, don't simply assume that they can't qualify for a good loan. Refer them to a lender and get an expert's opinion.

LOW-DOCUMENTATION LOANS

Lenders are willing to relax their income and asset verification requirements in certain circumstances. A buyer with a good credit history who can afford to make a substantial downpayment (greater than 20% of the purchase price) may be eligible for a low-documentation (or "low-doc") loan. The lender won't require the buyer to provide the standard proof of employment, income, and assets. This can be a great advantage for self-employed buyers and others with complicated financial situations. The lender may charge a slightly higher interest rate for a low-doc loan.

CHOOSING A LOAN

In many cases, a homebuyer will be offered a choice of different loans, either by a single lender or by competing lenders. Comparing the loans and choosing between them can be a challenge. The buyer must compare the cost of the loans and also consider how the structure of each loan (the downpayment, repayment period, and other features) would affect his circumstances in both the short term and the long term. Financing disclosure laws, including the Truth in Lending Act, the Mortgage Loan Broker Law, and the Seller Financing Disclosure Law, are designed to ensure that buyers will have the information they need to choose the best loan for their situation.

TRUTH IN LENDING ACT

To tell which of two or more possible loans is the least expensive, it isn't enough to compare the quoted interest rates. Loan fees and other financing charges also need to be taken into account.

The Truth in Lending Act, a federal law, requires lenders to disclose information about loan costs in consumer credit transactions. The disclosures help loan applicants compare credit costs and shop around for the best terms.

The Truth in Lending Act is implemented by **Regulation Z,** a regulation issued by the Federal Reserve Board. Regulation Z does not set limits on interest rates or other finance charges, but it does regulate the disclosure of these charges.

The most important disclosure required under Regulation Z is the loan's **annual percentage rate** (APR). The APR is the relationship between the total finance charges and the total amount financed. Like the loan's interest rate, the APR is expressed as a percentage, but the total finance charges used to calculate the APR include more than just interest on the loan principal. The total finance charges include interest, the loan origination fee, any discount points that will be paid by the borrower, and mortgage insurance costs (see Chapter 9).

Because it takes into account the other finance charges as well as the interest, the APR for a real estate loan is virtually always higher than the quoted interest rate. For example, a loan that bears an annual interest rate of 6% might have a 6.25% APR, because of the origination fee and mortgage insurance.

In a residential mortgage transaction, Regulation Z requires the lender to give the loan applicant a disclosure statement listing good faith estimates of the finance charges within three business days after receiving the written loan application. Most lenders give the disclosure statement to the applicant at the time of application. If any of the estimated figures change over the course of the transaction, new disclosures must be made before closing.

It is only by comparing the APRs quoted by different lenders that the least expensive loan can be found. By comparing only the interest rates, a buyer could easily be misled. A lender may quote a very low interest rate, but charge a large origination fee or several discount points. In that case, the total cost of the loan may actually be greater than the total cost of a loan from a competitor with a higher interest rate. The APRs of the two loans will reveal this difference in cost.

While a buyer won't get a Truth in Lending disclosure statement before actually applying for a loan, it's possible to find out the estimated APR of a loan with a phone call to the lender.

OTHER FINANCE DISCLOSURE LAWS

Whether or not a real estate finance transaction is subject to the federal Truth in Lending Act, other disclosures may be required by state law. California's finance disclosure laws include the Mortgage Loan Broker Law and the Seller Financing Disclosure Law. Like the Truth in Lending Act, they help buyers decide whether a particular loan meets their needs. In some cases, it's the real estate agent who has to make the disclosures required by these laws.

Mortgage Loan Broker Law. In order to get a sale closed, a real estate agent sometimes needs to take an active role in arranging financing. For instance, if it turns out that the buyer can't qualify for a large enough primary loan to purchase the property, the agent might arrange secondary financing with another lender. California law permits real estate agents to negotiate mortgage loans and also to be compensated for helping buyers in this way.

When a real estate agent arranges a loan, she is considered to be acting as a mortgage loan broker, and therefore must comply with the Mortgage Loan Broker Law. This law requires an agent negotiating a loan to make certain disclosures to the borrower. And as we'll discuss shortly, it also limits the commissions and costs that the agent may charge to a borrower.

A mortgage loan broker's disclosure statement should include the following information about the loan:

- the principal amount;
- estimated loan costs and expenses that will be deducted from the loan proceeds, including broker fees and commissions;
- the estimated balance that will be paid to the borrower;
- the loan interest rate and payment terms;
- a notice to the borrower regarding mortgage loan risks;
- any liens against the property and the order of their priority;
- any prepayment penalty; and
- the name(s) and real estate license number(s) of the broker and/or agent negotiating the loan.

The disclosure statement must be made on a form approved by the Real Estate Commissioner. As an example, the form used by the California Association of Realtors® is shown in Figure 8.4. The agent should give the statement to the borrower within three days of receiving the borrower's written loan application, or before the borrower becomes obligated on the loan, whichever happens first. Both the agent and the borrower must sign the disclosure statement. The agent or her broker must keep a signed copy of the statement for at least three years.

Commissions and loan costs. The Mortgage Loan Broker Law not only requires the disclosures described above, it also places limits on the commissions and costs that a real estate agent or other mortgage loan broker may charge to a borrower. These limits apply whenever an agent

FIG. 8.4   MORTGAGE LOAN DISCLOSURE STATEMENT

CALIFORNIA
ASSOCIATION
OF REALTORS®

MORTGAGE LOAN DISCLOSURE STATEMENT
(BORROWER)
(As required by the Business and Professions Code §10241
and Title 10, California Administrative Code, §2840)

_____
(Name of Broker/Arranger of Credit)

_____
(Business Address of Broker)

I. SUMMARY OF LOAN TERMS
   A. PRINCIPAL AMOUNT . . . . $ _____
   B. ESTIMATED DEDUCTIONS FROM PRINCIPAL AMOUNT
       1. Costs and Expenses (See Paragraph III-A). . . . . $ _____
      *2. Broker Commission/Organization Fee (See Paragraph III-B). . . . . $ _____
       3. Lender Origination Fee/Discounts (See Paragraph III-B) . . . . $ _____
       4. Additional compensation will/may be received from lender not deducted from loan proceeds.
           □ YES $ _____ (if known) or □ NO
       5. Amount to be Paid on Authorization of Borrower (See Paragraph III). . . . . $ _____
   C. ESTIMATED CASH PAYABLE TO BORROWER (A less B) . . . . $ _____

II. GENERAL INFORMATION ABOUT LOAN
   A. If this loan is made, Borrower will be required to pay the principal and interest at _____% per year, payable
       as follows: _____ payments of $ _____
                        (number of payments)   (monthly/quarterly/annually)
       and a **FINAL/BALLOON** payment of $ _____ to pay off the loan in full.

       **NOTICE TO BORROWER: IF YOU DO NOT HAVE THE FUNDS TO PAY THE BALLOON PAYMENT WHEN IT
       COMES DUE, YOU MAY HAVE TO OBTAIN A NEW LOAN AGAINST YOUR PROPERTY TO MAKE THE
       BALLOON PAYMENT. IN THAT CASE, YOU MAY AGAIN HAVE TO PAY COMMISSIONS, FEES AND EXPENSES
       FOR THE ARRANGING OF THE NEW LOAN. IN ADDITION, IF YOU ARE UNABLE TO MAKE THE MONTHLY
       PAYMENTS OR THE BALLOON PAYMENT, YOU MAY LOSE THE PROPERTY AND ALL OF YOUR EQUITY
       THROUGH FORECLOSURE. KEEP THIS IN MIND IN DECIDING UPON THE AMOUNT AND TERMS OF THIS
       LOAN.**

   B. This loan will be evidenced by a promissory note and secured by a deed of trust on property identified as (street
       address or legal description):
       _____
       _____

   C. 1. Liens presently against this property (do not include loan being applied for):

Nature of Lien	Priority	Lienholder's Name	Amount Owing
_____	_____	_____	_____
_____	_____	_____	_____
_____	_____	_____	_____

   2. Liens that will remain against this property after the loan being applied for is made or arranged (include loan
       being applied for):

Nature of Lien	Priority	Lienholder's Name	Amount Owing
_____	_____	_____	_____
_____	_____	_____	_____
_____	_____	_____	_____

       NOTICE TO BORROWER: Be sure that you state the amount of all liens as accurately as possible. If you contract
       with the broker to arrange this loan, but it cannot be arranged because you did not state these liens correctly, you
       may be liable to pay commissions, fees and expenses even though you do not obtain the loan.

Borrower acknowledges receipt of copy of this page.
   Borrower's Initials (_____)(_____)

EQUAL HOUSING
OPPORTUNITY

Reviewed by
Broker or Designee _____ Date _____

MORTGAGE LOAN DISCLOSURE STATEMENT (MS-11 PAGE 1 OF 3)

Reprinted with permission, California Association of Realtors®. Endorsement not implied.

Property Address: _____ Date: _____

D. If Borrower pays all or part of the loan principal before it is due, a PREPAYMENT PENALTY computed as follows may be charged:
_____
_____

E. Late Charges: ☐ YES, see loan documents   or   ☐ NO
F. The purchase of credit life or credit disability insurance by a borrower is not required as a condition of making this loan.
G. Is the real property which will secure the requested loan an "owner-occupied dwelling?" ☐ YES____ or ☐ NO____
(Borrower initial opposite YES or NO)

An "owner-occupied dwelling" means a single dwelling unit in a condominium or cooperative or residential building of four or fewer separate dwelling units, one of which will be owned and occupied by a signatory to the mortgage or deed of trust for this loan within 90 days of the signing of the mortgage or deed of trust.

III. DEDUCTIONS FROM LOAN PROCEEDS

A. Estimated Maximum Costs and Expenses of Arranging the Loan to be Paid Out of Loan Principal:

	PAYABLE TO	
	Broker	**Others**
1. Appraisal fee	_____	_____
2. Escrow fee	_____	_____
3. Title insurance policy	_____	_____
4. Notary fees	_____	_____
5. Recording fees	_____	_____
6. Credit investigation fees	_____	_____
7. Other costs and expenses:	_____	_____
	_____	_____
	_____	_____
Total Costs and Expenses	$ _____	

*B. Compensation | $ _____ |
1. Brokerage Commission/Origination Fee | $ _____ |
2. Lender Origination Fee/Discounts | $ _____ |

C. Estimated Payment to be Made out of Loan Principal on Authorization of Borrower

	PAYABLE TO	
	Broker	**Others**
1. Fire or other hazard insurance premiums	_____	_____
2. Credit life or disability insurance premiums (see Paragraph II-F)	_____	_____
3. Beneficiary statement fees	_____	_____
4. Reconveyance and similar fees	_____	_____
5. Discharge of existing liens against property:	_____	_____
	_____	_____
6. Other:	_____	_____
	_____	_____
	_____	_____
Total to be Paid on Authorization of Borrower	$ _____	

If this loan is secured by a first deed of trust on dwellings in a principal amount of less than $30,000 or secured by a junior lien on dwellings in a principal amount of less than $20,000, the undersigned licensee certifies that the loan will be made in compliance with Article 7 of Chapter 3 of the Real Estate Law.

*This loan **may / will / will not** (delete two) be made wholly or in part from broker-controlled funds as defined in Section 10241(j) of the Business and Professions Code.

Borrower acknowledges receipt of copy of this page.
Borrower's Initials (_____)(_____)

EQUAL HOUSING OPPORTUNITY

Reviewed by
Broker or Designee _____ Date _____

MORTGAGE LOAN DISCLOSURE STATEMENT (MS-11 PAGE 2 OF 3)

Property Address: _____ Date: _____

*NOTICE TO BORROWER: This disclosure statement may be used if the Broker is acting as an agent in arranging the loan by a third person or if the loan will be made with funds owned or controlled by the broker. If the Broker indicates in the above statement that the loan "may" be made out of Broker-controlled funds, the Broker must notify the borrower prior to the close of escrow if the funds to be received by the Borrower are in fact Broker-controlled funds.

_____   _____
Name of Broker   Broker Representative

_____   _____
License Number   License Number
                            OR
_____   _____
Signature of Broker   Signature

The Department of Real Estate License Information phone number is _____.

<u>NOTICE TO BORROWER:</u>

DO NOT SIGN THIS STATEMENT UNTIL YOU HAVE READ AND UNDERSTAND ALL OF THE INFORMATION IN IT. ALL PARTS OF THE FORM MUST BE COMPLETED BEFORE YOU SIGN.

Borrower hereby acknowledges the receipt of a copy of this statement.

DATED _____   _____
                                      (Borrower)

                                      _____
                                      (Borrower)

<u>Broker Review</u>: Signature of Real Estate Broker after review of this statement.

                                      _____
DATED _____   Real Estate Broker or Assistant Pursuant to Section 2725

Published and Distributed by:
REAL ESTATE BUSINESS SERVICES, INC.
a subsidiary of the CALIFORNIA ASSOCIATION OF REALTORS®
525 South Virgil Avenue, Los Angeles, California 90020

Reviewed by _____
Broker or Designee _____ Date _____

REVISION DATE 10/2000   Print Date
MS-11 (PAGE 3 OF 3)

MORTGAGE LOAN DISCLOSURE STATEMENT (MS-11 PAGE 3 OF 3)

or loan broker arranges a loan for a one- to four-unit residential property that is:

- a first deed of trust for less than $30,000, or
- a junior deed of trust for less than $20,000.

For these loans, a loan broker may charge no more than the following maximum commissions:

- for a first deed of trust:
  - 5% of the principal if the loan term is less than three years, or
  - 10% of the principal if the loan term is three years or more.
- for a junior deed of trust:
  - 5% of the principal if the loan term is less than two years,
  - 10% of the principal if the loan term is at least two years but less than three years, or
  - 15% of the principal if the loan term is three years or more.

Most loans have other costs associated with them, such as appraisal and credit report fees. These loan costs may not exceed 5% of the loan amount, or $390, whichever is greater. They may never exceed $700 or exceed the actual costs.

> **EXAMPLE:** In addition to their primary loan, the buyers need to borrow another $12,000 in order to purchase the seller's house. Their real estate broker arranges a $12,000 secondary loan with a five-year term. Because this is a junior deed of trust for less than $20,000, the Mortgage Loan Broker Law's commission limits apply. Since the term of the loan is longer than three years, the broker may charge no more than $1,800, or 15% of the principal, as a commission. The loan costs charged to the buyers may not exceed $600, which is 5% of the loan amount.

BALLOON PAYMENTS. The Mortgage Loan Broker Law also places limits on balloon payments in connection with first deeds of trust for less than $30,000 or junior deeds of trust for less than $20,000. (Seller-financed transactions are excluded from these limitations, however.)

For these types of loans, a balloon payment is prohibited if the loan is to be paid off in less than three years. If the property is an owner-occupied residence, a balloon payment is prohibited if the loan is to be paid off in less than six years. For the purposes of this law, a balloon payment is any payment that is more than twice the size of the smallest payment required by the loan agreement.

RESPA GOOD FAITH ESTIMATE. A real estate agent (or other loan broker) who negotiates a mortgage loan that is subject to the Real Estate Settlement Procedures Act (RESPA) must give the borrower a good faith estimate of closing costs. RESPA, which will be discussed in greater detail in Chapter 10, is a federal law that requires homebuyers to be given information about closing costs, to enable them to compare the cost of different settlement services. RESPA applies to federally related loans for the purchase of residential property, which covers almost all home purchase loans made by institutional lenders. RESPA does not cover seller-financed transactions, however.

To comply with RESPA, a real estate agent acting as a mortgage loan broker must give the borrower a good faith estimate of closing costs within three business days after receiving the loan application. The good faith estimate can be included on the mortgage loan disclosure statement; it does not have to be a separate document. In California, there are many forms available that meet the requirements of both the Mortgage Loan Broker Law and RESPA.

SELLER FINANCING DISCLOSURE LAW. A real estate agent who arranges seller financing in a transaction may need to make certain disclosures to the buyer and the seller regarding the terms of the financing. California's Seller Financing Disclosure Law applies to the purchase of a one- to four-unit residential property when the seller extends credit to the buyer with any arrangement that involves a finance charge and at least three payments in addition to the downpayment.

The seller financing disclosure form must disclose:

- the financing terms;
- existing liens against the property;
- a warning about the hazards of refinancing;
- an explanation of the possible effects of negative amortization;
- the buyer's credit and employment history;
- whether title insurance has been or will be obtained;
- whether a tax service has been arranged to ensure that property taxes are paid;

- whether the deed of trust will be recorded; and
- the amount, source, and purpose of any funds the buyer is to receive from the transaction.

The disclosure statement should be signed by the buyer, the seller, and the arranger of credit (the person who negotiates the financing). The statement must be delivered to the parties before a promissory note is executed. The arranger of credit must keep a signed copy of the disclosure statement on file for three years.

Note that a seller financing disclosure statement is not required if the transaction is already covered under another disclosure law, such as the Mortgage Loan Broker Law. An example of a seller financing addendum and disclosure statement can be found in Chapter 6 (Figure 6.2).

Locking in the Interest Rate

In addition to all of the other issues a buyer has to consider when applying for a loan, she'll need to decide whether to have the interest rate **locked in** for a certain period. If the rate is not locked in, the lender may change it at any time before closing. So even if the rate is 5.25% when the loan application is submitted, by the time the loan closes, the rate could be 5.5%. The buyer might end up with a much higher monthly loan payment than originally anticipated—even an unaffordable payment.

A buyer who wants to lock in the interest rate will usually be required to pay a lock-in fee; for example, the lender might charge 1.5% of the loan amount. The fee is typically applied to the buyer's closing costs if the transaction closes. If the lender rejects the loan application, the lock-in fee is refunded. But if the buyer withdraws the application, the fee is forfeited to the lender.

If the buyer thinks market interest rates may drop in the next few weeks, it probably doesn't make sense to lock in the rate. The lender may charge the buyer the locked-in rate even if market rates have gone down in the period before closing.

Other Considerations in Choosing a Loan

The interest rate and the overall cost of a loan are important considerations for any buyer, but they are by no means the only ones. In comparing different financing options, buyers should think about a variety of other issues: How much money will they have left in savings after the loan closes? How much spending money will they have left over each month after paying their mortgage payment? How long do they plan to stay in the home they're buying? With income ratios and other qualifying standards, a lender takes certain aspects of the buyers' situation into account before agreeing to make a loan. But only the buyers themselves can decide which financing alternative is most comfortable for them and fits in best with their own financial plans.

Some buyers are only planning to live in the house they're purchasing for a few years. These buyers generally want to minimize the short-term cost of the property, and they're less concerned with the long-term, overall cost. For example, this type of buyer might be a candidate for a loan with an adjustable interest rate. He can take advantage of a low starting rate without worrying about how high the rate may rise ten years from now.

Buyers who hope to retire early or reduce their workload may be most concerned with building equity and paying off their mortgage as soon as possible. They might prefer a loan with a 15-year or 20-year term, rather than the standard 30-year term, even though it means they will qualify

---

FIG. 8.5   BUYER'S CONSIDERATIONS IN CHOOSING A LOAN

- INTEREST RATE AND LOAN FEES

- SHORT-TERM COST OF FINANCING VS. OVERALL LONG-TERM COST

- SAVINGS REMAINING AFTER HOME PURCHASE

- SPENDING MONEY REMAINING AFTER MONTHLY MORTGAGE PAYMENT

- HOW LONG DOES THE BUYER INTEND TO OWN THIS HOME?

- HOW RAPIDLY WILL EQUITY BUILD?

- HOW SOON WILL THE MORTGAGE BE PAID OFF?

- HOW MUCH HOUSE WILL THIS FINANCING ENABLE THE BUYER TO PURCHASE?

- WHAT ALTERNATIVE INVESTMENT OPPORTUNITIES ARE AVAILABLE?

for a smaller loan amount and have to buy a less expensive home than they otherwise would.

Many first-time buyers with limited buying power want to purchase the largest, most expensive home they can possibly afford. They are interested in any and all financing arrangements that can boost their price range: an adjustable interest rate, a high loan-to-value ratio, a 40-year loan term, discount points, secondary financing, and so on.

On the other hand, some buyers don't want to borrow as much money for a house as lenders would allow them to. They may want to invest their money differently, or they may simply prefer to avoid the financial stress that the maximum monthly mortgage payment would represent for them.

In short, buyers must evaluate every potential loan in light of their own goals and preferences. The downpayment and other cash requirements, a fixed or adjustable interest rate, the monthly payment amount, and the loan term are all variables to consider in choosing a loan. We'll be discussing these and other loan features in the next chapter.

CHAPTER SUMMARY

1. A real estate agent or a lender may informally prequalify a buyer for a mortgage loan before she begins house-hunting, to determine how large a mortgage loan the buyer is likely to qualify for and what housing price range she should be considering. By contrast, only a lender may actually preapprove a buyer for a mortgage loan. Preapproval is a formal process that requires submission of a loan application and all supporting documentation.

2. To prequalify a buyer, calculate his stable monthly income and then apply income ratios to calculate the maximum PITI payment. Deduct a percentage of the payment for taxes and insurance to find the maximum principal and interest payment. Use the principal and interest payment to calculate a maximum loan amount. Divide the loan amount by an appropriate loan-to-value ratio to determine how expensive a house the buyer can afford.

3. When a mortgage loan application is submitted to a lender, the lender's underwriters evaluate it to determine whether the applicant is a good credit risk and can afford the proposed loan. The underwriter analyzes the applicant's income, net worth, and credit history.

4. Stable monthly income is income that meets the lender's standards of quality (how dependable the source is) and durability (how long the income is likely to continue). Verified income from employment, pensions, social security, spousal maintenance, child support, public assistance, dividends, interest, and rental property may be counted as stable monthly income.

5. Income ratios are used to measure the adequacy of a loan applicant's income. In many cases the underwriter will apply both a debt to income ratio and a housing expense to income ratio. A debt to income ratio states the applicant's monthly mortgage payment (PITI), plus any other monthly obligations, as a percentage of her stable monthly income. A housing expense to income ratio states the PITI payment alone as a percentage of stable monthly income.

6. Net worth is calculated by subtracting liabilities from assets. A loan applicant's net worth indicates to a lender whether the applicant knows how to manage money, has the cash required for closing, and has adequate reserves in case of a financial emergency. Liquid assets are generally more helpful to a loan application than non-liquid assets. If the loan applicant owns real estate, the lender will be concerned with the applicant's net equity. Lenders place limits on the amount of gift funds a buyer can use to close the transaction.

7. A credit report lists credit problems that have occurred within the past seven years (ten years for a bankruptcy). A loan applicant's credit score provides an overall measure of creditworthiness and may be used to determine the level of review applied to the application. It may also be a factor in setting the interest rate.

8. A buyer with a good credit history who can make a substantial downpayment may qualify for a low-documentation loan, so that he won't have to provide the standard proof of employment, income, and assets.

9. The Truth in Lending Act requires lenders to provide loan applicants with a disclosure statement within three days after receiving a written application. The statement must include the annual percentage rate (APR) of the proposed loan, as well as good faith estimates of all finance charges. When comparing loans, it's more accurate to consider APRs rather than the interest rates alone.

10. A real estate agent who helps a buyer obtain institutional financing or negotiates seller financing may be required to provide a disclosure statement to comply with the Mortgage Loan Broker Law or the Seller Financing Disclosure Law.

11. Remember that it is not always a good idea for buyers to borrow the maximum loan amount and buy the most expensive home they can. Buyers need to consider their entire financial situation, short-term and long-term, when choosing a home to buy and a loan to finance the purchase.

CHAPTER QUIZ

1. A buyer may find it useful to have a preapproval letter because it:

    a. does not commit the lender to making a loan

    b. gives the seller confidence that the financing contingency won't be a problem

    c. tells the seller the maximum amount the buyer can afford

    d. allows the buyer to extend the closing process

2. If a buyer comes to you after she has already found a house she wants to make an offer on, you should:

    a. advise her to prequalify herself using an online calculator

    b. tell her not to make an offer until the lender approves her loan application

    c. prequalify her or arrange for a lender to prequalify her

    d. skip the prequalification process and help her prepare an offer

3. Which of the following statements concerning computers and the loan application process is true?

    a. Loan applicants can submit financial information directly to an underwriting computer without disclosing it to the lender

    b. Many lenders underwrite their loans using software provided by Fannie Mae or Freddie Mac

    c. Most loan approval decisions are now made by computer, to eliminate human error

    d. Lenders are now able to get all the necessary information concerning the buyers and the property from online sources

4. If a loan applicant's primary source of income is self-employment, the lender will consider this stable monthly income if the loan applicant:

    a. does not have any other source of income

    b. also has secondary sources of income

    c. has been self-employed for at least five years

    d. has a history of employment in the same field and can document a reasonable chance for success

5. Which of the following would a lender consider an acceptable secondary income source?

   a. Rental income, with a percentage deducted to allow for vacancies or uncollected rent

   b. Interest on investments that the loan applicant will cash in to pay for closing costs

   c. Child support payments for the loan applicant's 17-year-old daughter

   d. Regular monthly income from a public assistance program, if the loan applicant's eligibility will expire at the end of the year

6. A housing expense to income ratio differs from a debt to income ratio because:

   a. a housing expense to income ratio takes into account principal and interest on the mortgage, but not taxes and insurance

   b. a housing expense to income ratio is based on the monthly mortgage payment alone, not on all of the loan applicant's debt payments

   c. a debt to income ratio does not include the proposed monthly mortgage payment

   d. a housing expense to income ratio takes into account the loan applicant's net worth as well as monthly income

7. Which of the following is true about how a lender evaluates net worth?

   a. When verifying bank accounts, the lender wants the present balance to be significantly higher than the average balance in the past

   b. The lender will prefer non-liquid assets to liquid assets

   c. The lender is primarily concerned with the appraised value of the real estate that the loan applicant owns

   d. If the loan applicant's income is marginal, the lender may approve the loan anyway if the applicant has significant net worth

8. How would a lender calculate the net equity in real estate the loan applicant owns?

   a. Take the market value of the property and deduct the sum of the liens against the property, plus the selling expenses

   b. Subtract the balance of the existing mortgage from the assessed value of the property

   c. Take the market value of the property and subtract between 10% and 13% for the estimated selling costs

   d. Add the buyer's downpayment to the market value of the property, then subtract the sum of the liens against the property

9. Which of the following would be most likely to have a negative effect on an individual's credit rating?

   a. Obtaining a copy of his own credit report

   b. Unemployment

   c. Debt consolidation

   d. A high FICO score

10. The APR for a real estate loan:

   a. must be disclosed before a loan application is submitted

   b. expresses the relationship of the total finance charges to the total amount financed

   c. includes interest, points, lock-in fees, closing costs, and the downpayment

   d. is usually lower than the quoted interest rate

ANSWER KEY

1. b. Preapproval makes a buyer's offer more attractive because the seller can be confident that the buyer will qualify for financing.

2. c. Even if the buyer has already found her dream home, the prequalification process will tell her whether she can qualify for a large enough loan to buy it or should look at more affordable houses instead.

3. b. The secondary market agencies encourage lenders to use their underwriting software. This makes it easier for lenders to make conforming loans and sell them on the secondary market.

4. d. A lender will count the income of a self-employed loan applicant who has been in business for a short time, but only if the loan applicant has a history of employment in the same field and can document a reasonable chance for success with pro forma financial statements and market feasibility studies.

5. a. Income from sources besides employment must still be reliable and durable. Rental income is acceptable if the loan applicant can prove that rental payments are made regularly, but the lender will usually consider only a certain percentage because vacancies and rent collection problems are unpredictable.

6. b. A housing expense to income ratio measures the adequacy of the loan applicant's income using only the monthly mortgage payment (principal, interest, taxes, and insurance). A debt to income ratio also takes payments on other debts into account.

7. d. Above-average net worth can mean the difference between approval and rejection if the loan applicant's income is marginal.

8. a. Net equity is the amount of money the loan applicant can expect to receive from the sale of the property. This is often the primary source of cash that will be used to buy the new property.

9. c. A pattern of increasing liabilities followed by debt consolidation suggests that the individual tends to live beyond his means.

10. b. The annual percentage rate (APR) helps loan applicants compare the overall cost of different loans by expressing the total finance charges as a percentage of the loan amount.

9

FINANCING PROGRAMS

BASIC LOAN FEATURES
- Repayment period
- Amortization
- Loan-to-value ratios
- Secondary financing
- Loan fees
- Fixed and adjustable interest rates

CONVENTIONAL LOANS
- Conventional loans and the secondary market
- Characteristics of conventional loans
- Underwriting conventional loans
- Making conventional loans more affordable

GOVERNMENT-SPONSORED LOAN PROGRAMS
- FHA-insured loans
- VA-guaranteed loans
- Cal-Vet loans

SELLER FINANCING
- How seller financing works
- Types of seller financing
- Other ways sellers can help

INTRODUCTION

As discussed in the previous chapter, the size of loan a particular buyer can get depends on the buyer's income, net worth, and credit history. But it also depends on the features of the loan and the way it's structured. How long is the repayment period? How much of a downpayment does the lender require? Is the interest rate fixed or adjustable? The types of loans that residential lenders offer change over time to reflect changing conditions in the mortgage finance market. Lenders want to make loans that will enable buyers to purchase homes, but they have to structure the loans to control the risk of default and protect their investments. The mortgage loans that make business sense to a lender vary with the state of the market: Are interest rates high or low, and are they headed up or down? Is this a buyer's market or a seller's market?

As a real estate agent, you can help your buyers get the financing they need by keeping abreast of currently available options. Lenders will frequently send you information about their latest loan programs, and you should keep an eye out for new developments. First-time buyers are especially likely to benefit from special programs. This chapter will provide you with the background information needed to understand the programs lenders offer. In the first part of the chapter, we'll review the basic features of a mortgage loan; it is differences in these features that distinguish the various loan programs. In the second part of the chapter, we'll look at the main categories of loan programs: conventional loans and government-sponsored loans. We'll also discuss seller financing.

BASIC LOAN FEATURES

The basic features of a mortgage loan include the repayment period; the amortization; the loan-to-value ratio; a secondary financing arrangement (in some cases); the loan fees; and a fixed or adjustable interest rate.

REPAYMENT PERIOD

The repayment period of a loan is the number of years the borrower has in which to repay the loan. The repayment period may also be referred to as the loan term.

Thirty years is generally considered the standard repayment period for a residential mortgage, but many lenders also offer 15-year and 20-year loans. In some programs a term as short as 10 years or as long as 40 years is allowed.

The length of the repayment period affects two important aspects of a mortgage loan:

1. the amount of the monthly payment, and
2. the total amount of interest paid over the life of the loan.

To see the impact that the repayment period has on the monthly payment and the total interest paid, let's compare a 30-year loan with a 15-year loan.

MONTHLY PAYMENT AMOUNT. The main reason 30 years became the standard term for a residential mortgage is that a longer repayment period reduces the amount of the monthly payment. Thus, a 30-year loan is more affordable than a 15-year loan.

> **EXAMPLE:** The monthly payment on a $100,000 30-year loan at 7% interest is $665.30. The monthly payment on the same loan amortized over a 15-year period is $898.83.

The higher monthly payment required for a 15-year loan means that the borrower will build equity in the home much faster. But the higher payment also makes it much more difficult to qualify for a 15-year loan than for the same size of loan with a 30-year term. A buyer who wants a 15-year loan and has sufficient funds might decide to make a larger downpayment and borrow less money in order to make the monthly payment amount more affordable. Or the buyer might choose instead to buy a much less expensive home than what he could afford with a 30-year loan.

TOTAL INTEREST. Probably the biggest advantage of a shorter repayment period is that it substantially decreases the amount of interest paid over the life of the loan. With a 15-year mortgage, a borrower will end up paying less than half as much interest over the life of the loan as a 30-year mortgage would require.

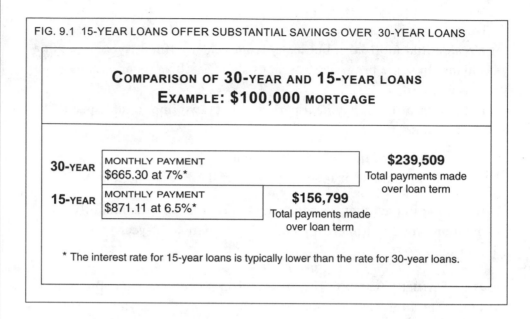

FIG. 9.1 15-YEAR LOANS OFFER SUBSTANTIAL SAVINGS OVER 30-YEAR LOANS

COMPARISON OF 30-YEAR AND 15-YEAR LOANS
EXAMPLE: $100,000 MORTGAGE

30-YEAR — MONTHLY PAYMENT $665.30 at 7%* — **$239,509** Total payments made over loan term

15-YEAR — MONTHLY PAYMENT $871.11 at 6.5%* — **$156,799** Total payments made over loan term

* The interest rate for 15-year loans is typically lower than the rate for 30-year loans.

EXAMPLE: Let's look at our $100,000 loan at 7% interest again. By the end of a 30-year loan term, the borrower will pay a total of $239,509. But by the end of a 15-year term, the borrower will pay only $161,789. After deducting the original $100,000 principal amount, you can see that the 30-year loan will require $139,509 in interest, while the 15-year loan will require only $61,789 in interest.

So the 30-year mortgage has affordable payments, but requires the borrower to pay a lot more interest over the life of the loan. On the other hand, the 15-year loan has much higher monthly payments, but allows the borrower to pay far less interest over the life of the loan.

INTEREST RATES FOR 15-YEAR LOANS. To simplify our comparison of a 15-year loan and a 30-year loan, we applied the same interest rate—7%—to both loans. In fact, however, a lender is likely to charge a significantly lower interest rate on a 15-year loan than it charges for a comparable 30-year loan. That's because a 15-year loan represents less of a risk for the lender.

The interest rate on a 15-year loan might be half a percentage point lower than the rate on a 30-year loan. If the interest rate on the 15-year loan in our example were only 6.5% instead of 7%, the monthly payment would be $871.11. The total interest paid over the life of the loan would be $56,799. (See Figure 9.1.)

AMORTIZATION

The amortization of a loan refers to how the principal and interest are paid over the repayment period. Most loans made by institutional lenders like banks and savings and loans are **fully amortized**. A fully amortized loan is completely paid off by the end of the repayment period by means of regular monthly payments. The amount of the monthly payment remains the same throughout the repayment period. Each monthly payment includes both a principal portion and an interest portion. As each payment is made, the principal amount of the debt is reduced. With each succeeding payment, a slightly smaller portion of the payment is applied to interest and a slightly larger portion is applied to the principal, until at last the final payment pays off the loan completely.

In the early years of a fully amortized loan, the principal portion of the payment is quite small, so it takes several years for the borrower's equity to increase significantly through debt reduction. But toward the end of the loan period, the borrower's equity increases more rapidly.

EXAMPLE: A fully amortized, 30-year $100,000 loan at 6% interest calls for monthly payments of $599.55. Only $99.55 of the first payment is applied to the principal. But by the twentieth year of the loan term, $327.89 of the $599.55 payment is applied to the principal.

FIG. 9.2   PAYMENTS FOR A FULLY-AMORTIZED LOAN

EXAMPLE: $100,000 LOAN @ 6%, 30-YEAR TERM, MONTHLY PAYMENTS

PAYMENT NUMBER	BEGINNING BALANCE	TOTAL PAYMENT	INTEREST PORTION	PRINCIPAL PORTION	ENDING BALANCE
1	$100,000.00	$599.55	$500.00	$99.55	$99,900.45
2	$99,900.45	$599.55	$499.50	$100.05	$99,800.40
3	$99,800.40	$599.55	$499.00	$100.55	$99,699.85
4	$99,699.85	$599.55	$498.50	$101.05	$99,598.80
5	$99,598.80	$599.55	$497.99	$101.56	$99,497.24

There are two alternatives to the fully amortized loan: the partially amortized loan and the interest-only loan. Like a fully amortized loan, a **partially amortized** loan requires monthly payments of both principal and interest. However, the monthly payments are not enough to completely pay off the debt by the end of the repayment period. At the end of the repayment period, some principal remains unpaid. It must then be paid off in one lump sum called a **balloon payment**.

> **EXAMPLE:** A partially amortized $100,000 loan might have a $71,000 balance at the end of the loan term. The borrower will have to make a balloon payment of $71,000 to pay off the loan.

In most cases, the borrower comes up with the funds for the balloon payment by refinancing. (Refinancing means using the funds from a new mortgage loan to pay off an existing mortgage.)

Unlike an amortized loan, an **interest-only** loan calls only for interest payments during the repayment period. No principal payments are made at all. At the end of the repayment period, the entire principal amount—the amount originally borrowed—is due and must be paid off with a balloon payment.

> **EXAMPLE:** If a $100,000 loan were an interest-only loan, the borrower would make monthly interest payments to the lender during the loan term. At the end of the loan term, the borrower would still owe the entire $100,000.

Since mortgage loans from institutional lenders are usually fully amortized, you're most likely to encounter a partially amortized loan or an interest-only loan as part of a secondary financing arrangement or a seller financing arrangement. (Secondary financing and seller financing are discussed later on in this chapter.)

LOAN-TO-VALUE RATIOS

A **loan-to-value ratio** (LTV) expresses the relationship between the loan amount and the value of the home being purchased. If a buyer is purchasing a $100,000 home with an $80,000 loan and a $20,000 downpayment, the loan-to-value ratio is 80%. If the loan amount were $90,000 and the downpayment were $10,000, the LTV would be 90%. The higher the LTV, the larger the loan amount and the smaller the downpayment.

A loan with a low LTV is generally less risky than one with a high LTV. The borrower's investment in her home is greater, so she'll try harder to avoid defaulting on the loan and losing the home. And if the borrower does default, the outstanding loan balance is less, so it's more likely that the lender will be able to recoup the entire amount in a fore-closure sale.

Lenders use LTVs to set maximum loan amounts. For example, under the terms of a particular loan program, the maximum loan amount might be 95% of the sales price or appraised value of the property, whichever is less. The borrower would be required to make a downpayment of at least 5%.

SECONDARY FINANCING

Sometimes a buyer may want to get two loans at the same time. One of the loans is a **primary loan** for most of the purchase price, and the other is used to pay part of the downpayment or closing costs required for the first loan. The second loan is referred to as **secondary financing**.

Secondary financing can come from a variety of sources. It may come from the same lender who is making the primary loan, it may come from a second lender, it may come from the seller, or it may come from a private third party.

A lender making a primary loan will usually place restrictions on the type of secondary financing arrangement the borrower may enter into. The borrower generally must be able to qualify for the combined payment on the primary and secondary loans. And in most cases the borrower will still be required to make at least a minimum downpayment out of his own funds.

LOAN FEES

Of course, lenders don't loan money free of charge. For mortgage loans, lenders not only charge borrowers interest on the principal, they also charge points. The term "point" is short for "percentage point." A point is one percentage point (1%) of the loan amount. For example, on a $100,000 loan, one point would be $1,000; six points would be $6,000.

There are two different types of points: loan origination fees and discount points.

ORIGINATION FEES. A loan origination fee is designed to pay administrative costs the lender incurs in processing a loan; it is sometimes called a service fee, an administrative charge, or simply a loan fee. An origination fee is charged in virtually every residential mortgage loan transaction. It's a closing cost, paid when the transaction closes, and it is usually paid by the buyer.

DISCOUNT POINTS. The second type of point is a discount point. Discount points are used to increase the lender's yield, or profit, on the loan. By charging discount points, the lender not only gets interest throughout the loan term, it collects an additional sum of money up front, when the loan is funded. As a result, the lender is willing to "discount" the loan—that is, make the loan at a lower interest rate than it would have without the discount points. In effect, the lender is paid a lump sum at closing so the borrower can avoid paying more interest later. A lower interest rate also translates into a lower monthly payment.

Discount points are not charged in all loan transactions, but they have become increasingly common. The number of discount points charged usually depends on how the loan's interest rate compares to market interest rates. Typically, a lender that offers an especially low rate charges more points to make up for it.

FIG. 9.3 BASIC FEATURES OF RESIDENTIAL MORTGAGE LOANS

BASIC LOAN FEATURES

- REPAYMENT PERIOD
- AMORTIZATION
- LOAN-TO-VALUE RATIO
- SECONDARY FINANCING (IN SOME CASES)
- LOAN FEES
  - ORIGINATION FEE (NEARLY ALWAYS)
  - DISCOUNT POINTS (IN SOME CASES)
- INTEREST RATE: FIXED OR ADJUSTABLE

FIXED AND ADJUSTABLE INTEREST RATES

A loan's interest rate can be either fixed or adjustable. With a fixed-rate loan, the interest rate charged on the loan remains constant throughout the entire loan term. If a borrower obtains a 30-year home loan with a 9% fixed interest rate, the interest rate remains 9% for the whole 30-year period, no matter what happens to market interest rates during that time. If market rates increase to 12%, or if they drop to 6%, the interest rate charged on the loan will still be 9%.

Until the early 1980s, virtually all mortgage loans had a fixed interest rate. During the 1980s, however, market interest rates rose dramatically and fluctuated constantly. Suddenly, many borrowers could no longer afford to take out a home loan. And many lenders (who were unable to predict future interest rates) became uncomfortable lending money for 30 years at a fixed interest rate. The **adjustable-rate mortgage** (ARM) was introduced as the solution to both of these problems.

An ARM allows the lender to periodically adjust the loan's interest rate to reflect changes in market interest rates. The lender's ability to change the loan's interest rate during the loan term passes on the risk of interest rate increases to the borrower. Because of this shift in risk, lenders are willing to charge a lower rate on ARMs. For example, if a borrower could get a fixed interest rate loan at 6%, he might be able to get an adjustable-rate loan at an initial rate between 3½% and 4%.

Of course, while the initial interest rate of an adjustable-rate loan appears attractive, the borrower is assuming a greater risk. With an ARM, it is the borrower who pays the price of an increase in market interest rates. When market rates go up, the borrower's interest rate and mortgage payments also go up. On the other hand, if market rates decrease, the borrower's interest rate and mortgage payments also decrease.

ARM FEATURES. An adjustable-rate loan has several special features, including the note rate, the index, the margin, a rate adjustment period, a payment adjustment period, rate caps, payment caps, a negative amortization cap, and a conversion option.

NOTE RATE. The note rate is the ARM's initial interest rate. It's commonly referred to as the note rate because it's the rate stated in the promissory note.

INDEX. An index is a widely published statistical report that is considered a reliable indicator of changes in the cost of money. Examples include the one-year Treasury securities index, the Eleventh District cost of funds index, and the LIBOR index.

Some indexes are more responsive to changes in the cost of money than others. For example, the one-year Treasury securities index is very responsive to economic fluctuations, while the cost of funds index is more stable. Most lenders choose the more responsive indexes. A borrower may want a more responsive index if he or she thinks rates will decrease, but a more stable index if he or she thinks rates will increase. This way, if the borrower is right and rates decrease, the borrower's interest rate will quickly reflect that change. On the other hand, if rates are increasing and a more stable index is used, the borrower's interest rate will increase more slowly.

MARGIN. An ARM's margin is the difference between the index rate and the interest rate the lender charges the borrower. The margin is how the lender earns a profit on the loan. A typical margin is between two and three percentage points.

> **EXAMPLE:** Suppose the current index rate is 5% and the lender's margin is 2%. 5% + 2% = 7%. The lender charges the borrower 7% on the loan. The 2% margin is the lender's income from the loan.

RATE ADJUSTMENT PERIOD. An ARM's rate adjustment period determines how often the lender has the right to adjust the loan's interest rate. The most common rate adjustment period is one year. But the rate adjustment period may be every 6 months, every 18 months, or some other time period. At the end of each period, the lender checks the index. If the index rate has increased, the lender can increase the borrower's interest rate. If the index rate has decreased, the lender must decrease the borrower's interest rate.

Some ARMs have a two-tiered rate adjustment structure. They provide for a longer initial period before the first rate adjustment, with more frequent rate adjustments after that.

> **EXAMPLE:** The borrowers are financing their home with a 30-year ARM that has an initial rate adjustment period of three years, with annual rate adjustments from then on. The interest rate charged on their loan won't change during the first three years of the repayment period, but it will change each year after that.

The loan in the example would be called a 3/1 ARM. There are also 5/1 ARMs, 7/1 ARMs, and 10/1 ARMs. In each case, the first number is the number of years in the initial rate adjustment period, and the second number means that subsequent rate adjustments will occur once a year. Some borrowers who choose these types of loans intend to sell or refinance their home before the end of the initial adjustment period. As a general rule, the longer the initial adjustment period, the higher the initial interest rate. But the initial rate will still be lower than the rate for a comparable fixed-rate loan.

MORTGAGE PAYMENT ADJUSTMENT PERIOD. An ARM's mortgage payment adjustment period determines when the lender changes the amount of the borrower's monthly payment to reflect a change in the interest rate charged on the loan. For most ARMs, the payment adjustment period coincides with the interest rate adjustment period. In that case, when the lender increases the interest rate on the loan, the payment amount immediately goes up as well. And when the lender decreases the loan's interest rate, the payment amount immediately goes down.

RATE CAPS. Not long after adjustable-rate loans were introduced, some ARM borrowers began suffering from "payment shock." Payment shock occurred when interest rates rose so rapidly that an ARM borrower could no longer afford her monthly mortgage payment.

To protect borrowers from payment shock, lenders began including interest rate caps in their ARMs. Rate caps limit how much the interest rate on the loan can go up, regardless of what its index does. By limiting interest rate increases, the rate cap prevents the monthly payment from increasing too much.

Most ARMs have two kinds of rate caps. One limits the amount that the interest rate can increase in any one adjustment period. The other limits the amount that the interest rate can increase over the entire life of the loan. Common rate caps are 2% per year and 5% over the life of the loan.

PAYMENT CAPS. Mortgage payments caps serve the same purpose as rate caps: limiting how much the borrower's monthly mortgage payment can increase. A payment cap directly limits how much the lender can raise the monthly mortgage payment, regardless of what is happening to the mortgage interest rate. A typical payment cap might limit payment increases to 7.5% annually.

FIG. 9.4   COMMON FEATURES OF ADJUSTABLE-RATE MORTGAGES

ARM F<small>EATURES</small>

- N<small>OTE RATE</small>: <small>INITIAL INTEREST RATE</small>
- I<small>NDEX</small>: <small>CHANGES IN ARM'S INTEREST RATE ARE TIED TO INDEX</small>
- M<small>ARGIN</small>: <small>DIFFERENCE BETWEEN INDEX RATE AND ARM RATE</small>
- R<small>ATE ADJUSTMENT PERIOD</small>: <small>HOW OFTEN ARM INTEREST RATE MAY CHANGE</small>
- P<small>AYMENT ADJUSTMENT PERIOD</small>: <small>HOW OFTEN PAYMENT AMOUNT MAY CHANGE</small>
- R<small>ATE CAPS</small>: <small>LIMIT RATE INCREASES (ANNUAL AND LIFE-OF-LOAN)</small>
- P<small>AYMENT CAPS</small>: <small>LIMIT PAYMENT INCREASES (ANNUAL AND LIFE-OF-LOAN)</small>
- N<small>EGATIVE AMORTIZATION CAP</small>: <small>LIMITS HOW MUCH INTEREST CAN BE ADDED TO PRINCIPAL BALANCE</small>
- C<small>ONVERSION OPTION</small>: <small>ALLOWS BORROWER TO CONVERT TO FIXED RATE</small>

N<small>EGATIVE AMORTIZATION CAP</small>. If an ARM has a payment cap but no rate cap, payment increases don't always keep up with increases in the loan's interest rate. The same thing can happen if the payment adjustment period differs from the rate adjustment period. As a result, the monthly payments don't cover the full amount of the interest that has accrued. So the lender adds the unpaid interest to the loan's principal balance. This is called **negative amortization**. A loan's principal balance ordinarily declines steadily over the loan term, but negative amortization makes the balance go up instead of down. The borrower can end up owing the lender more money than the original loan amount.

A negative amortization cap limits the amount of unpaid interest that can be added to the principal balance. A typical negative amortization cap limits the total amount a borrower can owe to 125% of the original loan amount. Most ARMs today are structured to prevent negative amortization in the first place.

C<small>ONVERSION OPTION</small>. An ARM may have a conversion option that allows the borrower to convert it to a fixed-rate loan. Most conversion options give the borrower a limited time in which to convert. For example, the borrower may be able to convert the ARM to a fixed-rate loan anytime between the first and fifth year of the loan term. Conversion is usually considerably less expensive than refinancing the loan.

ARM CHECKLIST. Adjustable-rate loans are complicated. To help your buyers understand ARMs and get all the information they need, you should give them the following list of questions to ask the lender:

- What will my initial interest rate be?
- How often will my interest rate change? Is the first rate adjustment period longer than later adjustment periods?
- How often will my payment change?
- Is there any limit to how much my interest rate can be increased?
- Is there any limit to how much my payment can be increased at any one time?
- Does my ARM allow negative amortization?
- Can my ARM be converted to a fixed-rate loan?

CONVENTIONAL LOANS

Now let's turn our attention to loan programs. Loans made by institutional lenders (such as banks, savings and loans, or mortgage companies) can be divided into two main categories: conventional loans and government-sponsored loans. A **conventional loan** is any institutional loan that is not insured or guaranteed by a government agency. For example, a loan made by a commercial bank and insured by a private mortgage insurance company is a conventional loan. A loan that is insured by the FHA (Federal Housing Administration) or guaranteed by the VA (Department of Veterans Affairs) is not a conventional loan. We'll discuss conventional loan programs first, and then look at government loan programs.

CONVENTIONAL LOANS AND THE SECONDARY MARKET

Lenders sometimes make conventional "portfolio" loans. A portfolio loan is one that the lender plans on keeping in its own portfolio of investments, as opposed to selling it on the secondary market. With some limitations, portfolio loans can be made according to the lender's own underwriting standards.

However, lenders generally want to have the option of selling their loans on the secondary market instead of keeping them in portfolio. Conventional loans are much easier to sell if the lender makes them in accordance with the underwriting standards and other rules set by the major secondary market agencies, Fannie Mae (the Federal National Mortgage Association) and Freddie Mac (the Federal Home Loan Mortgage Corporation). Loans that conform to the rules of Fannie Mae and Freddie Mac are called **conforming loans**; by contrast, loans made according to a lender's own standards are **nonconforming loans**. Because the standards of the secondary market agencies are so influential, our discussion of conventional loan programs is primarily based on rules set by Fannie Mae and Freddie Mac.

CHARACTERISTICS OF CONVENTIONAL LOANS

The elements that distinguish conventional loan programs from the government-sponsored programs include the loan-to-value rules, private mortgage insurance, and the qualifying standards (especially income ratios).

CONVENTIONAL LTVs. Traditionally, the standard conventional loan-to-value ratio has been 80%. That is, the loan is 80% of the sales price or appraised value (whichever is less) of the home being purchased. Lenders regard an 80% loan as a safe investment. The 20% downpayment gives the borrower a substantial incentive to avoid default, and if foreclosure becomes necessary, the lender is very likely to recover the full amount owed.

While 80% may be the preferred loan-to-value ratio, it's not the highest loan-to-value ratio allowed for conventional loans. Especially in areas where housing prices are high, 90% loans have become common, and even 95% loans are widely available. A 90% loan has a loan-to-value ratio over 80% but no higher than 90% of the home's value. A 95% loan has a loan-to-value ratio over 90% but no higher than 95%. (So a loan with an 81% LTV is considered a 90% loan rather than an 80% loan, and a loan with a 91% LTV is treated as a 95% loan, not a 90% loan.)

The lender's risk is greater with a 90% loan than with an 80% loan, and it is even greater with a 95% loan. If the loan amount is 90% or 95% of the home's value, it's quite possible that the foreclosure sale will bring in less money than the remaining debt on the property. So lenders make 90% and 95% loans (particularly 95% loans) more difficult to obtain than 80% loans. As we'll discuss later, lenders often apply stricter qualifying standards for higher-LTV loans.

Many lenders also charge higher fees and higher interest rates for 90% and 95% loans. And private mortgage insurance is required on all 90% and 95% conventional loans (see below).

Adjustable-rate mortgages with LTVs up to 95% are available. However, Fannie Mae and Freddie Mac generally do not purchase ARMs with LTVs over 90%. That's because the unpredictability of changes in interest rates and monthly payment amounts makes default more likely with an ARM than with a fixed-rate loan.

PRIVATE MORTGAGE INSURANCE. With a conventional loan, if the downpayment is less than 20% of the property's value, the lender requires the borrower to purchase private mortgage insurance (PMI). The mortgage insurance protects the lender against the extra risk that a higher loan-to-value ratio represents. Fannie Mae and Freddie Mac both require PMI on all conventional loans they purchase that have loan-to-value ratios greater than 80%.

When a borrower purchases PMI, the mortgage insurance company insures the lender against losses that might result if the borrower defaults on the loan. The mortgage insurance covers only the upper portion of the loan amount—typically, the upper 25% to 30%.

> **EXAMPLE:** Wilson is buying a $400,000 home. She's financing the purchase with a 90% loan, so the loan amount is $360,000. Because the LTV is over 80%, Wilson must purchase PMI. In exchange for the PMI premiums, the mortgage insurance company insures the top 25% of the loan amount, or $90,000. The insurance company is assuming the risk that the lender may lose up to $90,000 on a foreclosure sale in the event that Wilson defaults.

If the borrower defaults on a loan covered by PMI, the lender has two options. The lender can foreclose on the property, and if the foreclosure sale results in a loss, file a claim with the insurance company to cover the loss, up to the policy amount. Or the lender can simply relinquish the property to the insurer and make a claim for actual losses up to the policy amount. (Most lenders choose the first option.)

EXAMPLE: Returning to our previous example, suppose Wilson defaults on the loan when the principal balance is $352,000. The property is sold at a foreclosure sale for only $368,000. There is $7,626 of unpaid interest on the loan, and $1,950 in unpaid tax and insurance payments. The lender incurred $3,600 in attorney's fees and the foreclosure sale cost $9,350. After deducting the principal, the unpaid interest, taxes, and insurance, and all foreclosure costs, the lender ends up with a $6,526 loss. So the lender files a $6,526 claim with the insurance company. Since this amount is well within the $90,000 face amount of the insurance policy, the lender will be able to recoup the entire loss.

PREMIUMS. The borrower has to pay two fees to purchase private mortgage insurance. First, there is an initial premium that is paid when the loan is made, as part of the borrower's closing costs. This generally ranges from .5% of the loan amount to 1.5% of the loan amount, depending on the amount of coverage and the loan's LTV. Second, there is a recurring fee, called an annual renewal premium, that is added to the borrower's monthly mortgage payments. This ranges from .3% to .5% of the loan amount.

A one-time mortgage insurance premium can be paid as an alternative to the initial premium and the annual renewal premium. This one-time premium is usually financed over the loan term and added to the monthly mortgage payment in the same way as the renewal premium.

CANCELLATION OF PMI. If all goes well, the borrower will gradually pay off the principal. As the principal balance goes down, and assuming that the property does not depreciate in value, the loan-to-value ratio will decrease. Eventually the mortgage insurance should no longer be necessary.

A federal law called the Homeowners Protection Act requires lenders to cancel a conventional loan's PMI and refund any unearned premium to the borrower once certain conditions are met. The cancellation rules apply to loans closed on or after July 29, 1999, the date the law went into effect.

Here are the basic rules for standard loans covered by PMI (different rules apply to loans classified as high-risk and outside standard guidelines):

- The lender must automatically cancel the PMI when the loan's principal balance is scheduled to reach 78% of the home's original value, unless the borrower is delinquent on the payments.

- The borrower may send the lender a written request to cancel the PMI earlier, when the principal balance is scheduled to reach 80% of the original value. The request must be granted if the borrower's payment history is good, the value of the home has not decreased, and the borrower has not taken out any other loans on the home.

Although these rules don't apply to loans closed before July 29, 1999, the borrower can often get the PMI canceled on an earlier loan once the loan-to-value ratio has decreased sufficiently. Also, the Homeowners Protection Act requires lenders to send all borrowers with PMI (regardless of when their loans were closed) an annual notice concerning their PMI cancellation rights.

SECONDARY FINANCING AND CONVENTIONAL LOANS. Secondary financing can be used in conjunction with conventional loans, but most lenders require a series of rules to be met. These rules are designed to keep the borrower from overextending himself, and to reduce the risk that he will default on the primary loan. For example, one rule prohibits a repayment period of less than five years for the second loan. This prevents the second lender from requiring the borrower to make a balloon payment in the first five years of the loan, when the risk of default on the primary loan is the greatest. If your buyer is interested in secondary financing, he should check with the lender to see what types of secondary financing are acceptable.

PREPAYMENT PENALTIES. Some mortgage loan agreements allow the lender to charge the borrower a prepayment penalty if the borrower pays off all of the principal, or a substantial portion of it, before it is due. A prepayment penalty is not considered a standard provision in a conventional loan. However, some lenders offer reduced loan fees or a lower interest rate in exchange for including a prepayment penalty provision in the loan agreement. While this can be a reasonable arrangement, the borrower should carefully consider the consequences before agreeing to a prepayment penalty.

A prepayment penalty is usually charged only if the loan is prepaid during the first few years of the loan term. The borrower should find out how many years the prepayment penalty provision will be in effect. She also needs to ask under what circumstances the penalty will be charged.

Will she have to pay the penalty if the loan is paid off early because she has sold the property? What if she refinances? And how much will the penalty be? Imposing a heavy prepayment penalty with unreasonable terms is a predatory lending practice, and borrowers should beware.

ASSUMPTION. A conventional loan usually includes a due-on-sale clause (alienation clause), which means it can be assumed only with the lender's permission. The lender will evaluate the new buyers to make sure they are creditworthy. The buyers will be expected to pay an assumption fee, and the lender may also raise the interest rate on the loan.

UNDERWRITING CONVENTIONAL LOANS

When lenders qualify loan applicants for conventional loans, they evaluate the three characteristics of creditworthiness we discussed in Chapter 8: income, net worth, and credit history.

INCOME. As with any type of loan, the first step in analyzing a loan applicant's income for a conventional loan is to calculate the applicant's stable monthly income. (See Chapter 8.) The next step is to measure the adequacy of the stable monthly income using income ratios. Traditionally, lenders have used two income ratios for conventional loans: the total debt to income ratio and the housing expense to income ratio.

The total debt to income ratio measures the relationship between the loan applicant's monthly income and his total monthly debt. The total monthly debt is made up of the proposed housing expense, plus any other recurring liabilities. The housing expense includes PITI (principal, interest, taxes, hazard insurance, and any mortgage insurance), along with any dues owed to a homeowner's association or condominium association. The other recurring liabilities fall into three categories:

- installment debts (which have a definite beginning and ending date and fixed monthly payments);
- revolving debts (such as credit card payments); and
- other obligations (such as child support or spousal support).

Note that an installment debt is usually only counted as part of the applicant's monthly obligations if there are more than ten payments remaining.

EXAMPLE: Your buyer has a student loan with $100 payments. If there are only ten payments left until the loan is paid off, the $100 probably will not be included as part of the buyer's monthly obligations.

That rule also applies to child support or spousal support (alimony): if the required payments will end in ten months or less, they won't be counted as part of the loan applicant's monthly obligations.

There is an exception to the ten-payment rule, however. Even if there are ten payments or less remaining on a debt, if the payment amount is large enough to potentially interfere with the borrower's ability to pay the mortgage, then the lender may count the debt in calculating the total debt to income ratio.

The standard or benchmark total debt to income ratio for conventional loans is 36%. In other words, lenders generally consider a loan applicant's income adequate for a conventional loan if the total monthly obligations do not exceed 36% of stable monthly income.

EXAMPLE: The Browns have a stable monthly income of $4,800. Their monthly obligations include a $40 minimum payment on a credit card, a $300 car loan payment, and a $100 personal loan payment. First multiply $4,800 by 36%. *$4,800 × .36 = $1,728*. This is the maximum amount of total monthly obligations the lender will allow. Subtract the Browns' monthly debts: *$1,728 – $40 charge card payment – $300 car loan payment – $100 personal loan payment = $1,288*. This means that $1,288 is the maximum monthly housing expense the Browns can afford under the 36% total debt to income ratio guideline.

The second ratio that lenders have traditionally used for conventional loans is the housing expense to income ratio. The proposed housing expense generally must not exceed 28% of the borrower's stable monthly income.

EXAMPLE: Let's go back to the Browns' situation. They had a stable monthly income of $4,800. To apply the housing expense to income ratio, simply multiply $4,800 by 28%, or .28. *$4,800 × .28 = $1,344*. $1,344 is the maximum housing expense the Browns could afford under the housing expense to income ratio.

The lender compares the maximum housing expense figure arrived at with the total debt to income ratio to the one arrived at with the housing expense to income ratio, and the smaller of the two figures is treated as the maximum allowable housing expense. In our example, the Browns' maximum housing expense would be $1,288 (the figure indicated by the total debt to income ratio) rather than $1,344.

As you'll recall from the discussion of prequalifying in Chapter 8, you can use the Browns' maximum housing expense to determine a reasonable price range for them. First, estimate the maximum principal and interest payment by deducting a portion of their allowable monthly housing expense (for example, 15%) for taxes and insurance. Then use a financial calculator to calculate the maximum mortgage amount based on the maximum principal and interest payment. Add the amount of the Browns' anticipated downpayment to the maximum loan amount, and you have a sales price you can use as a guide in finding them homes they can afford.

> **EXAMPLE:** Subtract 15% from the Browns' maximum allowable monthly housing expense: $1,288 − 15% = $1,095. That's their estimated maximum principal and interest payment. If they could get a 30-year mortgage at 6% interest, the $1,095 payment translates into a maximum loan amount of approximately $182,600. If the Browns have $19,000 available for a downpayment, they could purchase a home costing about $201,000.

Lenders consider the total debt to income ratio a more reliable indicator than the housing expense to income ratio, because the total debt to income ratio takes all of the loan applicant's monthly obligations into account. In fact, Fannie Mae no longer sets a benchmark housing expense to income ratio; the monthly housing expense is now considered only as one of the components of the total debt to income ratio in Fannie Mae's underwriting.

Both Fannie Mae and Freddie Mac consider their income ratios as benchmarks or guidelines rather than rigid limits. They may be willing to purchase a loan even though the borrower's total debt to income ratio exceeds 36%, as long as there are compensating factors that justify making the loan in spite of the higher income ratio. For example, one or more of the following factors might offset the extra risk:

- a large downpayment,
- an excellent credit score,
- substantial net worth,
- demonstrated ability to incur few debts and accumulate savings,
- education, job training, or employment history that indicates strong potential for increased earnings, or
- significant energy-efficient features in the home being purchased.

On the other hand, when a proposed loan would involve other factors that represent increased rather than decreased risk, then a total debt to income ratio in excess of 36% is generally unacceptable. For example, a lender would be unlikely to accept a high total debt to income ratio for a loan with an LTV over 90% or for an adjustable-rate loan.

NET WORTH. Fannie Mae and Freddie Mac require most conventional loan applicants to have the equivalent of two months' mortgage payments in reserve after making the downpayment and paying all closing costs. Larger reserves may be required for riskier loans; for example, a lender might require three months' reserves for a 95% loan. The reserves must be cash or liquid assets that could easily be converted to cash if necessary (for example, the cash value of a life insurance policy, or the vested portion of a retirement account).

Fannie Mae and Freddie Mac also have rules regarding the use of gift funds to close a transaction. First of all, the donor must be the borrower's relative, fiancé, or domestic partner. Alternatively, the donor may be the borrower's employer, a municipality, or a nonprofit organization. Second, the gift must be accompanied by a gift letter that clearly states that the funds are a gift and not a loan. And third, the borrower usually must make a downpayment of at least 5% out of her own funds.

This 5% requirement doesn't apply if the loan-to-value ratio is 80% or less. So if the gift funds are at least 20% of the sales price, the borrower isn't required to contribute any of her own funds.

CREDIT HISTORY. Credit scores now play a significant role in conventional underwriting. Both Fannie Mae and Freddie Mac encourage lenders to use credit scores as a key tool in evaluating a loan applicant's creditworthiness.

FIG. 9.5 FEATURES OF CONVENTIONAL LOANS

CONVENTIONAL LOAN FEATURES

- LOAN-TO-VALUE RATIO CATEGORIES: 80%, 90%, 95%
- PRIVATE MORTGAGE INSURANCE REQUIRED IF LTV IS OVER 80%
- SECONDARY FINANCING ALLOWED IF CERTAIN RULES ARE MET
- PREPAYMENT PENALTIES NO LONGER STANDARD
- ASSUMPTION: LENDER'S PERMISSION USUALLY REQUIRED
- TRADITIONAL INCOME RATIO LIMITS
  - 36% MAXIMUM TOTAL DEBT TO INCOME RATIO
  - 28% MAXIMUM HOUSING EXPENSE TO INCOME RATIO
- GIFT FUNDS ALLOWED BUT LIMITED IF LTV IS OVER 80%
- CREDIT SCORES IMPORTANT

Fannie Mae treats the applicant's credit history, as reflected in his credit score, as one of two primary risk factors. The other is the cash investment the applicant will be making, measured by the loan-to-value ratio. Based on the credit score and the LTV, a proposed loan is ranked as having a low, moderate, or high primary risk, and that determines the level of review applied to the rest of the loan application. Fannie Mae treats the other aspects of the application, such as the total debt to income ratio and the cash reserves, as contributory risk factors that may increase or decrease the risk of default.

MAKING CONVENTIONAL LOANS MORE AFFORDABLE

Sometimes a buyer can't qualify for a standard fixed-rate loan and wouldn't be comfortable with an adjustable-rate loan. There are quite a few other options that can make a conventional loan more affordable. These include buydowns, loans with lower initial payments, low-down-payment programs, and programs targeted at low-income borrowers or low-income neighborhoods.

BUYDOWN PLANS. One of the easiest ways to make a loan less expensive is with a buydown. A buydown lowers the borrower's monthly payment and can make it easier to qualify for the loan. When the loan is made, the seller or a third party pays the lender a lump sum that is used to reduce the borrower's payments either early in the loan term or throughout the loan term.

A buydown has exactly the same effect as the loan discount points that lenders often charge. The lump sum payment at closing increases the lender's yield on the loan, and in return the lender charges a lower interest rate, which lowers the amount of the borrower's monthly mortgage payment.

Note that when a seller agrees to pay for a buydown, he doesn't have to come up with cash to do so. The amount of the buydown is simply deducted from the seller's net proceeds at closing and transferred to the lender. As you might expect, buydowns are especially popular when market interest rates are high.

A buydown can be permanent or temporary. With a permanent buydown, the borrower pays the lower interest rate (and a lower monthly payment) for the entire loan term. With a temporary buydown, the interest rate and the monthly payment are reduced only during the first years of the loan term.

PERMANENT BUYDOWNS. If a borrower's interest rate is bought down permanently, the buydown reduces the note rate, which is the interest rate stated in the promissory note. The cost of a permanent buydown depends on how much the interest rate is reduced and the amount of the loan. A rough rule of thumb is that it takes 6% of the loan amount (or six points) to reduce the interest rate on the loan by one percentage point.

> **EXAMPLE:** Bowen needs to borrow $150,000 to buy Sanderson's property. The lender quoted a 10% interest rate, and Bowen can't quite qualify for the loan at that rate. Sanderson agrees to buy down Bowen's interest rate by one percentage point. To estimate how much the buydown will cost Sanderson, multiply the loan amount by 6%. *$150,000 × .06 = $9,000.* At closing, the lender will withhold approximately $9,000 from the loan funds, reducing Sanderson's proceeds from the sale.
>
> The 1% buydown will reduce Bowen's mortgage payment by almost $100 per month, enabling her to qualify for the loan. The lender will charge Bowen 9% interest instead of 10% throughout the 30-year loan term, which will save Bowen nearly $35,800 over the life of the loan.

Keep in mind that the cost of a buydown varies from lender to lender. Six percent of the loan amount for each percentage point deducted from the interest rate is only a rule of thumb. The cost is affected by current market conditions, including market interest rates and the average time loans are outstanding before they are paid off. The amount that the lender will actually charge should be confirmed before the parties sign an agreement.

TEMPORARY BUYDOWNS. A temporary buydown reduces the buyer's monthly payment in the early years of the loan term. Temporary buydowns appeal to buyers who believe they can grow into a larger payment, but need time to get established. They also cost sellers less than permanent buydowns.

There are two types of temporary buydown plans: level payment and graduated payment. A level payment plan calls for an interest reduction that stays the same throughout the buydown period. For example, a seller might buy a buyer's interest rate down by 2% for two years. The buyer would pay the lower interest rate during the first two years, and then the lender would begin charging the note rate at the start of the third year.

With a graduated payment plan, the interest rate reduction changes at set points during the buydown period. One graduated payment plan is called a 3-2-1 buydown. It calls for a 3% reduction in the interest rate during the first year, 2% during the second year, and 1% during the third year. The lender begins charging the note rate in the fourth year. This gives the buyer the chance to get used to higher payments gradually.

With a temporary buydown, because the buyer will eventually have to afford a larger payment based on the full note rate, the lender may not be willing to qualify the buyer at the buydown rate. Instead, the lender may use a rate somewhere between the note rate and the buydown rate for qualifying. For instance, in the case of a 3% buydown, the lender might use a rate only 1% or 2% below the note rate to qualify the buyer. This would give the lender some assurance that the buyer will be able to handle the payment increase when the time comes. Alternatively, the lender might qualify the buyer at the buydown rate, but apply stricter income ratios to control the risk of default.

LIMITS ON BUYDOWNS AND OTHER CONTRIBUTIONS. Fannie Mae and Freddie Mac limit the financial contributions a buyer may accept from the seller or another interested party, such as the builder or a real estate agent involved in the transaction. If the loan-to-value ratio for the transaction is over 90%, these contributions can't exceed 3% of the property's sales price or appraised value (whichever is less). If the LTV is 90% or less, the contributions can't exceed 6%. And if the LTV is 75% or less, the contributions can't exceed 9%. These limits apply to buydowns, to payment of closing costs ordinarily paid by the buyer, and to similar contributions.

LOANS WITH LOWER INITIAL PAYMENTS. Many first-time homebuyers are just starting out in their careers. They expect their incomes to increase steadily, so that they'll eventually be able to afford a higher mortgage payment than they can now. These buyers may be able to buy a more expensive home without waiting if they get a loan that has lower payments at first and higher payments later on.

As we just discussed, a temporary buydown is one way of making a loan more affordable in the first years of the repayment period. Earlier in the chapter we also discussed adjustable-rate mortgages with two-tiered rate adjustment schedules. One example is the 5/1 ARM: the interest rate and payment amount start out lower than the rate and payment for a fixed-rate loan, and they don't change during the first five years; the lender makes annual adjustments after that. Other types of conventional loans with two-tiered structures that offer lower payments in the initial years than comparable fixed-rate loans include:

- two-step mortgages,
- balloon/reset mortgages, and
- interest-first mortgages.

TWO-STEP MORTGAGES. A two-step mortgage provides some of the advantages of an ARM, but less uncertainty for the borrower. A two-step mortgage is a 30-year loan that allows the lender to adjust the loan's interest rate at only one point during the loan term. The most common two-step programs are the 5/25 plan and the 7/23 plan.

The interest rate of a 5/25 loan is automatically adjusted after five years to the current market rate, and the monthly payment is adjusted accordingly. The interest rate and payment then stay at that level for the remaining 25 years of the loan term.

EXAMPLE: When your buyer obtained a loan, the current fixed interest rate was 6%. The buyer was able to get a 5/25 two-step loan at a 5.5% initial interest rate. Five years later, the market rate has increased by 2%, so the buyer's rate increases to 7.5%. He will continue to pay 7.5% interest for the remainder of the loan term, 25 years.

A "7/23" loan automatically adjusts after seven years to the current market rate, and then stays at that rate for the remaining 23 years of the loan term.

Because the lender will have an opportunity to adjust the loan's interest rate to reflect changes in the market rate, two-step mortgages are offered at a lower initial rate than fixed-rate loans. And while the borrower assumes the risk that interest rates will increase in the next five or seven years, he also gets to take advantage of lower rates without refinancing if market rates decrease during that five- or seven-year period. Because the interest rate on a two-step loan changes only once, many borrowers feel more comfortable with this type of loan than with an ARM.

BALLOON/RESET MORTGAGES. Balloon/reset mortgages are similar to two-step mortgages, with some key differences. Like two-step mortgages, balloon/reset mortgages come in two versions, 5/25 and 7/23. With a balloon/reset mortgage, however, the initial five- or seven-year period is actually the term of the loan. Although the payment amount is based on a 30-year amortization schedule, the entire mortgage balance becomes due at the end of the five- or seven-year term. In other words, a balloon/reset mortgage is a partially amortized loan.

At the end of the five- or seven-year term, the borrower may have to refinance in order to make the balloon payment. Alternatively, she may be allowed to "reset" the loan. Under the reset option, the loan stays in place and the interest rate is adjusted to the current market rate. The rate and payment are then level for 25 or 23 years.

By exercising the reset option, the borrower can avoid refinancing charges. To be entitled to reset the loan, the borrower has to meet certain conditions. For example, she must not have been delinquent on the mortgage payments during the preceding year. And she must not have placed other liens against the property.

FIG. 9.6   MAKING CONVENTIONAL LOANS MORE AFFORDABLE

CONVENTIONAL AFFORDABILITY PLANS AND PROGRAMS

- BUYDOWNS: PERMANENT OR TEMPORARY
- LOW INITIAL PAYMENT PROGRAMS
  - TWO-STEP MORTGAGES
  - BALLOON/RESET MORTGAGES
  - INTEREST-FIRST MORTGAGES
- LOW-DOWNPAYMENT PROGRAMS
  - 97% AND 100% LOANS
  - TARGETED PROGRAMS: LOW- OR MODERATE-INCOME BUYERS, OR NEIGHBORHOODS THAT NEED REVITALIZATION

INTEREST-FIRST MORTGAGES. With an interest-first mortgage, the monthly payments are lower in the earlier years of the loan because they are interest-only payments. The borrower isn't required to start paying off the principal until later on. The loan has a 30-year term, and the interest-only period is 15 years, with principal repayment beginning in the 16th year. The interest rate remains fixed throughout the 30-year term.

When it's time for the borrower to begin paying off the principal, the entire loan amount is fully amortized over the remaining 15 years of the loan term. As a result, the amount of the required monthly payment is likely to rise sharply at this point. However, the borrower is allowed to make prepayments of principal at any time during the initial 15-year period. Any prepayments will reduce the amount of the monthly payment later on.

LOW-DOWNPAYMENT PROGRAMS. For many potential homebuyers, especially first-time buyers, coming up with enough cash is the biggest challenge in buying a home. They have a steady, reliable income, but they don't have the savings to cover the downpayment, closing costs, and reserves required for a standard conventional loan. Even the 5% downpayment required for a 95% loan may be beyond their means. Buyers in this situation may want to consider special programs that have reduced cash requirements and allow them to draw on alternative sources for the cash they need.

The details of these programs vary. But here are examples of the types of loans that buyers can look for:

- A loan with a 95% LTV that requires a 3% downpayment from the borrower's own funds, with 2% from alternative sources.
- A loan with a 97% LTV that requires a 3% downpayment from the borrower's own funds, plus a 3% contribution to closing costs that may come from alternative sources.
- A loan with a 100% LTV that requires no downpayment from the borrower's funds, but a 3% contribution to closing costs that may come from alternative sources.

Depending on the program, the allowable alternative sources of funds may include gifts, grants, or unsecured loans. The funds may come from a relative, an employer, a public agency, a nonprofit organization, or a private foundation. More than one source may be tapped to get the necessary funds together.

Some of these programs don't require the borrower to have any reserves after closing. Others require only one month's mortgage payment in reserve.

TARGETED PROGRAMS. Although some conventional low-downpayment programs are open to any prospective homebuyer, many are specifically targeted at low- and moderate-income buyers. As a general rule, a buyer can qualify for one of these targeted programs if his stable monthly income does not exceed the median income in the metropolitan area in question. (An increased income limit applies in a high-cost area such as San Francisco.) To make it even easier for low- and moderate-income buyers to get a mortgage, these programs often allow a maximum debt to income ratio of 38% or even 40% and have no maximum housing expense to income ratio.

To encourage neighborhood revitalization, the targeted programs often waive their income limits for buyers who are purchasing homes in low-income or rundown neighborhoods. Thus, a buyer whose income is well above the area median could still qualify for a targeted low-downpayment program if she's buying a home in a neighborhood that meets the program's standards.

Other conventional low-downpayment programs are offered to specific groups such as teachers, police officers, and firefighters. These programs are intended to enable the borrowers to purchase homes in the urban communities they serve, instead of being priced out into the suburbs.

GOVERNMENT-SPONSORED LOAN PROGRAMS

Now let's turn to government-sponsored mortgage loan programs. The two major programs established by the federal government are the FHA-insured loan program and the VA-guaranteed loan program. In California, the state government also sponsors the Cal-Vet program. We'll look at each of these in turn.

FHA-INSURED LOANS

As we discussed in the previous section of the chapter, it's now possible for some buyers to obtain a conventional loan with a very low downpayment. But that's a relatively recent development. For most of the twentieth century, the FHA loan program was the main source of low-downpayment mortgage loans for U.S. homebuyers. The federal government created the Federal Housing Administration (FHA) in 1934, during the Great Depression, to help people with low and moderate incomes buy homes. Today the FHA is an agency within the U.S. Department of Housing and Urban Development, and it still plays a major role in residential financing.

The FHA does not make loans; it insures loans made by banks and other institutional lenders. In effect, the FHA is a giant mortgage insurance agency. Its insurance program, the Mutual Mortgage Insurance Plan, is funded with premiums paid by FHA borrowers. If a lender that makes an FHA-insured loan suffers a loss because the borrower defaults, the FHA will compensate the lender for its loss.

In exchange for insuring a loan, the FHA regulates many of the loan's terms and conditions. The FHA has various programs for specific types of mortgage loans, such as home rehabilitation loans and energy efficiency loans. But the central program for single-family home purchase loans is the 203(b) program. The rules we'll be discussing here apply to loans made through the 203(b) program.

CHARACTERISTICS OF FHA LOANS. Here are some of the key characteristics of FHA loans:

- FHA borrowers must intend to occupy the property as their primary residence. The FHA does not insure loans made to investors, as opposed to owner-occupants. The property purchased with an FHA loan may have up to four dwelling units.
- If there are any other mortgage loans against the property, the FHA loan must have first lien position.
- Most FHA loans have 30-year terms, although 15-year loans are also available. The interest rate may be fixed or adjustable.
- The origination fee for an FHA loan can't exceed 1%. The borrower may be charged discount points in addition to the origination fee, and these can be paid by either the borrower or the property seller.
- Mortgage insurance is required on all FHA loans.
- The minimum cash investment required for an FHA loan may be as little as 3% of the sales price. Closing costs that are paid by the borrower, as well as the downpayment, count toward the minimum cash investment.
- An FHA borrower can draw on a variety of sources for funds to make the minimum cash investment.
- The qualifying standards for an FHA loan are not as strict as those for a standard conventional loan.
- FHA loans never call for a prepayment penalty. They can be paid off at any time with no penalty.

DETERMINING THE FHA LOAN AMOUNT. The loan amount in an FHA transaction is determined by three sets of rules: the area maximum loan amount, the loan-to-value rules, and the minimum cash investment requirement.

AREA MAXIMUM LOAN AMOUNTS. Although the FHA program is intended to help low- and moderate-income buyers, eligibility for the program is not restricted to buyers with incomes under a certain limit. Instead, HUD sets maximum loan amounts for FHA programs, limiting the size of loans that can be insured. Maximum loan amounts vary from one place to another, because they are based on median housing costs in each area. For single-family homes, the basic maximum loan amount for the 203(b) program is currently $160,176. In high-cost areas, HUD may increase the maximum allowable loan amount up to 95% of the median home price in the area. But regardless of area prices, HUD may not raise its loan ceiling for single-family homes in any area to more than $290,319. (Exceptions are made for Alaska, Hawaii, Guam, and the Virgin Islands.)

FHA LOAN-TO-VALUE RATIOS. The size of an FHA loan is limited not only by the maximum loan amount for the area, but also by loan-to-value rules. The LTV limits that apply in a particular state depend on whether it is classified as a low or a high closing cost state. California is considered a low closing cost state, so the LTV limits shown on the following chart apply:

APPRAISED VALUE OR SALES PRICE (WHICHEVER IS LESS)	MAXIMUM ALLOWABLE LOAN-TO-VALUE RATIO
$50,000 or less	98.75%
Over $50,000, up to $125,000	97.65%
Over $125,000	97.15%

MINIMUM CASH INVESTMENT. One other factor that can limit the amount of an FHA loan in a particular transaction is the requirement that the borrower make a minimum cash investment of at least 3% of the sales price. The closing costs paid by the borrower, as well as any downpayment, are counted toward this 3% requirement.

> **EXAMPLE:** The sales price is $100,000, and the property has been appraised for the same amount. The required minimum cash investment is $3,000, 3% of the sales price.
>
> To calculate the loan amount, apply the appropriate LTV ratio: $100,000 × 97.65% = $97,650. With this loan amount, the borrower would need to make a downpayment of $2,350. She is also paying $1,000 in closing costs, so her total cash investment will be $3,350. This fulfills the requirement for a minimum cash investment of at least $3,000.
>
> On the other hand, suppose the seller has agreed to pay the borrower's closing costs. A $2,350 downpayment from the borrower would not be enough to fulfill the minimum cash investment requirement. As a result, the loan amount would be reduced from $97,650 to $97,000, requiring a $3,000 downpayment from the borrower.

Note that any discount points the borrower is paying do not count toward the required minimum cash investment. Neither do "prepaid expenses," which include interim interest on the loan and impounds for property taxes and hazard insurance.

FHA INSURANCE PREMIUMS. The mortgage insurance premiums for FHA loans are called the MIP. Usually, an FHA borrower pays both a one-time premium and annual premiums.

The one-time premium is sometimes called the "upfront MIP." The one-time premium is 1.5% of the loan amount. Either the borrower or the seller can pay the one-time premium in cash at closing. The borrower also has the option of financing the one-time premium over the loan term. When the one-time premium is financed, it is simply added to the base loan amount (the amount determined by the loan-to-value and minimum cash investment rules). The monthly payments are then set to pay off the total amount financed by the end of the loan term.

In addition to the one-time MIP, an annual premium is also required. The annual premium is .5% of the loan balance if the loan term is over 15 years, or .25% if the term is 15 years or less. The annual premium is paid in monthly installments: one-twelfth of the annual premium is added to each monthly payment. The annual premium is generally charged until the loan balance has been paid down to 78% of the original sales price or appraised value. (The mortgage insurance remains in effect throughout the life of the loan, however.)

SELLER CONTRIBUTIONS. As you've seen, to make the home more affordable, sometimes a seller agrees to buy down the buyer's interest rate. Or the seller might help pay all or part of the buyer's closing costs or discount points. When the sale is financed with an FHA loan, such seller contributions may not exceed 6% of the sales price.

SECONDARY FINANCING. An FHA borrower is not allowed to use secondary financing—a second mortgage against the home being purchased with the FHA loan—from the seller, another interested party, or an institutional lender to pay the required minimum cash investment, closing costs, or other expenses required to close the FHA loan. However, secondary financing may be used to cover the minimum cash investment and other costs if it is provided by a member of the borrower's immediate family (the borrower's parent, child, or grandparent). The total financing can't exceed the property's value or sales price plus the closing costs, prepaid expenses, and discount points; the borrower must be able to afford the payments on both loans; and the secondary financing can't call for a balloon payment within five years after closing.

Also, it's permissible to have a second mortgage (from anyone, not necessarily a family member) along with the FHA-insured first mortgage to make up the base loan amount. For this type of secondary financing arrangement, certain conditions must be met. You should have your buyers consult the lender if they wish to use secondary financing.

UNDERWRITING FHA LOANS. To qualify a buyer for an FHA loan, the lender examines both the creditworthiness of the loan applicant and the value of the property. As with conventional loans, examining the creditworthiness of the loan applicant involves analyzing his income, net worth, and credit history. However, the FHA's underwriting standards are not as strict as the standards used for conventional loans. The less stringent FHA standards make it easier for low- and moderate-income homebuyers to qualify for a mortgage.

INCOME RATIOS. When an FHA underwriter evaluates a loan applicant's income, the first step is to add up her monthly effective income. "Effective income" is the applicant's gross income from all sources that can be expected to continue for the first three years of the loan term. The FHA's effective income is essentially the same thing as a conventional lender's stable monthly income.

Once the applicant's effective income has been determined, the FHA underwriter applies two ratios to evaluate the adequacy of the income. These two ratios are the fixed payment to income ratio and the housing expense to income ratio. As a general rule, an FHA loan applicant's fixed payment to income ratio may not exceed 41%. In addition, the applicant's housing expense to income ratio may not exceed 29%. The applicant must qualify under both ratios.

When computing the applicant's fixed payment to income ratio, the underwriter will take into account the proposed monthly housing expense plus all recurring monthly charges. The housing expense includes principal and interest (based on the total amount financed), property taxes, hazard insurance, one-twelfth of the annual premium for the FHA mortgage insurance, and any dues owed to a homeowner's association or condominium association. Recurring monthly charges include the monthly payments on any debt with ten or more payments remaining. Alimony and child support payments, installment debt payments, and payments on revolving credit accounts are all counted.

EXAMPLE: O'Neill is applying for an FHA loan. She has a reliable monthly salary of $2,750. She also receives $740 a month in Social Security payments for her young children, which began when their father died three years ago. O'Neill's effective income totals $3,490 a month. She pays the following monthly recurring charges: a $235 car payment, a $50 minimum MasterCard payment, and a $125 personal loan payment.

To see how large a house payment O'Neill can qualify for, use the FHA's two income ratios. First multiply her effective income by 41% to see how much she can spend per month on her total fixed payments. *$3,490 × .41 = $1,431.* Then subtract her recurring monthly charges from her maximum total fixed payments. *$1,431 − $235 car payment − $50 MasterCard payment − $125 personal loan payment = $1,021.* O'Neill could qualify for a $1,021 monthly housing expense under the fixed payment to income ratio.

Next, apply the housing expense to income ratio by multiplying O'Neill's effective income by 29%. *$3,490 × .29 = $1,012.* $1,012 is the maximum monthly housing expense O'Neill could qualify for under this ratio. Since O'Neill must qualify under both ratios, you must take the lesser housing expense figure. The largest monthly housing expense O'Neill could qualify for is $1,012.

If a loan applicant's income ratios exceed the 41% and 29% limits, he might not qualify for an FHA loan. However, the underwriter is allowed to approve the loan if there are compensating factors that will reduce the risk of default. For example, if the applicant has a conservative attitude toward credit and has at least three months' mortgage payments in reserve after closing, the underwriter could approve the loan in spite of a fixed payment to income ratio over 41%.

A temporary buydown can be used with an FHA loan to help the applicant qualify for the loan. There are limits on how much the interest rate on an FHA loan can be bought down for qualifying purposes, however. No matter how large the temporary buydown actually is, the FHA underwriter will use an interest rate reduction of no more than two percentage

---

FIG. 9.7   FEATURES OF FHA-INSURED LOANS

FHA LOAN FEATURES

- FOR RESIDENTIAL PROPERTIES WITH ONE TO FOUR UNITS
- BORROWER MUST OCCUPY PROPERTY AS PRIMARY RESIDENCE
- 1% ORIGINATION FEE (DISCOUNT POINTS ALSO ALLOWED)
- FHA MORTGAGE INSURANCE (MIP) ON ALL LOANS
- MAXIMUM LOAN AMOUNT DEPENDS ON AREA MAXIMUM, LTV RULES, AND MINIMUM CASH INVESTMENT REQUIREMENT
- BORROWER'S MINIMUM CASH INVESTMENT:
  - MAY BE AS LITTLE AS 3% OF SALES PRICE
  - CLOSING COSTS AND DOWNPAYMENT COUNT TOWARD IT
- SECONDARY FINANCING ALLOWED BUT LIMITED
- INCOME RATIO GUIDELINES:
  - 41% FIXED PAYMENT TO INCOME RATIO
  - 29% HOUSING EXPENSE TO INCOME RATIO
- ASSUMPTION: LENDER'S APPROVAL REQUIRED

---

points to qualify the borrower. So even if the interest rate on the loan were bought down from 11% to 7.5% for the first year, the buyer would still be required to qualify for the loan at 9%, two percentage points below the note rate.

FUNDS FOR CLOSING. At closing, an FHA borrower must have enough cash to cover the minimum cash investment, discount points, prepaid expenses, and other out-of-pocket expenses. Ordinarily, no reserves are required. The borrower may use gift funds to help close the transaction. The donor of the gift funds must be the borrower's employer or labor union, a close relative, a close friend with a clearly defined interest in the borrower, a charitable organization, or a government agency.

An FHA borrower also has other options for coming up with the necessary funds. As we discussed earlier, a close family member may provide secondary financing to cover the minimum cash investment and other funds needed for closing. Alternatively, a close family member may simply loan the funds to the borrower without requiring a second mortgage or any form of security in return.

Also, the borrower may be permitted to borrow the cash needed for closing from someone other than a family member, as long as the loan is secured by collateral other than the property being purchased with the FHA mortgage. For example, if the applicant can borrow money against his car or vacation property, the loan funds may be used to close the sale. Note that this loan must be from an independent third party, not from the seller or a real estate agent involved in the transaction. It must be clear that the loan is a bona fide business transaction and that the collateral is truly worth the loan proceeds.

ASSUMPTION. FHA loans contain due-on-sale clauses, and various limitations on assumption apply. With some exceptions, the buyer must intend to occupy the property as his primary residence. And an assumption will only be allowed if the buyer meets FHA qualifying standards.

VA-GUARANTEED LOANS

The VA home loan program allows veterans to finance the purchase of their homes with low-cost loans that offer a number of advantages over conventional and FHA loans. A VA loan is a government-sponsored loan, but, like an FHA loan, it is made by an institutional lender, not a government agency. However, the loan is guaranteed by the Department of Veterans Affairs (VA), which sharply reduces the lender's risk. If the borrower defaults, the VA will reimburse the lender for its losses.

A VA loan can be used to finance the purchase or construction of an owner-occupied single-family residence, or a multifamily residence with up to four units, as long as the veteran will occupy one of the units.

CHARACTERISTICS OF VA LOANS. One of the biggest advantages of VA financing is that, unlike most loans, a typical VA loan does not require a downpayment. Within certain limitations, a VA loan can equal the sales price or appraised value of the home, whichever is less. This allows many veterans who would otherwise be unable to buy homes to do so.

Equally important to many veteran buyers, the underwriting standards for VA loans are more relaxed than the standards for either conventional or FHA-insured loans. Therefore, not only is a veteran able to purchase a home with less cash, he or she will also find it easier to qualify for the loan.

There are no income limits on VA borrowers, nor are there official restrictions on the size of a VA loan. This means that VA loans are not limited to low- or moderate-income buyers.

VA loans are fully amortized and typically have 30-year terms. The lender may not impose any prepayment penalties.

The VA doesn't set a maximum interest rate for VA loans; the interest rate is negotiable between the lender and borrower. The lender may charge the borrower a flat fee of no more than 1% of the loan amount to cover administrative costs (the equivalent of an origination fee). The lender may also charge reasonable discount points, which can be paid by the borrower, the seller, or a third party.

VA loans do not require mortgage insurance. The borrower doesn't have to pay for the private mortgage insurance required for many conventional loans, or the MIP required for all FHA-insured loans. However, a VA borrower usually has to pay a **funding fee**. (Veterans with service-connected disabilities are exempt.) For a no-downpayment loan, the funding fee is 2% of the loan amount. If the borrower makes a downpayment of 5% or more, the fee is reduced. The funding fee can be financed along with the loan amount.

Another important feature of VA loans is the leniency extended to VA borrowers who are experiencing temporary financial difficulties, such as illness, injury, unemployment, or the death of a spouse. A VA loan officer can help a borrower whose loan becomes delinquent to negotiate a repayment plan with the lender.

ELIGIBILITY. To obtain a VA loan, a veteran must have a Certificate of Eligibility issued by the VA. To be eligible, the veteran must have served a minimum amount of continuous active duty. This minimum amount varies depending on when the veteran served, and it ranges from 90 days to two years of active duty. A buyer who is unsure about his or her eligibility should check with the local VA office.

VA GUARANTY. Lenders are willing to make no-downpayment loans to veterans because the federal government is backing each loan with a loan guaranty. Because of the VA guaranty, the lender's risk of loss if the borrower defaults on the loan is minimal.

Like private mortgage insurance, the VA guaranty covers only a portion of the loan amount. Currently, the maximum guaranty amount is $60,000 for a loan amount over $144,000. The lender could lose up to $60,000 due to borrower default and the entire loss would be covered by the VA.

Just because a loan is guaranteed by the VA doesn't mean that the veteran has no personal liability for the loan. A veteran who has been found guilty of fraud, misrepresentation, or bad faith may be required to repay the VA the amount that the VA paid to the lender. In that case, the amount owed constitutes a delinquent federal debt. The veteran's income tax refund can be taken and applied against the debt, as can any federal pay owed to the veteran. The veteran will not be eligible for any further federal loans until arrangements to repay the debt have been made.

ASSUMPTION AND RELEASE OF LIABILITY. A VA loan can be assumed by anyone, either a veteran or a non-veteran, as long as the person is credit-worthy. The interest rate on a VA loan is not changed on assumption, and the lender can charge no more than a 0.5% funding fee on the assumption.

The original borrower is released from further liability in connection with the loan if the following conditions are met:

1. the loan payments are current;
2. the new buyer is an acceptable credit risk; and
3. the new buyer contractually assumes the veteran's obligations on the loan.

RESTORATION OF ENTITLEMENT. The guaranty amount available to a particular veteran is sometimes called the veteran's "entitlement." After using his entitlement, a veteran can obtain another VA loan only if the entitlement is restored.

EXAMPLE: McDowell used a VA loan to buy a home in 1990. He used up his entire guaranty entitlement at that time. This year McDowell decided to sell the property. With the sale proceeds, he paid off the entire remaining balance of his VA loan. When he repaid the loan, McDowell's full guaranty entitlement was restored. If McDowell decides to buy another home, he can use his entitlement to get another VA loan.

It's possible for a veteran to have his entitlement restored even if the loan is assumed instead of paid off when the home is sold. For this to work, the new homebuyer must also be a veteran who agrees to substitute his or her entitlement for the seller's entitlement. The loan payments must be current, and the buyer must also be an acceptable credit risk. If all of these conditions are met, the veteran can formally request a substitution of entitlement from the VA.

LOAN AMOUNT. The amount of a VA loan cannot exceed the appraised value of the home or the sales price. The VA puts no other restrictions on the loan amount. However, most lenders do have rules about VA loan amounts. The most common one is that for a no-downpayment loan, most lenders require the guaranty amount to equal at least 25% of the value or sales price of the property, whichever is less. Since the current maximum guaranty amount is $60,000, this restriction means that most lenders will not make a no-downpayment loan for more than $240,000.

These lenders will still approve a larger loan if the borrower can make a downpayment. They typically want the total of the guaranty amount and the veteran's downpayment to equal 25% of the value or the sales price, whichever is less. This 25% rule means that the downpayment a veteran may have to make is still likely to be fairly modest.

> **EXAMPLE:** Vickers has her full VA guaranty entitlement. She wants to buy a home for $248,500. Her lender won't make a no-downpayment loan larger than $240,000, so Vickers will have to make a downpayment in order to purchase the home. However, because of the lender's 25% rule, Vickers doesn't have to pay the difference between the $248,500 sales price and $240,000 to get the loan. Her downpayment only has to equal 25% of the difference. The combination of Vickers's entitlement and downpayment must equal 25% of the sales price. 25% of $248,500 is $62,125. Her entitlement is $60,000. *$62,125 – $60,000 entitlement = $2,125.* Vickers only has to make a $2,125 downpayment in order to purchase the home.

The other situation in which a VA borrower is required to make a downpayment is when the property's sales price exceeds its appraised value. The borrower has to make up the difference out of her own funds.

SECONDARY FINANCING. If he doesn't have enough cash, a VA borrower can obtain secondary financing to cover a downpayment required by the lender. The total financing (the VA loan plus the secondary financing) can't exceed the appraised value of the property, the borrower must be able to qualify for the payments on both loans, and the second loan cannot have more stringent conditions than the VA loan. The interest rate on the second loan can be higher than the rate on the VA loan, but not higher than industry standards for second mortgage interest rates.

Secondary financing that meets these standards can be used for the borrower's closing costs, as well as for a downpayment required by the lender. But secondary financing cannot be used when the downpayment is required because the sales price exceeds the property's appraised value.

SELLER CONCESSIONS. When a sale is financed with a VA loan, the seller is allowed to make certain concessions to help the buyer purchase the property. The seller's concessions generally must be no more than 4% of the property's value. But payment of the buyer's closing costs and normal discount points are not subject to this 4% limit. For example, suppose a lender would ordinarily charge two points on a loan, and the seller has offered to pay five points. The three extra points would be counted against the 4% limit on seller concessions.

QUALIFYING FOR A VA LOAN. To qualify for a VA loan, a veteran must meet the underwriting standards set by the Department of Veterans Affairs. A VA loan applicant's income is analyzed with two different methods, an income ratio method and a residual income method. The veteran must qualify under both methods.

The income ratio method for analyzing a veteran's income is very similar to the method used for conventional and FHA loans. However, only one ratio—the total debt to income ratio—is used, instead of two ratios. As a general rule, the vet's total debt to income ratio should not be more than 41%.

> **EXAMPLE:** Garcia is eligible for a VA loan. He makes $3,800 a month, and his total monthly obligations add up to $475 a month. To see how large a house payment he could qualify for, multiply $3,800 by 41%. *$3,800 × .41 = $1,558.* Now subtract his monthly obligations of $475 from $1,558. *$1,558 − $475 = $1,083.* Garcia would be able to qualify for a $1,083 monthly housing expense under the total debt to income ratio.

FIG. 9.8   VA RESIDUAL INCOME REQUIREMENTS

Table of Residual Incomes by Region
For loan amounts of $79,999 and below

Family Size	Northeast	Midwest	South	West
1	$390	$382	$382	$425
2	$654	$641	$641	$713
3	$788	$772	$772	$859
4	$888	$868	$868	$967
5	$921	$902	$902	$1,004

Over 5: Add $75 for each additional member up to a family of 7.

Table of Residual Incomes by Region
For loan amounts of $80,000 and above

Family Size	Northeast	Midwest	South	West
1	$450	$441	$441	$491
2	$755	$738	$738	$823
3	$909	$889	$889	$990
4	$1,025	$1,003	$1,003	$1,117
5	$1,062	$1,039	$1,039	$1,158

Over 5: Add $80 for each additional member up to a family of 7.

The second method used to qualify a VA loan applicant is the **residual income method**, also called cash flow analysis. To determine the veteran's residual income, the underwriter subtracts the proposed housing expense, all other recurring obligations, and certain taxes from the veteran's gross income. The taxes that are deducted include all of the taxes that are ordinarily deducted from a paycheck, including federal, state, and local income taxes, Social Security taxes, and Medicare taxes.

The loan applicant's residual income should be at least one dollar more than the VA's minimum requirement. The minimum requirement varies, depending on where the veteran lives, his family size, and the size of the proposed loan (see Figure 9.8). For example, the residual income required for a family of three living in California when the loan amount is less than $80,000 is $859. The residual income required for a family of four living in California when the loan amount is $80,000 or more is $1,117.

EXAMPLE: Returning to our previous example, let's calculate Garcia's residual income. He lives in California and has a family of four, and he wants to buy a $180,500 home. The VA requires him to have at least $1,117 in residual income to qualify for a loan.

Start with Garcia's monthly income, $3,800. First, subtract all of the taxes deducted from his paycheck (federal and state income taxes, social security, and Medicare), which come to $950. Next, subtract his recurring monthly obligations, which are $475. And finally, subtract his proposed housing expense, which is, at most, $1,083 (the figure we obtained from applying the 41% total monthly obligations to income ratio). *$3,800 – $950 – $475 – $1,083 = $1,292.* Garcia's residual income is well above his required minimum ($1,117) so he should have no problem qualifying for the $1,083 proposed monthly housing expense.

FIG. 9.9 FEATURES OF VA-GUARANTEED LOANS

VA LOAN FEATURES

- FOR RESIDENTIAL PROPERTIES WITH ONE TO FOUR UNITS
- BORROWER MUST OCCUPY PROPERTY AS PRIMARY RESIDENCE
- 100% FINANCING ALLOWED — NO DOWNPAYMENT REQUIRED
- 1% ORIGINATION FEE (DISCOUNT POINTS ALSO ALLOWED)
- 2% FUNDING FEE FOR NO DOWNPAYMENT LOAN
- NO VA MAXIMUM LOAN AMOUNT
- MAXIMUM GUARANTY $60,000
- LENDERS MAY REQUIRE DOWNPAYMENT FOR LOAN OVER $240,000
- SECONDARY FINANCING ALLOWED FOR DOWNPAYMENT
- INCOME RATIO GUIDELINE: 41% TOTAL DEBT TO INCOME RATIO
- RESIDUAL INCOME REQUIREMENTS
- LOAN CAN BE ASSUMED BY NON-VETERAN (WITH LENDER'S APPROVAL)
- RESTORATION OF ENTITLEMENT: LOAN MUST BE PAID OFF UNLESS ASSUMED BY ANOTHER VETERAN

The VA emphasizes that its minimum residual income figures are only guidelines. If the veteran fails to meet the guidelines, it should not mean an automatic rejection of the loan application. The underwriter should take other factors into consideration, such as the applicant's ability to accumulate a significant net worth, and the number and ages of any dependents.

The VA's 41% income ratio is also flexible. A lender can approve a VA loan even though the applicant's income ratio is above 41% if the application presents other favorable factors, such as a substantial amount of liquid assets, a substantial downpayment, or significantly more residual income than the minimum amount required by the VA. Extra residual income is an especially important compensating factor. If the applicant's residual income is at least 20% over the required minimum, the lender can approve the loan even though the income ratio is well over 41% and there are no other compensating factors.

CAL-VET LOANS

Veterans who live in California may also be eligible for a loan to purchase a single-family residential or farm property through the California Veterans Farm and Home Purchase Program. The California Department of Veterans Affairs processes, originates, and services loans made through this program, which are known as Cal-Vet loans.

The Cal-Vet program works very differently from the federal programs, which directly insure or guarantee loans made by lenders. Instead, when a veteran purchases property using a Cal-Vet loan, the state of California actually purchases the property and takes title to it, and then sells the property to the veteran using a land contract. The buyer holds only an equitable interest in the property until the land contract is fully paid, at which point he receives a grant deed.

ELIGIBILITY. To be eligible for most types of Cal-Vet loans, a veteran must have:
- served at least 90 days of active duty, part of which was during a wartime period or certain other foreign campaigns;
- received an honorable discharge; and
- applied for the loan within 30 years of discharge from active duty (with exceptions for veterans who were wounded in action, were prisoners of war, or are disabled).

FIG. 9.10 CAL-VET LOAN CHARACTERISTICS

CAL-VET LOAN CHARACTERISTICS

- STATE SELLS PROPERTY TO VETERAN THROUGH LAND CONTRACT
- BELOW-MARKET VARIABLE INTEREST RATES WITH 0.5% CAP
- HIGH LOAN-TO-VALUE RATIOS (95% TO 97%)
- LOAN AMOUNT VARIES AMONG COUNTIES (MAXIMUM $322,700)
- AVAILABLE ONLY FOR OWNER-OCCUPIED SINGLE-FAMILY RESIDENCES

All veterans, regardless of whether they served during wartime, are eligible for Cal-Vet loans if they are first-time homebuyers, or if they are purchasing a home in an area targeted as economically distressed. First-time homebuyers and "targeted area" purchasers are subject to limitations on both the property's purchase price and family income. The limits vary, depending on the size of the family and the county where the property is located.

A veteran's surviving spouse may apply for a Cal-Vet loan if the veteran died of injuries suffered in the line of duty, is designated as missing or a prisoner of war, or died after applying for a Cal-Vet loan.

CHARACTERISTICS OF CAL-VET LOANS. Cal-Vet loans have a number of benefits for borrowers, such as low downpayments and below-market interest rates. A small downpayment is always required, but loan-to-value ratios of 95% or 97% are common. Interest rates may vary over the loan's term, according to prevailing interest rates, but have never exceeded 8%. The interest rate cannot increase more than 0.5% over the loan term.

Cal-Vet loans are subject to a maximum loan amount that varies from county to county. The highest loan amount available anywhere in the state is $322,700.

Even though the state is selling the property to the veteran through a land contract, the state obtains a guaranty on the loan either through the federal VA-guaranteed loan program or with private mortgage insurance. For this guaranty, the veteran must pay a funding fee between 1.25% and 3.3% of the loan amount, depending on the size of the downpayment. If the downpayment is at least 20% of the property's value, no funding fee is charged. In some cases the fee may be financed over the contract term, but it is a one-time charge. The veteran will not be required to make monthly PMI payments.

A veteran may originate a Cal-Vet loan through a mortgage broker or directly through the California Department of Veterans Affairs, but in either case the veteran must pay a $50 application fee for a Cal-Vet loan. The veteran must also pay a 1% origination fee, but does not pay any discount points. The only other fee is for a property appraisal, which costs $350 if performed by a Cal-Vet appraiser. Cal-Vet loans do not have a prepayment penalty.

Cal-Vet loans are fully amortized and typically have a 30-year loan term. Mobile home purchase loans more commonly have 15- or 20-year terms.

Secondary financing is allowed, but only if the Cal-Vet loan amount and secondary loan amount do not exceed 98% of the property's appraised value.

The Cal-Vet borrower must occupy the home within 60 days after signing the contract. The property may not be transferred, encumbered, or leased without the permission of the California Department of Veterans Affairs. The property may be leased if the borrower shows a compelling need, but only for a maximum of four years. A Cal-Vet loan may be assumed only by another qualified veteran.

A Cal-Vet borrower must purchase life insurance through the Cal-Vet program. If the borrower dies during the loan term, part or all of the loan balance will be paid out of the insurance proceeds. In addition, the Cal-Vet borrower purchases low-cost homeowner's insurance through the program, which includes flood and earthquake protection.

SELLER FINANCING

Institutional lenders such as banks, savings and loans, and mortgage companies are not the only sources of residential financing. In some cases, the home seller may also be a source. When a seller helps a buyer finance the purchase of a home, it's called **seller financing**. Seller financing can take a variety of forms, ranging from the simple to the complex.

FIG. 9.11 ADVANTAGES OF SELLER FINANCING

WHY USE SELLER FINANCING?

- MAY MAKE PROPERTY MORE MARKETABLE
- SELLER CAN HELP BUYER QUALIFY FOR INSTITUTIONAL LOAN
- BUYER MAY SAVE MONEY ON FINANCING COSTS
- BUYER MAY BE WILLING TO PAY MORE FOR HOME
- POSSIBLE TAX BENEFITS FOR SELLER (INSTALLMENT SALE REPORTING)

HOW SELLER FINANCING WORKS

As you know, institutional lenders require both a promissory note and a security instrument (a mortgage or a deed of trust) when they make a loan. The promissory note is evidence of the debt, and the security instrument makes the property collateral for the loan. In many cases, these same documents are used in seller financing. The homebuyer signs a promissory note, promising to pay the seller the amount of the debt, and then signs a mortgage or deed of trust that gives the seller a security interest in the home being purchased. This kind of seller financing arrangement is often called a **purchase money loan**.

Purchase money loans are quite different from institutional loans. With an institutional loan, the lender gives the borrower cash, which is then given to the seller in return for the deed to the property. With a purchase money loan, the seller simply extends credit to the buyer. Essentially, the buyer is allowed to pay off the purchase price in installments over time, instead of having to pay the total purchase price in cash at closing.

In some instances, the seller may choose to use a land contract instead of the promissory note and mortgage or deed of trust. With a land contract, the buyer takes immediate possession of the land, but does not acquire legal title until the entire purchase price is paid off. A land contract is another way a seller can offer credit to the buyer.

In a seller-financed transaction, the seller usually decides which type of financing documents to use. If your seller is unsure about which type to use, you should recommend that she speak to an attorney. Never advise a seller about the legal consequences of using the various types of documents. And always recommend that an attorney prepare any documents used in a seller-financed transaction. If your seller wishes to prepare the documents herself, strongly recommend that an attorney review them before they are signed by the parties.

WHY USE SELLER FINANCING? Setting up a seller-financed transaction can be complicated. The seller has to decide what kinds of documents to use and, typically, one or more attorneys get involved somewhere along the way. But there are several good reasons to use seller financing. One important reason is to make the property more marketable. This is especially true when market interest rates are high or loans are difficult to obtain. When interest rates are high, mortgage payments are also high. Potential buyers may have a difficult time qualifying for a loan with high mortgage payments, or they may be simply unwilling to take on a long-term loan at such high interest rates. By offering seller financing at a lower-than-market interest rate, a seller can make his home more attractive to potential buyers.

Seller financing can also help a buyer who could not qualify for institutional financing to complete the purchase of a home. With seller financing, the buyer avoids some of the costs of borrowing money from a lender, such as the loan origination fee and any discount points. Also, the seller may agree to a smaller downpayment than an institutional lender would require. Both of these factors mean a buyer can close a seller-financed sale with much less cash than an institutional loan would demand.

Because of the potential advantages that seller financing has for buyers, the seller may be able to get more for her property. For example, if the seller was asking $350,000 cash, a buyer might be willing to pay $360,000 for the property and attractive seller financing terms. In essence, the buyer would pay an additional $10,000 for the property to get the advantages of a low downpayment, fewer closing costs, a favorable interest rate, and lower monthly payments.

Seller financing can also provide the seller with important tax benefits. Because the buyer will be paying the purchase price of the property in installments, over a period of years, the seller is allowed to spread out her profit from the sale over that same period. In other words, the seller does not have to report the full profit from the sale on her tax return in the year of sale. Only the amount of profit actually received in a given year is taxed in that year. The seller can spread the tax payments out over a longer period, and may be able to take advantage of a lower tax rate as a result.

Always advise a seller to consult an accountant or attorney about the tax implications of seller financing. There may be some tax disadvantages to a particular transaction that the seller may not be aware of.

CONCERNS OF THE PARTIES. When structuring a seller financing arrangement, it's important to pay close attention to the particular needs of the buyer and the seller. The buyer will be concerned with the cost of the financing, especially the interest rate and the amount of the downpayment. If the seller requires a balloon payment in a few years, the buyer should have some idea where he is going to get the money to make that payment. Will the buyer have the cash to make the balloon payment, or will he have to refinance the property? Financing that involves a balloon payment always presents a risk for the buyer. For the most part, this kind of arrangement works out fine, but the buyer should make plans about the balloon payment sooner rather than later.

Seller financing raises different concerns for the seller. Obviously, the seller doesn't want to extend financing to a buyer who can't afford the monthly payments. And the seller should also be concerned about whether the buyer will be able to make any required balloon payment. But there are other equally important issues for the seller to consider.

First of all, the seller needs to decide whether she can really afford to offer seller financing, or whether she needs to be cashed out. For example, if the seller is purchasing a new home, she may need all of her equity from the old home in cash at closing. And even if the seller does not need all of the equity right away, is the buyer's anticipated downpayment enough cash to meet the seller's needs?

Most sellers who offer seller financing do so because they don't need the cash right away and a steady monthly income is attractive. Is the mortgage payment the buyer is going to pay on the seller financing enough to meet the seller's monthly needs? Is the interest rate charged on the seller financing a good rate of return? If the seller would charge 5% interest on the second mortgage, but could get a 7% return from investing in a mutual fund, the seller may want to rethink the transaction.

FIG. 9.12 POTENTIAL ISSUES WITH SELLER FINANCING

SELLER FINANCING CONCERNS

- BALLOON PAYMENT: HOW WILL BUYER PAY IT WHEN THE TIME COMES?

- HOW MUCH IMMEDIATE CASH DOES SELLER NEED FROM SALE?

- IS INTEREST RATE CHARGED A GOOD RATE OF RETURN FOR SELLER?

- COULD THE SALE CREATE TAX PROBLEMS FOR SELLER?

- PRIORITY OF SELLER'S LIEN

And depending on the rate of interest charged, the seller could be faced with tax penalties based on the "imputed interest" rule. Under the imputed interest rule, if a seller charges an interest rate that is below a specified minimum, the IRS will treat some of the principal received in each installment payment as interest, and thus taxable. If the seller runs afoul of the imputed interest rule, many of the benefits the seller thought he was getting by offering seller financing could be eliminated. Again, it is imperative to advise your sellers to seek competent tax advice before they enter into a seller-financed transaction.

Finally, lien priority is an important consideration in any seller financing arrangement. It is almost certain that any new or existing institutional loan will have a higher priority than the seller's loan. In the event of default, the higher priority loan will be repaid first. If there is nothing left after the institutional loan has been repaid, the seller will get nothing. Thus, like an institutional lender, the seller must consider the relationship between the liens and the property's value. Would the property sell for enough at a foreclosure sale to pay off the seller financing as well as the liens with higher priority?

TYPES OF SELLER FINANCING

Seller financing can be used alone or in conjunction with institutional financing.

SELLER SECONDS. One of the most common forms of seller financing is the seller second. With a seller second, the buyer pays most of the purchase price with an institutional loan, and the seller finances some of what would normally be the buyer's downpayment with a second mortgage.

> **EXAMPLE:** Schmidt is buying Earnshaw's home for $200,000. She is getting an institutional loan for $170,000. However, she doesn't have enough cash to make a $30,000 downpayment, so Earnshaw agrees to take back a second mortgage in the amount of $15,000. Now Schmidt only has to come up with $15,000 for the downpayment.

There are several advantages to a seller second. As in this example, a seller second allows the buyer to make a smaller downpayment than she might otherwise have to make. A seller second can also help a marginal buyer qualify for an institutional loan. Institutional lenders have certain rules that must be followed when the buyer is going to use secondary financing. The lender should always be consulted to make sure the seller second is acceptable.

As long as the parties stay within the institutional lender's guidelines, they can come up with virtually unlimited ways to structure their financing package.

PRIMARY SELLER FINANCING. Seller financing may also be used as the only source of financing. This is called primary seller financing. Seller financing is at its most flexible when it is the primary financing. Lender guidelines for secondary loans no longer have to be followed, and qualifying standards can be ignored if the parties choose to do so.

UNENCUMBERED PROPERTY. Seller financing can be used when the property is either encumbered by a previous mortgage or unencumbered. Property is unencumbered when the seller owns it free and clear of any liens. When the property is unencumbered, seller financing is usually very straightforward. All the buyer and seller have to do is negotiate the sales price and the terms of the financing, and then have the appropriate finance documents prepared.

Since the seller financing is the primary, or only, source of financing, the seller will have first lien position, as long as she properly records the loan documents. However, the seller still has to be prepared to protect her security interest. A first mortgage does not have priority over all other liens. For example, real property tax liens and special assessment liens take priority over mortgages, no matter what the recording date. If the buyer fails to pay the property taxes, the property could be foreclosed on and the seller could take a loss at the foreclosure sale.

Destruction of the premises is another danger. Suppose the buyer fails to keep the property insured and the house burns down. The buyer then defaults on the loan, and the seller has to foreclose. Since the property is now probably worth much less than the amount of the remaining debt, the seller is likely to lose a great deal of money in the foreclosure sale.

The seller can protect her interest in the property by setting up an impound account for taxes and insurance, just as many institutional lenders do. Along with the loan payment, the buyer would make monthly tax and insurance payments, which would be deposited into the impound account. The funds in the impound account would then be used to pay off the property taxes and insurance premiums when they become due. Many banks, savings and loans, and mortgage companies are willing to provide and service impound accounts for private parties.

ENCUMBERED PROPERTY. It's relatively uncommon for a seller to own his property free and clear of any other mortgage liens. Typically, the seller financed the purchase of the property and still owes money on that loan when he decides to sell. When the property is encumbered with a mortgage loan, it's a rare seller who can pay off the first loan with savings or the buyer's downpayment alone.

For instance, suppose Clark is selling his home for $100,000. He'd prefer to finance the sale and receive payments on an installment basis. However, there's a first mortgage on the property in the amount of $55,000. Clark doesn't have enough cash to pay off a $55,000 loan at closing, and a buyer is unlikely to have that much cash to invest in the home as a downpayment. It's possible that the buyer could assume Clark's existing mortgage, and Clark could finance the rest of the purchase price with a seller second. But there is another alternative that may be more attractive: wraparound financing.

With a **wraparound loan**, the buyer does not assume the seller's mortgage. Nor does the seller try to pay off this mortgage at closing. Instead, the buyer takes the property "subject to" the existing mortgage. This means the seller remains primarily responsible for making the payments on this mortgage. The seller finances the complete purchase price for the buyer, less the downpayment. The seller then uses part of the monthly payment received from the buyer to make the monthly payment on the existing mortgage (referred to as the **underlying mortgage**), and keeps the balance.

> **EXAMPLE:** Clark owes $55,000 on his $100,000 house. The mortgage payment is $500. Clark sells his house to Moore for $100,000. Moore gives him a $5,000 downpayment, and Clark finances the remaining $95,000 purchase price at 8% interest. Moore's monthly payment is $700. Clark uses part of the $700 to make the $500 payment on the underlying mortgage, then keeps the remaining $200 for himself.

Wraparound financing is only possible if the underlying loan does not have a due-on-sale clause. If there's a due-on-sale clause, the lender may call the underlying note, and it will become immediately due and payable.

When there is a due-on-sale clause in the underlying mortgage, it is dangerous to try to get away with a wraparound loan by keeping the lender in the dark about the sale. This is called a "silent" wrap, and it could easily backfire. Real estate agents should never get involved in silent wraps.

With wraparound financing, the buyer typically needs a little extra protection. If the seller fails to make the payments on the underlying loan, the institutional lender could foreclose, and the buyer could lose the property as well as all the monthly payments she has already made.

The best way to protect the buyer is to set up an escrow account for the loan payments. An independent third party in charge of the escrow account uses part of the buyer's payment to make the underlying loan payments and sends the remainder to the seller. Thus, the buyer is assured that the underlying loan payments will always be made in a timely manner. The seller can require the buyer to deposit tax and hazard insurance payments into the same account, thus protecting the seller's security interest in the property as well.

OTHER WAYS SELLERS CAN HELP

In many cases a seller can't afford to offer seller financing to a buyer, usually because the seller can't wait several years to be cashed out. However, there are a number of other ways in which a seller can help a buyer close the transaction, including all of the following:

- **BUYDOWNS.** As we discussed earlier, the seller can help the buyer by agreeing to a buydown. To buy down the interest rate on the buyer's institutional loan, the seller doesn't have to pay the lender a lump sum at closing. Instead, the seller's net proceeds from the sale are reduced by the amount of the buydown. From the seller's point of view, a buydown is similar to a price reduction. However, a buydown may help the buyer more than a straight price reduction, by enabling him to qualify for an institutional loan more easily.

- **CONTRIBUTIONS TO CLOSING COSTS.** By paying for some of the closing costs that are typically the buyer's responsibility, the seller enables the buyer to close the transaction with less cash. Remember, however, that lenders place limitations on the amount a seller can contribute toward the buyer's closing costs.

- **EQUITY EXCHANGES.** Instead of cash, the seller may be willing to accept another asset, such as recreational property, a car, or a boat, as all or part of the downpayment. Again, this kind of transaction enables the buyer to close the sale with significantly less cash.

- **LEASE/OPTIONS.** Sometimes a prospective buyer may simply not be ready to purchase a home. The buyer may need time to save up for a downpayment, pay off debts, or improve her credit rating. Or perhaps the buyer needs more time to sell a property she already owns. In these circumstances, a lease/option arrangement may help the buyer purchase the seller's home. A lease/option is a combination of a lease and an option to buy. The seller leases the property to a prospective buyer for a specific period of time. At the same time, the seller gives the buyer an option to purchase the property at a certain price during the lease period.

Whenever you're handling a sale that involves seller financing, you should make sure that both parties understand all the ramifications of the transaction. While you can't give them legal advice, it is appropriate to raise the concerns we've discussed here, such as the seller's lien priority and the importance of an impound account. As a real estate agent, you should never prepare the documents used in a seller-financed transaction, and you should always strongly recommend that both the buyer and the seller get advice from their attorneys or accountants, or both.

CHAPTER SUMMARY

1. Conventional loans may be 30-year or 15-year, fixed- or adjustable-rate, and fully or partially amortized. A conventional loan is classified as an 80%, 90%, or 95% loan, depending on the loan-to-value ratio. Private mortgage insurance is required for conventional loans with LTVs over 80%.

2. Lenders charge an origination fee to cover their administrative costs, and may charge discount points to increase the yield on the loan. A seller may pay for a buydown to help the buyer qualify for financing.

3. A conventional loan applicant's total debt to income ratio should not exceed 36%, and the housing expense ratio should not exceed 28%. The applicant should have two months' mortgage payments in reserve after closing.

4. FHA loans are characterized by less stringent qualifying standards, low minimum cash investment requirements, and mortgage insurance (both a one-time premium and annual premiums).

5. An FHA loan applicant's fixed payment to income ratio should not exceed 41%, and the housing expense to income ratio should not exceed 29%.

6. VA loans generally require no downpayment and no mortgage insurance. VA qualifying standards are lenient. The VA guarantees up to $60,000 of the loan amount. Although the VA does not set a maximum loan amount, most lenders require the guaranty to cover at least 25% of the loan amount.

7. A VA loan applicant is generally required to have a total debt to income ratio of 41% or less, and also have residual income that meets VA standards.

8. In a Cal-Vet loan transaction, the California Department of Veterans Affairs actually purchases the property and sells it back to the veteran through a land contract. A Cal-Vet loan requires only a small downpayment and has a favorable interest rate. The maximum loan amount varies from county to county.

9. When a seller helps the buyer finance the transaction, it's called seller financing. The most common form of seller financing is the seller second: the buyer pays most of the purchase price with an institutional loan, and the seller finances some of the buyer's downpayment.

10. Seller financing may also be used as the only source of financing. If the property is already encumbered by a mortgage, the parties may decide to use wraparound financing. In a wraparound arrangement, the buyer takes the property subject to the first mortgage, and the seller uses part of the monthly payment received from the buyer to make the payment on the underlying mortgage. Wraparound financing can't be used if there is a due-on-sale clause in the underlying mortgage.

CHAPTER QUIZ

1. A loan that requires monthly payments of both principal and interest, but leaves some of the principal to be paid off in a balloon payment at the end of the loan term, is:

    a. fully amortized

    b. negatively amortized

    c. non-amortized

    d. partially amortized

2. A lender will usually charge a higher interest rate in which of the following situations?

    a. The borrower wants an ARM instead of a fixed-rate mortgage

    b. The seller is offering a buydown

    c. The borrower wants a 5/1 ARM instead of an ARM with a one-year initial rate adjustment period

    d. The borrower wants a two-step mortgage instead of a fixed-rate mortgage

3. A portfolio loan is a loan that:

    a. the lender plans to keep as an investment

    b. conforms to the rules of Fannie Mae and Freddie Mac

    c. is insured or guaranteed by a government agency

    d. is sold on the secondary market

4. A conforming loan with a 95% LTV:

    a. may involve stricter qualifying standards

    b. generally cannot be an ARM

    c. requires private mortgage insurance

    d. All of the above

5. The Homeowners Protection Act requires:

    a. borrowers to send a written request to their lender in order to cancel private mortgage insurance

    b. all loans closed on or after July 29, 1999, to be covered by private mortgage insurance

    c. lenders to send all borrowers with private mortgage insurance an annual notice concerning their PMI cancellation rights

    d. lenders to automatically cancel the PMI when a loan's principal balance reaches 78% of the home's current appraised value

6. All of the following factors might justify making a loan when the borrower exceeds income ratio benchmarks, except:

    a. substantial net worth

    b. significant energy-efficient features in the home being purchased

    c. a high loan-to-value ratio

    d. education that indicates strong potential for increased earnings

7. With a graduated payment buydown plan, what rate will a lender probably use to qualify the buyer for the loan?

    a. A rate somewhere between the initial rate the borrower will pay and the full note rate

    b. The index rate

    c. A rate 1% or 2% above the note rate

    d. The buydown rate

8. Which of the following can the borrower count as part of the minimum cash investment required for an FHA loan?

    a. Discount points

    b. Closing costs

    c. Buydown paid for by seller

    d. Prepaid expenses

9. Parker has full guaranty entitlement for a VA loan. If the lender uses the 25% rule, how much of a downpayment will Parker have to make in order to buy a $254,000 home?

   a. $48,500

   b. $15,000

   c. $14,000

   d. $3,500

10. If a seller wants to help a prospective buyer qualify for an institutional loan, which of the following options will reduce the buyer's interest rate?

   a. Buydown

   b. Lease/option

   c. Silent wrap

   d. Equity exchange

ANSWER KEY

1. d. With a partially amortized loan, not all of the principal is paid off through the monthly payments, and the borrower must make a balloon payment at the end of the loan term.

2. c. With adjustable-rate loans, as a general rule, the longer the initial rate adjustment period, the higher the interest rate. The interest rate on a 5/1 ARM is not adjusted during the first five years, but may be adjusted annually after that.

3. a. If a lender plans to keep a loan as an investment instead of selling it on the secondary market, the lender is keeping the loan "in portfolio."

4. d. For a 95% loan, the secondary market agencies may require the lender to apply stricter qualifying standards, and they usually will not buy a 95% loan if it has an adjustable interest rate. Private mortgage insurance is required on any loan with an LTV over 80%.

5. c. The Homeowners Protection Act requires lenders to send an annual notice to borrowers with PMI, regardless of whether their loans are subject to the other provisions of the act. (PMI must be canceled automatically when the principal balance reaches 78% of the home's original value, not 78% of the current appraised value.)

6. c. If the borrower exceeds the income ratio guidelines, the lender may consider other factors that indicate the borrower will be able to make the monthly payments. A high loan-to-value ratio, however, means the borrower has less invested in the property and is more likely to default.

7. a. Because a buyer with a graduated payment buydown will eventually have to pay interest at the full note rate, the lender wants to make sure the buyer will be able to handle the increased monthly payments. As a result, the lender will often qualify the buyer using a rate that is lower than the full note rate but higher than the initial buydown rate.

8. b. The downpayment and closing costs paid by the borrower count toward the required minimum cash investment for an FHA loan. Discount points paid by the borrower do not count, nor does a buydown or closing costs paid for by the seller or a third party.

9. d. Using the 25% rule, the lender will want the maximum guaranty amount ($60,000) plus the veteran's downpayment to be at least 25% of the sales price or appraised value, whichever is less. $254,000 × 25% = $63,500. $63,500 − $60,000 (guaranty) = $3,500 (downpayment).

10. a. With a buydown, the seller can lower the interest rate on the buyer's loan, which may allow the buyer to get a loan he might not otherwise qualify for.

CHAPTER 10

CLOSING THE TRANSACTION

THE CLOSING PROCESS

- Escrow
- Steps in closing a transaction
  - Overview
  - Inspections
  - Financing
  - Appraisal
  - Hazard insurance
  - Title insurance
- The real estate agent's role

CLOSING COSTS

- Costs and credits
- Estimating the buyer's net cost
- Estimating the seller's net proceeds

LAWS THAT AFFECT CLOSING

- Income tax regulations
  - 1099 reporting
  - Foreign Investment in Real Property Tax Act
  - California withholding law
- Real Estate Settlement Procedures Act

INTRODUCTION

You helped your buyers find an affordable house that suits their needs. They made an offer on the house, and the sellers accepted it. The buyers must now order inspections, apply for or finalize their financing, and obtain a preliminary title report. The sellers must pay off the liens against the property, arrange for required repairs, and execute the deed. In other words, the buyers and the sellers must go through the closing process.

As a real estate agent, you will be shepherding your buyers and sellers through closing. Many of your clients will be unfamiliar with the process; you'll need to calm their anxieties and answer their questions. How long will it take to close the sale? What responsibilities does each party have? How much cash will the buyer need to close the sale? How much cash will the seller receive at closing?

In this chapter, we will discuss the closing process, closing costs and which party usually pays them, and how to estimate the buyer's net cost and the seller's net proceeds. We'll also cover some laws that affect closing, including the Real Estate Settlement Procedures Act.

THE CLOSING PROCESS

The phrase "closing a sale" actually has two meanings in the real estate field. Sometimes it refers to getting a buyer to make an offer, or getting a seller to accept one. For instance, a seller's agent can "close a sale" by overcoming the buyer's objections and convincing the buyer that it's the right time to make an offer on the house. Here, however, we'll be using "closing the sale" in its other sense, to mean completing all the tasks that have to be taken care of before title can be transferred to the buyer and the purchase price can be disbursed to the seller.

For every sale you handle as a real estate agent, it's part of your job to make sure that all of the closing requirements are met on time. You probably won't be completing all, or even most, of the necessary tasks yourself, but you have to know what needs to be done, who's responsible for doing it, and whether it's being done in a timely manner. If the closing process doesn't go smoothly, it can cause considerable delay and inconvenience, and in some cases the transaction will fall apart altogether.

FIG. 10.1   CHECKLIST FOR CLOSING

Closing Checklist

Property: _____

Buyer: _____

Seller: _____

Other party's agent: _____

Financing		**Inspection 1**	
Lender: _____		Company: _____	
Loan application submitted	_____	Inspection ordered	_____
Appraisal ordered	_____	Inspection report issued	_____
Appraisal completed	_____	Approval or disapproval	_____
Loan package submitted	_____	Seller's response	_____
Loan approved	_____	Repairs completed	_____
Loan documents signed	_____	Repairs reinspected	_____
Loan funds disbursed	_____	Reinspection approved	_____

Closing Requirements		**Inspection 2**	
Good faith deposit	_____	Company: _____	
Escrow opened	_____	Inspection ordered	_____
Escrow instructions	_____	Inspection report issued	_____
Seller's information	_____	Approval or disapproval	_____
Title search ordered	_____	Seller's response	_____
Preliminary title report	_____	Repairs completed	_____
Demand for payoff	_____	Repairs reinspected	_____
All conditions fulfilled	_____	Reinspection approved	_____
All documents signed	_____		
Buyer deposits funds	_____	**Moving**	
Hazard insurance policy	_____	Seller's belongings out	_____
Documents recorded	_____	Yard cleanup	_____
Title policies issued	_____	Interior cleaning	_____
Settlement statements	_____	Keys for buyer	_____

To help keep track of the steps in the closing process and make sure that everything's getting done, you might want to use a closing checklist, such as the one shown in Figure 10.1. Review the deposit receipt to remind yourself of the basic terms and any unusual provisions; add any special requirements to the checklist. As the days go by, refer to your list on a regular basis, check off what has been accomplished and fill in the date of completion, and note what still needs to be done.

ESCROW

Most transactions in California are closed through the escrow process. The closing is handled by a neutral third party called an **escrow agent** or **closing agent**. The escrow agent holds money and documents on behalf of the buyer and seller in accordance with their written **escrow instructions**. The agent will release the money and documents to the appropriate parties only when all of the conditions set forth in the escrow instructions have been fulfilled.

BENEFITS OF ESCROW. There are two major benefits to closing a transaction through escrow. First, escrow helps ensure that both parties will go through with the transaction as agreed. For example, once a signed deed has been placed in escrow, it's much more difficult for the seller to change his mind at the last moment and refuse to transfer title to the buyer. The escrow agent has legally binding instructions to deliver the deed to the buyer when the buyer pays the purchase price. The seller can't just demand the deed back from the escrow agent. So if the seller changes his mind, a lawsuit may be required to resolve the matter.

The second benefit of escrow is convenience. It isn't necessary for everyone involved in the transaction to be present at the same time for the sale to close.

ESCROW AGENTS. In addition to holding items on behalf of the parties and disbursing them at the proper time, the escrow agent or closing agent is also responsible for seeing that legal documents are prepared and recorded, prorating the settlement costs, preparing the settlement statements, and various other tasks.

LICENSING AND EXEMPTIONS. In California, escrow agents (independent escrow companies) must be licensed with the Department of Corporations. Only a corporation—not a partnership or an individual—can be licensed as an escrow agent.

However, attorneys, title companies, banks, savings and loans, and insurance companies may provide escrow services without an escrow license. Real estate brokers who provide escrow services for transactions they are handling are also exempt from the escrow licensing requirement, and they may charge a fee for their escrow services.

EXAMPLE: Yamamoto is buying Farley's house, and you're the broker representing Farley. You may act as the closing agent for the transaction; you don't need a special escrow license. You may provide the closing services free of charge, or you may charge Yamamoto and Farley an escrow fee in addition to your regular commission.

TERMINOLOGY. Sometimes the term "escrow agent" is reserved for a licensed independent escrow company, while "closing agent" is used as a general term that refers to any person or entity providing escrow services in a real estate transaction (whether that's a lawyer, a bank, a real estate broker, or a licensed escrow agent). In other cases, the two terms are used interchangeably in the more general sense, to mean any person or entity that is providing escrow services in a real estate transaction. Thus, when a lawyer or a real estate broker is performing the same tasks as an escrow company, you may hear the lawyer or the broker referred to either as the closing agent or as the escrow agent for the transaction.

The escrow process is handled differently in different parts of the state. In northern California, closing services are usually provided by title insurance companies. In southern California, many transactions are closed by independent escrow companies. Also, statewide, many lenders have in-house escrow departments to handle transactions that they are financing.

STEPS IN CLOSING A TRANSACTION

Certain steps must be completed during the closing process in almost every residential transaction. We'll give you an overview of these steps, and then consider some of them in more detail.

OVERVIEW. If the sale is contingent on one or more inspections—for example, a home inspection and a soil test—the inspections should be ordered as soon as possible after the deposit receipt is signed. This is usually done by the buyer or the buyer's real estate agent.

BUYER'S LOAN. Another step that should be taken as soon as possible is arranging for financing. The buyer must either apply for a loan or, if he has been preapproved for a loan, fulfill any additional requirements set by the lender. In any case, the lender will order a property appraisal before issuing a final loan commitment.

Opening escrow. Escrow may be opened when the buyer's lender delivers a copy of the deposit receipt to its escrow department. Alternatively, a real estate agent may open escrow by delivering a copy of the agreement to the escrow agent specified by the parties.

Either way, the escrow agent will set up the escrow and conduct the closing based on escrow instructions signed by the buyer and seller. The C.A.R. deposit receipt form (see Figure 6.1 in Chapter 6) includes the escrow instructions for the transaction. If a deposit receipt form that doesn't include escrow instructions is used, the escrow agent will prepare a separate document for the parties to sign, based on the deposit receipt. The conditions and deadlines in the escrow instructions must match the terms of the deposit receipt.

Appraisal. The appraisal report is sent to the buyer's lender, because the lender is the appraiser's client. To find out what the appraiser concluded, the parties or their real estate agents usually have to ask the lender.

Title report. The escrow agent orders a preliminary title report, if the lender has not already done so. This report, which describes the current condition of the seller's title to the property, is sent to the lender and the buyer for approval. Any unexpected title problems revealed in the report must be addressed.

Loan payoff. In most transactions, the seller has a mortgage or deed of trust on the property that will be paid off at closing. The escrow agent requests a final payoff figure from the seller's lender. A form called a "Demand for Payoff" or a "Request for Beneficiary's Statement" is used to make this request. The escrow agent will also need to obtain exact figures for any other liens that must be removed or judgments that must be paid.

Inspection reports. After an inspection has been completed, the inspection report may be sent to the buyer or the buyer's real estate agent, who in turn may be expected to provide a copy to the buyer's lender. If the report shows that repairs are needed, there may be negotiations between the buyer and the seller about which of them will pay for the repairs (see Chapter 7). For any lender-required repairs, the lender will want proof that the repairs have been completed.

Loan approval. When the buyer's loan is approved, the lender informs the buyer of the exact terms on which it was approved and the date on which the loan commitment will expire. The lender also gives the buyer

FIG. 10.2 STEPS IN THE CLOSING PROCESS

- INSPECTIONS ORDERED BY BUYER OR REAL ESTATE AGENT
- FINANCING APPLIED FOR OR FINALIZED BY BUYER
- APPRAISAL ORDERED BY LENDER
- ESCROW OPENED BY LENDER OR REAL ESTATE AGENT
- ESCROW INSTRUCTIONS SIGNED BY THE PARTIES
- PRELIMINARY TITLE REPORT ORDERED BY CLOSING AGENT
- LOAN PAYOFF AMOUNT REQUESTED FROM SELLER'S LENDER BY CLOSING AGENT
- LOAN DOCUMENTS SIGNED BY BUYER
- DOWNPAYMENT AND CLOSING COSTS DEPOSITED BY BUYER
- LOAN FUNDS DEPOSITED BY LENDER
- SETTLEMENT STATEMENTS PREPARED BY CLOSING AGENT
- FUNDS DISBURSED BY CLOSING AGENT
- TITLE POLICY ISSUED BY TITLE COMPANY
- DOCUMENTS FILED FOR RECORDING
- HAZARD INSURANCE POLICY ISSUED TO BUYER

an updated good faith estimate of her closing costs. The lender sends all of the new loan documents—the promissory note and the mortgage or deed of trust—to the escrow agent, who arranges for the buyer to review and sign them. Once the loan documents have been signed, they are returned to the lender, who then coordinates loan funding with the escrow agent.

BUYER'S FUNDS. When all of the contingencies listed in the deposit receipt (such as the inspections, the financing arrangements, or the sale of the buyer's home) have been satisfied, the buyer deposits the downpayment and the closing costs into escrow. Some lenders disburse the loan funds to the escrow agent at this point, but many lenders wait until the title has been transferred and the buyer's deed and mortgage or deed of trust have been recorded.

SETTLEMENT STATEMENTS. Once he knows how much each of the specific closing costs will be (how much the recording fees come to, how much the title insurance policies cost, etc.), the escrow agent prepares the final settlement statements and disburses the funds held in escrow to the seller, the real estate broker, and other individuals or entities that are entitled to payment. The title insurance policies are issued, as is the buyer's hazard or homeowner's insurance policy. The deed and the other documents are filed with the county clerk for recording. Once this has all been done, the sale has officially closed.

Next, let's look at certain aspects of the closing process in more detail. We'll discuss property inspections, financing and the appraisal, hazard insurance, and title insurance.

INSPECTIONS. As we discussed in Chapter 7, many residential deposit receipts have one or more inspection contingency provisions. For the benefit of the buyer, the sale is conditioned on a satisfactory inspection of the property by an expert. In addition, many lenders make one or more satisfactory inspections a condition of loan approval. Thus, inspections are a key part of the closing process.

For each inspection required by the parties' agreement or by the lender, not only must an initial inspection be ordered, but the inspection report must be approved or rejected by the buyer or the lender, repairs must be completed and reinspected, and the parties must be notified about the results of the reinspection. (For more information about the types of addenda and notice forms that can be used for inspection contingencies, see Chapter 7.) It's very important for inspections to be ordered early in the closing process; if repairs are required, they need to be completed early enough so that they don't delay the closing.

TYPES OF INSPECTIONS. There are many different types of real estate inspections. Here are brief descriptions of the inspections most commonly required in residential transactions. The first three on the list may be carried out by a single expert called a home inspector.

- **STRUCTURAL INSPECTION.** The inspector identifies the materials used in the construction, the type of construction, and the accessibility of the various areas that are to be inspected. In addition, the inspector checks for major and minor problems in the structural systems of the building, including the foundation and the floor, wall, and roof framing.

- **ELECTRICAL AND PLUMBING INSPECTION.** The inspector checks the existing electrical and plumbing systems for capacity, safety, and life expectancy. Plumbing systems are also checked for unsanitary conditions. Upgrades and repairs may be recommended. If the property's water source is a private well, it may also be inspected for water quality and quantity.
- **INTERIOR INSPECTION.** The inspector checks the walls, floors, and ceilings for signs of water damage, settling, fire hazards, or other problems. Ventilation and energy conservation issues are noted. Appliances may also be examined for operational problems.
- **PEST INSPECTION.** A pest inspector checks for damage caused by wood-eating insects such as termites, wood-boring beetles, and carpenter ants.
- **SOIL INSPECTION.** A soil inspector or geologist examines the soil conditions to see if there are existing or potential settling or drainage problems.
- **ENVIRONMENTAL INSPECTION.** An environmental inspection addresses concerns about radon, urea formaldehyde, asbestos, lead-based paint, underground storage tanks, or contaminated water. (These problems are discussed in Chapter 3.)

CHOOSING AN INSPECTOR. For a particular inspection, your buyer may have an inspector in mind, or he may ask you to recommend someone reputable. If possible, give the buyer at least three names to choose from. (Ask your broker or the other agents in your office for suggestions, if necessary.)

To help a buyer make the selection, you can suggest that he ask the home inspector the following questions:

1. How long has the firm (or individual inspector) been in business? (A minimum of five years' experience is recommended.)
2. Does the firm belong to the American Society of Home Inspectors? (Membership requires actual experience, passing a written examination, inspection reviews, and continuing education.)
3. Has the firm changed its name recently? If so, why?
4. What type of report does the firm prepare? How long does it take to complete the report and get it back to the client?
5. How many inspectors does the firm have? Are they full-time or part-time?

6. Does the firm engage in other businesses in addition to inspections? (In other words, is home inspection only a sideline?)
7. Does the firm also offer to make any of the repairs recommended by the inspection? (Inspection companies that also make repairs may not give unbiased reports.)
8. Does the firm provide references? If the buyer requests them, an inspector should be willing to give several references.

It is also a good idea to check with the Better Business Bureau to see if any complaints have been lodged against the inspection firm.

INSPECTION REPORTS. After an inspection is completed, the inspector prepares an inspection report. The report should summarize the major points of concern and state which problems need to be repaired or otherwise addressed promptly. This should include information about substandard workmanship and also about deterioration, such as dry rot or old wiring.

The report should put the property into perspective by comparing it to similar properties. A 15-year-old house can't be expected to be in the same condition as a brand new one.

In addition, the report should project a five-year budget for anticipated repair work and identify potential remodeling problems. For instance, if the buyer were to add rooms onto the house, the entire electrical system might need to be upgraded. Or the septic system might only be adequate for a three-bedroom house, and if another bedroom were added, a new septic tank would be required.

REPAIRS. After an inspection report has been issued, the party who requested it (the buyer or the lender) must either approve or disapprove the report. Depending on the terms of the inspection contingency provision, the repairs may have to be completed before the transaction can close. (See Chapter 7.) If the buyer's lender ordered the inspection, the repairs may be a condition of loan approval.

Ideally, the parties will already have agreed who will pay for any required repairs, but that isn't always the case. The deposit receipt may commit the seller to paying up to a specified amount, but no more than that. If the repair costs significantly exceed that amount, it may be necessary for the seller to negotiate a price adjustment or some other concession to persuade the buyer to go forward.

In many cases, the repairs have to be completed and reinspected—and the buyer or lender has to approve the reinspection report—before the sale can close or the loan can be funded. In some circumstances, however, the closing can take place even though the repairs won't be completed by the closing date.

STRUCTURAL PEST CONTROL INSPECTIONS. Structural pest control inspections can be particularly important, and most lenders in California require one. In addition, this type of inspection is required by the FHA and the VA in certain parts of the state. Copies of structural pest inspection reports must be filed with the state Structural Pest Control Board and kept for two years.

Typically, a seller will order a structural pest control inspection when the house is first listed so that any problems found can be corrected as soon as possible. In most cases, the seller will pay for corrective repairs, but the buyer is responsible for any preventive measures.

FINANCING. A home sale can't close unless the buyers have enough money to pay the purchase price. The buyers nearly always borrow the money they need from a bank or other lender. As explained in Chapter 8, it's now common for buyers to get preapproved for financing. Before choosing a house to buy, the buyers submit a fully completed loan application and the supporting documentation. The lender performs a credit analysis and qualifies the buyers for a certain loan amount at a specified interest rate. If they find a house that can be purchased with that loan amount, and if the property meets the lender's standards, the lender will issue a final loan commitment. By taking care of many matters beforehand, loan preapproval can streamline the closing process.

Employees of the buyer's lender are actively involved in closing the transaction. Even if the buyer has been preapproved for a loan, the lender's team orders and evaluates the appraisal, reviews the preliminary title report, and may also order inspections and require repairs. They prepare the financing documents for the buyer to sign, and they are responsible for funding the loan—that is, depositing the loan amount into escrow so that it can be disbursed at closing. As we indicated earlier, in some cases the entire closing is handled by the lender's escrow department.

Because of their role, the loan officer and other employees of the lender can have a big impact on the closing. If they're reputable and competent, they'll make sure that the loan process is completed smoothly and quickly, with a minimum of errors. Find out which lenders have good or bad reputations by asking experienced real estate agents, and pass that information along to your buyers before they choose their lender.

APPRAISAL. The buyer's lender orders the appraisal as part of the loan underwriting process. The property as well as the buyer must be qualified for the requested loan. Regardless of the buyer's financial situation, it's the property that serves as the security for the debt. If the loan is not repaid as agreed, the lender will foreclose on the property to recover the money owed. Before approving the loan, the lender must be certain that the property is worth enough to protect the lender's investment in case the borrower defaults.

The residential appraisal process has a lot in common with the competitive market analysis that real estate agents use to help price a home (see Chapter 4). In fact, the CMA method is based on the sales comparison approach to appraisal, which is the most important approach for residential appraisals.

You should understand the basic appraisal process well enough to give a brief explanation of the process to the buyer and seller. They are often anxious about the appraisal, since their transaction depends on the appraiser's opinion.

In addition, understanding the appraisal process will help you prevent and cope with the problem of a low appraisal, when the appraiser concludes that the property is worth less than the sales price. (See Chapter 4.) Of course, pricing the property realistically in the first place is the best way to avoid a low appraisal. But it can also help if you assist the appraiser in any way you can. If possible, arrange to be there when the appraiser inspects the property. Don't get in the way, but answer the appraiser's questions and make sure none of the property's strong points get overlooked.

You can offer the appraiser an updated competitive market analysis that includes at least three good comparable sales. Most appraisers don't have much time to spend on any one property, so if your comparables are convincing, the appraiser could decide to use them.

HAZARD INSURANCE. Virtually all lenders require the escrow agent to make sure the mortgaged property is insured up to the property's replacement cost before the loan funds are disbursed. In most cases the minimum insurance policy is the HO-2 policy. This type of policy provides coverage against the following perils:

- fire and lightning;
- windstorm and hail;
- explosion;
- riot or civil commotion;
- vehicles;
- smoke;
- vandalism and malicious mischief;
- theft;
- breakage of glass;
- falling objects;
- weight of ice, snow, and sleet;
- collapse of a building or any part of a building;
- accidental discharge or overflow of water or steam;
- sudden accidental tearing apart of heating, air conditioning, or hot water systems;
- freezing of plumbing, heating, air conditioning systems, or household appliances; and
- sudden accidental damage from artificially generated electrical current.

In addition to insuring the real property, these policies usually provide coverage for personal property on the premises. They also provide a limited amount of liability coverage for personal injury and property damage that the policy holder causes.

Note that the HO-2 policy doesn't cover damage resulting from floods or earthquakes. A buyer who is concerned about floods or earthquakes should consider buying supplemental coverage. But this type of coverage can be expensive, and it isn't available in all areas or for all properties.

TITLE INSURANCE. Title insurance insures the buyer or the buyer's lender against financial losses that could result from as yet undiscovered problems with the seller's title. As we said earlier, the escrow agent or the lender orders a preliminary title report on the property.

The title report should be ordered early in the closing process to allow time for problems to be resolved. For example, if the title report indicates that there is a judgment lien against the property, the seller will have to clear away the lien so that marketable title can be transferred to the buyer at closing. Depending on the circumstances, the seller may simply arrange to pay the lienholder at closing. Or the seller may need to prove to the title company's satisfaction that there is no lien against the property. Perhaps the title searcher overlooked a recorded release, or the lien might be against a completely different person who has the same name as the seller.

TYPES OF TITLE POLICIES. The two main types of title insurance policies are the mortgagee's policy, also called an ALTA policy, and the owner's policy, also called a CLTA policy. (ALTA stands for American Land Title Association, CLTA for California Land Title Association.)

The buyer's lender will require the buyer to purchase a **mortgagee's policy** as a condition of the loan. The mortgagee's policy protects the lender's security interest.

> **EXAMPLE:** After closing, it comes to light that there's a lien against the property that has higher priority than the lender's deed of trust. That other lien was not discovered by the title searcher and listed in the title report. As a result, the lien was not paid off before closing; but it also wasn't listed as an exception to coverage in the title policy. If the lender suffers a financial loss because it doesn't have first lien position, the title company will have to reimburse the lender, up to the face amount of the policy.

By contrast, an **owner's policy** benefits the buyer. It will protect the buyer's ownership interest against undiscovered title problems, such as a forged deed or a gap in the chain of title. It will cover the legal fees paid to defend the buyer's title against a covered claim, and it will also pay off successful claims, up to the face amount of the policy. In northern California, it's customary for the buyer to pay for the owner's policy, while in southern California, the seller typically pays for the owner's policy.

It's never wise for a buyer to purchase a home without an owner's title insurance policy. (Keep in mind that the lender's policy offers no protection to the buyer.) The coverage is not particularly expensive, and although title problems are unlikely to surface, they could be very costly if they did.

STANDARD COVERAGE VS. EXTENDED COVERAGE. Standard coverage title insurance protects the policy holder against title problems that concern matters of record—that is, deeds and liens and other interests that have been recorded so that they appear in the public record. Extended coverage protects against all of the same problems that a standard coverage policy does, plus problems that should be discovered in an actual inspection of the property. These include encroachments, adverse possession, construction that may result in a lien that hasn't been recorded yet, and other problems that do not show up in the public record. The title company sends an inspector to the property to look for indications that there may be one of these problems.

Lenders require mortgagee's policies to be extended coverage policies. Owner's policies have traditionally provided standard coverage, but it's becoming more common for buyers to want extended coverage. If the seller is going to pay for the owner's policy, a provision in which the seller agrees to pay for extended coverage could be added to the deposit receipt. Alternatively, the seller could pay the amount that standard coverage would cost, and the buyer could pay the additional amount required for extended coverage.

THE REAL ESTATE AGENT'S ROLE IN THE CLOSING PROCESS

As your sale progresses toward closing, it's important to keep track of the details. Don't assume that everything's going smoothly while you turn your attention to other listings and other buyers.

COMMUNICATION. Throughout the closing process, keep your client up to date on what's happening. Let her know when the appraisal is completed, when the loan is approved, and so on. This will ease her anxieties and reassure her that someone—you—is looking after her interests. Communication is especially important when problems crop up. If there's a delay in getting a preliminary title report or the pest inspection looks bad, tell your client immediately. Explain the problem, suggest what can be done about it, and then work with the client to find a solution.

Communication with the other party's agent is also very important. You need to promote your client's interests, but you should always do your best to get along with the other agent and the other party. Although their interests will sometimes conflict with those of your client, in most cases all of you ultimately want the sale to close. Don't agree to unreasonable demands, but work with the other agent to complete the transaction successfully.

PREVENTING PROBLEMS. Here is a list of questions and suggestions that will help you prevent problems and make the closing process smoother. Of course, what you do in a particular transaction will depend in part on whether you're representing the buyer or the seller.

PREPARING THE DEPOSIT RECEIPT. Have the forms used for the buyer's offer and any counteroffers been filled out carefully? Do the parties understand the terms of their agreement? Is the legal description of the property complete and correct? Consider whether the deadlines in the agreement make sense under all of the current conditions. How long will it take to fulfill the contingencies in this market? The contingencies may include inspections, financing, and even the sale of the buyer's current home. When does the buyer need to move? Is it realistic to expect that the seller can be completely moved out by that date?

OPENING ESCROW. Does the escrow agent have a copy of every addendum and amendment as well as a copy of the deposit receipt itself? If the escrow instructions are separate from the deposit receipt form, do they accurately reflect all the terms of the deposit receipt? The parties can sign amended instructions if necessary.

INSPECTIONS. Are you responsible for ordering any inspections? If so, do it right away. And if someone else has that responsibility, make sure they take care of it as soon as possible. Later, check to see whether the inspection report has been delivered to the appropriate parties. Does the report seem thorough and accurate? If the report recommends repairs, do the recommendations seem reasonable? If the transaction is contingent on the results of this inspection, help your client prepare or respond to the inspection notice (see Chapter 7). If repairs are agreed to, they should be ordered and completed as soon as possible. Have arrangements for a timely reinspection been made?

FINANCING. If the buyer hasn't been preapproved for a loan, has she gathered all of the personal information that she'll need for the loan application? Has she chosen a competent lender? Check with the lender periodically to find out how the loan process is going.

APPRAISAL. Can you be on hand when the appraiser inspects the seller's home? Do you have recent comparable sales you can show the appraiser? If the appraisal comes in low, does a request for reconsideration of value seem appropriate? (See Chapter 4.)

SPECIAL PROVISIONS. Are there any special provisions in the deposit receipt that require your attention? Are both parties clear on which personal property items and fixtures are included in the sale, and which the seller is going to take with him?

TITLE INSURANCE. Has a preliminary title report been ordered? When the report becomes available, find out whether there are any title problems that need to be cleared up.

HAZARD INSURANCE. Has the buyer applied for and obtained a new homeowner's insurance policy? Has a copy of the policy been delivered to the escrow agent or the lender?

MOVING OUT. Is the seller packing his belongings and preparing to move out on time? Has he arranged for his mail to be forwarded? When the seller leaves, will the house be reasonably clean? Will the yard be in reasonably good shape? Many sellers will be glad to pay to have junk hauled away, or to have a team of house cleaners go over the house once it's empty. You should be able to recommend junk hauling services and house cleaning services. Ask the other agents in your office which companies they recommend.

MOVING IN. If the buyer wants to move in before closing, has an interim rental agreement been prepared and signed? (See Chapter 6.) Whenever the buyer moves in, will the seller have all of the house keys ready to turn over to the buyer? If the buyer finds personal property that may have been left behind accidentally, or if there's unforwarded mail for the seller, it's usually more appropriate to contact the seller's agent rather than the seller himself.

LAST-MINUTE PROBLEMS. In the closing process, the risk that the transaction will fall apart is usually greatest before the contingencies have been fulfilled, but something can go wrong at any point, right up through the last few days before closing.

EXAMPLE: The sale of your client's house to the Friedmans has been going well. The seller and the buyers have been taking care of their responsibilities on time, and the financing contingency and inspection contingencies have been satisfied.

But just a week before the date set for closing, you get a call from the seller. He says that there's a problem with the house that he never told you about. There's some dry rot in the crawl spaces. He should have listed this in the transfer disclosure statement, but he decided not to. The home inspector apparently missed the problem. Now the seller's conscience (and fear of liability) has prompted him to let you know about it. He wants to know what he should do.

How you handle this situation may mean the difference between closing the sale on time and not closing it at all. The problem must be disclosed to the buyers, and they could use it as grounds for canceling the contract. You should do whatever you can to prevent that. For instance, you might go to the house and investigate the extent of the problem, consult with your broker and a home inspector, help the seller decide on an appropriate price concession to offer the buyers, and then call the buyers' agent. By dealing with this problem in a straightforward and professional manner, you can make it much more likely that the sale will go through.

To summarize, always stay on top of the closing process. Keep in touch with your client, with the other party's agent, and with the escrow agent. Handle any problems that come up as promptly as you can. Your role in getting the transaction to close can be just as important as your role in negotiating the sale in the first place.

CLOSING COSTS

One of your primary tasks as a real estate agent is explaining the various costs of closing a real estate transaction to your clients. Some examples of closing costs are inspection fees, title insurance fees, recording fees, escrow fees, and loan fees. Some of these are paid by the buyer, some are paid by the seller, and some are split between the two parties.

The closing costs, along with the other financial details of the transaction, are set forth in a **settlement statement** (also called a **closing statement**). The final settlement statement prepared for the buyer shows exactly how much money the buyer must pay at closing. The final statement for the seller shows exactly how much the seller will take away from closing.

Preliminary and final settlement statements are prepared for the parties by the closing agent. As a real estate agent, you might never be responsible for filling out a settlement statement form. Even so, you should be able to read one. And you need to be able to give the buyers and sellers you work with a reasonable estimate of how much their closing costs will be. For a seller, even before he lists his property, one of the most important pieces of information is the answer to the question, "How much money will I get from this sale?"

To explain the seller's estimated **net proceeds** (the amount of cash the seller will walk away with) and the buyer's estimated **net cost** (the amount of cash the buyer must pay at closing), you have to know how the various closing costs are typically allocated on a settlement statement. Many agents use worksheets to help them calculate—and explain—the net costs and net proceeds. A buyer's estimated net cost worksheet is shown later in the chapter, in Figure 10.4. A seller's estimated net proceeds worksheet is shown in Figure 10.5. Your broker may have similar worksheets available for you to use.

You'll need to do some math to calculate the amount of certain closing costs. And some expenses will have to be **prorated** between the buyer and the seller. To prorate an expense is to divide and allocate it proportionately between two or more parties, according to time, interest, or benefit. Figure 10.3 shows the steps involved in proration.

COSTS AND CREDITS

On a settlement statement, the costs that a party must pay at closing are referred to as that party's **debits** (the opposite of credits). The buyer's debits increase the amount of money the buyer will have to bring to closing. The seller's debits decrease the seller's net proceeds.

In addition to their debits, each party will usually have some credits that also must be taken into account (and in some cases prorated). Credits are payments that will be made to the buyer or the seller at closing. The buyer's credits decrease the buyer's net cost. The seller's credits increase the seller's net proceeds.

FIG. 10.3 PRORATING AN EXPENSE

STEP 1
Divide the expense by the number of days it covers to find the per diem (daily) rate.
- Divide annual expenses by 365 (or by 360, for an estimate).
- Divide monthly expenses by the number of days in the month in question (or by 30, for an estimate).

STEP 2
Determine the number of days for which one party is responsible for the expense.

STEP 3
Multiply the number of days by the per diem rate to find that party's share of the expense.

Expense paid in arrears (overdue):
- Seller's share is a debit for the seller.

Expense paid in advance:
- Seller's share is a credit for the seller.

Expense continues after closing:
- Buyer's share is a credit for the buyer if paid in arrears.
- Buyer's share is a debit for the buyer if paid in advance.

Note that some closing costs are charges that one party owes the other party. At closing, each of these will be treated as a debit for the party that must pay it and as a credit for the other party. For example, the buyer may be required to pay the seller a prorated share of the annual property taxes, because the seller paid the taxes in advance. The prorated amount is a debit for the buyer and a credit for the seller on the settlement statement. On your worksheets, add it to the buyer's net cost, and also add it to the seller's net proceeds.

Other closing costs are charges that one party must pay to a third party. For example, the seller will have to pay the broker the sales commission. This is a debit for the seller (subtracted from the net proceeds), but it does not affect the buyer.

Also, some of the credits a party receives at closing come from a third party. For example, the seller's lender must refund any unused tax and insurance reserves to the seller at closing. This is a credit for the seller (added to the net proceeds), and it does not affect the buyer.

Residential transactions involve many standard closing costs. Some are allocated according to custom, some are allocated according to the terms of the deposit receipt, and a few are allocated according to law. We'll first go through the process of estimating a buyer's net cost. After that, we'll turn to the seller's net proceeds.

ESTIMATING THE BUYER'S NET COST

Certain costs are the buyer's responsibility in every transaction, or almost every transaction. Responsibility for other costs—whether they'll be paid by the buyer or by the seller, or shared between them—may vary. To estimate a buyer's net cost, you add up all of the charges the buyer will have to pay to close the sale and offset them with the credits owed to the buyer.

PURCHASE PRICE. Of course, the purchase price is the major cost for the buyer in every transaction. Use this as the starting point on your buyer's net cost worksheet (see Figure 10.4). The price is offset by the buyer's good faith deposit and the financing.

GOOD FAITH DEPOSIT. The buyer gives the seller a good faith deposit when the deposit receipt is signed, and the deposit is applied to the purchase price if the sale closes. Since the buyer has already paid the good faith deposit, it is treated as a credit for the buyer on the settlement statement. On the net cost worksheet, subtract the amount of the deposit from the purchase price.

FINANCING. Most buyers pay a large part of the purchase price with borrowed money. Any financing arrangement—a new loan, the assumption of the seller's loan, or seller financing—is treated as a credit for the buyer. On the buyer's worksheet, subtract the loan amount and/or the amount of other financing from the purchase price.

LOAN COSTS. Borrowing money isn't free. In addition to the interest the buyer will have to pay over the life of the loan, she will incur a number of closing costs in the course of obtaining the loan. Unless the seller has agreed to pay some of them, the buyer will pay all of the closing costs

FIG. 10.4   BUYER'S ESTIMATED NET COST WORKSHEET

Buyer's Estimated Net Cost	
Purchase Price	**$370,000.00**
Good faith deposit (credit)	− 10,000.00
Financing (credit)	− 335,000.00
Remainder (price less offsets)	**$25,000.00**
Buyer's Closing Costs	
Appraisal fee	+ 275.00
Credit report	+ 40.00
Origination fee	+ 3,350.00
Discount points	+ 10,050.00
Prepaid interest	+ 1,028.33
Lender's title insurance	+ 600.00
Inspection fees	+ 400.00
Hazard insurance	+ 375.00
Attorney's fees	+ 350.00
Recording fees	+ 50.00
Escrow fee	+ 250.00
Property taxes	+ 890.97
Estimated Net Cost	**$42,659.30**

associated with the loan. That means you should add these closing costs to the purchase price on your buyer's net cost worksheet.

APPRAISAL. The appraisal is required by the buyer's lender, so the appraisal fee is ordinarily paid by the buyer.

CREDIT REPORT. The buyer's lender charges the buyer for the credit investigation, so this is also a cost for the buyer.

ORIGINATION FEE. This is the lender's one-time charge to the borrower for setting up the loan (see Chapter 9). It's almost always paid by the buyer. If the buyer is assuming the seller's loan, an assumption fee will be charged instead of an origination fee.

DISCOUNT POINTS. The discount points are paid by the buyer, unless the seller has agreed to pay for a buydown (see Chapter 9). In that case, some or all of the points are paid by the seller.

PREPAID INTEREST. As a general rule, the first payment date of a new loan is not the first day of the month immediately following closing, but rather the first day of the next month after that. For instance, if a sale closes on April 14, the first payment on the new loan is due on June 1 instead of May 1. This gives the buyer a chance to recover a little from the financial strain of closing.

Even though the first loan payment isn't due for an extra month, interest begins accruing on the loan on the closing date. Interest on a real estate loan is almost always paid in arrears. In other words, the interest that accrues during a given month is paid at the end of that month. For instance, a loan payment that is due on September 1 includes the interest that accrued during August. So if the transaction closes on April 14, the first payment will be due on June 1, and that payment will cover the interest accrued in May. However, it won't cover the interest accrued between April 14 and April 30. Instead, the lender will require the buyer to pay the interest for those 17 days in April at closing. This is called **prepaid interest** or **interim interest**. It is almost always paid by the buyer.

> **EXAMPLE:** The buyer is borrowing $335,000 at 6.5% interest to finance the purchase. The annual interest on the loan during the first year will be $21,775 ($335,000 × .065 = $21,775). The escrow agent divides that annual figure by 360 to get the per diem interest rate.
>
> $$\$21,775 \div 360 = \$60.49 \text{ per diem}$$
>
> There are 17 days between the closing date (April 14) and the first day of the following month, so the lender will expect the buyer to prepay 17 days' worth of interest at closing.
>
> $$\$60.49 \times 17 \text{ days} = \$1,028.33 \text{ prepaid interest}$$
>
> The escrow agent will enter $1,028.33 as a debit to the buyer on the settlement statement. When you are preparing your estimated net cost worksheet for the buyer, you can go through the same process to come up with a figure for the prepaid interest. Add it to the buyer's net cost.

LENDER'S TITLE INSURANCE PREMIUM. As explained earlier, the lender requires the buyer to provide a policy to protect the lender's lien priority. The premium for the lender's policy is paid by the buyer, unless otherwise agreed. Don't forget that in northern California, the buyer will also typically pay for the owner's title insurance policy.

INSPECTION FEES. The cost of an inspection is allocated by agreement between the parties. Customarily, the buyer pays for the inspection fees.

HAZARD INSURANCE. The lender generally requires the buyer to pay for one year of hazard insurance coverage in advance, at closing.

ATTORNEY'S FEES. A buyer who is represented by an attorney in the transaction is responsible for her own attorney's fees. (The same is true for the seller.) In many transactions, the attorney's fees are not handled through escrow. Instead, each lawyer simply bills his or her client directly.

RECORDING FEES. The fees for recording the various documents involved in the transaction are usually charged to the party who benefits from the recording. The fees for recording the deed and the new mortgage or deed of trust are normally paid by the buyer.

ESCROW FEE. Also called a settlement fee or closing fee, this is the escrow agent's charge for his or her services. The buyer and the seller commonly agree to split the escrow fee, so that each of them pays half.

PROPERTY TAXES. The seller is responsible for the property taxes up to the day of closing; the buyer is responsible for them on the day of closing and thereafter. If the seller has already paid some or all of the property taxes in advance, he is entitled to a prorated refund from the buyer at closing. The amount of the refund is a debit for the buyer and a credit for the seller.

EXAMPLE: The sale is closing on April 14. This year the property taxes on the house are $2,996.65. The escrow agent calculates the per diem rate by dividing that figure by 360.

$$2,996.65 \div 360 = 8.32 \text{ per diem}$$

The seller is responsible for the property taxes from January 1 through April 13—in other words, for the first 73 days of the year. The buyer is responsible for them from April 14 to the end of the tax year, which in California is June 30. Annual property taxes in California are paid in two equal installments, so each installment for this property would be $1,498.33 ($2,996.65 ÷ 2 = $1,498.33).

The seller has already paid taxes through the end of June, so at closing he will be entitled to a credit for the share that is the buyer's responsibility. The escrow agent multiplies the number of days for which the seller is responsible by the per diem rate to determine the seller's share of the taxes. The escrow agent subtracts the seller's share from the annual figure to find the buyer's share.

$$73 \text{ days} \times \$8.32 = \$607.36 \text{ (Seller's share)}$$

$$\$1,498.33 - \$607.36 = \$890.97 \text{ (Buyer's share)}$$

This $890.97 will appear on the buyer's settlement statement as a debit and on the seller's statement as a credit. Again, you can do a similar proration for your net cost and net proceeds estimates. Add the buyer's debit to the buyer's net cost, and add the seller's credit to the seller's net proceeds.

ESTIMATED TOTAL COST. When all of the appropriate items on your net cost worksheet have been filled in, you're ready to calculate the buyer's estimated net cost. Subtract the buyer's credits from the purchase price, and then add all of the buyer's costs. The result is the net cost, the amount of money that the buyer will have to give to the escrow agent in order to close the sale.

Be sure your buyer knows what kind of check the escrow agent will accept. A certified check or cashier's check, rather than a personal check, is usually required.

ESTIMATING THE SELLER'S NET PROCEEDS

Now let's look at the costs and credits that you should take into consideration when estimating a seller's net proceeds.

SALES PRICE. The largest credit for the seller is, naturally, the sales price. It should be the starting point in your net proceeds calculation (see Figure 10.5). You'll add any other credits that the seller will receive at closing to the price, then subtract the costs that the seller must pay.

REFUNDS. The seller may be entitled to certain refunds at closing. As you've already seen, if the seller has paid the property taxes in advance,

FIG. 10.5   SELLER'S ESTIMATED NET PROCEEDS WORKSHEET

Seller's Estimated Net Proceeds	
Sales Price	**$370,000.00**
Prorated property taxes (credit)	+ 890.97
Reserve account (credit)	+ 1,000.64
Total Proceeds to Seller	**$371,891.61**
Seller's Closing Costs	
Loan payoff	− 156,000.00
Interest due on loan	− 424.62
Prepayment penalty	− 0.00
Other liens and assessments	− 0.00
Brokerage commission	− 25,900.00
Owner's title insurance	− 725.00
Seller-paid discount points	− 0.00
Documentary transfer tax	− 407.00
Repairs	− 500.00
Attorney's fees	− 0.00
Recording fees	− 24.00
Escrow fee	− 250.00
Estimated Net Proceeds	**$187,660.99**

the buyer will have to refund the share that she's responsible for to the seller. That will increase the seller's net proceeds. (On the other hand, if the seller hasn't paid the taxes yet, he will have to pay a prorated share of them at closing, which will decrease the net proceeds.)

Another possible credit for the seller is a refund of funds remaining in the reserve account (or impound account) for the seller's loan. A seller often has reserves on deposit with his lender to cover future property taxes and hazard insurance premiums. When the seller's loan is paid off, the unused balance in the reserve account is refunded to the seller by the lender. If your seller will receive this type of refund, add it to the seller's net proceeds. The seller's lender can help you determine how much the refund of reserves will be.

Any other refunds that the seller will receive at closing should be treated in the same way.

TOTAL PROCEEDS. On your net proceeds worksheet, add all of the seller's credits to the sales price to determine the seller's total proceeds. You'll be subtracting the seller's costs from this figure.

SELLER FINANCING OR LOAN ASSUMPTION. We explained earlier that any type of financing is a credit for the buyer. Thus, just like a new loan, seller financing or an assumed loan is subtracted from the buyer's net cost. But unlike a new loan, seller financing or an assumed loan is also subtracted from the seller's net proceeds. That's because either of these financing arrangements will reduce the amount of cash the seller will receive at closing. (Note, however, that if the buyer obtains a new loan from a bank or other third-party lender, the loan amount has no effect on the seller's net proceeds.)

PAYOFF OF SELLER'S LOAN. If, like most sellers, your seller will have to pay off his existing mortgage loan, his net will be reduced by the payoff amount. This is the unpaid principal balance, plus any unpaid interest, as of the closing date. Even if you don't yet know when the closing date will be, you can calculate a good estimate of the payoff amount by asking the seller's lender for the current principal balance.

The actual payoff amount will probably be somewhat less than the estimated payoff (because the principal balance will be less), but you don't need to worry about the difference. Since your estimate of the seller's net proceeds won't match the actual net proceeds exactly, it's better if the estimate turns out to be a little lower than the actual figure, rather than a little higher. That way, the seller will be pleased rather than disappointed at closing. (For the same reason, it's better if the buyer's estimated net cost is a little higher than the actual figure.)

INTEREST ON SELLER'S LOAN. Because interest on a real estate loan is paid in arrears, when a transaction closes in the middle of the payment period, the seller owes his lender some interest after paying off the principal balance.

> **Example:** The closing date is April 14. Although the seller made a mortgage payment on his loan on April 1, that payment did not include any of the interest that is accruing during April. The seller owes the lender interest for the period from April 1 through April 14. The escrow agent prorates the interest, charging the seller only for those days, rather than for the whole month.
>
> Suppose the remaining principal balance is $156,000 and the annual interest rate is 7%. First find the per diem amount.

$$\$156,000 \times .07 = \$10,920 \text{ annual interest}$$

$$\$10,920 \div 360 = \$30.33 \text{ per diem interest}$$

$$\$30.33 \times 14 \text{ days} = \$424.62$$

> The seller owes the lender $424.62 in interest. Subtract this from the seller's net proceeds.

Suppose the seller in this example had arranged for the buyer to assume his loan. In that case, the buyer's first payment to the lender would be due May 1, and it would pay all of the interest for April. The seller would be debited for the interest owed up to April 14, and the buyer will be credited for the same amount.

Note that the FHA loan program does not allow proration of interest when a loan is paid off in the middle of a payment period. The seller must pay for a full month's interest regardless of the closing date.

Prepayment Penalty. This is a charge the seller's lender may impose on the seller for paying the loan off before the end of its term. If the seller must pay a prepayment penalty, contact the lender to determine approximately how much the penalty will be. Subtract the estimated penalty from the seller's net proceeds.

Sales Commission. The real estate broker's commission is almost always paid by the seller. The amount of the commission is usually determined by multiplying the sales price by the commission rate.

> **Example:** Your listing agreement says that the seller will pay a brokerage commission of 7% of the sales price. The house sells for $370,000.

$370,000 \times .07 = \$25,900$. The amount of the brokerage commission is $25,900.

Since the commission is one of the seller's costs, you should subtract it from the sales price when you're calculating the seller's net proceeds.

OWNER'S TITLE INSURANCE PREMIUM. As explained earlier, the premium for the owner's title insurance policy (which protects the buyer) is customarily paid by the seller in southern California. In northern California, the premium for the owner's policy is usually paid by the buyer.

DISCOUNT POINTS. If the seller has agreed to pay discount points or other costs involved in the buyer's loan, these will be a debit for the seller on the settlement statement. Subtract them from the seller's net proceeds.

DOCUMENTARY TRANSFER TAX. A documentary transfer tax is imposed on most sales of real property in California. The amount of the tax is 55 cents per every $500 of the selling price, or fraction thereof. The documentary transfer tax is customarily paid by the seller.

> **EXAMPLE:** A property's selling price is $370,000. The seller would owe $407 in documentary transfer tax. The documentary transfer tax would be calculated this way:
>
> $$\$370,000 \div \$500 = 740$$
> $$740 \times \$0.55 = \$407.00$$

REPAIR COSTS. The cost of repairs that the seller agreed to pay for will be deducted from the seller's proceeds at closing, unless the seller has already paid for them.

ATTORNEY'S FEES. Again, the seller will pay his own attorney's fees if he is represented by a lawyer. These will not necessarily be handled through the closing process.

RECORDING FEES. The seller will pay the recording fees for the documents that are recorded for his benefit. For instance, the seller customarily pays the fee for recording a deed of reconveyance to release the property from the lien of the deed of trust he has paid off.

ESCROW FEE. As mentioned earlier, the seller customarily pays half of the escrow fee.

ESTIMATED NET PROCEEDS. When you subtract the seller's loan payoff and all of the seller's closing costs from the seller's total proceeds, you arrive at the seller's estimated net proceeds, the amount he can expect to take away from closing. The escrow agent may offer the seller different options for receiving these funds, such as a cashier's check or direct deposit.

LAWS THAT AFFECT CLOSING

To end the chapter, we'll discuss some laws that must be complied with in closing a real estate transaction. These include certain income tax laws and the Real Estate Settlement Procedures Act.

INCOME TAX REGULATIONS

There are some income tax requirements connected with closing that you should be familiar with. The escrow agent (or other closing agent) is primarily responsible for ensuring that these requirements are met.

1099 REPORTING. The person responsible for closing a real estate sale generally must report the sale to the Internal Revenue Service. (Certain transactions may be exempt, but most are not.) IRS Form 1099-S is used to report the seller's name and social security number and the gross proceeds from the sale. In most cases, the gross proceeds figure is the same as the property's sales price.

Note that the closing agent is not permitted to charge an extra fee for filling out the 1099-S form.

FIRPTA. The Foreign Investment in Real Property Tax Act (FIRPTA) was passed in 1980 to help prevent foreign investors from evading tax liability on income generated from the sale of real estate. To comply with FIRPTA, the buyer must determine whether the seller is a U.S. citizen. If the seller is not a citizen, then the buyer must withhold 10% of the sales price and forward that amount to the Internal Revenue Service. In most cases, the closing agent handles these requirements on behalf of the buyer.

Many deposit receipt forms have a provision concerning FIRPTA compliance. The seller and the buyer agree to sign any documents necessary to comply with FIRPTA (or with the state withholding law discussed below).

Unless the transaction is exempt from FIRPTA, the closing agent will usually prepare a certification for the seller to sign, stating that the seller is not a "foreign person" under the terms of this law. But if the seller is a foreign person, the closing agent will withhold the required amount instead.

FIRPTA's exemptions cover various types of transactions. Most notably for our purposes, some residential transactions are exempt from the law. For the exemption to apply, the buyer must be purchasing the property for use as his or her home, and the purchase price must be $300,000 or less.

CALIFORNIA WITHHOLDING LAW. In some transactions, the closing agent will withhold 3.33% of the sales price from the seller to comply with state income tax law. The funds withheld must be transmitted to the Franchise Tax Board. Real estate sales are exempt from this requirement if the sales price is $100,000 or less, or if the property being conveyed was the seller's principal residence.

REAL ESTATE SETTLEMENT PROCEDURES ACT

The Real Estate Settlement Procedures Act (RESPA) affects how closing is handled in most residential transactions financed with institutional loans. The law has two main goals:

- to provide borrowers with information about their closing costs; and
- to eliminate kickbacks and referral fees that unnecessarily increase the costs of settlement.

TRANSACTIONS COVERED BY RESPA. RESPA applies to "federally related" loan transactions. A loan is federally related if:

1. it will be secured by a mortgage or deed of trust against:
   - property on which there is (or on which the loan proceeds will be used to build) a dwelling with four or fewer units;
   - a condominium unit or a cooperative apartment;
   - a lot with (or on which the loan proceeds will be used to place) a mobile home; and
2. the lender is federally regulated, has federally insured accounts, is assisted by the federal government, makes loans in connection with a federal program, sells loans to Fannie Mae, Ginnie Mae, or Freddie Mac, or makes real estate loans that total more than $1,000,000 per year.

In short, the act applies to almost all institutional lenders and to most residential loans.

EXEMPTIONS. RESPA does not apply to the following loan transactions:

- a loan used to purchase 25 acres or more;
- a loan primarily for a business, commercial, or agricultural purpose;
- a loan used to purchase vacant land, unless there will be a one- to four-unit dwelling built on it or a mobile home placed on it;
- temporary financing, such as a construction loan;
- an assumption for which the lender's approval is neither required nor obtained.

Note that RESPA also does not apply to seller-financed transactions, since they are not federally regulated.

RESPA REQUIREMENTS. RESPA has these requirements for federally related loan transactions:

1. Within three days after receiving a written loan application, the lender must give all loan applicants:
   - a copy of a booklet about settlement procedures, prepared by HUD, which explains RESPA, closing costs, and the settlement statement;
   - a good faith estimate of closing costs, which must also include information about any provider of settlement services (such as a particular title insurance company or escrow agent) that the lender requires the borrower to use; and
   - a mortgage servicing disclosure statement, which discloses whether the lender intends to service the loan or transfer it to another lender.
2. The closing agent is required to itemize all loan settlement charges on a Uniform Settlement Statement form (discussed below).
3. If the borrower will have to make deposits into an impound account to cover taxes, insurance, and other recurring costs, the lender cannot require excessive deposits (more than necessary to cover the expenses when they come due).

4. A lender or a provider of settlement services (such as a title company) may not:
   - pay kickbacks or referral fees to anyone for referring customers;
   - accept unearned fees—that is, fees for settlement services that were not actually provided; or
   - charge a fee for the preparation of the Uniform Settlement Statement, an impound account statement, or the disclosure statement required by the Truth in Lending Act.
5. The seller may not require the buyer to use a particular title company.

RESPA's prohibition on referral fees (number 4 above) put an end to practices that were once widespread and that generally benefited real estate agents, lenders, and settlement service providers at the expense of homebuyers.

UNIFORM SETTLEMENT STATEMENT. The closing agent must provide completed Uniform Settlement Statement forms to the buyer, the seller, and the lender on or before the closing date. Although the same form is used for both the buyer and the seller, in most cases a different statement is prepared for each party. The one given to the buyer presents only the buyer's closing information, and the one given to the seller presents only the seller's closing information.

A copy of the Uniform Settlement Statement form is shown in Figure 10.6. The back of the form (that is, the second page shown here) is used to itemize each party's closing costs. The buyer's statement will show the buyer's costs in the left column. The seller's statement will show the seller's costs in the right column. On each statement, the costs are added up and the total is transferred to the front of the form. On the buyer's statement, the buyer's total costs are entered on line 103. On the seller's statement, the seller's total costs are entered on line 502.

On the front of the buyer's statement, lines 101 through 120 list the buyer's debits, and lines 201 through 301 list the buyer's credits. On the front of the seller's statement, lines 401 through 420 list the seller's credits, and lines 501 through 601 list the seller's debits. The amount of cash the buyer must bring to closing appears on line 303, and the amount of cash the seller will receive at closing is shown on line 603.

FIG. 10.6   UNIFORM SETTLEMENT STATEMENT

A. **Settlement Statement**	U.S. Department of Housing and Urban Development	OMB Approval No. 2502-0265

B. Type of Loan

1. ☐ FHA 2. ☐ FmHA 3. ☐ Conv. Unins.	6. File Number:	7. Loan Number:	8. Mortgage Insurance Case Number:
4. ☐ VA 5. ☐ Conv. Ins.			

C. Note: This form is furnished to give you a statement of actual settlement costs. Amounts paid to and by the settlement agent are shown. Items marked "(p.o.c.)" were paid outside the closing; they are shown here for informational purposes and are not included in the totals.

D. Name & Address of Borrower:	E. Name & Address of Seller:	F. Name & Address of Lender:

G. Property Location:	H. Settlement Agent:
	Place of Settlement:	I. Settlement Date:

J. Summary of Borrower's Transaction		**K. Summary of Seller's Transaction**	
100. Gross Amount Due From Borrower		**400. Gross Amount Due To Seller**	
101. Contract sales price		401. Contract sales price	
102. Personal property		402. Personal property	
103. Settlement charges to borrower (line 1400)		403.	
104.		404.	
105.		405.	
Adjustments for items paid by seller in advance		**Adjustments for items paid by seller in advance**	
106. City/town taxes to		406. City/town taxes to	
107. County taxes to		407. County taxes to	
108. Assessments to		408. Assessments to	
109.		409.	
110.		410.	
111.		411.	
112.		412.	
120. Gross Amount Due From Borrower		**420. Gross Amount Due To Seller**	
200. Amounts Paid By Or In Behalf Of Borrower		**500. Reductions In Amount Due To Seller**	
201. Deposit or earnest money		501. Excess deposit (see instructions)	
202. Principal amount of new loan(s)		502. Settlement charges to seller (line 1400)	
203. Existing loan(s) taken subject to		503. Existing loan(s) taken subject to	
204.		504. Payoff of first mortgage loan	
205.		505. Payoff of second mortgage loan	
206.		506.	
207.		507.	
208.		508.	
209.		509.	
Adjustments for items unpaid by seller		**Adjustments for items unpaid by seller**	
210. City/town taxes to		510. City/town taxes to	
211. County taxes to		511. County taxes to	
212. Assessments to		512. Assessments to	
213.		513.	
214.		514.	
215.		515.	
216.		516.	
217.		517.	
218.		518.	
219.		519.	
220. Total Paid By/For Borrower		**520. Total Reduction Amount Due Seller**	
300. Cash At Settlement From/To Borrower		**600. Cash At Settlement To/From Seller**	
301. Gross Amount due from borrower (line 120)		601. Gross amount due to seller (line 420)	
302. Less amounts paid by/for borrower (line 220)	( )	602. Less reductions in amt. due seller (line 520)	( )
303. Cash ☐ From ☐ To Borrower		**603. Cash** ☐ To ☐ From Seller	

Section 5 of the Real Estate Settlement Procedures Act (RESPA) requires the following: • HUD must develop a Special Information Booklet to help persons borrowing money to finance the purchase of residential real estate to better understand the nature and costs of real estate settlement services; • Each lender must provide the booklet to all applicants from whom it receives or for whom it prepares a written application to borrow money to finance the purchase of residential real estate; • Lenders must prepare and distribute with the Booklet a Good Faith Estimate of the settlement costs that the borrower is likely to incur in connection with the settlement. These disclosures are manadatory.

Section 4(a) of RESPA mandates that HUD develop and prescribe this standard form to be used at the time of loan settlement to provide full disclosure of all charges imposed upon the borrower and seller. These are third party disclosures that are designed to provide the borrower with pertinent information during the settlement process in order to be a better shopper.

The Public Reporting Burden for this collection of information is estimated to average one hour per response, including the time for reviewing instructions, searching existing data sources, gathering and maintaining the data needed, and completing and reviewing the collection of information.

This agency may not collect this information, and you are not required to complete this form, unless it displays a currently valid OMB control number.

The information requested does not lend itself to confidentiality.

L. Settlement Charges

700. Total Sales/Broker's Commission based on price $	@ % =		Paid From Borrowers Funds at Settlement	Paid From Seller's Funds at Settlement
Division of Commission (line 700) as follows:				
701. $	to			
702. $	to			
703. Commission paid at Settlement				
704.				
800. Items Payable In Connection With Loan				
801. Loan Origination Fee	%			
802. Loan Discount	%			
803. Appraisal Fee	to			
804. Credit Report	to			
805. Lender's Inspection Fee				
806. Mortgage Insurance Application Fee to				
807. Assumption Fee				
808.				
809.				
810.				
811.				
900. Items Required By Lender To Be Paid In Advance				
901. Interest from to	@$	/day		
902. Mortgage Insurance Premium for		months to		
903. Hazard Insurance Premium for		years to		
904.		years to		
905.				
1000. Reserves Deposited With Lender				
1001. Hazard insurance	months@$	per month		
1002. Mortgage insurance	months@$	per month		
1003. City property taxes	months@$	per month		
1004. County property taxes	months@$	per month		
1005. Annual assessments	months@$	per month		
1006.	months@$	per month		
1007.	months@$	per month		
1008.	months@$	per month		
1100. Title Charges				
1101. Settlement or closing fee	to			
1102. Abstract or title search	to			
1103. Title examination	to			
1104. Title insurance binder	to			
1105. Document preparation	to			
1106. Notary fees	to			
1107. Attorney's fees	to			
(includes above items numbers:		)		
1108. Title insurance	to			
(includes above items numbers:		)		
1109. Lender's coverage	$			
1110. Owner's coverage	$			
1111.				
1112.				
1113.				
1200. Government Recording and Transfer Charges				
1201. Recording fees: Deed $	; Mortgage $	; Releases $		
1202. City/county tax/stamps: Deed $	; Mortgage $			
1203. State tax/stamps: Deed $	; Mortgage $			
1204.				
1205.				
1300. Additional Settlement Charges				
1301. Survey to				
1302. Pest inspection to				
1303.				
1304.				
1305.				
1400. Total Settlement Charges (enter on lines 103, Section J and 502, Section K)				

form **HUD-1** (3/86)
ref Handbook 4305.2

CHAPTER SUMMARY

1. Most real estate transactions in California are closed through the escrow process. Money and documents are given to a neutral third party (the escrow agent), who holds them until they can be disbursed or delivered to the proper parties. The escrow agent may also handle a variety of other tasks, such as preparing documents for the parties to execute, ordering the preliminary title report, calculating and prorating closing costs, and preparing settlement statements.

2. Some of the most important aspects of the closing process are inspections and repairs, approval of the buyer's loan, the appraisal, and the purchase of hazard insurance and title insurance. As a real estate agent, you should have a checklist of what needs to be done and make sure everything is getting done in time for the closing date. It's part of your job to keep the sale on track.

3. You should be able to provide good estimates of the buyer's net cost and the seller's net proceeds. To do this, you need to be familiar with the standard closing costs and who typically pays them. You must also be able to prorate certain expenses, such as property taxes and hazard insurance.

4. The income tax regulations that apply to real estate closings include 1099 reporting rules, the Foreign Investment in Real Property Tax Act, and the California withholding law. In some transactions, FIRPTA or the state withholding law requires a portion of the seller's proceeds to be withheld and sent to the IRS or the Franchise Tax Board.

5. The Real Estate Settlement Procedures Act, another federal law, helps home buyers and sellers understand their closing costs. RESPA applies to most residential real estate transactions financed with institutional loans. Key requirements include the good faith estimate of closing costs and the Uniform Settlement Statement. The prohibition on kickbacks and referral fees is another important aspect of RESPA.

CHAPTER QUIZ

1. Although the terms are often used interchangeably, the technical difference between an escrow agent and a closing agent is that:

    a. an escrow agent is a licensed escrow company, while a closing agent is anyone providing escrow services

    b. a closing agent represents the interests of only one party to a transaction, while an escrow agent acts on behalf of both parties and is supposed be neutral

    c. the term "closing agent" refers specifically to a real estate broker who is providing escrow services

    d. None of the above; there is no difference

2. Which of the following is not one of the steps in the inspection process?

    a. Ordering the inspection

    b. Approval or disapproval of the inspection report

    c. Appraisal of the property

    d. Reinspection of any required repairs

3. When choosing a home inspector, a buyer should look for a firm that:

    a. has recently changed its name

    b. will offer to make the repairs recommended by the inspection

    c. belongs to the American Society of Home Inspectors

    d. does other business in addition to inspections

4. An HO-2 hazard insurance policy will cover damages resulting from:

    a. floods

    b. vehicles

    c. earthquakes

    d. encroachments

5. If the buyer is concerned about title problems that do not show up in the public record, he should:

   a. make sure there are no problems on the preliminary title report

   b. require the seller to purchase a standard coverage title insurance policy

   c. rely on the lender's title insurance policy

   d. get an extended coverage title insurance policy

6. On a settlement statement, the debits represent:

   a. the amount of financing in the transaction

   b. amounts that are owed to a party at closing

   c. costs that a party must pay at closing

   d. costs that the buyer must pay to the seller

7. The good faith deposit is:

   a. retained by the broker at closing as her commission

   b. applied toward the purchase price at closing

   c. a credit for the buyer on the settlement statement

   d. Both b and c

8. Prepaid interest refers to:

   a. the charge that the buyer must pay at closing to cover interest that will accrue on his loan during the last part of the month in which closing occurs

   b. the refund to the seller of reserves on deposit in an impound account with her lender

   c. the interest owed by the seller at closing after paying off the principal balance of her loan

   d. the fact that mortgage interest is usually paid in advance

9. The seller customarily pays the fee for recording the:

   a. deed of reconveyance

   b. deed from the seller to the buyer

   c. new mortgage or deed of trust

   d. None of the above

10. A loan secured by a deed of trust on the home the buyer is purchasing will be considered a "federally related" loan if the:

    a. person responsible for closing must report the sale to the IRS

    b. lender sells loans to Fannie Mae

    c. closing agent is required to withhold part of the proceeds under FIRPTA

    d. loan is used to purchase more than 25 acres

ANSWER KEY

1. a. The two terms are often used interchangeably, but technically the term "escrow agent" refers to a licensed escrow company. "Closing agent" refers to anyone providing escrow services—a lawyer, an escrow company, a broker, a lender, etc.

2. c. During the closing process, the initial inspection needs to be ordered, and then the inspection report must be approved or rejected by the buyer and/or the lender. If the seller makes repairs, a reinspection will be necessary. (The appraisal is a separate matter, not part of the inspection process.)

3. c. Membership in the American Society of Home Inspectors requires actual experience, passing a written examination, inspection reviews, and continuing education.

4. b. Floods and earthquakes are not covered by a typical hazard insurance policy, although supplemental coverage may be available. (Protection against encroachments would be provided by extended coverage title insurance, not by hazard insurance.)

5. d. Only an extended coverage title insurance policy will protect against problems that do not appear in the public record, such as an encroachment or adverse possession.

6. c. Debits are costs that a party must pay at closing, either to the other party or to a third party. The buyer's debits increase the amount of money the buyer will need to pay at closing. The seller's debits decrease the seller's net proceeds.

7. d. The good faith deposit is applied toward the purchase price at closing; it's part of the buyer's downpayment. Because the buyer has already paid the good faith deposit, it is treated as a credit for the buyer on his settlement statement.

8. a. The buyer's first payment on a new loan is not due the first day of the month immediately after closing, but the first day of the month after that. To cover the interest that accrues during the remainder of the month in which closing occurs, the buyer must pay prepaid or interim interest at closing.

9. a. The seller would pay the fee for recording a deed of reconveyance to release the property from the lien of a deed of trust. The recording fee for a document is generally paid by the party who benefits most from having that document recorded.

10. b. For RESPA purposes, a loan is federally related if the lender is federally regulated, has federally insured accounts, is assisted by the federal government, makes loans in connection with a federal program, sells loans to Fannie Mae, Ginnie Mae, or Freddie Mac, or makes real estate loans that total more than $1,000,000 per year.

CHAPTER 11

Property Management

Investing in Real Estate
- Investment characteristics
- Advantages of investing in real estate

Types of Managed Properties
- Residential rental property
- Other types of property

The Property Management Agreement

The Management Plan
- Preliminary study
- Management proposal

Management Functions
- Leasing and tenant relations
- Recordkeeping and manager/owner relations
- Maintenance

INTRODUCTION

You successfully helped the Herreras complete the purchase of a new home. Now, perhaps a few years later, they are doing well financially and are looking to buy an investment property. They liked working with you and ask you to represent them again this time. Not only do they want your help with the purchase, they also want to know if you can manage the property for them.

Many brokerage offices engage in property management to some degree, so all real estate agents should have an understanding of property management principles. In this chapter, we will discuss the basics of investing in real estate and the differences between types of managed properties. With a focus on income-producing residential property, we will also discuss how the management of real estate is organized, examining the property management agreement, the management plan, and the various functions of a property manager.

INVESTING IN REAL ESTATE

Real property has value for two basic reasons: it has value because it can be used, and it also has investment value. For property owners who do not live on or otherwise make use of their property, the investment aspect is the most important. Someone who owns property as an investment may not have time to devote a lot of attention to it, but still wants the investment to perform well. To ensure this, the owner usually hires someone else to manage the property. A person other than the owner who supervises the operation of income-producing property in exchange for a fee is called a **property manager**.

A property manager's job begins after someone has decided to invest in income-producing property, such as an apartment building, office building, or shopping center. The manager's primary function is to help the property owner achieve his or her investment goals. So before discussing the nuts and bolts of property management, let's take a brief look at general investment principles and at real estate as an investment. (A word of caution: Real estate agents should not act as investment counselors; they should always refer clients to an accountant, attorney, or investment specialist for investment advice.)

INVESTMENT CHARACTERISTICS

An investment is an asset that is expected to generate a **return** (a profit). A return on an investment can take various forms, including interest, dividends, or appreciation in value. An asset appreciates in value because of inflation, and may also appreciate because of a rising demand for the asset. For example, a parcel of prime vacant land appreciates in value as developable land becomes increasingly scarce.

An investor considers any investment in terms of three potential advantages: liquidity, safety, and total return on the investment (sometimes called **yield**). These three characteristics are interrelated. For example, liquidity and safety generally go together. On the other hand, in exchange for a high return an investor often sacrifices safety or liquidity, or both.

A **liquid asset** is one that can be converted into cash quickly. Money in a bank account is extremely liquid: to convert it into cash, the investor need only present the bank with a withdrawal slip or check. Mutual funds, stocks, and bonds are less liquid—they take a little longer (perhaps a week or so) to convert into cash. Other items, such as jewelry or coin collections, are not considered liquid at all, because an investor might have to wait months to exchange those assets for cash. Real estate is not considered a liquid asset.

Liquid investments do not offer very high returns. In general, the more liquid the asset, the lower the return. For example, the money in your wallet is the most liquid asset you can have, but it earns no return (interest) at all. Money in a savings account is a little less liquid—you have to go to the bank to withdraw it—but it offers a modest return in the form of a low rate of interest. By contrast, real estate can offer a very high rate of return, but it is not at all liquid.

The most liquid investments are generally considered the safest. With liquid assets, there is little risk of losing the asset itself. Money in the bank is both liquid and safe. Since your deposit is insured by the federal government (up to $100,000), there is little chance of losing your investment. Other, less liquid types of investments, such as gold or real estate, are not as safe. For example, if a property owner must sell when real estate values are low, the owner may lose a good portion of his original investment in the property.

Investments that are both safe and liquid offer the lowest returns. In a sense, investors "pay" for safety and liquidity with a low return. Savings accounts and certificates of deposit, both safe investments, offer relatively low returns. Mutual funds, gold, and real estate can generate high returns, but at a considerable risk to the investor. For some types of assets, such as real estate, the safety of the investment will increase if the investor can afford to keep the investment for a long period of time. For example, if an investor does not need to cash out her investment in real estate for ten or fifteen years, chances are good that she will reap a high return. This is true because the investor will have more control over when to sell the asset, and will be able to take full advantage of healthy market conditions.

> **Example:** Jeanne and Harold both invest $20,000 in rental homes in the same year. One year later, Jeanne desperately needs some cash and is forced to sell her rental home at a loss. She ends up with only $17,000 out of her original $20,000 investment.
>
> Harold, on the other hand, keeps his rental home for twelve years. He's in no hurry to sell his property, so he can wait for optimal market conditions. He sells at the peak of a real estate cycle, when property values are high. Because Harold could afford to choose when to sell the property, he walked away from the transaction with $45,000, a very healthy return on his original $20,000 investment.

Advantages of Investing in Real Estate

People invest in real estate for many reasons. The advantages of investing in real estate can be broken down into three general categories:

- appreciation,
- leverage, and
- cash flow.

Appreciation. Appreciation refers to an increase in a property's value due to changes in the economy or other outside factors. Although real estate values may fluctuate, over a period of several years real estate usually increases in value at a rate equal to or higher than the rate of inflation. Thus, real estate is considered an effective hedge against inflation. And when buildable property becomes scarce, the value of properties in prime locations increases even more rapidly.

Appreciation causes a property owner's equity to increase. **Equity** is the difference between the value of the property and the liens against it, so an increase in the property's value increases the owner's equity in the property. Also, each monthly mortgage payment increases the owner's equity, in proportion to the reduction of the principal amount of the loan. Equity adds to the investor's net worth and can also be used to secure an equity loan (a mortgage against the owner's equity in the property). So even though real estate is not considered a liquid asset, equity in real estate can be used to generate cash funds.

LEVERAGE. Real estate investors can take advantage of **leverage**, which is defined as using borrowed money to invest in an asset. If the asset appreciates, then the investor earns money on the money borrowed, as well as on the money he invested.

> **EXAMPLE:** Martin purchases a rental home for $315,000. He makes a $63,000 downpayment and borrows the rest of the purchase price. The rent generated by the property covers all the expenses of operating the property, plus the mortgage payment and income taxes. The property appreciates at 3% per year for five years. At the end of the five years, Martin sells the property for $365,000. He's made a $50,000 profit over five years on his $63,000 investment. This represents a 79% return over the five-year period. The property appreciated at 3% per year, but because he only invested 20% of the purchase price, Martin was able to generate a 79% return on his investment.

CASH FLOW. Many real estate investments not only appreciate in value, but also generate a positive cash flow. **Cash flow** is the difference between the income generated by the property and the expenses associated with it, including operating costs, mortgage payments, and taxes.

Cash flow may be either positive or negative, depending on whether or not the income from the investment exceeds the expenses. Some investors are primarily interested in generating a return through appreciation, and may be willing to accept a negative cash flow, but most real estate investors probably expect a positive cash flow. When a real estate investment generates a positive cash flow, the investor's monthly income increases. Thus, a real estate investment can increase both the investor's net worth (through appreciation of the property) and her income (through positive cash flow).

Another way in which a property can generate cash flow is through a **sale-leaseback** arrangement. In a sale-leaseback, the owner of a building (typically a commercial property) sells the building to an investor, but then leases the property back from the investor and continues to use it. The money generated by the sale can be used for expansion, acquiring inventory, or investment elsewhere. At the same time, the seller can deduct the rent paid to lease the property from his or her income taxes as a business expense.

TYPES OF MANAGED PROPERTIES

Now let's consider the different types of properties that a property manager may be called upon to manage. There are four basic types of income-producing properties:

1. residential rental property,
2. office buildings,
3. retail property, and
4. industrial property.

Each type of property has its own unique characteristics and management needs. Because each type of property demands a different kind of expertise, property managers often specialize in one particular type.

RESIDENTIAL RENTAL PROPERTY

A property owner may need the services of a property manager to operate anything from a single-family rental home to a large apartment complex. The homeowners' associations that run condominiums and co-ops also frequently rely on outside property managers.

Apartment buildings are the most common type of managed residential property. They typically offer six-month or one-year leases and have a relatively high turnover rate. As a result, residential property managers tend to spend a lot of time marketing and leasing out space.

The owner and property manager of a residential rental property must fulfill certain legal requirements that do not apply to other types of property. The operation of a residential rental property must comply with the landlord-tenant laws, which are designed to protect the rights of residential tenants. In addition, a number of cities in California have rent control ordinances. If the property is located in an area that has rent controls, the property manager must determine whether the property is subject to the provisions of the ordinance.

OTHER TYPES OF PROPERTY

Obviously, properties used for business and commercial purposes are very different from residential properties. Our discussion will focus primarily on managing residential properties, but most of the principles and practices we'll be describing apply to the management of any type of property. Let's look briefly at the special characteristics of different types of nonresidential property.

OFFICE BUILDINGS. Office buildings have very different maintenance requirements than residential buildings. For example, they have facilities that get continuous use, such as elevators and public restrooms, and thus need frequent cleaning and maintenance. Also, management is often responsible for cleaning the tenants' spaces as well as the common areas of the building.

Lease negotiations are also very different for office space than for residential units. Office leases are for longer periods of time, and rent payments are set up differently. Rent is typically based on a price per square foot (rather than per unit), and the lease often includes an escalation clause that provides for automatic increases in rent. Landlords commonly offer major concessions to attract tenants, such as extensive remodeling to suit the tenant's needs, or free rent for a limited period.

RETAIL PROPERTY. Leasing space to an appropriate tenant is a concern with any type of property, but it's especially important when managing a shopping center. The success of each tenant in a shopping center depends in part on the customers that each of the other tenants attracts, so it is vital to lease to strong tenants. Also, a portion of the rent is often based on the tenant's income, so the owner has a vested interest in the financial success of each tenant. The tenant mix must appeal to the widest variety of potential shoppers, while avoiding direct competition within the shopping center itself.

INDUSTRIAL PROPERTY. Many industrial properties are specialized and expensive to build. As a result, the lease for an industrial property is usually for a much longer term than for other properties. An industrial lease often lasts anywhere from 10 to 25 years.

Because of the long lease term, it's essential to find the right tenant for an industrial property. Many property managers rely on leasing agents to find industrial tenants. The leasing agent will study the physical aspects of the property, the nearby transportation services, and the supply of and demand for the prospective tenant's products, to find a suitable tenant.

Warehouse and storage space is one type of industrial property where long-term leases are not generally used. This is because the property is not specialized to a particular tenant's needs. Many different tenants can use the space, and tenants tend to come and go more frequently. So for the manager of a warehouse property, finding new tenants would be an important part of the job, much as it is with a residential rental property.

THE PROPERTY MANAGEMENT AGREEMENT

The first step in the management process is entering into a property management agreement. The property management agreement establishes the working relationship between the property manager and the property owner. In the same way that a listing agreement creates an agency relationship between a broker and a seller, the management agreement creates an agency relationship between the manager and the owner.

The property management agreement should always be in writing and signed by both the manager and the owner. The written document should contain all the terms and conditions of the agreement. In particular, it should explicitly state what powers and duties the manager has. This includes addressing which kinds of decisions the manager can freely make, and which issues must be referred to the owner. For example, suppose several units in an apartment building need new carpets. Could the manager replace the carpets without consulting the owner, or is this a decision the owner wants to make? Other areas where questions might arise include the manager's authority to execute leases, hire and fire employees, make major repairs, choose an insurance company and policy for the property, or embark on a major advertising campaign.

At a minimum, the following elements should be included in the property management agreement:

- the term of the agreement;
- the scope of the manager's authority;
- the manager's compensation;
- the type of property; and
- the description of the property (as always, it's best to use a legal description).

The property manager's compensation may be based on a percentage of gross income, a commission on new rentals, a fixed fee, or some combination of these. Sometimes different forms of compensation apply to different duties, such as renting units, handling evictions, preparing units for rental or sale, or managing units during periods of vacancy. The property management agreement should state exactly how the compensation will be determined.

A typical property management agreement goes into considerable detail, as you can see from the C.A.R. property management agreement form shown in Figure 11.1. Some of the additional provisions that should be included in a property management agreement include:

- whether the manager is authorized to collect and disburse funds, and if so, for what purposes;
- whether the manager is authorized to hold and disburse tenant security deposits;
- a description of other management responsibilities (duties should be stated, exceptions noted);
- any reports the manager must provide to the owner, specifying the frequency and level of detail of the reports; and
- how costs will be allocated (whether the manager or the owner will pay for specific expenses, such as office help, advertising, or telephone expenses).

The property manager must bear in mind that after the management agreement is signed, an agency relationship exists between the manager and the owner, and thus the manager is bound by all the duties and responsibilities of an agent (see Chapter 1).

FIG. 11.1 PROPERTY MANAGEMENT AGREEMENT

CALIFORNIA ASSOCIATION OF REALTORS®

PROPERTY MANAGEMENT AGREEMENT
(C.A.R. Form PMA, Revised 4/03)

_____ ("Owner"), and
_____ ("Broker"), agree as follows:

1. **APPOINTMENT OF BROKER:** Owner hereby appoints and grants Broker the exclusive right to rent, lease, operate and manage the property(ies) known as _____
   _____ and any additional property that may later be added to this Agreement ("Property"), upon the terms below, for the period beginning (date) _____ and ending (date) _____, at 11:59 PM.
   (If checked:) ☐ Either party may terminate this Property Management Agreement ("Agreement") on at least 30 days written notice _____ months after the original commencement date of this Agreement. After the exclusive term expires, this Agreement shall continue as a non-exclusive agreement that either party may terminate by giving at least 30 days written notice to the other.

2. **BROKER ACCEPTANCE:** Broker accepts the appointment and grant, and agrees to:
   A. Use due diligence in the performance of this Agreement.
   B. Furnish the services of its firm for the rental, leasing, operation and management of the Property.

3. **AUTHORITY AND POWERS:** Owner grants Broker the authority and power, at Owner's expense, to:
   A. ADVERTISING: Display FOR RENT/LEASE and similar signs on the Property and advertise the availability of the Property, or any part thereof, for rental or lease.
   B. RENTAL;LEASING: Initiate, sign, renew, modify or cancel rental agreements and leases for the Property, or any part thereof; collect and give receipts for rents, other fees, charges and security deposits. Any lease or rental agreement executed by Broker for Owner shall not exceed _____ year(s) or ☐ shall be month-to-month. Unless Owner authorizes a lower amount, rent shall be: ☐ at market rate; OR ☐ a minimum of $ _____ per _____;
   OR ☐ see attachment.
   C. TENANCY TERMINATION: Sign and serve in Owner's name notices that are required or appropriate; commence and prosecute actions to evict tenants; recover possession of the Property in Owner's name; recover rents and other sums due; and, when expedient, settle, compromise and release claims, actions and suits and/or reinstate tenancies.
   D. REPAIR;MAINTENANCE: Make, cause to be made, and/or supervise repairs, improvements, alterations and decorations to the Property; purchase, and pay bills for, services and supplies. Broker shall obtain prior approval of Owner for all expenditures over $ _____ for any one item. Prior approval shall not be required for monthly or recurring operating charges or, if in Broker's opinion, emergency expenditures over the maximum are needed to protect the Property or other property(ies) from damage, prevent injury to persons, avoid suspension of necessary services, avoid penalties or fines, or suspension of services to tenants required by a lease or rental agreement or by law, including, but not limited to, maintaining the Property in a condition fit for human habitation as required by Civil Code §§ 1941 and 1941.1 and Health and Safety Code §§ 17920.3 and 17920.10.
   E. REPORTS, NOTICES AND SIGNS: Comply with federal, state or local law requiring delivery of reports or notices and/or posting of signs or notices.
   F. CONTRACTS;SERVICES: Contract, hire, supervise and/or discharge firms and persons, including utilities, required for the operation and maintenance of the Property. Broker may perform any of Broker's duties through attorneys, agents, employees, or independent contractors and, except for persons working in Broker's firm, shall not be responsible for their acts, omissions, defaults, negligence and/or costs of same.
   G. EXPENSE PAYMENTS: Pay expenses and costs for the Property from Owner's funds held by Broker, unless otherwise directed by Owner. Expenses and costs may include, but are not limited to, property management compensation, fees and charges, expenses for goods and services, property taxes and other taxes, Owner's Association dues, assessments, loan payments and insurance premiums.
   H. SECURITY DEPOSITS: Receive security deposits from tenants, which deposits shall be ☐ given to Owner, or ☐ placed in Broker's trust account and, if held in Broker's trust account, pay from Owner's funds all interest on tenants' security deposits if required by local law or ordinance. Owner shall be responsible to tenants for return of security deposits and all interest due on security deposits held by Owner.
   I. TRUST FUNDS: Deposit all receipts collected for Owner, less any sums properly deducted or disbursed, in a financial institution whose deposits are insured by an agency of the United States government. The funds shall be held in a trust account separate from Broker's personal accounts. Broker shall not be liable in event of bankruptcy or failure of a financial institution.
   J. RESERVES: Maintain a reserve in Broker's trust account of $ _____.
   K. DISBURSEMENTS: Disburse Owner's funds held in Broker's trust account in the following order:
   (1) Compensation due Broker under paragraph 6.
   (2) All other operating expenses, costs and disbursements payable from Owner's funds held by Broker.
   (3) Reserves and security deposits held by Broker.
   (4) Balance to Owner.
   L. OWNER DISTRIBUTION: Remit funds, if any are available, monthly (or ☐ _____), to Owner.
   M. OWNER STATEMENTS: Render monthly (or ☐ _____), statements of receipts, expenses and charges for each Property.
   N. BROKER FUNDS: Broker shall not advance Broker's own funds in connection with the Property or this Agreement.
   O. ☐ (If checked) Owner authorizes the use of a keysafe/lockbox to allow entry into the Property and agrees to sign a keysafe/lockbox addendum (C.A.R. Form KLA).

PMA REVISED 4/03 (PAGE 1 OF 3) Print Date

Owner's Initials (_____)(_____)
Broker's Initials (_____)(_____)

Reviewed by _____ Date _____

EQUAL HOUSING OPPORTUNITY

PROPERTY MANAGEMENT AGREEMENT (PMA PAGE 1 OF 3)

Reprinted with permission, California Association of Realtors®. No endorsement implied.

Owner Name: _____ Date: _____

4. OWNER RESPONSIBILITIES: Owner shall:

   A. Provide all documentation, records and disclosures as required by law or required by Broker to manage and operate the Property, and immediately notify Broker if Owner becomes aware of any change in such documentation, records or disclosures, or any matter affecting the habitability of the Property.

   B. Indemnify, defend and hold harmless Broker, and all persons in Broker's firm, regardless of responsibility, from all costs, expenses, suits, liabilities, damages, attorney fees and claims of every type, including but not limited to those arising out of injury or death of any person, or damage to any real or personal property of any person, including Owner, for: **(i)** any repairs performed by Owner or by others hired directly by Owner; or **(ii)** those relating to the management, leasing, rental, security deposits, or operation of the Property by Broker, or any person in Broker's firm, or the performance or exercise of any of the duties, powers or authorities granted to Broker.

   C. Maintain the Property in a condition fit for human habitation as required by Civil Code §§ 1941 and 1941.1 and Health and Safety Code §§ 17920.3 and 17920.10 and other applicable law.

   D. Pay all interest on tenants' security deposits if required by local law or ordinance.

   E. Carry and pay for: **(i)** public and premises liability insurance in an amount of no less than $1,000,000; and **(ii)** property damage and worker's compensation insurance adequate to protect the interests of Owner and Broker. Broker shall be, and Owner authorizes Broker to be, named as an additional insured party on Owner's policies.

   F. Pay any late charges, penalties and/or interest imposed by lenders or other parties for failure to make payment to those parties, if the failure is due to insufficient funds in Broker's trust account available for such payment.

   G. Immediately replace any funds required if there are insufficient funds in Broker's trust account to cover Owner's responsibilities.

5. LEAD-BASED PAINT DISCLOSURE:

   A. ☐ The Property was constructed on or after January 1, 1978.

OR B. ☐ The Property was constructed prior to 1978.

     (1) Owner has no knowledge of lead-based paint or lead-based paint hazards in the housing except: _____
_____.

     (2) Owner has no reports or records pertaining to lead-based paint or lead-based paint hazards in the housing. except the following, which Owner shall provide to Broker: _____

6. COMPENSATION:

   A. Owner agrees to pay Broker fees in the amounts indicated below for:

     (1) Management: _____.

     (2) Renting or Leasing: _____.

     (3) Evictions: _____.

     (4) Preparing Property for rental or lease: _____.

     (5) Managing Property during extended periods of vacancy: _____.

     (6) An overhead and service fee added to the cost of all work performed by, or at the direction of, Broker: _____.

     (7) Other: _____

   B. This Agreement does not include providing on-site management services, property sales, refinancing, preparing Property for sale or refinancing, modernization, fire or major damage restoration, rehabilitation, obtaining income tax, accounting or legal advice, representation before public agencies, advising on proposed new construction, debt collection, counseling, attending Owner's Association meetings or _____
_____

   If Owner requests Broker to perform services not included in this Agreement, a fee shall be agreed upon before these services are performed.

   C. Broker may divide compensation, fees and charges due under this Agreement in any manner acceptable to Broker.

   D. Owner further agrees that:

     (1) Broker may receive and keep fees and charges from tenants for: **(i)** requesting an assignment of lease or sublease of the Property; **(ii)** processing credit applications; **(iii)** any returned checks and/or (iv) if checked) late payments; and **(iv)** any other services that are not in conflict with this Agreement.

     (2) Broker may perform any of Broker's duties, and obtain necessary products and services, through affiliated companies or organizations in which Broker may own an interest. Broker may receive fees, commissions and/or profits from these affiliated companies or organizations. Broker has an ownership interest in the following affiliated companies or organizations: _____

     Broker shall disclose to Owner any other such relationships as they occur. Broker shall not receive any fees, commissions or profits from unaffiliated companies or organizations in the performance of this Agreement, without prior disclosure to Owner.

     (3) Other: _____

7. AGENCY RELATIONSHIPS: Broker shall act, and Owner hereby consents to Broker acting, as dual agent for Owner and tenant(s) in any resulting transaction. If the Property includes residential property with one-to-four dwelling units and this Agreement permits a tenancy in excess of one year, Owner acknowledges receipt of the "Disclosure Regarding Agency Relationships" (C.A.R. Form AD). Owner understands that Broker may have or obtain property management agreements on other property, and that potential tenants may consider, make offers on, or lease through Broker, property the same as or similar to Owner's Property. Owner consents to Broker's representation of other owners' properties before, during and after the expiration of this Agreement.

8. NOTICES: Any written notice to Owner or Broker required under this Agreement shall be served by sending such notice by first class mail or other agreed-to delivery method to that party at the address below, or at any different address the parties may later designate for this purpose. Notice shall be deemed received three (3) calendar days after deposit into the United States mail OR ☐ _____

Owner's Initials (_____)(_____)
Broker's Initials (_____)(_____)

Reviewed by _____ Date _____

PMA REVISED 4/03 (PAGE 2 OF 3)

PROPERTY MANAGEMENT AGREEMENT (PMA PAGE 2 OF 3)

Owner Name: _____   Date: _____

9.   DISPUTE RESOLUTION

A.   MEDIATION: Owner and Broker agree to mediate any dispute or claim arising between them out of this Agreement, or any resulting transaction before resorting to arbitration or court action, subject to paragraph 9B(2) below. Paragraph 9B(2) below applies whether or not the arbitration provision is initialed. Mediation fees, if any, shall be divided equally among the parties involved. If, for any dispute or claim to which this paragraph applies, any party commences an action based on a dispute or claim to which this paragraph applies, without first attempting to resolve the matter through mediation, or refuses to mediate after a request has been made, then that party shall not be entitled to recover attorney fees, even if they would otherwise be available to that party in any such action. THIS MEDIATION PROVISION APPLIES WHETHER OR NOT THE ARBITRATION PROVISION IS INITIALED.

B.   ARBITRATION OF DISPUTES: (1) Owner and Broker agree that any dispute or claim in law or equity arising between them regarding the obligation to pay compensation under this agreement, which is not settled through mediation, shall be decided by neutral, binding arbitration, including and subject to paragraph 9B(2) below. The arbitrator shall be a retired judge or justice, or an attorney with at least 5 years of residential real estate law experience, unless the parties mutually agree to a different arbitrator, who shall render an award in accordance with substantive California Law. The parties shall have the right to discovery in accordance with Code of Civil Procedure § 1283.05. In all other respects, the arbitration shall be conducted in accordance with Title 9 of Part III of the California Code of Civil Procedure. Judgment upon the award of the arbitrator(s) may be entered in any court having jurisdiction. Interpretation of this agreement to arbitrate shall be governed by the Federal Arbitration Act.

(2) EXCLUSIONS FROM MEDIATION AND ARBITRATION: The following matters are excluded from mediation and arbitration hereunder: **(i)** a judicial or non-judicial foreclosure or other action or proceeding to enforce a deed of trust, mortgage, or installment land sale contract as defined in Civil Code § 2985; **(ii)** an unlawful detainer action; **(iii)** the filing or enforcement of a mechanic's lien; and **(iv)** any matter that is within the jurisdiction of a probate, small claims, or bankruptcy court. The filing of a court action to enable the recording of a notice of pending action, for order of attachment, receivership, injunction, or other provisional remedies, shall not constitute a waiver of the mediation and arbitration provisions.

"NOTICE: BY INITIALING IN THE SPACE BELOW YOU ARE AGREEING TO HAVE ANY DISPUTE ARISING OUT OF THE MATTERS INCLUDED IN THE 'ARBITRATION OF DISPUTES' PROVISION DECIDED BY NEUTRAL ARBITRATION AS PROVIDED BY CALIFORNIA LAW AND YOU ARE GIVING UP ANY RIGHTS YOU MIGHT POSSESS TO HAVE THE DISPUTE LITIGATED IN A COURT OR JURY TRIAL. BY INITIALING IN THE SPACE BELOW YOU ARE GIVING UP YOUR JUDICIAL RIGHTS TO DISCOVERY AND APPEAL, UNLESS THOSE RIGHTS ARE SPECIFICALLY INCLUDED IN THE 'ARBITRATION OF DISPUTES' PROVISION. IF YOU REFUSE TO SUBMIT TO ARBITRATION AFTER AGREEING TO THIS PROVISION, YOU MAY BE COMPELLED TO ARBITRATE UNDER THE AUTHORITY OF THE CALIFORNIA CODE OF CIVIL PROCEDURE. YOUR AGREEMENT TO THIS ARBITRATION PROVISION IS VOLUNTARY."

"WE HAVE READ AND UNDERSTAND THE FOREGOING AND AGREE TO SUBMIT DISPUTES ARISING OUT OF THE MATTERS INCLUDED IN THE 'ARBITRATION OF DISPUTES' PROVISION TO NEUTRAL ARBITRATION."

Owner's Initials _____ / _____   Broker's Initials _____ / _____

10.   EQUAL HOUSING OPPORTUNITY: The Property is offered in compliance with federal, state and local anti-discrimination laws.

11.   ATTORNEY FEES: In any action, proceeding or arbitration between Owner and Broker regarding the obligation to pay compensation under this Agreement, the prevailing Owner or Broker shall be entitled to reasonable attorney fees and costs from the non-prevailing Owner or Broker, except as provided in paragraph 9A.

12.   ADDITIONAL TERMS: ☐ Keysafe/Lockbox Addendum (C.A.R. Form KLA); ☐ Lead-Based Paint and Lead-Based Paint Hazards Disclosure (C.A.R. Form FLD)
_____

13.   TIME OF ESSENCE; ENTIRE CONTRACT; CHANGES: Time is of the essence. All understandings between the parties are incorporated in this Agreement. Its terms are intended by the parties as a final, complete and exclusive expression of their Agreement with respect to its subject matter, and may not be contradicted by evidence of any prior agreement or contemporaneous oral agreement. If any provision of this Agreement is held to be ineffective or invalid, the remaining provisions will nevertheless be given full force and effect. Neither this Agreement nor any provision in it may be extended, amended, modified, altered or changed except in writing. This Agreement and any supplement, addendum or modification, including any copy, may be signed in two or more counterparts, all of which shall constitute one and the same writing.

Owner warrants that Owner is the owner of the Property or has the authority to execute this contract. Owner acknowledges Owner has read, understands, accepts and has received a copy of the Agreement.

Owner _____
Owner _____ Date _____
              Print Name
Address _____ City _____ Social Security/Tax ID # (for tax reporting purposes
Telephone _____ Fax _____ State _____ Zip _____
                                                     E-mail _____

Owner _____
Owner _____ Date _____
              Print Name
Address _____ City _____ Social Security/Tax ID # (for tax reporting purposes
Telephone _____ Fax _____ State _____ Zip _____
                                                     E-mail _____

Real Estate Broker (Firm) _____ Date _____
By (Agent) _____
Address _____ City _____ State _____ Zip _____
Telephone _____ Fax _____ E-mail _____

THIS FORM HAS BEEN APPROVED BY THE CALIFORNIA ASSOCIATION OF REALTORS® (C.A.R.). NO REPRESENTATION IS MADE AS TO THE LEGAL VALIDITY OR ADEQUACY OF ANY PROVISION IN ANY SPECIFIC TRANSACTION. A REAL ESTATE BROKER IS THE PERSON QUALIFIED TO ADVISE ON REAL ESTATE TRANSACTIONS. IF YOU DESIRE LEGAL OR TAX ADVICE, CONSULT AN APPROPRIATE PROFESSIONAL.

This form is available for use by the entire real estate industry. It is not intended to identify the user as a REALTOR®. REALTOR® is a registered collective membership mark which may be used only by members of the NATIONAL ASSOCIATION OF REALTORS® who subscribe to its Code of Ethics.

SURE TRAC
The System for Success™

Published by the
California Association of REALTORS®

PMA REVISED 4/03 (PAGE 3 OF 3)

Reviewed by _____ Date _____

EQUAL HOUSING OPPORTUNITY

PROPERTY MANAGEMENT AGREEMENT   (PMA PAGE 3 OF 3)

THE MANAGEMENT PLAN

Once a property manager has entered into a management agreement, the actual business of managing begins. The first (and often most important) step in managing a property is drawing up a management plan. A management plan outlines the manager's strategy for financial management and physical upkeep, and focuses on achieving the owner's goals.

The management plan should implement the owner's goals in the most effective way possible. Since there are many different reasons for investing in income property, different property owners have different management goals. For instance, one property owner may simply want a steady, reliable stream of income. Another owner may want a tax shelter. Another may want to increase the property's value in order to reap a bigger profit in later years.

An owner's goals can also change over the period of ownership. The property manager should review the management plan periodically with the owner's goals in mind. If circumstances have changed, the management plan may need to be updated accordingly.

> **EXAMPLE:** When he's in his early forties, Greg decides to purchase a small apartment building. He has other sources of income, so he's most interested in the long-term investment and tax shelter aspects of real estate ownership. However, as the years pass, Greg's needs change. After he retires, he is suddenly more interested in receiving a steady cash flow from his property. The management plan for the property needs to be revised to reflect Greg's new goals.

THE PRELIMINARY STUDY

A management plan can be created only after a comprehensive study of all aspects of the property, including its location, physical characteristics, financial status, and policies of operation. This preliminary study includes a regional analysis, neighborhood analysis, property analysis, and market analysis.

REGIONAL ANALYSIS. Preparing a management plan begins with a study of the region (the city or metropolitan area) in which the property is located. The manager analyzes the general economic conditions, physical attributes, and population growth and distribution. Among the most significant considerations are trends in occupancy rates, market rental rates, employment levels, and (for residential property) family size and lifestyle.

OCCUPANCY RATES. According to the law of supply and demand, when the demand for an item is greater than the supply, the price or value of the item increases. And when the supply exceeds the demand, the price or value of the item decreases. This basic rule applies to rental properties just as it applies to other commodities.

From a property manager's point of view, the supply of rental units is the total number of units available for occupancy in the area where the managed property is located. The demand for rental units is the total number of potential tenants in that area who are able to pay the rent for those units. When demand exceeds supply, rental rates go up; when supply exceeds demand, rental rates go down.

There is a **technical oversupply** of property when there are more units than potential tenants. There is an **economic oversupply** when there are enough potential tenants, but they are unable to pay the current rent. Likewise, there may be a **technical shortage** (when there are more potential tenants than units) or an **economic shortage** (when there are more able-to-pay tenants than units).

To set rental rates for a managed property, a property manager must determine the occupancy trend for the area. If the trend is toward higher occupancy levels, the value of the units will increase because space is becoming more scarce. It is during these times that managers raise rents and reduce services. On the other hand, if there is a trend toward higher vacancy rates, a unit's value will decrease. In periods of high vacancy, tenants are likely to resist rent increases or make more demands for services or repairs when leases are renewed.

Occupancy levels are constantly fluctuating. The direction and speed in which they are moving will have a significant impact on the property manager's operating and marketing policies.

MARKET RENTAL RATES. In addition to evaluating occupancy trends, a property manager should keep track of market rental rates, which are the rates currently being charged for comparable rental units. The manager should set rental rates for the managed units at a level that will enable them to compete in the current market.

There are published reports that provide information about rental rates, such as the Department of Labor's statistics on rents paid for residential units. A property manager may also evaluate the properties that he or she is managing to determine the average monthly rent per unit or square foot. Statistics kept by an individual property manager can be combined with statistics kept by other managers in the area to get a broader perspective. Rental rates stated in classified ads can also be considered. These methods, while not precise, can give a manager a basic picture of market trends.

EMPLOYMENT LEVELS. The property manager should be aware of local employment trends, since employment levels affect how many potential tenants can afford to rent. A property manager should also know whether earnings are increasing or decreasing, and about savings rates in the community. If potential tenants cannot afford a particular rental unit or would rather save than spend, the property manager's product is not going to be sold.

FAMILY SIZE AND LIFESTYLE. Family size has a great deal to do with the value of particular residential units. If the average family size were three (two parents and one child), five-bedroom units would have little appeal and two-bedroom units would be very attractive. Thus, the two-bedroom units will command a higher price per square foot than the five-bedroom units. A property manager needs to be aware of the national trend toward smaller and even single-person households, and also any local trends in family size and lifestyle.

NEIGHBORHOOD ANALYSIS. After the regional analysis, the next step in the preliminary study is to analyze the specific neighborhood where the property is located. The definition of a neighborhood varies considerably from one place to another. In rural areas, a neighborhood may consist of many square miles. In an urban area, a neighborhood may be only a few blocks.

The qualities of the neighborhood have a significant bearing on the property's value and use. Important neighborhood characteristics include:

- the character of the buildings and amenities of the neighborhood;
- the level of maintenance (whether the buildings are well cared for, or in poor condition);

- a growth or decline in population; and
- the economic status of the residents.

A property manager should discover the reasons behind any neighborhood trends. Is the population density increasing because of further development or because single-family homes are changing into rooming houses? Development is a sign of economic prosperity; rooming house tenancies are not.

A neighborhood analysis helps a property manager factor location into the management plan. No matter how effectively a property is operated, its profitability will be strongly affected by its location. Once the characteristics of the location have been determined, realistic management goals can be set.

Property Analysis. Of course, to develop a management plan the manager must become very familiar with the physical characteristics of the property itself. She will inspect the property, noting its architectural design, physical condition, facilities, and general layout.

The following characteristics are particularly important:

- the number and size of the living units, or the number of rentable square feet;
- the appearance of the property and the rental spaces (age, architectural style, layout, view, fixtures, etc.);
- the physical condition of the building (roof, elevators, windows, etc.);
- the physical condition of the rental spaces (floor coverings, stairways, shades or blinds, walls, entryways);
- the amenities provided (laundry room, recreational facilities, etc.);
- the services provided (janitorial services, repair services, or security);
- the relationship of the land to the building (Is the land used efficiently? Is there adequate parking?);
- the current occupancy rate and tenant composition; and
- the size and efficiency of the current staff.

Market Analysis. The last step in the preliminary study for a management plan is the market analysis, which provides information on competing properties. To do a market analysis, the manager must first define the pertinent market. The major divisions of the real estate market are residential, commercial, retail, and industrial. Each of these can be broken down into subcategories. For instance, the residential market can be divided into single-family rental homes, duplexes, townhouses, walk-up apartments, small multistory apartments, and large apartment complexes.

Once the manager has identified the market that the managed property competes in, there are several characteristics that must be examined:

- the number of units available in the area;
- the average age and character of the buildings in which the units are located;
- the quality of the average unit in the market (size, condition, layout, facilities, etc.);
- the number of potential tenants in the area;
- the current price for the average unit; and
- the occupancy rate for the average unit.

The property manager compares the managed property to comparable properties in the neighborhood. In this way, the manager can evaluate what the property has to offer and what its disadvantages are. Armed with this information, the manager can establish an effective management strategy.

THE MANAGEMENT PROPOSAL

After completing the preliminary study, the property manager develops a management proposal and submits it to the property owner for approval. The manager's proposal will include a rental schedule, income and expense projections, a schedule of day-to-day operations, and perhaps suggestions for physical changes to the property itself.

RENTAL SCHEDULE. A rental schedule is a list of all the rental rates assigned to the different types of units. For example, an apartment building may consist of studio apartments, one-bedroom apartments, and two-bedroom apartments. Some apartments may have views, others may not. A rental schedule lists the various types of units and their rental rates.

Rental schedules are based on all the data collected during the regional, neighborhood, property, and market analyses. This information helps the manager determine the maximum rent that can be charged while maintaining the desired occupancy level. To set the rate for a particular type of unit, the manager can adjust the market rental rate for the average comparable unit up or down to reflect the differences between the comparable and the type of unit in question. In other words, the manager can apply competitive market analysis to rental rates (see Chapter 4). Because this method of setting rates depends on market conditions, the rental schedule should be reexamined periodically to see if it's current. Either an unusually high vacancy rate or an unusually low vacancy rate is an indication that the property's rental rates are out of line with the market. If the vacancy rate is too high, the rent may be too expensive; if the vacancy rate is unusually low, the rent may be below the norm.

BUDGETS. The property manager also sets up a budget of income and operating expenses. The manager lists the total value of all rentable space at the scheduled rental rates, then subtracts a figure for delinquent rental payments and vacancies (sometimes called a **bad debt and vacancy factor**). Any other income sources, such as laundry facilities, vending machines, or parking, should also be listed.

Next, the estimated operating expenses—both fixed expenses and variable expenses—are listed. **Fixed expenses** include such items as property taxes, insurance premiums, and employee salaries. **Variable expenses** include utilities, maintenance, and repairs. Finally, the manager deducts projected operating expenses from projected revenues to arrive at a cash flow figure.

DAY-TO-DAY OPERATIONS. In addition to long-range financial planning, the management proposal should include the manager's plans for the day-to-day operations of the property. This means that the manager has to decide how much (if any) staffing will be required and what the employment policies and procedures will be. The manager should also address what marketing and maintenance will be needed.

PHYSICAL ALTERATIONS. In some cases, the property manager's proposal will include recommendations for remodeling, rehabilitation, or other physical alterations to the property. For instance, after a thorough exami-

FIG. 11.2 PROPERTY MANAGEMENT DOCUMENTS

MANAGEMENT AGREEMENT

- CONTRACT BETWEEN PROPERTY MANAGER AND OWNER
- CREATES AN AGENCY RELATIONSHIP
- ESTABLISHES SCOPE OF MANAGER'S AUTHORITY

MANAGEMENT PLAN

- IMPLEMENTS OWNER'S GOALS
- BASED ON A COMPREHENSIVE STUDY OF THE PROPERTY AND MARKET CONDITIONS

MANAGEMENT PROPOSAL

- INCLUDES RENTAL SCHEDULE AND PLANS FOR DAY-TO-DAY OPERATIONS
- BUDGET PROJECTS FUTURE INCOME AND EXPENSES
- WHEN APPROVED BY OWNER, PROPOSAL BECOMES MANAGEMENT PLAN

nation of the property, the customer base, and the market, a manager might decide that the property would be worth much more to the owner if the building were altered to match current family size and lifestyle trends.

EXAMPLE: An older building is made up of three- and four-bedroom units in a neighborhood predominantly made up of one- and two-person households. If the apartments were converted to smaller units, the owner's profits would probably increase significantly.

OWNER'S APPROVAL. Once completed, the management proposal is presented to the property owner. If the owner has suggestions or concerns, the management proposal may need to be adjusted. When the proposal is approved, it becomes the management plan: the blueprint for managing the property.

MANAGEMENT FUNCTIONS

Property managers must possess the skills necessary to perform a variety of management functions. They must be able to market the property, negotiate leases, and handle tenant relations. They must be able to keep and understand detailed financial records and report to the property owner on a regular basis. They must also be able to arrange for the maintenance and repairs that will preserve the value of the property.

LEASING AND TENANT RELATIONS

The property manager's tasks involved in leasing and tenant relations include marketing the rental spaces, negotiating leases, addressing tenants' complaints, and collecting rents.

MARKETING. The more people who view a rental space, the more likely it is to be rented out. So property managers generally use advertising to bring potential tenants to their properties.

Different types of properties require different types and amounts of advertising. For some properties, advertising is necessary only when there is a vacancy to fill. Or if the property is in a prominent location and attractive to potential tenants, advertising may not be necessary at all. On the other hand, if the property is in an isolated location, continuous advertising may be required to generate enough interest to fill vacancies when they occur.

Successful advertising brings in a good number of potential tenants in the least amount of time for the lowest cost. Property managers often evaluate the effectiveness of their advertising in terms of the number of potential tenants for the advertising dollars spent. For example, based on experience, a property manager might have a general rule of thumb that the cost of advertising should not exceed $25 to $35 per prospect. Thus, newspaper advertising that costs $300 should bring in nine to twelve prospective tenants to view the property.

To reach the greatest number of potential tenants for the lowest possible cost, the property manager must be familiar with the various types of advertising and know which will be most effective for the property in question. The manager may consider using signs, newspaper ads, radio or television spots, direct mail, or some combination of these tools.

SIGNS. Small, tasteful signs are often used, whether there is a vacancy or not, to inform passersby of the name of the manager and how to acquire rental information. The use of signs is most successful for large apartment complexes, office buildings, and shopping centers.

NEWSPAPER ADVERTISING. Newspaper advertising includes classified ads and display ads. Classified ads (inexpensive line-type advertising that appears in the newspaper's classified ads section) are the most popular way to advertise residential rental space. Display ads are larger and more expensive than classified ads. A display ad often includes a photograph of the property, and it may appear in any section of the newspaper. Display advertising is generally an effective way to advertise space in a new office building, industrial park, or shopping center.

RADIO AND TELEVISION. Property managers occasionally use radio and television ads for large commercial and residential properties. Although broadcast advertising reaches a large audience, there usually aren't many potential tenants in the audience. Since broadcast advertising (especially television advertising) is quite expensive, it generally isn't cost-effective for most rental properties.

DIRECT MAIL. To be effective, direct mail advertising must be received by potential tenants, not just the general public. So a property manager who wants to use direct mail must compile or purchase a mailing list. With a good mailing list and a brochure designed to appeal to prospective tenants, direct mail can be an effective means of advertising. Also, the same brochure can be handed out to those who visit the property.

LEASING. A prospect sees an advertisement and comes to look at the available rental space. Now it is the property manager's job to convince the prospect that the rental space is desirable. They will usually tour the property together, and during the tour the manager will emphasize all of the property's positive qualities and amenities. He will point out traffic patterns and access to public transportation, the characteristics of the other tenants, the exterior and interior condition of the property, and its overall maintenance. If it's commercial property, the manager and the prospect may discuss how the space could be altered to suit the prospect's requirements.

After the tour, if the prospect is still interested in the property, it's the property manager's responsibility to make sure that the prospect is a suitable tenant. Naturally, financial stability is a key consideration, but the manager must also look at other factors. The manager should consider whether the prospect is likely to be a responsible and cooperative tenant. For certain types of property, the tenant must be appropriate for the property. In the case of a shopping center, for example, the manager must make sure that the prospect's business complements that of the other retail tenants.

Ultimately, whether to accept a particular tenant is up to the property manager's judgment. However, the manager must be very careful to avoid violating antidiscrimination laws (see Chapter 3). If the manager decides in favor of the prospect, the next step is to execute a rental agreement or lease.

SIGNING A LEASE. A lease is a contract between the landlord (the property owner) and the tenant, allowing the tenant to occupy and use the property. In exchange, the tenant pays rent to the landlord. For the protection of both parties, a lease should always be put into writing and signed by the landlord and the tenant. A lease for a fixed term must be in writing to be enforceable. The property manager may sign the lease as the landlord's agent, if the manager is authorized to execute leases.

The written lease should include the names of the parties, a description of the property, the amount of the rent, and the duration of the tenancy. The lease should also clearly spell out the responsibilities of the parties and any restrictions imposed on the tenant. These additional terms could cover issues such as utilities or maintenance that will be the tenant's responsibility, restrictions on alterations to the property, and whether the tenant is allowed to sublease the property or assign the lease to another party.

SECURITY DEPOSITS. Both commercial and residential tenants are typically required to provide a security deposit at the beginning of the lease term. The security deposit gives the property owner some protection if the tenant damages the property or defaults on rent payments.

The lease agreement should include the amount of the security deposit and clearly state the conditions under which the deposit will be returned to the tenant. California law limits the amount of residential security deposits to no more than two months' rent for an unfurnished property, and no more than three months' rent for a furnished property. When a tenant moves out, the landlord must provide the tenant with an itemized list of deposit deductions within three weeks, and refund any balance of the deposit that remains.

USE OF PREMISES. Unless specific limitations are stated in the lease, a tenant may use the property for any legal purpose. However, many leases place additional restrictions on the tenant's use of the property. A lease for retail space in a shopping center would typically restrict the tenant to a specific kind of business, to maintain the desired mix of stores and prevent harm to the business of other tenants.

LEASE RENEWAL. Unless the tenant has caused problems, in most cases a property manager would much rather renew an existing lease than find a new tenant. Renewal avoids a vacancy between the time one tenant moves out and another moves in. A building has greater stability with long-term tenants, and it is usually easier and less expensive to satisfy the requirements of an existing tenant than to improve the space for a new tenant.

A property manager should be aware of which tenants are nearing the end of their lease terms and notify them that their leases are about to expire. Then the manager should follow up on the notices, by phone or in person, to inquire whether the tenant wants to renew. If the tenant is going to renew the lease, the terms of the new lease must be negotiated.

Some leases contain an **automatic renewal clause**, which provides that the lease will be automatically renewed on the same terms unless one party notifies the other of his or her intent to terminate the lease.

TENANT COMPLAINTS. Of course, keeping tenants happy is an important part of the property manager's job. Making sure that the property is kept clean and in good repair is essential, and so is responding promptly and professionally to requests and complaints.

RENT COLLECTION. Rental property cannot be profitable unless the rents are collected when due. Careful selection of tenants in the first place is one of the most effective ways of avoiding delinquent rents. A high occupancy rate doesn't benefit the property owner unless the tenants meet their financial obligations.

The manager of a residential property should check every rental applicant's references and employment information, and contact the applicant's previous landlord. Credit checks are also helpful in determining whether a prospective tenant is likely to meet financial obligations in a timely manner. For a commercial lease, the prospective tenant is usually required to provide extensive financial information.

The amount of the rent, the time and place of rent payment, and any penalties imposed for late payment should be clearly stated in the lease. The manager needs to follow a collection plan that includes adequate recordkeeping, immediate notification of late payments, and consistent enforcement. When all collection attempts fail, the manager must be prepared to take legal action to evict the tenant. The legal eviction process is called an **unlawful detainer action**.

RECORDKEEPING AND MANAGER/OWNER RELATIONS

A property manager must account to the owner for all money received and disbursed. It's up to the owner to decide how frequent and detailed operating reports should be. This often depends on how involved the owner wants to be in the management of the property. For example, an owner with extensive property holdings who is also engaged in another full-time occupation may not want to be bothered with detailed, time-consuming reports. But a retired person with only one or two income-producing properties may want to be very involved in their management.

STATEMENT OF OPERATIONS. In many cases, the property manager's report to the owner takes the form of a monthly statement of operations. A statement of operations typically includes the following sections: a summary of operations, the rent roll, a statement of disbursements, and a narrative report of operations.

The **summary of operations** is a brief description of the property's income and expenses that makes it easier for the owner to evaluate the property's monthly financial performance. The summary is supported by the accompanying information in the rest of the statement of operations.

The **rent roll** is a report on rent collection. Both occupied and vacant units are listed in the rent roll, as well as the total of rental income earned, both collected and uncollected. (The combined rental values of the leased and the vacant space should equal the total rental value of the building.) The rent roll breaks down rental figures into the previous balance, current rent, total amount received, and balance due.

The information in the rent roll is obtained from the individual ledger sheets kept on each tenant and rental space. A ledger sheet typically shows the tenant's name, unit, phone number, regular rent, other recurring charges, security deposit information, move-in date, lease term, payments made, and balances owed.

The **statement of disbursements** lists all of the expenses paid during the pertinent time period. A written order should be prepared for every purchase and payment so that an accurate account can be made of all expenditures, including the purpose of each one. Disbursements are usually classified according to type, to make analysis easier. For example, all maintenance expenses should be listed together, and so should all tax and insurance expenses, all administrative expenses, and so on.

In addition to the numerical accounts given to the owner, it is often helpful to include a **narrative report of operations** in the statement of operations. This is simply a letter explaining the information set forth in the other sections of the statement. The narrative report adds a personal touch, and it is especially important if the income was lower or the expenses were higher than expected. If there is a deviation from the normal cash flow, the owner will want a clear explanation. If the reason for a drop in cash flow is not explained, the owner may doubt the competence or integrity of the property manager.

KEEPING IN TOUCH. In addition to sending the owner reports and statements, the manager should contact the owner in person from time to time. A telephone call or an appointment to explain a particular proposal or problem or to ask a question is much more effective than a letter. A formal meeting is a good idea if the monthly report is especially unusual.

MAINTENANCE

In addition to leasing, tenant relations, recordkeeping, and reporting to the owner, a property manager is responsible for the supervision of property maintenance. There are four basic categories of maintenance activities:

1. **Preventive maintenance:** Work done to preserve the physical condition of the premises and prevent deterioration. (Cleaning the gutters is an example of preventive maintenance.) Good preventive maintenance reduces corrective maintenance costs.
2. **Corrective maintenance:** Actual repairs that keep equipment, utilities, and amenities functioning in a proper manner. (Fixing a leaking faucet is an example of corrective maintenance.)

3. **Housekeeping:** Cleaning the common areas and grounds on a regular basis to keep the property attractive (for example, vacuuming hallways and cleaning elevators).

4. **New construction:** This includes alterations made for the benefit of a tenant, as well as cosmetic changes designed to make the building more attractive (for example, redecorating the lobby).

When managing commercial or industrial property, a property manager is often required to alter the interior of the building to meet the needs of a new tenant. These alterations can range from a simple repainting job to completely redesigning or rebuilding the space. (If the property is new construction, the interior is often left incomplete so that it can be built to fit the needs of the individual tenants.) Property managers dealing with remodeling or new construction must be aware of the Americans with Disabilities Act, the federal law that requires public accommodations to be accessible to the disabled (see Chapter 3).

Property managers are not expected to know how to fix the building's plumbing or electrical wiring themselves. Most maintenance activities are handled by building maintenance employees or by outside maintenance services. However, a property manager must be able to recognize the maintenance needs of the property and see that they are fulfilled.

The manager should direct the activities of the maintenance staff or independent contractors with a schedule of inspection and maintenance. First, the manager should inventory the building's equipment and physical elements (plumbing, furnace, roof, walls, etc.). Then a schedule of regular inspections, cleaning, and repairs should be set. For instance, walls and roofs should be scheduled for periodic inspection, painting, and repairs. Elevators should be serviced on a regular basis.

It's also important for the property manager to keep accurate and up-to-date records on when the various elements were inspected, serviced, replaced, or repaired. These routine inspections and maintenance activities will help preserve the value of the building and prevent major repair expenses.

CHAPTER SUMMARY

1. An investment is an asset that is expected to generate a return for the investor. Three basic characteristics of an investment are the liquidity, safety, and yield. The advantages of real estate investment include appreciation, leverage, and cash flow.

2. There are four main types of income-producing properties: residential, office, retail, and industrial. Each type has unique characteristics and management needs. Property managers often specialize in one type of property.

3. A property manager must have a written management agreement with the property owner. The agreement should include all of the terms and conditions of the management arrangement, including compensation, the type of property, the manager's duties and authority, allocation of costs, and provisions for reporting to the owner.

4. Before preparing a management plan, the manager should conduct a regional analysis, a neighborhood analysis, a property analysis, and a market analysis. The information gathered during this preliminary study will help the manager set a rental schedule, prepare a budget, and plan the day-to-day operations.

5. The functions of a property manager include marketing the property, leasing, handling tenant complaints, rent collection, recordkeeping, preparing reports for the owner, and arranging for the maintenance of the property.

CHAPTER QUIZ

1. The main disadvantage of investing in real estate is:

   a. the use of leverage to increase returns

   b. lack of liquidity

   c. uniformly low returns

   d. a constantly increasing supply, which decreases values

2. The contract between a property manager and the owner of the property is called a:

   a. property management agreement

   b. management plan

   c. lease

   d. management proposal

3. The property manager's main purpose must be to fulfill:

   a. his or her career goals

   b. the owner's objectives

   c. the government's affordable housing goals

   d. his or her office's cash flow goals

4. If a regional analysis shows that the typical family size is four, with two parents and two children, which of the following apartment units would be the most marketable?

   a. Studio

   b. Five-bedroom

   c. Three-bedroom

   d. It is unlikely that one type of unit would be preferred over any another

5. The type of property that ordinarily demands the most marketing is:

   a. residential

   b. office

   c. retail

   d. industrial

6. By completing a market analysis, a property manager discovers that the average rental rate for comparable residential units is $1,650. For the subject property, the property manager should set a rental rate of approximately:

   a. $1,550 per unit, to undercut the competition

   b. $1,725 per unit, because tenants are not very well informed and will probably pay a higher-than-average price

   c. $1,650 per unit, to remain competitive

   d. None of the above; a fixed rental rate should not be set

7. The least cost-effective way to advertise a rental property is with:

   a. television

   b. direct mail

   c. classified advertising

   d. full-color brochures

8. Insurance premiums would be considered a:

   a. variable expense

   b. daily expense

   c. fixed expense

   d. pro rata expense

9. To see which tenants are behind in their rent, a property owner should examine the:

   a. rent schedule

   b. statement of disbursements

   c. narrative report of operations

   d. rent roll

10. The most effective way to reduce expensive repair bills is to:

   a. emphasize preventive maintenance

   b. put off repairs for as long as possible

   c. institute a policy of tenant-paid repairs

   d. find cheap repair companies

Answer Key

1. b. Because it takes some time to convert real property into cash, the lack of liquidity is the main disadvantage of investing in real estate.

2. a. A property management agreement should contain all the terms of the contract between the owner and the property manager. It creates an agency relationship between the manager and the owner. Entering into a property management agreement is the first step in the management process.

3. b. A property manager's primary responsibility is to work to achieve the property owner's objectives. The property manager should design a management plan that focuses on achieving the owner's goals as effectively as possible.

4. c. In this situation, a family of typical size would be more likely to rent a three-bedroom unit than either a studio or a five-bedroom apartment.

5. a. Because residential lease terms are relatively short, managing residential property tends to involve more marketing than managing other types of property.

6. c. Rental rates should not be much lower or much higher than the rates for competitive properties. The rental schedule should be reexamined periodically to make sure it is current.

7. a. Television is usually the most expensive form of advertising. Although it reaches a large audience, there aren't many potential tenants in the audience. Property managers rarely use television as a form of advertising.

8. c. Fixed expenses remain the same, regardless of rental income. Insurance premiums are a fixed expense.

9. d. The rent roll is a report on rent collection. It lists all units individually and breaks down rental figures in detail, including uncollected amounts.

10. a. Preventive maintenance preserves the physical integrity of the property and reduces the need for corrective maintenance.

GLOSSARY

The definitions given here explain how the listed terms are used in the real estate field. Some of the terms have additional meanings, which can be found in a standard dictionary.

ABSTRACT OF TITLE—*See:* Title, Abstract of.

ACCELERATION CLAUSE—A provision in a promissory note or security instrument allowing the lender to declare the entire debt due immediately if the borrower breaches one or more provisions of the loan agreement. Also referred to as a call provision.

ACCEPTANCE—1. Agreeing to the terms of an offer to enter into a contract, thereby creating a binding contract. 2. Taking delivery of a deed from the grantor.

ACCEPTANCE, QUALIFIED—*See:* Counteroffer.

ACCRUED ITEMS OF EXPENSE—Expenses that have been incurred but are not yet due or payable; in a settlement statement, the seller's accrued expenses are credited to the buyer.

ACQUISITION COST—The amount of money a buyer was required to expend in order to acquire title to a piece of property; in addition to the purchase price, this might include closing costs, legal fees, and other expenses.

ACRE—A measure of area for land; one acre is 43,560 square feet.

Adjustable-Rate Mortgage—*See:* Mortgage, Adjustable-Rate.

Administrator's Deed—*See:* Deed, Administrator's.

Ad Valorem—A Latin phrase that means "according to value," used to refer to taxes that are assessed on the value of property.

Affirm—1. To confirm or ratify. 2. To make a solemn declaration that is not under oath.

Agency—A relationship of trust created when one person (the principal) grants another (the agent) authority to represent the principal in dealings with third parties.

Agency, Apparent—When third parties are given the impression that someone who has not been authorized to represent another is that person's agent, or else given the impression that an agent has been authorized to perform acts which are in fact beyond the scope of his or her authority. Also called ostensible agency.

Agency, Dual—When an agent represents both parties to a transaction, as when a broker represents both the buyer and the seller.

Agency, Exclusive—*See:* Listing, Exclusive.

Agency, Ostensible—*See:* Agency, Apparent.

Agency Coupled with an Interest—When an agent has a claim against the property that is the subject of the agency, so that the principal cannot revoke the agent's authority.

Agent—A person authorized to represent another (the principal) in dealings with third parties.

Agent, Dual—*See:* Agency, Dual.

Agent, General—An agent authorized to handle all of the principal's affairs in one area or in specified areas.

Agent, Gratuitous—An agent who does not have a legal right to claim compensation for his or her services (such as a broker who does not have a written employment contract with the seller).

Agent, Special—An agent with limited authority to do a specific thing or conduct a specific transaction.

AGENT, UNIVERSAL—An agent authorized to do everything that can be lawfully delegated to a representative.

AGREEMENT—*See:* Contract.

ALIENATION—The transfer of ownership or an interest in property from one person to another, by any means.

ALIENATION, INVOLUNTARY—Transfer of an interest in property against the will of the owner, or without action by the owner, occurring through operation of law, natural processes, or adverse possession.

ALIENATION, VOLUNTARY—When an owner voluntarily transfers an interest to someone else.

ALIENATION CLAUSE—A provision in a security instrument that gives the lender the right to declare the entire loan balance due immediately if the borrower sells or otherwise transfers the security property. Also called a due-on-sale clause.

ALL-INCLUSIVE TRUST DEED—*See:* Mortgage, Wraparound.

ALTA—American Land Title Association, a nationwide organization of title insurance companies. An extended coverage title policy is sometimes referred to as an ALTA policy.

AMENITIES—Features of a property that contribute to the pleasure or convenience of owning it, such as a fireplace, a beautiful view, or its proximity to a good school.

AMORTIZATION, NEGATIVE—When unpaid interest on a loan is added to the principal balance, increasing the amount owed.

AMORTIZE—To gradually pay off a debt with installment payments that include both principal and interest. *See also:* Loan, Amortized.

ANNUAL PERCENTAGE RATE (APR)—All of the charges that the borrower will pay for the loan (including the interest, loan fee, discount points, and mortgage insurance costs), expressed as an annual percentage of the loan amount.

ANTICIPATION, PRINCIPLE OF—An appraisal principle which holds that value is created by the expectation of benefits to be received in the future.

ANTITRUST LAWS—Laws that prohibit any agreement that has the effect of restraining trade, including conspiracies.

APPORTIONMENT—A division of property (as among tenants in common when the property is sold or partitioned) or liability (as when responsibility for closing costs is allocated between the buyer and seller) into proportionate, but not necessarily equal, parts.

APPRAISAL—An estimate or opinion of the value of a piece of property as of a particular date. Also called valuation.

APPRAISER—One who estimates the value of property, especially an expert qualified to do so by training and experience.

APPRECIATION—An increase in value; the opposite of depreciation.

APPURTENANCES—Rights that go along with ownership of a particular piece of property, such as air rights or mineral rights; they are ordinarily transferred with the property, but may, in some cases, be sold separately.

APR—*See:* Annual Percentage Rate.

AREA—The size of a surface, usually in square units of measure, such as square feet or square miles. The area of a piece of land may also be stated in acres.

ARM—*See:* Mortgage, Adjustable-Rate.

ARM'S LENGTH TRANSACTION—1. A transaction in which both parties are informed of the property's merits and shortcomings, neither is acting under unusual pressure, and the property has been exposed on the open market for a reasonable length of time. 2. A transaction in which there is no pre-existing family or business relationship between the parties.

ARTIFICIAL PERSON—A legal entity such as a corporation, which the law treats as an individual with legal rights and responsibilities; as distinguished from a natural person, a human being. Sometimes called a legal person.

ASSESSMENT—The valuation of property for purposes of taxation.

ASSESSOR—An official who determines the value of property for taxation.

ASSET—Anything of value that a person owns.

ASSETS, LIQUID—Cash and other assets that can be readily liquidated (turned into cash), such as stock.

ASSIGN—To transfer rights (especially contract rights) or interests to another.

ASSIGNEE—One to whom rights or interests have been assigned.

ASSIGNMENT—1. A transfer of contract rights from one person to another. 2. In the case of a lease, when the original tenant transfers his or her entire leasehold estate to another. *Compare:* Sublease.

ASSIGNMENT OF CONTRACT AND DEED—The instrument used to substitute a new vendor for the original vendor in a land contract.

ASSIGNOR—One who has assigned his or her rights or interest to another.

ASSUMPTION—When a buyer takes on personal liability for paying off the seller's existing mortgage or deed of trust.

ASSUMPTION FEE—A fee paid to the lender, usually by the buyer, when a mortgage or deed of trust is assumed.

ATTORNEY IN FACT—Any person authorized to represent another by a power of attorney; not necessarily a lawyer (an attorney at law).

AUTHORITY, ACTUAL—Authority actually given to an agent by the principal, either expressly or by implication.

AUTHORITY, APPARENT—Authority to represent another that someone appears to have and that the principal is estopped from denying, although no actual authority has been granted.

AUTHORITY, IMPLIED—An agent's authority to do everything reasonably necessary to carry out the principal's express orders.

BAD DEBT/VACANCY FACTOR—A percentage deducted from a property's potential gross income to determine the effective gross income, estimating the income that will probably be lost because of vacancies and tenants who don't pay.

BALLOON PAYMENT—A payment on a loan (usually the final payment) that is significantly larger than the regular installment payments.

BANKRUPTCY—1. When the liabilities of an individual, corporation, or firm exceed the assets. 2. When a court declares an individual, corporation, or firm to be insolvent, so that the assets and debts will be administered under bankruptcy laws.

BENEFICIARY—1. One for whom a trust is created and on whose behalf the trustee administers the trust. 2. The lender in a deed of trust transaction. 3. One entitled to receive real or personal property under a will; a legatee or devisee.

BILL OF SALE—A document used to transfer title to personal property from one person to another.

BINDER—1. An instrument providing immediate insurance coverage until the regular policy is issued. 2. Any payment or preliminary written statement intended to make an agreement legally binding until a formal contract has been drawn up.

BLIND AD—An advertisement placed by a real estate licensee that does not include the broker's name.

BLOCKBUSTING—Attempting to induce owners to list or sell their homes by predicting that members of another race or ethnic group, or people suffering from some disability, will be moving into the neighborhood; this violates antidiscrimination laws. Also called panic selling.

BLUE SKY LAWS—Laws that regulate the promotion and sale of securities in order to protect the public from fraud.

BOARD OF DIRECTORS—The body responsible for governing a corporation on behalf of the shareholders, which oversees the corporate management.

BONA FIDE—In good faith; genuine; not fraudulent.

BREACH—Violation of an obligation, duty, or law; especially an unexcused failure to perform a contractual obligation.

BROKER—One who is licensed to represent members of the public in real estate transactions for compensation; may be an individual, a corporation, or a partnership.

BROKER, ASSOCIATE—A person who has qualified as a broker, but is affiliated with another broker.

BROKER, DESIGNATED—A corporate officer or general partner who is authorized to act as the broker for a licensed corporation or partnership.

BROKER, FEE—A real estate broker who allows another person to use his or her license to operate a brokerage, in violation of the license law.

BROKERAGE—A real estate broker's business.

BROKERAGE FEE—The commission or other compensation charged for a real estate broker's services.

BUSINESS OPPORTUNITY—A business that is for sale.

BUYDOWN—When discount points are paid to a lender to reduce (buy down) the interest rate charged to the borrower; especially when a seller pays discount points to help the buyer/borrower qualify for financing.

CALL PROVISION—*See:* Acceleration Clause.

CANCELLATION—Termination of a contract without undoing acts that have been already performed under the contract. *Compare:* Rescission.

CAPACITY—The legal ability or competency to perform some act, such as enter into a contract or execute a deed or will.

CAPITAL—Money (or other forms of wealth) available for use in the production of more money.

CAPITALIZATION—A method of appraising real property by converting the anticipated net income from the property into the present value. Also called the income approach to value.

CAPITALIZE—1. To provide with cash, or another form of capital. 2. To determine the present value of an asset using capitalization.

CAR—The California Association of Realtors®.

CARRYBACK LOAN—*See:* Loan, Purchase Money.

CASH FLOW—The residual income after deducting all operating expenses and debt service from gross income. Also called spendable income.

CERTIFICATE OF ELIGIBILITY—A document issued by the Department of Veterans Affairs as evidence of a veteran's eligibility for a VA-guaranteed loan.

CERTIFICATE OF REASONABLE VALUE—A document issued by the Department of Veterans Affairs, setting forth the current market value of a property, based on a VA-approved appraisal.

CERTIFICATE OF SALE—The document given to the purchaser at a mortgage foreclosure sale, instead of a deed; replaced with a sheriff's deed only after the redemption period expires.

CHAIN OF TITLE—*See:* Title, Chain of.

CHANGE, PRINCIPLE OF—An appraisal principle which holds that property values are in a state of flux, increasing and decreasing in response to social, economic, and governmental forces.

CIVIL LAW—The body of law concerned with the rights and liabilities of one individual in relation to another; includes contract law, tort law, and property law. *Compare:* Criminal Law.

CIVIL RIGHTS—Fundamental rights guaranteed to individuals by the law. The term is primarily used in reference to constitutional and statutory protections against discrimination or government interference.

CIVIL SUIT—A lawsuit in which one private party sues another private party (as opposed to a criminal suit, in which an individual is sued—prosecuted—by the government).

CLIENT—One who employs a broker, lawyer, or appraiser. A real estate broker's client can be a seller, a buyer, a landlord, or a tenant.

CLOSING—The final stage in a real estate transaction, when the seller receives the purchase money, the buyer receives the deed, and title is transferred. Also called settlement.

CLOSING COSTS—Expenses incurred in the transfer of real estate in addition to the purchase price; for example, the appraisal fee, title insurance premium, broker's commission, and excise tax.

CLOSING DATE—The date on which all the terms of a purchase agreement must be met, or the contract is terminated.

CLOSING STATEMENT—*See:* Settlement Statement.

CLOUD ON TITLE—A claim, encumbrance, or apparent defect that makes the title to a property unmarketable. *See:* Title, Marketable.

CODE OF ETHICS—A body of rules setting forth accepted standards of conduct, reflecting principles of fairness and morality; especially one that the members of an organization are expected to follow.

COLLATERAL—Anything of value used as security for a debt or obligation.

COLOR OF TITLE—*See:* Title, Color of.

COMMISSION—1. The compensation paid to a broker for services in connection with a real estate transaction (usually a percentage of the sales price). 2. A group of people organized for a particular purpose or function; usually a governmental body, such as the Real Estate Advisory Commission.

COMMITMENT—In real estate finance, a lender's promise to make a loan. A loan commitment may be "firm" or "conditional"; a conditional commitment is contingent on something, such as a satisfactory credit report on the borrower.

COMMUNITY PROPERTY—In California and other community property states, property owned jointly by a married couple, as distinguished from each spouse's separate property; generally, any property acquired through the labor or skill of either spouse during marriage.

CO-MORTGAGOR—Someone (usually a family member) who accepts responsibility for the repayment of a mortgage loan along with the primary borrower, to help the borrower qualify for the loan.

COMPETENT—1. Of sound mind, for the purposes of entering into a contract or executing an instrument. 2. Both of sound mind and having reached the age of majority.

COMPETITION, PRINCIPLE OF—An appraisal principle which holds that profits tend to encourage competition, and excess profits tend to result in ruinous competition.

COMPETITIVE MARKET ANALYSIS—A comparison of homes that are similar in location, style, and amenities to the subject property, in order to set a realistic listing price. Similar to the sales comparison approach to value.

COMPLIANCE INSPECTION—A building inspection to determine, for the benefit of a lender, whether building codes, specifications, or conditions established after a prior inspection have been met before a loan is made.

CONDITION—1. A provision in a contract that makes the parties' rights and obligations depend on the occurrence (or non-occurrence) of a particular event. Also called a contingency clause. 2. A provision in a deed that makes title depend on compliance with a particular restriction.

CONDITIONAL COMMITMENT—*See:* Commitment.

CONFORMING LOAN—*See:* Loan, Conforming.

CONFORMITY, PRINCIPLE OF—An appraisal principle which holds that the maximum value of property is realized when there is a reasonable degree of social and economic homogeneity in the neighborhood.

CONSIDERATION—Anything of value (such as money, goods, services, or a promise) given to induce another to enter into a contract. Sometimes called valuable consideration.

CONSPIRACY—An agreement or plan between two or more persons to perform an unlawful act.

CONSTRUCTION LIEN—*See:* Lien, Mechanic's.

CONTINGENCY CLAUSE—*See:* Condition.

CONTOUR—The shape or configuration of a surface. A contour map depicts the topography of a piece of land by means of lines (contour lines) that connect points of equal elevation.

CONTRACT—An agreement between two or more persons to do or not do a certain thing, for consideration.

CONTRACT, BILATERAL—A contract in which each party has made a binding promise to perform (as distinguished from a unilateral contract).

CONTRACT, BROKER AND SALESPERSON—An employment contract between a broker and an affiliated salesperson, outlining their mutual obligations.

CONTRACT, CONDITIONAL SALES—*See:* Contract, Land.

CONTRACT, EXECUTED—A contract in which both parties have completely performed their contractual obligations.

CONTRACT, EXECUTORY—A contract in which one or both parties have not yet completed performance of their obligations.

CONTRACT, EXPRESS—A contract that has been put into words, either spoken or written.

CONTRACT, IMPLIED—A contract that has not been put into words, but is implied by the actions of the parties.

CONTRACT, INSTALLMENT SALES—*See:* Contract, Land.

CONTRACT, LAND—A contract for the sale of real property in which the buyer (the vendee) pays in installments; the buyer takes possession of the property immediately, but the seller (the vendor) retains legal title until the full price has been paid. Also called a conditional sales contract, installment sales contract, real estate contract, or contract for deed.

CONTRACT, ORAL—A spoken agreement that has not been written down. Also called a parol contract.

CONTRACT, PAROL—*See:* Contract, Oral.

CONTRACT, REAL ESTATE—1. Any contract pertaining to real estate. 2. A land contract.

CONTRACT, SALES—*See:* Purchase Agreement.

CONTRACT, UNENFORCEABLE—An agreement that a court would refuse to enforce; for example, because its contents can't be proven or the statute of limitations has run out.

CONTRACT, UNILATERAL—A contract that is accepted by performance; the offeror has promised to perform his or her side of the bargain if the other party performs, but the other party has not promised to perform. *Compare:* Contract, Bilateral.

CONTRACT, VALID—A binding, legally enforceable contract.

CONTRACT, VOID—An agreement that is not an enforceable contract, because it lacks a required element (such as consideration) or is defective in some other respect.

CONTRACT, VOIDABLE—A contract that one of the parties can disaffirm without liability, because of lack of capacity or a negative factor such as fraud or duress.

CONTRACT FOR DEED—*See:* Contract, Land.

CONTRACT OF ADHESION—A contract that is one-sided and unfair to one of the parties; a "take it or leave it" contract, in which the offeror had much greater bargaining power than the offeree.

CONTRACT OF SALE—*See:* Purchase Agreement.

CONTRIBUTION, PRINCIPLE OF—An appraisal principle which holds that the value of real property is greatest when the improvements produce the highest return commensurate with their cost (the investment).

CONVENTIONAL FINANCING—*See:* Loan, Conventional.

CONVERSION—Misappropriating property or funds belonging to another; for example, converting trust funds to one's own use.

CONVEYANCE—The transfer of title to real property from one person to another by means of a written document, especially a deed.

COOPERATIVE SALE—A sale in which the buyer and the seller are brought together by salespersons working for different brokers.

CORPORATION—An association organized according to certain laws, in which individuals may purchase ownership shares; treated by the law as an artificial person, separate from the individual shareholders. *Compare:* Partnership.

CORRECTION DEED—*See*: Deed, Correction.

COST—The amount paid for anything in money, goods, or services.

COST, REPLACEMENT—In appraisal, the current cost of constructing a building with the same utility as the subject property using modern materials and construction methods.

COST, REPRODUCTION—In appraisal, the cost of constructing a replica (an exact duplicate) of the subject property, using the same materials and construction methods that were originally used, but at current prices.

COST APPROACH TO VALUE—One of the three main methods of appraisal, in which an estimate of the subject property's value is arrived at by estimating the cost of replacing (or reproducing) the improvements, then deducting the estimated accrued depreciation and adding the estimated market value of the land.

COUNTEROFFER—A response to a contract offer, changing some of the terms of the original offer; it operates as a rejection of the original offer (not as an acceptance). Also called qualified acceptance.

COVENANT—1. A contract. 2. A promise. 3. A guarantee (express or implied) in a document such as a deed or lease. 4. A restrictive covenant.

COVENANT, RESTRICTIVE—A promise to do or not do an act relating to real property, especially a promise that runs with the land; usually an owner's promise not to use the property in a specified manner.

CREDIT—A payment receivable (owed to you), as opposed to a debit, which is a payment due (owed by you).

CREDITOR—One who is owed a debt.

CREDITOR, SECURED—A creditor with a security interest in or a lien against specific property; if the debt is not repaid, the creditor can repossess the property or (in the case of real estate) foreclose on the property and collect the debt from the sale proceeds.

CRIMINAL LAW—The body of law under which the government can prosecute an individual for crimes, wrongs against society. *Compare:* Civil Law.

CRV—*See:* Certificate of Reasonable Value.

CUL-DE-SAC—A dead end street, especially one with a semicircular turnaround at the end.

CUSTOMER—From the point of view of a real estate agent, a prospective property buyer.

DAMAGES—In a civil lawsuit, an amount of money the defendant is ordered to pay the plaintiff.

DAMAGES, COMPENSATORY—Damages awarded to a plaintiff as compensation for injuries (personal injuries, property damage, or financial losses) caused by the defendant's act or failure to act.

DAMAGES, LIQUIDATED—A sum that the parties to a contract agree in advance (at the time the contract is made) will serve as full compensation in the event of a breach.

DAMAGES, PUNITIVE—In a civil lawsuit, an award added to compensatory damages, to punish the defendant for outrageous or malicious conduct and discourage others from similar conduct.

DEBIT—A charge or debt owed to another.

DEBTOR—One who owes money to another.

DEBT SERVICE—The amount of money required to make the periodic payments of principal and interest on an amortized debt, such as a mortgage.

DEED—An instrument which, when properly executed and delivered, conveys title to real property from the grantor to the grantee.

DEED, ADMINISTRATOR'S—A deed used by the administrator of an estate to convey property owned by the deceased person to the heirs.

DEED, CORRECTION—A deed used to correct minor mistakes in an earlier deed, such as misspelled names or typographical errors in the legal description. Also called a deed of confirmation or a reformation deed.

DEED, GIFT—A deed that is not supported by valuable consideration; often lists "love and affection" as consideration.

DEED, GRANT—A deed that uses the word "grant" in its words of conveyance and carries two implied warranties: (1) the grantor has not previously conveyed title to anyone else, and (2) the grantor has not caused any encumbrances to attach to the property other than those already disclosed to the grantee.

DEED, QUITCLAIM—A deed that conveys any interest in a property that the grantor has at the time the deed is executed, without warranties.

DEED, REFORMATION—*See:* Deed, Correction.

DEED, SHERIFF'S—A deed delivered, on court order, to the holder of a certificate of sale when the redemption period after a mortgage foreclosure has expired.

DEED, SPECIAL WARRANTY—A deed in which the grantor warrants title only against defects that may have arisen during his or her period of ownership; rarely used in California.

DEED, TAX—A deed given to a purchaser of property at a tax foreclosure sale.

DEED, TRUST—*See:* Deed of Trust.

DEED, TRUSTEE'S—A deed given to a purchaser of property at a trustee's sale.

DEED, WARRANTY—1. A deed in which the grantor warrants the title against defects that might have arisen before or during his or her period of ownership; rarely used in California. 2. Any type of deed that carries warranties.

DEED, WILD—A deed that won't be discovered in a standard title search, because of a break in the chain of title.

DEED EXECUTED UNDER COURT ORDER—A deed that is the result of a court action, such as judicial foreclosure or partition.

DEED IN LIEU OF FORECLOSURE—A deed given by a borrower to the lender, relinquishing ownership of the security property, to satisfy the debt and avoid foreclosure.

DEED OF CONFIRMATION—*See:* Deed, Correction.

DEED OF PARTITION—Deed used by co-owners (such as tenants in common or joint tenants) to divide up the co-owned property so that each can own a portion in severalty.

DEED OF RECONVEYANCE—The instrument used to release the security property from the lien created by a deed of trust when the debt has been repaid.

DEED OF TRUST—An instrument that creates a voluntary lien on real property to secure the repayment of a debt, and which includes a power of sale clause permitting nonjudicial foreclosure; the parties are the grantor or trustor (borrower), the beneficiary (the lender), and the trustee (a neutral third party).

DEED RELEASE PROVISION—*See:* Release Clause.

DEED RESTRICTIONS—Provisions in a deed that restrict use of the property, and which may be either covenants or conditions.

DEFAULT—Failure to fulfill an obligation, duty, or promise, as when a borrower fails to make payments, or a tenant fails to pay rent.

DEFENDANT—1. The person being sued in a civil lawsuit. 2. The accused person in a criminal lawsuit.

DEFERRED MAINTENANCE—Depreciation resulting from maintenance or repairs that were postponed, causing physical deterioration of the building.

DELIVERY—The legal transfer of a deed from the grantor to the grantee, which results in the transfer of title.

DEPARTMENT OF REAL ESTATE—The state agency in charge of administering the Real Estate Law in California.

DEPOSIT—Money offered as an indication of commitment or as a protection, and which may be refunded under certain circumstances, such as an earnest money deposit or a tenant's security deposit.

DEPOSIT RECEIPT—*See:* Purchase Agreement.

DEPRECIATION—1. A loss in value (caused by deferred maintenance, functional obsolescence, or external obsolescence). 2. For the purpose of income tax deductions, apportioning the cost of an asset over a period of time.

DISBURSEMENTS—Money paid out or expended.

DISCLAIMER—A denial of legal responsibility.

DISCOUNT—1. (verb) To sell a promissory note at less than its face value. 2. (noun) An amount withheld from the loan amount by the lender when the loan is originated; discount points.

DISCOUNT POINTS—A percentage of the principal amount of a loan, collected by the lender at the time a loan is originated, to give the lender an additional yield.

DISCRIMINATION—Treating people unequally because of their race, religion, sex, national origin, age, or some other characteristic.

DONATIVE INTENT—The intent to transfer title immediately and unconditionally; required for proper delivery of a deed.

DOWNPAYMENT—The part of the purchase price of property that the buyer is paying in cash; the difference between the purchase price and the financing.

DRAINAGE—A system to draw water off land, either artificially (e.g., with pipes) or naturally (e.g., with a slope).

DUAL AGENCY—*See:* Agency, Dual.

DUE-ON-SALE CLAUSE—*See:* Alienation Clause.

DURESS—Unlawful force or constraint used to compel someone to do something (such as sign a contract) against his or her will.

EARNEST MONEY—*See:* Good Faith Deposit.

EASEMENT—An irrevocable right to use some part of another person's real property for a particular purpose.

ELEMENTS OF COMPARISON—In the sales comparison approach to appraisal, considerations taken into account in selecting comparables and comparing comparables to the subject property; they include date of sale, location, physical characteristics, and terms of sale.

EMPLOYEE—Someone who works under the direction and control of another. *Compare:* Independent Contractor.

ENCUMBER—To place a lien or other encumbrance against the title to a property.

ENCUMBRANCE—A nonpossessory interest in real property; a right or interest held by someone other than the property owner, which may be a lien, an easement, a profit, or a restrictive covenant.

ENCUMBRANCE, FINANCIAL—A lien.

ENCUMBRANCE, NON-FINANCIAL—An easement, a profit, or a restrictive covenant.

EQUITABLE REMEDY—In a civil lawsuit, a judgment granted to the plaintiff that is something other than an award of money (damages); an injunction, rescission, and specific performance are examples.

EQUITY—1. An owner's unencumbered interest in his or her property; the difference between the value of the property and the liens against it.
2. A judge's power to soften or set aside strict legal rules, to bring about a fair and just result in a particular case.

ESCROW—An arrangement in which something of value (such as money or a deed) is held on behalf of the parties to a transaction by a disinterested third party (an escrow agent) until specified conditions have been fulfilled.

ESTATE—1. An interest in real property that is or may become possessory; either a freehold or a leasehold. 2. The property left by someone who has died.

ESTOPPEL—A legal doctrine that prevents a person from asserting rights or facts that are inconsistent with his or her earlier actions or statements.

ESTOPPEL CERTIFICATE—A document that prevents a person who signs it from later asserting facts different from those stated in the document. Also called an estoppel letter.

ETHICS—A system of accepted principles or standards of moral conduct. *See:* Code of Ethics.

EXCLUSIVE LISTING—*See:* Listing, Exclusive.

EXCULPATORY CLAUSE—A clause in a contract that relieves one party of liability for certain defaults or problems; such provisions are not always enforceable.

EXECUTE—1. To sign an instrument and take any other steps (such as acknowledgment) that may be necessary to its validity. 2. To perform or complete. *See:* Contract, Executed.

EXEMPTION—A provision holding that a law or rule does not apply to a particular person or group; for example, a person entitled to a tax exemption is not required to pay the tax.

EXPRESS—Stated in words, whether spoken or written. *Compare:* Implied.

EXTENDER CLAUSE—*See:* Safety Clause.

EXTERNAL OBSOLESCENCE—*See:* Obsolescence, External.

FAILURE OF PURPOSE—When the intended purpose of an agreement or arrangement can no longer be achieved; in most cases, this releases the parties from their obligations.

FANNIE MAE—Popular name for the Federal National Mortgage Association (FNMA).

FED—The Federal Reserve.

FEE—*See:* Fee Simple.

FEE, QUALIFIED—A fee simple estate that is subject to termination if a certain condition is not met or if a specified event occurs. It may be a fee simple determinable or a fee simple subject to condition subsequent. Also called a conditional fee or defeasible fee.

FEE BROKER—*See:* Broker, Fee.

FEE SIMPLE—The highest and most complete form of ownership, which is of potentially infinite duration. Also called a fee or a fee simple absolute.

FHA—Federal Housing Administration. *See also:* Loan, FHA.

FIDUCIARY RELATIONSHIP—A relationship of trust and confidence, where one party owes the other (or both parties owe each other) loyalty and a higher standard of good faith than is owed to third parties. For example, an agent is a fiduciary in relation to the principal; husband and wife are fiduciaries in relation to one another.

FINANCE CHARGE—Any charge a borrower is assessed, directly or indirectly, in connection with a loan. *See also:* Total Finance Charge.

FINANCIAL STATEMENT—A summary of facts showing the financial condition of an individual or a business, including a detailed list of assets and liabilities. Also called a balance sheet.

FINANCING STATEMENT—A brief instrument that is recorded to perfect and give constructive notice of a creditor's security interest in an article of personal property.

FINDER—Someone who introduces a real estate buyer and seller, but does not help them negotiate their contract. A finder is not the agent of either party and does not have to be licensed. Also called a middleman.

FIRM COMMITMENT—*See:* Commitment.

FIRST LIEN POSITION—The position held by a mortgage or deed of trust that has higher lien priority than any other mortgage or deed of trust against the property.

FIXED-RATE LOAN—*See:* Loan, Fixed-Rate.

FIXED TERM—A period of time that has a definite beginning and ending.

FORECLOSURE—When a lienholder causes property to be sold against the owner's wishes, so that the unpaid lien can be satisfied from the sale proceeds.

FORECLOSURE, JUDICIAL—1. The sale of property pursuant to court order to satisfy a lien. 2. A lawsuit filed by a lender to foreclose on the security property when the borrower has defaulted.

FORECLOSURE, NONJUDICIAL—Foreclosure by a trustee under the power of sale clause in a deed of trust.

FORFEITURE—Loss of a right or something else of value as a result of failure to perform an obligation or fulfill a condition.

FOR SALE BY OWNER—A property that is being sold by the owner without the help of a real estate agent. Also called a FSBO (often pronounced "fizz-bo").

FRANCHISE—A right or privilege granted by a government to conduct a certain business, or a right granted by a private business to use its trade name in conducting business.

FRAUD—An intentional or negligent misrepresentation or concealment of a material fact, which is relied upon by another, who is induced to enter a transaction and harmed as a result.

FRAUD, ACTUAL—Deceit or misrepresentation with the intention of cheating or defrauding another.

FRAUD, CONSTRUCTIVE—A breach of duty that misleads the person the duty was owed to, without an intention to deceive; for example, if a seller gives a buyer inaccurate information about the property without realizing that it is false, that may be constructive fraud.

FREDDIE MAC—Popular name for the Federal Home Loan Mortgage Corporation (FHLMC).

FREE AND CLEAR—Ownership of real property completely free of any liens.

FREEHOLD—A possessory interest in real property that has an indeterminable duration; it can be either a fee simple or an estate for life. Someone who has a freehold estate has title to the property (as opposed to someone with a leasehold estate, who is only a tenant).

FRONTAGE—The distance a property extends along a street or a body of water; the distance between the two side boundaries at the front of the lot.

FRONT FOOT—A measurement of property for sale or valuation, with each foot of frontage presumed to extend the entire depth of the lot.

FUNCTIONAL OBSOLESCENCE—*See*: Obsolescence, Functional.

GIFT DEED—*See*: Deed, Gift.

GIFT FUNDS—Money that a relative (or other third party) gives to a buyer who otherwise would not have enough cash to close the transaction.

GINNIE MAE—Popular name for the Government National Mortgage Association (GNMA).

GOOD FAITH DEPOSIT—A deposit that a prospective buyer gives the seller (usually when the buyer's offer is presented) as evidence of his or her good faith intent to complete the transaction. The deposit is applied to the purchase price if the sale closes.

GRANT—To transfer or convey an interest in real property by means of a written instrument.

GRANT DEED—*See*: Deed, Grant.

GRANTEE—One who receives a grant of real property.

GRANTING CLAUSE—Words in a deed that indicate the grantor's intent to transfer an interest in property.

GRANTOR—One who grants an interest in real property to another.

GROUP BOYCOTT—An agreement between two or more real estate brokers to exclude other brokers from equal participation in real estate activities.

GUARDIAN—A person appointed by a court to administer the affairs of a minor or an incompetent person.

HABENDUM CLAUSE—A clause included after the granting clause in many deeds; it begins "to have and to hold" and describes the type of estate the grantee will hold.

HEIR—Someone entitled to inherit another's property under the laws of intestate succession.

HEIRS AND ASSIGNS—A phrase used in legal documents to cover all successors to a person's interest in property; assigns are successors who acquire title in some manner other than inheritance, such as by deed.

HIGHEST AND BEST USE—The use which, at the time of appraisal, is most likely to produce the greatest net return from the property over a given period of time.

HOLDER IN DUE COURSE—A person who obtains a negotiable instrument for value, in good faith, without notice that it is overdue or notice of any defenses against it.

HUD—The U.S. Department of Housing and Urban Development.

HYPOTHECATE—To make property security for an obligation without giving up possession of it. *Compare:* Pledge.

IMPLIED—Not expressed in words, but understood from actions or circumstances. *Compare:* Express.

IMPOUND ACCOUNT—A bank account maintained by a lender for payment of property taxes and insurance premiums on the security property; the lender requires the borrower to make regular deposits, and then pays the expenses out of the account when they are due. Also called a reserve account or escrow account.

IMPROVEMENTS—Manmade additions to real property.

IMPROVEMENTS, MISPLACED—Improvements that do not fit the most profitable use of the site; they can be overimprovements or underimprovements.

INCOME, DISPOSABLE—Income remaining after income taxes have been paid.

INCOME, EFFECTIVE GROSS—A measure of a rental property's capacity to generate income; calculated by subtracting a bad debt/vacancy factor from the economic rent (potential gross income).

INCOME, GROSS—A property's total income before making any deductions (for bad debts, vacancies, operating expenses, etc.).

INCOME, NET—The income left over after subtracting the property's operating expenses (fixed expenses, maintenance expenses, and reserves for replacement) from the effective gross income. In the income approach to value, it is capitalized to estimate the subject property's value.

INCOME, POTENTIAL GROSS—A property's economic rent; the income it could earn if it were available for lease in the current market.

INCOME, RESIDUAL—The amount of income that an applicant for a VA loan has left over after taxes, recurring obligations, and the proposed housing expense have been deducted from his or her gross monthly income.

INCOME, SPENDABLE—The income that remains after deducting operating expenses, debt service, and income taxes from a property's gross income. Also called net spendable income or cash flow.

INCOME APPROACH TO VALUE—One of the three main methods of appraisal, in which an estimate of the subject property's value is based on the net income it produces; also called the capitalization method or investor's method of appraisal.

INCOME PROPERTY—Property that generates rent or other income for the owner, such as an apartment building. In the federal income tax code, it is referred to as property held for the production of income.

INCOME RATIO—A standard used in qualifying a buyer for a loan, to determine whether he or she has sufficient income; the buyer's debts and proposed housing expense should not exceed a specified percentage of his or her income.

INCOMPETENT—Not legally competent; not of sound mind.

INDEPENDENT CONTRACTOR—A person who contracts to do a job for another, but retains control over how he or she will carry out the task, rather than following detailed instructions. *Compare:* Employee.

INDEX—A published statistical report that indicates changes in the cost of money; used as the basis for interest rate adjustments in an ARM.

INDEX, TRACT—An index of recorded documents in which all documents that carry a particular legal description are grouped together.

INDEXES, GRANTOR/GRANTEE—Indexes of recorded documents maintained by the recorder, with each document listed in alphabetical order according to the last name of the grantor (in the grantor index) and the grantee (in the grantee index); the indexes list the recording number of each document, so that it can be located in the public record.

IN-HOUSE TRANSACTION—A sale in which the buyer and the seller are brought together by salespersons working for the same broker.

INJUNCTION—A court order prohibiting someone from performing an act, or commanding performance of an act.

INSTALLMENT SALE—Under the federal income tax code, a sale in which less than 100% of the sales price is received in the year the sale takes place.

INSTRUMENT—A legal document, usually one that transfers title (such as a deed), creates a lien (such as a mortgage), or establishes a right to payment (such as a promissory note or contract).

INSURANCE, HAZARD—Insurance against damage to real property caused by fire, flood, theft, or other mishap. Also called casualty insurance.

INSURANCE, HOMEOWNER'S—Insurance against damage to a homeowner's real property and personal property; a form of hazard insurance.

INSURANCE, MORTGAGE—Insurance that protects a lender against losses resulting from the borrower's default.

INSURANCE, MUTUAL MORTGAGE—The mortgage insurance provided by the FHA to lenders who make loans through FHA programs.

INSURANCE, PRIVATE MORTGAGE (PMI)—Insurance provided by private companies to conventional lenders for loans with loan-to-value ratios over 80%.

INSURANCE, TITLE—Insurance that protects against losses resulting from undiscovered title defects. An owner's policy protects the buyer, while a mortgagee's policy protects the lien position of the buyer's lender.

INSURANCE, TITLE, EXTENDED COVERAGE—Title insurance that covers problems that should be discovered by an inspection of the property (such as encroachments and adverse possession), in addition to the problems covered by standard coverage policies. An extended coverage policy is sometimes referred to as an ALTA (American Land Title Association) policy.

INSURANCE, TITLE, STANDARD COVERAGE—Title insurance that protects against latent title defects (such as forged deeds) and undiscovered recorded encumbrances, but does not protect against problems that would only be discovered by an inspection of the property. A standard coverage policy is sometimes referred to as a CLTA (California Land Title Association) policy.

INTEREST—1. A right or share in something (such as a piece of real estate). 2. A charge a borrower pays to a lender for the use of the lender's money.

INTEREST, COMPOUND—Interest computed on both the principal and the interest that has already accrued. *Compare:* Interest, Simple.

INTEREST, INTERIM—*See:* Interest, Prepaid.

INTEREST, PREPAID—Interest on a new loan that must be paid at the time of closing; covers the interest due for the first month of the loan term. Also called interim interest.

INTEREST, SIMPLE—Interest that is computed on the principal amount of the loan only, which is the type of interest charged in connection with real estate loans. *Compare:* Interest, Compound.

INTERPLEADER—A court action filed by someone who is holding funds that two or more people are claiming. The holder turns the funds over to the court; the court resolves the dispute and delivers the funds to the party who is entitled to them.

INVALID—Not legally binding or legally effective; not valid.

JOINT TENANCY—A form of co-ownership in which the co-owners have unity of time, title, interest, and possession and the right of survivorship. *Compare:* Tenancy in Common.

JUDGMENT—1. A court's binding determination of the rights and duties of the parties in a lawsuit. 2. A court order requiring one party to pay the other damages.

JUDGMENT, DEFICIENCY—A personal judgment entered against a borrower in favor of the lender if the proceeds from a foreclosure sale of the security property are not enough to pay off the debt.

JUDGMENT CREDITOR—A person who is owed money as a result of a judgment in a lawsuit.

JUDGMENT DEBTOR—A person who owes money as a result of a judgment in a lawsuit.

JUDGMENT LIEN—*See:* Lien, Judgment.

JUDICIAL FORECLOSURE—*See:* Foreclosure, Judicial.

LAND CONTRACT—*See:* Contract, Land.

LANDLORD—A landowner who has leased his or her property to another (a tenant). Also called a lessor.

LATENT DEFECT—A defect that is not visible or apparent. *Compare:* Patent Defect.

LAWFUL OBJECT—An objective or purpose of a contract that does not violate the law or a judicial determination of public policy.

LEASE—A conveyance of a leasehold estate from the fee owner to a tenant; a contract in which one party pays the other rent in exchange for the possession of real estate. Also called a rental agreement.

LEASEBACK—*See:* Sale-Leaseback.

LEGAL DESCRIPTION—A precise description of a parcel of real property that would enable a surveyor to locate its exact boundaries. It may be a lot and block description, a metes and bounds description, or a government survey description.

LENDER, INSTITUTIONAL—A bank, savings and loan, or similar organization that invests other people's funds in loans; as opposed to an individual or private lender, which invests its own funds.

LESSOR—A landlord.

LESSEE—A tenant.

LEVERAGE—The effective use of borrowed money to finance an investment such as real estate.

LEVY—To impose a tax.

LIABILITY—1. A debt or obligation. 2. Legal responsibility.

LIABILITY, JOINT AND SEVERAL—A form of liability in which two or more persons are responsible for a debt both individually and as a group.

LIABILITY, LIMITED—When a business investor is not personally liable for the debts of the business, as in the case of a limited partner or a corporate shareholder.

LIABILITY, VICARIOUS—A legal doctrine holding that a principal can be held liable for harm to third parties resulting from an agent's actions.

LIABLE—Legally responsible.

LICENSE—1. Official permission to do a particular thing that the law does not allow everyone to do. 2. Revocable, non-assignable permission to use another person's land for a particular purpose. *Compare:* Easement.

LIEN—A nonpossessory interest in real property, giving the lienholder the right to foreclose if the owner doesn't pay a debt owed to the lienholder; a financial encumbrance on the owner's title.

LIEN, ATTACHMENT—A lien intended to prevent transfer of the property pending the outcome of litigation.

LIEN, CONSTRUCTION—*See:* Lien, Mechanic's.

LIEN, EQUITABLE—A lien arising as a matter of fairness, rather than by agreement or by operation of law.

LIEN, GENERAL—A lien against all the property of a debtor, rather than a particular piece of his or her property. *Compare:* Lien, Specific.

LIEN, INVOLUNTARY—A lien that arises by operation of law, without the consent of the property owner. Also called a statutory lien.

LIEN, JUDGMENT—A general lien against a judgment debtor's property, which the judgment creditor creates by recording an abstract of judgment in the county where the property is located.

LIEN, MATERIALMAN'S—A construction lien in favor of someone who supplied materials for a project (as opposed to labor).

LIEN, MECHANIC'S—A lien on property in favor of someone who provided labor or materials to improve it. Also called a construction lien or materialman's lien.

LIEN, PROPERTY TAX—A specific lien on property to secure payment of property taxes.

LIEN, SPECIFIC—A lien that attaches only to a particular piece of property. *Compare:* Lien, General.

LIEN, STATUTORY—*See:* Lien, Involuntary.

LIEN, TAX—A lien on property to secure the payment of taxes.

LIEN, VOLUNTARY—A lien placed against property with the consent of the owner; a deed of trust or a mortgage.

LIENHOLDER, JUNIOR—A secured creditor whose lien is lower in priority than another's lien.

LIEN PRIORITY—The order in which liens are paid off out of the proceeds of a foreclosure sale.

LIEN THEORY—The theory holding that a mortgage or deed of trust does not involve a transfer of title to the lender, but merely creates a lien against the property in the lender's favor. *Compare:* Title Theory.

LIMITED LIABILITY—*See:* Liability, Limited.

LIQUIDATED DAMAGES—*See:* Damages, Liquidated.

LIQUIDITY—The ability to convert an asset into cash quickly.

LISTING—A written agency contract between a seller and a real estate broker, stipulating that the broker will be paid a commission for finding (or attempting to find) a buyer for the seller's property. Also called a listing agreement.

LISTING BROKER—The broker who takes a listing, and thus represents the seller.

LISTING, EXCLUSIVE—Either an exclusive agency listing or an exclusive right to sell listing.

LISTING, EXCLUSIVE AGENCY—A listing agreement that entitles the broker to a commission if anyone other than the seller finds a buyer for the property during the listing term.

LISTING, EXCLUSIVE RIGHT TO SELL—A listing agreement that entitles the broker to a commission if anyone—including the seller—finds a buyer for the property during the listing term.

LISTING, MULTIPLE—A listing (usually an exclusive right to sell listing) that includes a provision allowing the broker to submit the listing to his or her multiple listing service for dissemination to cooperating brokers.

LISTING, NET—A listing agreement in which the seller sets a net amount he or she is willing to accept for the property; if the actual selling price exceeds that amount, the broker is entitled to keep the excess as his or her commission.

LISTING, OPEN—A nonexclusive listing, given by a seller to as many brokers as he or she chooses. If the property is sold, a broker is only entitled to a commission if he or she was the procuring cause of the sale.

LOAN, AMORTIZED—A loan that requires regular installment payments of both principal and interest (as opposed to an interest-only loan). It is fully amortized if the installment payments will pay off the full amount of the principal and all of the interest by the end of the repayment period. It is partially amortized if the installment payments will cover only part of the principal, so that a balloon payment of the remaining principal balance is required at the end of the repayment period.

LOAN, CAL-VET—A loan made through the California Veterans Farm and Home Purchase Program.

LOAN, CALLED—A loan that has been accelerated by the lender. *See:* Acceleration Clause.

Loan, Carryback—*See:* Loan, Purchase Money.

Loan, Conforming—A loan made in accordance with the standardized underwriting criteria of the major secondary market agencies, Fannie Mae and Freddie Mac, and which therefore can be sold to those agencies.

Loan, Construction—A loan to finance the cost of constructing a building, usually providing that the loan funds will be advanced in installments as the work progresses. Also called an interim loan.

Loan, Conventional—An institutional loan that is not insured or guaranteed by a government agency.

Loan, FHA—A loan made by an institutional lender and insured by the Federal Housing Administration, so that the FHA will reimburse the lender for losses that result if the borrower defaults.

Loan, Fixed-rate—A loan on which the interest rate will remain the same throughout the entire loan term. *Compare:* Mortgage, Adjustable-rate.

Loan, G.I.—*See:* Loan, VA-Guaranteed.

Loan, Guaranteed—A loan in which a third party has agreed to reimburse the lender for losses that result if the borrower defaults.

Loan, Home Equity—A loan secured by the borrower's equity in the home he or she already owns. *Compare:* Loan, Purchase Money.

Loan, Interest-only—A loan that requires the borrower to pay only the interest during the loan term, with the principal due at the end of the term.

Loan, Interim—*See:* Loan, Construction.

Loan, Participation—A loan in which the lender receives some yield on the loan in addition to the interest, such as a percentage of the income generated by the property, or a share in the borrower's equity.

Loan, Permanent—*See:* Loan, Take-out.

Loan, Purchase Money—1. When a seller extends credit to a buyer to finance the purchase of the property, accepting a deed of trust or mortgage instead of cash. Sometimes called a carryback loan. 2. In a more general sense, any loan the borrower uses to buy the security property (as opposed to a loan secured by property the borrower already owns).

Loan, Rollover—A loan in which the interest rate is renegotiated at specified intervals.

LOAN, TAKE-OUT—Long-term financing used to replace a construction loan (an interim loan) when construction has been completed. Also called a permanent loan.

LOAN, VA-GUARANTEED—A home loan made by an institutional lender to an eligible veteran and guaranteed by the Department of Veterans Affairs. The VA will reimburse the lender for losses if the borrower defaults.

LOAN CORRESPONDENT—An intermediary who arranges loans of an investor's money to borrowers, and then services the loans.

LOAN FEE—A loan origination fee, an assumption fee, or discount points.

LOAN-TO-VALUE RATIO (LTV)—The relationship between the loan amount and either the sales price or the appraised value of the property (whichever is less), expressed as a percentage.

LOCAL MARKET—*See:* Primary Mortgage Market.

LOCK-IN CLAUSE—A clause in a promissory note or land contract that prohibits prepayment before a specified date, or prohibits it altogether.

LTV—*See:* Loan-to-Value Ratio.

M.A.I.—Member of the Appraiser's Institute. The initials identify a member of the American Institute of Real Estate Appraisers of the National Association of Realtors.®

MAJORITY, AGE OF—The age at which a person becomes legally competent; in California, 18 years old. *See:* Minor.

MAKER—The person who signs a promissory note, promising to repay a debt. *Compare:* Payee.

MARGIN—In an adjustable-rate mortgage, the difference between the index rate and the interest rate charged to the borrower.

MARKETABLE TITLE—*See:* Title, Marketable.

MARKET DATA APPROACH—*See:* Sales Comparison Approach.

MARKET PRICE—1. The current price generally being charged for something in the marketplace. 2. The price actually paid for a property. *Compare:* Value, Market.

MASTER/SERVANT RELATIONSHIP—A legal term for a standard employer/employee relationship.

MATERIAL FACT—An important fact; one that is likely to influence a decision.

MATURITY DATE—The date by which a loan is supposed to be paid off in full.

MEETING OF MINDS—*See:* Mutual Consent.

MIDDLEMAN—*See:* Finder.

MINIMUM PROPERTY REQUIREMENTS (MPRs)—A lender's requirements concerning the physical condition of a building, which must be met before a loan can be approved.

MINOR—A person who has not yet reached the age of majority; in California, a person under 18.

MIP—Mortgage insurance premium; especially a premium charged in connection with an FHA-insured loan.

MISREPRESENTATION—A false or misleading statement. *See:* Fraud.

MLS—*See:* Multiple Listing Service.

MONOPOLY—When a single entity or group has exclusive control over the production or sale of a product or service.

MORTGAGE—1. An instrument that creates a voluntary lien on real property to secure repayment of a debt, and which (unlike a deed of trust) ordinarily does not include a power of sale, so it can only be foreclosed judicially; the parties are the mortgagor (borrower) and mortgagee (lender). 2. The term is often used more generally, to refer to either a mortgage or a deed of trust—i.e., to any loan secured by real property. *Note: If you do not find the specific term you are looking for here under "Mortgage," check the entries under "Loan."*

MORTGAGE, ADJUSTABLE-RATE (ARM)—A loan in which the interest rate is periodically increased or decreased to reflect changes in the cost of money. *Compare:* Loan, Fixed-Rate.

MORTGAGE, BALLOON—A partially amortized mortgage loan that requires a large balloon payment at the end of the loan term.

MORTGAGE, BLANKET—A mortgage that is a lien against more than one parcel of property.

MORTGAGE, BUDGET—A loan in which the monthly payments include a share of the property taxes and insurance, in addition to principal and interest; the lender places the money for taxes and insurance in an impound account.

MORTGAGE, CLOSED—A loan that cannot be paid off early.

MORTGAGE, CLOSED-END—A loan that does not allow the borrower to increase the balance owed; the opposite of an open-end mortgage.

MORTGAGE, DIRECT REDUCTION—A loan that requires a fixed amount of principal to be paid in each payment; the total payment becomes steadily smaller, because the interest portion becomes smaller with each payment as the principal balance decreases.

MORTGAGE, FIRST—The mortgage on a property that has first lien position; the one with higher lien priority than any other mortgage against the property.

MORTGAGE, HARD MONEY—A mortgage given to a lender in exchange for cash, as opposed to one given in exchange for credit.

MORTGAGE, JUNIOR—A mortgage that has lower lien priority than another mortgage against the same property. Sometimes called a secondary mortgage.

MORTGAGE, LEVEL PAYMENT—An amortized loan with payments that are the same amount each month, although the portion of the payment that is applied to principal steadily increases and the portion of the payment applied to interest steadily decreases. *See:* Loan, Amortized.

MORTGAGE, OPEN-END—A loan that permits the borrower to reborrow the money he or she has repaid on the principal, usually up to the original loan amount, without executing a new loan agreement.

MORTGAGE, PACKAGE—A mortgage that is secured by certain items of personal property (such as appliances) in addition to the real property.

MORTGAGE, SATISFACTION OF—The document a mortgagee gives the mortgagor when the mortgage debt has been paid in full, acknowledging that the debt has been paid and the mortgage is no longer a lien against the property.

MORTGAGE, SECONDARY—*See:* Mortgage, Junior.

MORTGAGE, SENIOR—A mortgage that has higher lien priority than another mortgage against the same property; the opposite of a junior mortgage.

MORTGAGE, WRAPAROUND—A purchase money loan arrangement in which the seller uses part of the buyer's payments to make the payments on an existing loan (called the underlying loan); the buyer takes title subject to the underlying loan, but does not assume it. When the security instrument used for wraparound financing is a deed of trust instead of a mortgage, it may be referred to as an all-inclusive trust deed.

MORTGAGE BANKER—An intermediary who originates and services real estate loans on behalf of investors.

MORTGAGE BROKER—An intermediary who brings real estate lenders and borrowers together and negotiates loan agreements between them.

MORTGAGE COMPANY—A type of real estate lender that originates and services loans on behalf of large investors (acting as a mortgage banker) or for resale on the secondary mortgage market.

MORTGAGE LOAN—Any loan secured by real property, whether the actual security instrument used is a mortgage or a deed of trust.

MORTGAGEE—A lender who accepts a mortgage as security for repayment of the loan.

MORTGAGING CLAUSE—A clause in a mortgage that describes the security interest given to the mortgagee.

MORTGAGOR—A property owner (usually a borrower) who gives a mortgage to another (usually a lender) as security for payment of an obligation.

MULTIPLE LISTING SERVICE (MLS)—An organization of brokers who share their exclusive listings.

MUTUAL CONSENT—When all parties freely agree to the terms of a contract, without fraud, undue influence, duress, menace, or mistake. Mutual consent is achieved through offer and acceptance; it is sometimes referred to as a "meeting of the minds."

NAR—National Association of Realtors.®

NARRATIVE REPORT—A thorough appraisal report in which the appraiser summarizes the data and the appraisal methods used, to convince the reader of the soundness of the estimate; a more comprehensive presentation than a form report or an opinion letter.

NATIONAL MARKET—*See:* Secondary Mortgage Market.

NEGLIGENCE—Conduct that falls below the standard of care that a reasonable person would exercise under the circumstances; carelessness or recklessness.

NEGOTIABLE INSTRUMENT—An instrument containing an unconditional promise to pay a certain sum of money, to order or to bearer, on demand or at a particular time. It can be a check, promissory note, bond, draft, or stock.

NET INCOME—*See:* Income, Net.

NET LISTING—*See:* Listing, Net.

NET WORTH—An individual's personal financial assets, minus his or her personal liabilities.

NOMINAL INTEREST RATE—The interest rate stated in a promissory note. Also called the note rate or coupon rate. *Compare:* Annual Percentage Rate.

NONCONFORMING LOAN—*See:* Loan, Conforming.

NOTARIZE—To have a document certified by a notary public.

NOTARY PUBLIC—Someone who is officially authorized to witness and certify the acknowledgment made by someone signing a legal document.

NOTE—*See:* Note, Promissory.

NOTE, DEMAND—A promissory note that is due whenever the holder of the note demands payment.

NOTE, INSTALLMENT—A promissory note that calls for regular payments of principal and interest until the debt is fully paid.

NOTE, JOINT—A promissory note signed by two or more persons with equal liability for payment.

NOTE, PROMISSORY—A written promise to repay a debt; it may or may not be a negotiable instrument.

NOTE, STRAIGHT—A promissory note that calls for regular payments of interest only, so that the entire principal amount is due in one lump sum at the end of the loan term.

NOTICE, ACTUAL—Actual knowledge of a fact, as opposed to knowledge imputed by law (constructive notice).

NOTICE, CONSTRUCTIVE—Knowledge of a fact imputed to a person by law. A person is held to have constructive notice of something when he or she should have known it (because he or she could have learned it through reasonable diligence or an inspection of the public record), even if he or she did not actually know it.

NOTICE OF DEFAULT—A notice sent by a secured creditor to the debtor, informing the debtor that he or she has breached the loan agreement.

NOTICE OF SALE—A notice stating that foreclosure proceedings have been commenced against a property.

NOVATION—1. When one party to a contract withdraws and a new party is substituted, relieving the withdrawing party of liability. 2. The substitution of a new obligation for an old one.

OBSOLESCENCE—Any loss in value (depreciation) due to reduced desirability and usefulness.

OBSOLESCENCE, EXTERNAL—Loss in value resulting from factors outside the property itself, such as proximity to an airport. Also called economic obsolescence or external inadequacy.

OBSOLESCENCE, FUNCTIONAL—Loss in value due to inadequate or outmoded equipment, or as a result of poor or outmoded design.

OFFER—When one person (the offeror) proposes a contract to another (the offeree); if the offeree accepts the offer, a binding contract is formed.

OFFER, ILLUSORY—An offer that is not a valid contract offer, because it requires something more than simple acceptance in order to create a contract.

OFFER, TENDER—*See:* Tender.

OFFEREE—One to whom a contract offer is made.

OFFEROR—One who makes a contract offer.

OFFICER—In a corporation, an executive authorized by the board of directors to manage the business of the corporation.

OFF-SITE IMPROVEMENTS—Improvements that add to the usefulness of a site but are not located directly on it, such as curbs, street lights, and sidewalks.

ONE-PARTY LISTING—A listing agreement that is only effective in regard to one particular buyer.

OPEN HOUSE—Showing a listed home to the public for a specified period of time.

OPTION—A contract giving one party the right to do something, without obligating him or her to do it.

OPTIONEE—The person to whom an option is given.

OPTIONOR—The person who gives an option.

OPTION TO PURCHASE—An option giving the optionee the right to buy property owned by the optionor at an agreed price during a specified period.

ORDINANCE—A law passed by a local legislative body, such as a city or county council. *Compare:* Statute.

ORIENTATION—The placement of a house on its lot, with regard to its exposure to the sun and wind, privacy from the street, and protection from outside noise.

ORIGINATION FEE—A fee a lender charges a borrower upon making a new loan, intended to cover the administrative costs of making the loan. Also called a loan fee or points.

"OR MORE"—A provision in a promissory note that allows the borrower to prepay the debt.

OWNERSHIP—Title to property, dominion over property; the rights of possession and control.

OWNERSHIP, CONCURRENT—When two or more individuals share ownership of one piece of property, each owning an undivided interest in the property (as in a tenancy in common or joint tenancy, or with community property). Also called co-ownership or co-tenancy.

OWNERSHIP IN SEVERALTY—Ownership by a single individual.

PANIC SELLING—*See:* Blockbusting.

PARCEL—A lot or piece of real estate, especially a specified part of a larger tract.

PARTIAL RECONVEYANCE—The instrument given to the borrower when part of the security property is released from a blanket deed of trust under a partial release clause.

PARTIAL RELEASE CLAUSE—*See:* Release Clause.

PARTIAL SATISFACTION—The instrument given to the borrower when part of the security property is released from a blanket mortgage under a partial release clause.

PARTNER, GENERAL—A partner who has the authority to manage and contract for a general or limited partnership, and who is personally liable for the partnership's debts.

PARTNER, LIMITED—A partner in a limited partnership who is primarily an investor and does not participate in the management of the business, and who is not personally liable for the partnership's debts.

PARTNERSHIP—An association of two or more persons to carry on a business for profit. The law regards a partnership as a group of individuals, not as an entity separate from its owners. *Compare:* Corporation.

PARTNERSHIP, GENERAL—A partnership in which each member has an equal right to manage the business and share in the profits, as well as equal responsibility for the partnership's debts.

PARTNERSHIP, LIMITED—A partnership made up of one or more general partners and one or more limited partners.

PARTNERSHIP PROPERTY—All property that partners bring into their business at the outset or later acquire for their business.

PATENT DEFECT—A problem that is readily observable in an ordinary inspection of the property. *Compare:* Latent Defect.

PAYEE—In a promissory note, the party who is entitled to be paid; the lender. *Compare:* Maker.

PERCOLATION TEST—A test to determine the ability of the ground to absorb or drain water; used to determine whether a site is suitable for construction, particularly for installation of a septic tank system.

PERSONAL PROPERTY—Any property that is not real property; movable property not affixed to land. Also called chattels or personalty.

PERSONALTY—Personal property.

PHYSICAL DETERIORATION—Loss in value (depreciation) resulting from wear and tear or deferred maintenance.

PLAINTIFF—The party who brings or starts a civil lawsuit; the one who sues.

PLEDGE—When a debtor transfers possession of property to the creditor as security for repayment of the debt. *Compare:* Hypothecate.

PMI—*See:* Insurance, Private Mortgage.

POINT—One percent of the principal amount of a loan.

POINTS—*See:* Discount Points; Origination Fee.

PORTFOLIO—The mix of investments owned by an individual or company.

POSSESSION—1. The holding and enjoyment of property. 2. Actual physical occupation of real property.

POTABLE WATER—Water that is safe to drink.

POWER OF ATTORNEY—An instrument authorizing one person (the attorney in fact) to act as another's agent, to the extent stated in the instrument.

POWER OF SALE CLAUSE—A clause in a deed of trust giving the trustee the right to foreclose nonjudicially (sell the debtor's property without a court action) if the borrower defaults.

PREPAYMENT—Paying off part or all of a loan before payment is due.

PREPAYMENT PENALTY—A penalty charged to a borrower who prepays.

PREPAYMENT PRIVILEGE—A provision in a promissory note allowing the borrower to prepay.

PREVENTIVE MAINTENANCE—A program of regular inspection and care of a property and its fixtures, allowing the prevention of potential problems or their immediate repair.

PRICE FIXING—The cooperative setting of prices by competing firms. Price fixing is an automatic violation of antitrust laws.

PRIMARY MORTGAGE MARKET—The market in which mortgage loans are originated, where lenders make loans to borrowers. Also called the local market. *Compare:* Secondary Mortgage Market.

PRIME RATE—The interest rate a bank charges its largest and most desirable customers.

PRINCIPAL—1. One who grants another person (an agent) authority to represent him or her in dealings with third parties. 2. One of the parties to a transaction (such as a buyer or seller), as opposed to those who are involved as agents or employees (such as a broker or escrow agent). 3. In regard to a loan, the amount originally borrowed, as opposed to the interest.

PROCURING CAUSE—The real estate agent who is primarily responsible for bringing about a sale; for example, by negotiating the agreement between the buyer and seller.

PROFIT—A nonpossessory interest; the right to enter another person's land and take something (such as timber or minerals) away from it.

PROGRESSION, PRINCIPLE OF—An appraisal principle which holds that a property of lesser value tends to be worth more when it is located in an area with properties of greater value than it would be if located elsewhere. The opposite of the principle of regression.

PROMISEE—Someone who has been promised something; someone who is supposed to receive the benefit of a contractual promise.

PROMISOR—Someone who has made a contractual promise to another.

PROMISSORY NOTE—*See:* Note, Promissory.

PROPERTY—1. The rights of ownership in a thing, such as the right to use, possess, transfer, or encumber it. 2. Something that is owned.

PROPERTY TAX—*See:* Tax, Property.

PROPRIETORSHIP, INDIVIDUAL OR SOLE—A business owned and operated by one person.

PRORATION—The process of dividing or allocating something (especially a sum of money or an expense) proportionately, according to time, interest, or benefit.

PROTECTION CLAUSE—*See:* Safety Clause.

PUBLIC RECORD—The official collection of legal documents that individuals have filed with the county recorder in order to make the information contained in them public.

PUFFING—Superlative statements about the quality of a property that should not be considered assertions of fact.

PURCHASE AGREEMENT—A contract in which a seller promises to convey title to real property to a buyer in exchange for the purchase price. Also called a deposit receipt in California. Elsewhere, also called a purchase and sale agreement, earnest money agreement, sales contract, or contract of sale.

PURCHASER'S ASSIGNMENT OF CONTRACT AND DEED—The instrument used to assign the vendee's equitable interest in a contract to another.

QUALIFYING STANDARDS—The standards a lender requires a loan applicant to meet before a loan will be approved. Also called underwriting standards.

QUITCLAIM DEED—*See*: Deed, Quitclaim.

RATIFY—To confirm or approve after the fact an act that was not authorized when it was performed.

REAL ESTATE—*See:* Real Property.

REAL ESTATE BROKERAGE—1. A real estate broker's business. 2. As a licensed real estate agent, bringing a buyer and a seller together and negotiating a sales contract between the two parties.

REAL ESTATE CONTRACT—1. A purchase and sale agreement. 2. A land contract. 3. Any contract having to do with real property.

REAL ESTATE INVESTMENT SYNDICATE—A group of people or companies who join together to purchase and develop a piece of real estate.

REAL ESTATE INVESTMENT TRUST (REIT)—A real estate investment business with at least 100 investors, organized as a trust and entitled to special tax treatment under IRS rules.

REAL ESTATE MORTGAGE INVESTMENT CONDUIT (REMIC)—A special business entity that must invest a substantial amount of its funds in qualified mortgage loans to qualify for special tax treatment.

REAL PROPERTY—Land and everything attached to or appurtenant to it. Also called realty or real estate. *Compare:* Personal Property.

REALTOR®—A real estate agent who is an active member of a state and local real estate board that is affiliated with the National Association of Realtors.®

REALTY—*See:* Real Property.

RECONCILIATION—The final step in an appraisal, when the appraiser assembles and interprets the data in order to arrive at a final value estimate. Also called correlation.

RECONVEYANCE—Releasing the security property from the lien created by a deed of trust, by recording a deed of reconveyance.

RECORDING—Filing a document at the county recorder's office, so that it will be placed in the public record.

RECORDING NUMBERS—The numbers stamped on documents when they're recorded, used to identify and locate the documents in the public record.

REDEMPTION—1. When a defaulting borrower prevents foreclosure by paying the full amount of the debt, plus costs. 2. When a mortgagor regains the property after foreclosure by paying whatever the foreclosure sale purchaser paid for it, plus interest and expenses.

REDLINING—When a lender refuses to make loans secured by property in a certain neighborhood because of the racial or ethnic composition of the neighborhood.

REDUCTION CERTIFICATE—A signed statement from a lender certifying the present balance on the loan, the rate of interest, and the maturity date. A form of estoppel certificate.

REFORMATION—A legal action to correct a mistake, such as a typographical error, in a deed or other document. The court will order the execution of a correction deed.

REFORMATION DEED—*See*: Deed, Reformation.

REGRESSION, PRINCIPLE OF—An appraisal principle which holds that a valuable property surrounded by properties of lesser value will tend to be worth less than it would be in a different location; the opposite of the principle of progression.

REGULATION Z—The Federal Reserve Board's regulation that implements the Truth in Lending Act.

REINSTATE—To prevent foreclosure by curing the default.

RELEASE—1. To give up a legal right. 2. A document in which a legal right is given up.

RELEASE CLAUSE—1. A provision in a purchase agreement that allows the seller to keep the property on the market while waiting for a contingency to be fulfilled; if the seller receives another good offer, he can require the buyer to either waive the contingency clause or terminate the contract. (Also called a 72-hour clause, since the buyer is typically given 72 hours to respond.) 2. A clause in a blanket mortgage or deed of trust which allows the borrower to get part of the security property released from the lien when a certain portion of the debt has been paid or other conditions are fulfilled. Also called a partial release clause.

RENT—Compensation paid by a tenant to the landlord in exchange for the possession and use of the property.

REPLACEMENT COST—*See:* Cost, Replacement.

REPRODUCTION COST—*See:* Cost, Reproduction.

RESCISSION—When a contract is terminated and each party gives anything acquired under the contract back to the other party. (The verb form is rescind.) *Compare:* Cancellation.

RESERVE ACCOUNT—*See:* Impound Account.

RESERVE REQUIREMENTS—The percentage of deposits commercial banks must keep on reserve with the Federal Reserve Bank.

RESERVES FOR REPLACEMENT—For income-producing property, regular allowances set aside to pay for the replacement of structures and equipment that are expected to wear out.

RESIDUALS—Commissions in the form of delayed payments (when a part of the commission is paid with each installment on an installment sales contract, for example).

RESPA—Real Estate Settlement Procedures Act.

RESPONDEAT SUPERIOR, DOCTRINE OF—A legal rule holding that an employer is liable for torts committed by an employee within the scope of his or her employment.

RESTITUTION—Restoring something (especially money) that a person was unjustly deprived of.

RESTRICTION—A limitation on the use of real property.

RESTRICTION, DEED—A restrictive covenant in a deed.

RESTRICTION, PRIVATE—A restriction imposed on property by a previous owner, a neighbor, or the subdivision developer; a restrictive covenant or a condition in a deed.

RESTRICTION, PUBLIC—A law or regulation limiting or regulating the use of real property.

RESTRICTIVE COVENANT—*See:* Covenant, Restrictive.

RISK ANALYSIS—*See:* Underwriting.

SAFETY CLAUSE—A clause in a listing agreement providing that for a specified period after the listing expires, the broker will still be entitled to a commission if the property is sold to someone the broker dealt with during the listing term. Also called a protection clause or extender clause.

SALE-LEASEBACK—A form of real estate financing in which the owner of industrial or commercial property sells the property and leases it back from the buyer. In addition to certain tax advantages, the seller/lessee obtains more cash through the sale than would normally be possible by borrowing and mortgaging the property, since lenders will not often lend 100% of the value.

SALES COMPARISON APPROACH—One of the three main methods of appraisal, in which the sales prices of comparable properties are used to estimate the value of the subject property. Also called the market data approach.

SATISFACTION OF MORTGAGE—*See:* Mortgage, Satisfaction of.

SECONDARY FINANCING—Money borrowed to pay part of the required down-payment or closing costs for a first loan, when the second loan is secured by the same property that secures the first loan.

SECONDARY MORTGAGE MARKET—The market in which investors (including Fannie Mae, Freddie Mac, and Ginnie Mae) purchase real estate loans from lenders; also called the national market.

SECRET PROFIT—A financial benefit that an agent takes from a transaction without informing the principal.

SECURITY AGREEMENT—Under the Uniform Commercial Code, a document that creates a lien on personal property being used to secure a loan.

SECURITY INSTRUMENT—A document that creates a voluntary lien, to secure repayment of a loan; for debts secured by real property, it is either a mortgage or a deed of trust.

SECURITY INTEREST—The interest a creditor may acquire in the debtor's property to ensure that the debt will be paid.

SECURITY PROPERTY—The property that a borrower gives a lender a voluntary lien against, so that the lender can foreclose if the borrower defaults.

SELLING BROKER—The broker responsible for procuring a buyer for real estate; may represent either the seller or the buyer.

SEPARATE PROPERTY—Property owned by a married person that is not community property; includes property acquired before marriage or by gift or inheritance after marriage.

SERVANT—*See:* Master/Servant Relationship.

SETTLEMENT—1. An agreement between the parties to a civil lawsuit, in which the plaintiff agrees to drop the suit in exchange for money or the defendant's promise to do or refrain from doing something. 2. Closing.

SETTLEMENT STATEMENT—A document that presents a final, detailed accounting for a real estate transaction, listing each party's debits and credits and the amount each will receive or be required to pay at closing. Also called a closing statement.

SEVENTY-TWO HOUR CLAUSE—*See:* Release Clause.

SEVERALTY—*See:* Ownership in Severalty.

SHAREHOLDER—An individual who holds ownership shares (shares of stock) in a corporation, and has limited liability in regard to the corporation's debts. Also called a stockholder.

SHERIFF'S DEED—*See:* Deed, Sheriff's.

SHERIFF'S SALE—A foreclosure sale held after a judicial foreclosure. Sometimes called an execution sale.

SPECIAL ASSESSMENT—A tax levied only against the properties that have benefited from a public improvement (such as a sewer or a street light), to cover the cost of the improvement; creates a special assessment lien. Also called an improvement tax.

SPECIAL WARRANTY DEED—*See:* Deed, Special Warranty.

SPECIFIC PERFORMANCE—A legal remedy in which a court orders someone who has breached to actually perform the contract as agreed, rather than simply paying money damages.

S.R.A.—A member of the Society of Real Estate Appraisers.

STABLE MONTHLY INCOME—A loan applicant's gross monthly income that meets the lender's tests of quality and durability.

STATUTE—A law enacted by a state legislature or the U.S. Congress. *Compare:* Ordinance.

STATUTE OF FRAUDS—A law that requires certain types of contracts to be in writing and signed in order to be enforceable.

STATUTE OF LIMITATIONS—A law requiring a particular type of lawsuit to be filed within a specified time after the event giving rise to the suit occurred.

STATUTORY WARRANTY DEED—*See:* Deed, Statutory Warranty.

STEERING—Channeling prospective buyers or tenants to or away from particular neighborhoods based on their race, religion, national origin, or ancestry.

STOCKHOLDER—*See:* Shareholder.

SUBAGENT—A person that an agent has delegated authority to, so that the subagent can assist in carrying out the principal's orders; the agent of an agent.

SUBCONTRACTOR—A contractor who, at the request of the general contractor, provides a specific service, such as plumbing or drywalling, in connection with the overall construction project.

SUBJECT TO—When a purchaser takes property subject to a trust deed or mortgage, he or she is not personally liable for paying off the loan; in case of default, however, the property can still be foreclosed on.

SUBLEASE—When a tenant grants someone else the right to possession of the leased property for part of the remainder of the lease term; as opposed to a lease assignment, where the tenant gives up possession for the entire reminder of the lease term. Also called a sandwich lease. *Compare:* Assignment.

SUBORDINATION CLAUSE—A provision in a mortgage or deed of trust that permits a later mortgage or deed of trust to have higher lien priority than the one containing the clause.

SUBROGATION—The substitution of one person in the place of another with reference to a lawful claim or right. For instance, a title company that pays a claim on behalf of its insured, the property owner, is subrogated to any claim the owner successfully undertakes against the former owner.

SUBSTITUTION, PRINCIPLE OF—A principle of appraisal holding that the maximum value of a property is limited by the cost of obtaining another equally desirable property, assuming that there would not be a long delay or significant incidental expenses involved in obtaining the substitute property.

SUBSTITUTION OF LIABILITY—A buyer wishing to assume an existing loan may apply for the lender's approval; once approved, the buyer assumes liability for repayment of the loan, and the original borrower (the seller) is released from liability.

SURVEY—The process of precisely measuring the boundaries and determining the area of a parcel of land.

SYNDICATE—An association formed to operate an investment business. A syndicate is not a recognized legal entity; it can be organized as a corporation, partnership, or trust.

TAX, AD VALOREM—A tax assessed on the value of property.

TAX, DOCUMENTARY TRANSFER—A state tax levied on most real estate sales, to be paid by the seller.

TAX, GENERAL REAL ESTATE—An annual ad valorem tax levied on real property.

TAX, IMPROVEMENT—*See:* Special Assessment.

TAX, PROPERTY—1. The general real estate tax. 2. Any ad valorem tax levied on real or personal property.

TAX DEED—*See:* Deed, Tax.

TAX SALE—Sale of property after foreclosure of a tax lien.

TENANCY IN COMMON—A form of concurrent ownership in which two or more persons each have an undivided interest in the entire property, but no right of survivorship. *Compare:* Joint Tenancy.

TENANT—Someone in lawful possession of real property; especially, someone who has leased the property from the owner (also called a lessee).

TENDER—An unconditional offer by one of the parties to a contract to perform his or her part of the agreement; made when the offeror believes the other party is breaching, it establishes the offeror's right to sue if the other party doesn't accept it. Also called a tender offer.

TERM—A prescribed period of time; especially, the length of time a borrower has to pay off a loan, or the duration of a lease.

THIRD PARTY—1. A person seeking to deal with a principal through an agent. 2. In a transaction, someone who is not one of the principals.

TIE-IN ARRANGEMENT—An agreement to sell one product, only on the condition that the buyer also purchases a different product.

TIGHT MONEY MARKET—When loan funds are scarce, leading lenders to charge high interest rates and discount points.

TILA—Truth in Lending Act.

TIME IS OF THE ESSENCE—A clause in a contract that means performance on the exact dates specified is an essential element of the contract; failure to perform on time is a material breach.

TITLE—Lawful ownership of real property. Also, the deed or other document that is evidence of that ownership.

TITLE, ABSTRACT OF—A brief, chronological summary of the recorded documents affecting title to a particular piece of real property.

TITLE, AFTER-ACQUIRED—Title acquired by a grantor after he or she attempted to convey property he or she didn't own.

TITLE, CHAIN OF—1. The chain of deeds (and other documents) transferring title to a piece of property from one owner to the next, as disclosed in the public record. 2. A listing of all recorded documents affecting title to a particular property; more complete than an abstract.

TITLE, CLEAR—A good title to property, free from encumbrances or defects; marketable title.

TITLE, COLOR OF—Title that appears to be good title, but which in fact is not; commonly based on a defective instrument, such as an invalid deed.

TITLE, EQUITABLE—The vendee's interest in property under a land contract. Also called an equitable interest.

TITLE, LEGAL—The vendor's interest in property under a land contract.

TITLE, MARKETABLE—Title free and clear of objectionable liens, encumbrances, or defects, so that a reasonably prudent person with full knowledge of the facts would not hesitate to purchase the property.

TITLE COMPANY—A title insurance company.

TITLE INSURANCE—*See:* Insurance, Title.

TITLE REPORT—A report issued by a title company, disclosing the condition of the title to a specific piece of property, before the actual title insurance policy is issued. Sometimes called a preliminary title report.

TITLE SEARCH—An inspection of the public record to determine the rights and encumbrances affecting title to a piece of property.

TITLE THEORY—The theory holding that a mortgage or deed of trust gives the lender legal title to the security property while the debt is being repaid. *Compare:* Lien Theory.

TOPOGRAPHY—The contours of the surface of the land (level, hilly, steep, etc.).

TORT—A breach of a duty imposed by law (as opposed to a duty voluntarily taken on in a contract) that causes harm to another person, giving the injured person the right to sue the one who breached the duty. Also called a civil wrong (in contrast to a criminal wrong, a crime).

TOTAL FINANCE CHARGE—Under the Truth in Lending Act, the total finance charge on a loan includes interest, any discount points paid by the borrower, the loan origination fee, and mortgage insurance costs.

TRACT—1. A piece of land of undefined size. 2. In the rectangular survey system, an area made up of 16 townships; 24 miles on each side.

TRUST—A legal arrangement in which title to property (or funds) is vested in one or more trustees, who manage the property on behalf of the trust's beneficiaries, in accordance with instructions set forth in the document establishing the trust.

TRUST ACCOUNT—A bank account, separate from a real estate broker's personal and business accounts, used to segregate trust funds from the broker's own funds.

TRUST DEED—*See:* Deed of Trust.

TRUST FUNDS—Money or things of value received by an agent, not belonging to the agent but being held for the benefit of others.

TRUSTEE—1. A person appointed to manage a trust on behalf of the beneficiaries. 2. A neutral third party appointed in a deed of trust to handle the nonjudicial foreclosure process in case of default.

TRUSTEE IN BANKRUPTCY—An individual appointed by the court to handle the assets of a person in bankruptcy.

TRUSTEE'S DEED—*See*: Deed, Trustee's.

TRUSTEE'S SALE—A nonjudicial foreclosure sale under a deed of trust.

TRUSTOR—The borrower in a deed of trust. Also called the grantor.

UNDERWRITING—In real estate lending, the process of evaluating a loan application to determine the probability that the applicant would repay the loan, and matching the risk to an appropriate rate of return. Sometimes called risk analysis.

UNDUE INFLUENCE—Exerting excessive pressure on someone so as to overpower the person's free will and prevent him or her from making a rational or prudent decision; often involves abusing a relationship of trust.

UNENFORCEABLE—*See:* Contract, Unenforceable.

Uniform Commercial Code—A body of law adopted in slightly varying versions in most states (including California), which attempts to standardize commercial law dealing with such matters as negotiable instruments and sales of personal property. Its main applications to real estate law concern security interests in fixtures and bulk transfers.

Uniform Settlement Statement—A settlement statement required for any transaction involving a loan that is subject to the Real Estate Settlement Procedures Act (RESPA).

Uniform Standards of Professional Appraisal Practice—Guidelines for appraisers adopted by the Appraisal Foundation, a nonprofit organization of professional appraiser associations.

Unilateral Contract—*See:* Contract, Unilateral.

Unjust Enrichment—An undeserved benefit; a court generally will not allow a remedy (such as forfeiture of a land contract) if it would result in the unjust enrichment of one of the parties.

Usury—Charging an interest rate that exceeds legal limits.

VA—The U.S. Department of Veterans Affairs (formerly the Veterans Administration).

Vacancy Factor—*See:* Bad Debt/Vacancy Factor.

Valid—The legal classification of a contract that is binding and enforceable in a court of law.

Valuable Consideration—*See:* Consideration.

Valuation—*See:* Appraisal.

Value—The present worth of the future benefits of owning a piece of real or personal property.

Value, Assessed—The value placed on property by the taxing authority (the county assessor, for example) for the purposes of taxation.

Value, Face—The value of an instrument, such as a promissory note or a security, that is indicated on the face of the instrument itself.

Value, Market—The most probable price which a property should bring in a competitive and open market under all conditions requisite to a fair sale, the buyer and seller each acting prudently and knowledgeably, and assuming the price is not affected by undue stimulus. (This is the definition from the Uniform Standards of Professional Appraisal Practice.) Market value is also called fair market value, value in exchange, or objective value. *Compare:* Market Price.

VALUE, SUBJECTIVE—The value of a property in the eyes of a particular person, as opposed to its market value (objective value).

VALUE, UTILITY—The value of a property to its owner or to a user. (A form of subjective value.) Also called value in use.

VALUE IN EXCHANGE—*See:* Value, Market.

VALUE IN USE—*See:* Value, Utility.

VARIABLE INTEREST RATE—A loan interest rate that can be adjusted periodically during the loan term, as in the case of an adjustable-rate mortgage.

VENDEE—A buyer or purchaser; particularly, someone buying property under a land contract.

VENDOR—A seller; particularly, someone selling property by means of a land contract.

VERIFY—1. To confirm or substantiate. 2. To confirm under oath.

VOID—Having no legal force or effect.

VOIDABLE—*See:* Contract, Voidable.

WAIVER—The voluntary relinquishment or surrender of a right.

WARRANTY, IMPLIED—In a sale or lease of property, a guarantee created by operation of law, whether or not the seller or landlord intended to offer it.

WARRANTY DEED—*See*: Deed, Warranty.

WASTE—Destruction, damage, or material alteration of property by someone in possession who holds less than a fee estate (such as a life tenant or lessee), or by a co-owner.

WATER TABLE—The level at which water may be found, either at the surface or underground.

WILD DEED—*See*: Deed, Wild.

WRAPAROUND FINANCING—*See:* Mortgage, Wraparound.

YIELD—The return of profit to an investor on an investment, stated as a percentage of the amount invested.

INDEX

A

(Continued)